Proceedings of the
Danish Institute at Athens

Proceedings of the Danish Institute at Athens

VOLUME VIII

Edited by *Kristina Winther-Jacobsen, Rune Frederiksen & Søren Handberg*

Athens 2017

Proceedings of the Danish Institute at Athens Volume VIII

General editor: Kristina Winther-Jacobsen
Graphic design: Jørgen Sparre
Typeset: Ryevad Grafisk
Cover illustration: View from the Saint Elijah Stone Quarry on
the southern slopes of Mount Parnassus. Delphi is situated
far to the left in the picture 300 metres higher up. In the background
is the port of Kirrha situated on the Bay of Corinth (See p. 214).
Printed at Narayana Press, Denmark

ISSN 1108 149X
ISBN 978 87 7184 148 0

AARHUS UNIVERSITY PRESS
Langelandsgade 177
DK-8200 Aarhus N
www.unipress.dk

Gazelle Book Services Ltd.
White Cross Mills, Hightown
Lancaster LA1 4XS, England
www.gazellebooks.com

ISD
70 Enterprise Drive
Bristol, CT 06010
USA
www.isdistribution.com

This volume was financed by a private Danish foundation wishing to remain anonymous.

Contents

7   Celebrating 25 years of archaeological research
     at the Danish Institute at Athens
     KRISTINA WINTHER-JACOBSEN, RUNE FREDERIKSEN
     & SØREN HANDBERG

Ancient Studies

25   A Late Roman building complex in the Papaz Tarlası, Vezirköprü
     (ancient Neoklaudiopolis, northern Asia Minor)
     KRISTINA WINTHER-JACOBSEN & TØNNES BEKKER-NIELSEN

     Appendix: Two Byzantine Coins from the Papaz Tarlası
     VERA SAUER

59   True to type?
     Archaic Cypriot male statues made of limestone
     LONE WRIEDT SØRENSEN

89   Vroulia revisited
     From K. F. Kinch's excavations in the early 20th century
     to the present archaeological site
     ERIPHYLE KANINIA & STINE SCHIERUP

131 The cults of Kalydon
     Reassessing the miniaturised votive objects
     SIGNE BARFOED

149 Colour shifts
     On methodologies in research on the polychromy
     of Greek and Roman sculpture
     JAN STUBBE ØSTERGAARD

Art Historical Studies and Modern Greece

179   The Parthenon in Danish art and architecture,
      from Nicolai Abildgaard to Theophil Hansen
      PATRICK KRAGELUND

Reports on Danish Fieldwork in Greece

191   The Lower Acropolis of Kalydon in Aitolia
      Preliminary report on the excavations carried out in 2013-15
      OLYMPIA VIKATOU & SØREN HANDBERG

209   A short-cut to Delphi
      *Indications of a vehicle track from a stone quarry
      to the Sanctuary of Apollo at Delphi*
      ERIK HANSEN, GREGERS ALGREEN-USSING AND RUNE FREDERIKSEN

265   The Greek-Swedish-Danish Excavations 2013
      A short preliminary report
      ERIK HALLAGER & MARIA ANDREADAKI-VLAZAKI

281   The Greek-Swedish-Danish Excavations 2014
      A preliminary report
      ERIK HALLAGER & MARIA ANDREADAKI-VLAZAKI

293   The Pit L Baby Burial – Hermeneutics
      Implications for immigration into Kydonia in MMIII/LMI
      P. J. P. MCGEORGE

305   'Finding Old Sikyon', 2015
      A preliminary report
      RUNE FREDERIKSEN, KONSTANTINOS KISSAS, JAMIESON DONATI,
      GIORGOS GIANNAKOPOULOS, SILKE MÜTH, VASSILIOS PAPATHANASIOU,
      WOLFGANG RABBEL, HARALD STÜMPEL, KATHARINA RUSCH & KRISTINA
      WINTHER-JACOBSEN

Celebrating 25 years of archaeological research at the Danish Institute at Athens

KRISTINA WINTHER-JACOBSEN,
RUNE FREDERIKSEN & SØREN HANDBERG[1]

After the Second World War it was no longer possible for foreigners to get permission to do archaeological fieldwork in Greece without the mediation of an official foreign archaeological school based in Greece. Danish archaeologists such as Søren Dietz,[2] Erik Hallager,[3] and Klavs Randsborg managed to work on permits generously provided by the Swedish Institute at Athens. However, in 1992, the combined efforts of representatives of several institutions and Bertel Haarder, then Minister of Education, succeeded in establishing a Danish Institute. On the birthday of the famous Danish writer Hans Christian Andersen, the Danish Institute at Athens opened, on April 2, 1992, with Søren Dietz as its first director.

The privileged situation the institute finds itself in today – located in the Plaka, one of the old central neighbourhoods of Athens on top of the Archaic agora, in two beautifully restored neoclassical buildings associated with a large modern auditorium – is due to generous donations from the Carlsberg Foundation in 1993 and 1995 and the Velux Foundation in 2000.

According to Greek law, the foreign institutes or schools are registered by the Greek Ministry of Culture as archaeological schools, i.e. they are non-profit, archaeological research institutions. The function of the schools are defined in the Greek law *on the protection of antiquities and cultural heritage* from 2002, according to which schools are obliged to administer all archaeological research conducted in Greece by scholars of their native countries. The schools are privileged to conduct archaeological fieldwork on Greek soil under a number of conditions, including the maintenance of a research library accessible to Greek scholars, and the publications of the results of their work in a scientific journal. The Nordic Library, a collaborative institution shared by the four Nordic institutes which opened in 1995, responds to the first condition, and *Proceedings of the Danish Institute at Athens* and *Monographs of the Danish Institute at Athens* to the second (see below).

25 years of field projects

Under the privilege of Greek law each international school is allowed three *synergasias*, collaborative projects involving the school and one of the Greek ephorates, and three autonomous projects at any given time. Archaeologically speaking, the Danish Institute at Athens has been very active. Since its inauguration in 1992, DIA has mediated twelve fieldwork permissions for Danish scholars, including the Swedish–Greek–Danish collaboration at Khania. Some projects have taken up previous Danish engagements in Greece, e.g. the excavations of Karl Frederik Kinch on Rhodes between 1902 and 1914,[4] the excavations

---

1   With contributions and insights from Thomas Roland, Pernille Foss, Søren Dietz, Bjørn Lovén, Niels Andreasen and Erik Hallager, for which we are very grateful.
2   See Rathje & Lund 1991, 40-1.
3   See Rathje & Lund 1991, 41.
4   Blinkenberg 1931, 1941; Dietz 1984; Dietz & Trolle 1974; Dyggve 1960; Friis Johansen 1957; Kinch 1914; Sørensen & Pentz 1992; see also Rathje & Lund 1991, 39.

Fig. 1. *Kefallénia, Circular alter at Palaiocastro (Photo: Thomas Roland).*

of Frederik Poulsen, later Einar Dyggve and Konstantinos Romaios at Kalydon between 1926 and 1938,[5] and the work of Knud Friis Johansen on 'Sikyonean'" pottery.[6]

The Danish archaeological projects are all committed to the education of students through participation in fieldwork and publication preparations. In fact the Kalydon Lower Acropolis Project acted as a seminar excavation for Danish students of classical archaeology in 2013-6, and more recently also Norwegian students. We owe a debt of gratitude to the Central Archaeological Council and the Greek Ministry of Culture and Sports for granting us the permits and thereby supporting this important element in the education of Danish archaeologists and to the ephorates (mentioned individually below under the relevant projects) for their collaboration in this important endeavour.

Throughout the history of the Danish Institute at Athens the Carlsberg Foundation has been the main supporter of Danish fieldwork in Greece. We remain ever grateful for this vital support to the work of the Danish Institute at Athens. However, many more foundations have supported the field projects and our gratitude is also owed to the Danish Ministry of Education, the Consul General Gösta Enboms Foundation, the New Carlsberg Foundation, the Danish Council for Independent Research, the Institute of Aegean Prehistory, the Costopoulos Foundation, Queen Margrethe II's Archaeological Foundation, the Augustinus Foundation, the Danish Research Council, Agency for Science, Technology and Innovation, the Eleni Nakou Foundation, the Velux Foundation, the G.E.C. Gads Foundation, the Sonning Foundation, The American Friends of the Zea Harbour Project, the RPM Nautical Foundation, the Leverhulme Trust, Interspiro AB, the Gunvor & Josef Anérs Stiftelse, the Kungl. Vitterhets Historie och Antikvitets Akademien and the Herbert och Karin Jacobssons Stiftelse.

---

5   Poulsen & Rhomaios 1927; Dyggve, Poulsen & Rhomaios 1934; Dyggve & Poulsen 1948; Dyggve 1951. See also Rathje & Lund 1991, 40.
6   Friis Johansen 1918; 1923.

Kefallénia

In 1992 the survey began in the western part of Kefallénia, the largest of the Ionian Islands, directed by Klavs Randsborg from the University of Copenhagen and under the aegis of the Swedish Institute at Athens. With the establishment of the Danish Institute the permit was transferred and fieldwork continued in 1993 and 1994 funded by the Danish Ministry of Education.

The projects applied a combination of topographical and extensive and intensive archaeological survey to the investigation of prehistoric and ancient/historical settlement patterns. Much effort was also put into mapping and describing architectural sites, for example a group of smaller Archaic forts and the ancient town of Sami.

The archaeological survey revealed a total of more than five hundred sites dating from the Middle Paleolithic to the early Modern period, with an emphasis, however, on the Classical, Hellenistic and Roman periods. As a novelty in the island's history, it was established by the lithic inventories that occupation was present in the Late Neolithic period. The project has been instrumental in making the archaeology of the island available to an English-speaking audience through the two volumes published in the Danish journal *Acta Archaeologica*.[7] On several occasions, Klavs Randsborg expressed his strong interest in returning to Greek archaeology, but regrettably he passed away in 2016.

Fig. 2. *Rhodes, Kattavia 1994 (Photo: Søren Dietz).*

Rhodes

The fieldwork of Karl Frederik Kinch and Christian Blinkenberg on Rhodes is probably the largest Danish investment in the archaeology of Greece to date. Publication of the results took 90 years,[8] but the data continue to generate interest, including two PhD projects in recent years.[9] Two Danish attempts to return to Rhodes took place in 1975 and 1994, both revisiting southern Rhodes where K.F. Kinch worked in 1907-8.[10] In 1994, former Director of the Danish Institute at Athens Søren Dietz directed a survey campaign in the valley around the village

Kattavia in southern Rhodes in collaboration with the National Museum in Copenhagen and the Ephorate of the Dodecanese, represented by Effy Karantzaly, with Mette Korsholm as field director. The survey examined an area of about 5 km² and the collected material documented settlements in the valley from the Neolithic Age into the modern period.[11] The project succeeded in locating the centre of the ancient deme, Kattavia, a workshop for 7th-century BC relief-decorated amphorae and a large workshop producing transport amphorae. The survey was funded by the Consul General Gösta Enboms Foundation.

---

7   Randsborg 2002.

8   See n. 3.

9   Cecilie Brøns, University of Copenhagen/National Museum, Copenhagen and Sanne Hoffmann, University of Aarhus/National Museum, Copenhagen. See also Kaninia & Schierup, this volume.

10 Rathje & Lund 1991, 39.

11 The project awaits publication.

Fig. 3. *Chalkis, Aghia Triadha 1996 (Photo: Søren Dietz).*

Danish commitment to the archaeology of Rhodes continues. In 2016, the Carlsberg Foundation funded the four-year 'Rhodes Centennial Project'. In close collaboration with the Ephorate of Antiquities for the Dodecanese, this project will undertake the study and publication of six rescue excavations in the city and the necropolis of Rhodes. The project is directed by Vincent Gabrielsen, with Stella Skaltsa acting as vice-director, both of the Saxo Institute at the University of Copenhagen.

Chalkis

Between 1995 and 2001, the Danish Institute at Athens conducted surveys and excavations near the village of Kato Vassiliki, on the northern coast of the Corinthian gulf, in co-operation with the ephorate of Patras. The research was directed by former Director of the Institute, Søren Dietz, and former Ephor of Patras, Keeper of National Antiquities Lazaros Kolonas, with Iannis Moschos and Sanne Houby-Nielsen as field directors. The project was supported by the Consul General Gösta Enboms Foundation. In 2014, Søren Dietz returned to Chalkis with Tatiana Smekalova and Bruce Bevan in order to carry out geomagnetic investigations to identify more precisely the port and the residential and industrial facilities associated with it.

The efforts were concentrated partly on the locality of Pangali, on the eastern slope of Mount Varassova, and partly on the hill of Aghia Triadha, named after its large Early Byzantine Basilica.[12] In 1995, the two already known Classical fortification walls in Pangali were measured, and an intensive survey revealed that the area between the walls was probably never inhabited. A trial trench excavated in 1996 showed that a Final Neolithic settlement existed in Pangali in the latter half of the 5th millennium BC.[13]

In 1996-8, the Byzantine, Archaic, Classical and Hellenistic fortification walls surrounding the hill of Aghia Triadha were cleaned and measured, and foundations of Archaic/Classical and Hellenistic houses, primarily situated outside these walls, were excavated and measured. At the eastern terrace of the hill, layers of an EHI habitation with indications of an additional earlier mid 4th-millenium habitation were uncovered in a trial trench.[14] A small excavation was carried out from 1998 onwards on the flat land; the area west of the hill of Aghia Triada revealed both rich pre-historic layers (Middle to Late Bronze Age) at a depth of 3-4 m, thick layers from the Archaic periods and a rich Early Hellenistic tomb. Geological investigations made in 1997-8 in the Bay of Kato Vassiliki and geomagnetic surveys in 2014 indicated that the ancient harbour was situated at the shore of the bay, just west of the hill of Aghia Triadha.

Kalydon

The Kalydon project has been the flagship of the Danish Institute at Athens since 2001. The project takes up the baton of Frederik Poulsen and Einar Dyggve, who carried out fieldwork at the site in the 1920s and 30s.[15] Since the inauguration of the Danish Institute at Athens, three projects have taken place at Kalydon: the Kalydon urban project, the Kalydon Theatre project, and the Kalydon Lower Acropolis project. In 2016 Signe Barfoed received permission from the Ministry of Culture and Sports to study and publish the unpublished pottery and terracotta figurines from Poulsen and Rhomaios' excavations in the Sanctuary of Artemis Laphria.

---

12   See list of MoDIA volumes below: Dietz & Moschos (eds) 2006; Dietz & Kolonas (eds) 2016; Houby-Nielsen forthcoming.

13   F. Mavridis & L. Sørensen in Dietz & Moschos (eds) 2006.

14   Dietz & Kolonas (eds) 2016.

15   See n. 4.

Fig. 4. *Kalydon, East Gate (Photo: Søren Dietz).*

The Kalydon urban project

In 2001 the Danish Institute commenced large-scale archaeological fieldwork in ancient Kalydon in Aitolia. Kalydon is located around 8 km as the crow flies from Chalkis, on the west side of Mount Varassova and 12 km from Messolonghi further to the west. The project was directed by the Institute's first director, Søren Dietz, in collaboration with Maria Stavropoulou-Gatsi and Ioannis Moschos from the ephorate in Patras. The project was later transferred to the new administration in Messolonghi with Maria Stavropoulou-Gatsi as ephor. The excavations were sponsored by the Consul General Gösta Enboms Foundation and the New Carlsberg Foundation.

While the old excavations in Kalydon between the two world wars concentrated on the Sanctuary of Artemis Laphria (illuminating the Homeric epics) and a palaestra, the so-called Heroon of Leon, outside the city walls, the 2001 fieldwork focused on the city itself, and on Kalydonian urbanism – the economic and social life of an ancient city state.

From the beginning several types of survey were conducted: geomagnetic surveys – in an attempt to get an overall view of the town plan – estimating the economic and social divisions of the town; topographical surveys aiming towards a total topographic registration of visible remains on the surface (including the remaining parts of the fortification walls, tombs etc.) and the town in the landscape; geological surveys mapping the geology of the landscape between the town and the sea and estimating the fluctuations of the coastline/coastal morphology and the changing course of the river Evinos; and finally, larger parts of the areas underwent archaeological survey.

Excavations were carried out on strategic topics. An examination of the so-called 'bouleuterion' was initiated in 2001 in order to clarify the function of the installation – if a 'bouleuterion', it would have tremendous consequences for the estimation of the town planning. In the end it was shown to be a theatre of a rather unconventional layout (see below). Based on the results of the geomagnetic surveys, excavation was carried out from the beginning on the Acropolis in order to understand the chronology and function of installations in this important part of the town. Excavations were also carried out in the area near the large West Gate leading

11

Fig. 5. *Kalydon, Theatre (Photo: Rune Frederiksen).*

to the Artemis Laphria sanctuary. Here a large peristyle building, older than the Heroon, was partly uncovered. The find of a shrine to the Anatolian mother goddess Kybele was rather exceptional; it was well-preserved since the roof collapsed around 50 AD, preserving the context almost in situ. The sloping, terraced area inside the West Gate was called the Lower Town, where industrial activities took place, in contrast to the habitation area in the centre of the town. The commercial agora was placed near the ancient East Gate, leading to the agricultural areas close to the river Evinos and the harbour area near present day Krioneri, at the foot of Mount Varassova. A well-preserved kiln was excavated in a building further up the main street from the peristyle building. The layout of the excavation was based on the results from the geomagnetic surveys.

The results are published in Monographs of the Danish Institute at Athens (MoDIA) 12 (see below).

The Kalydon theatre project

The theatre at Kalydon was found during rescue excavations in the 1960s, and in 2002 the Danish–Greek project directed by Maria Stavropoulou-Gatzi and Søren Dietz identified the structure as a theatre following partial analytic excavations. Rune Frederiksen – then director of the Danish Institute at Athens – was given four subsequent grants from the Carlsberg Foundation (2011-4)

to carry out a complete excavation, study and publication of the theatre. This project was conducted as a new Danish–Greek collaborative project, under the direction of Frederiksen and the Ephor of Aitolia and Akarnania, Olympia Vikatou. The theatre is a structure of great significance, first because of its idiosyncratic form: almost all of the some 250 ancient Greek theatre ruins known are of semicircular design, whereas this theatre is rectangular, and perfectly designed to be so. In addition to posing important questions relating to ancient architecture, this unusual form questions the role of the circular form as a central physical frame of the ancient Greek drama. The scene-building with proskenion of the Ionic order is well–preserved and its meticulous excavation will answer basic questions on the development of this element of ancient dramatic architecture. Frederiksen, Vikatou and some 15 other Greek and Danish archaeologists, architects and university students are currently amassing vast amounts of excavation data into chapters for a monograph which will present this exciting monument to the international scholarly community.

Kalydon Lower Acropolis project

A new research project which includes fieldwork on the Lower Acropolis of Kalydon was, with the support of the Carlsberg Foundation, initiated in 2013. The project is a collaboration between the Danish Institute and the

Fig. 6. *View over the excavations on the Lower Acropolis of Kalydon. The Hellenistic house is seen in the foreground, the test trenches at the fortification wall are visible further down the hill. The South Hill, the plateau with the extra-urban sanctuary of Artemis Laphria and the Gulf of Patra are visible in the back ground (Photo: Søren Handberg).*

Ephorate of Antiquities of Aitolia-Acarnania and Lefkada, under the direction of Søren Handberg and the ephor Olympia Vikatou. The main aim of the project is to enhance our understanding of the early period of the city's history, of which we have very little knowledge.

During four years of excavations in 2013-6, the project has fully excavated a private house dating to the Hellenistic period and investigated part of an earlier fortification wall that surrounds the acropolis.[16] The investigations showed that the house was most likely destroyed around the middle of the 2nd century BC and that many of the objects in it had been preserved in their original culture-historical context. Test trenches at the fortification wall revealed a 3.6 m-thick double-faced wall, which is likely to date to the Early Classical period. Across most of the excavated area, but especially associated with the fortification wall, pottery dating to the Late Geometric

through to the Classical period was observed. These finds suggest that the acropolis was occupied in the early period of the city's history. The new finds increase the knowledge of the topography of the early city, and show that, in terms of size, it was comparable to other ancient Greek cities. The excavations have also produced a substantial amount of Roman pottery that can be dated from the late 1st century BC to the early 1st century AD, which reveals that the city was not completely abandoned when the later Roman Emperor Augustus founded the city of Nikopolis in 27 BC, as the ancient literary sources suggest.

Piraeus

From 2002 to 2012 the Zea Harbour Project conducted fieldwork on land and under water in and around two naval harbours in the Piraeus, Mounichia and Zea. Working

---

16   For a preliminary report on the project see Vikatou & Handberg, this volume.

Fig. 7. *An archaeologist excavates the early shipsheds at Mounichia Harbour in the Piraeus on one of the very rare days of good visibility (Photo: V. Tsiairis © ZHP 2012).*

under the auspices of the Danish Institute at Athens, the project was directed by Bjørn Lovén in close collaboration with the Ephorate of Underwater Antiquities and the Ephorate of West Attica, Piraeus and Islands. The project was mainly funded by the Carlsberg Foundation, but it also received support from the Eleni Nakou Foundation, the Velux Foundation, the G.E.C. Gads Foundation, the Sonning Foundation, the Augustinus Foundation, The American Friends of the Zea Harbour Project, the RPM Nautical Foundation, the Leverhulme Trust and Interspiro AB.

The Zea Harbour Project made a number of significant discoveries within Zea, the largest and most important naval harbour of antiquity, and the smaller naval base of Mounichia. These included the identification of so-called double-shipsheds at Zea and the discovery that two shipsheds in Mounichia date to 520-480 BC, thus showing that Athens stored its warships in shipsheds in the Piraeus before or just after the Persian Wars. The project also defined and mapped coastal fortifications on the Koumoundourou Hill and in the Piraiki, the harbour fortifications of Zea and Mounichia, thereby producing important knowledge of the fortifications of the Piraeus. The project has been a model of modern, careful and meticulous fieldwork under challenging conditions in the polluted waters of modern Piraeus. The methods included digital and geophysical survey as well as excavation.

The results of the Zea Harbour Project are published in Monographs of the Danish Institute at Athens (MoDIA) 15 (see below). The first volume was published in 2012, and two additional volumes are being prepared for publication.

Mount Pelion

The three-year Pelion Cave Project in Thessaly, directed by Niels H. Andreasen, was initiated in 2006 by the Danish Institute at Athens in co-operation with the Ephorate of Palaeoanthropology and Speleology of Northern Greece. While the use of caves goes back to the earliest humans, the original and innovative purpose of the Pelion

Fig. 8. *Survey of cave with WWII remains on North Pelion (Photo: Markos Vaxevanopoulos).*

Cave Project was to understand the diversity, complexity and development of cave-use on the mountain, mainly from 1881 – the end of the Ottoman period in that region – until today.

Husbandry, local history and folklore related to caves have rarely been documented systematically in this region. The physical traces and knowledge of cave-use are rapidly disappearing, but caves remain a valuable source of information concerning local history and regional economy. The conditions on Mount Pelion in southeast Thessaly provided a unique opportunity to ask key questions of both ethnographic and historical interest, as well as demonstrating nuances in cave-use that would otherwise have remained undetected. The methodology included archaeological survey, systematic collection of objects from the cave floors, local historical research and interviews with local informants.

The 2006-8 survey on Mount Pelion documented 158 caves and rock shelters, and compiled a rich collection of ethnographic material. Drawing on archaeological and topographical data from the caves as well as documentary records, oral history and folklore, the project has raised interesting issues about cave-use prior to and following the onset of the industrialized period. The rich dataset demonstrates complexities beyond the picture usually perceived by archaeologists and provides a fascinating glimpse of a humanized landscape existing outside the cultural landscape of villages and fields.

The Pelion Cave Project was supported by the Danish Council for Independent Research, the Institute of Aegean Prehistory, the Costopoulos Foundation, Queen Margrethe II's Archaeological Foundation and the Augustinus Foundation. Scientific adaptation of the data for publication in the Institutes monograph series volume 19, expected in 2017 (see below), has been made possible due to a grant from the Danish Research Council, Agency for Science, Technology and Innovation.

Khania

In 2010 the Danish Institute at Athens joined the long-term Greek–Swedish excavations at Kastelli, Khania, in

Fig. 9. *The impressive walls of the LM IIIA:2/IIIB:1 Building 2 were very well preserved between the wall foundations of an Early Christian Basilica. Facing east. Excavation photo 2010 (Photo: Erik Hallager).*

sensational find of Linear B tablets came to light, in Crete otherwise only known from the Palace at Knossos. The tablets are dated from context to the LM IIIB:1 period (c. 1250 BC) and prove that Dionysos was considered a god as early as the Bronze Age. The way the tablets were made is exactly the same as that of the Knossos tablets, the date of which is still uncertain: an observation which may allow for the dating of the Knossos tablets.

The aim of the Greek–Swedish–Danish Excavations was to excavate as far as the modern habitation permitted the building where the Linear B tablets were found. The excavations stopped in 2014, and as discussed in the two reports, they revealed one of the largest and most impressive non-palatial buildings yet discovered in LM III Crete.[17]

The sponsors for the project have been the Institute for Aegean Prehistory, the Carlsberg Foundation, Gunvor & Josef Anérs Stiftelse. Kungl. Vitterhets Historie och Antikvitets Akademien, Herbert och Karin Jacobssons Stiftelse and the Augustinus Foundation.

Lechaion

The Lechaion Harbour Project was initiated in 2014 by the Danish Institute at Athens in co-operation with the University of Copenhagen and the Ephorate of Underwater Antiquities. The project is under the direction of Bjørn Lovén and Dimitris Kourkoumelis, aided by assistant directors Paraskevi Micha and Panagiotis Athanasopoulos. In 2013 it received a grant from Queen Margrethe II's Archaeological Foundation. The Augustinus Foundation and the Carlsberg Foundation have committed to funding the project until 2018.

Lechaion, together with Kenchreai, served as a harbour town of ancient Corinth. Throughout antiquity Corinth took advantage of its position astride the Isthmus to control land routes north and south and sea routes east and west. Lechaion, positioned north of the city on the Gulf of Corinth, offered convenient access to the central and western Mediterranean, and according to ancient sources, Corinth derived a great deal of its wealth from this trade.

The aim of the project is to document the physical remains of Lechaion's harbours in light of Corinth's 25

Crete. The project was directed by Yannis Tzedakis (former General Director of Antiquities, Ministry of Culture), followed in 2011 by Maria Andreadaki-Vlazaki (General Secretary of the Ministry of Culture and Sports), Ann-Louise Schallin (the Swedish Institute) and Erik Hallager (the Danish Institute). The previous excavations at Minoan Kydonia revealed that Khania has existed for 5000 years, and showed that the site was continuously inhabited with the exception of a 400-year period from the end of the Bronze Age (c. 1150) till the end of the Geometric period (c. 725).

The most important discoveries were those from the end of the Bronze Age, the Late Minoan period (c. 1600-1150 BC), from which – uniquely for Crete – seven subsequent settlements could be documented. In 1990 a

17   For reports on seasons 2013 and 2014 see Hallager & Andreadakis-Vlazakis as well as McGeorge, this volume.

Fig. 10. *Archaeologist excavating wooden caisson in Area 2 (Photo: V. Tsiairis © LHP 2015).*

centuries of recorded history. The methods include digital and geophysical survey of the inner and outer harbours as well as the harbour canal, using innovative technologies such as a newly-developed 3D parametric sub-bottom profiler, and excavation.

The project will generate data pertaining to the development of commercial harbours, and, by extension, shed essential light on the nature and development of the ancient world. Its early discoveries are already yielding unique and critical archaeological information on the use of wooden caissons in underwater construction techniques during the Byzantine era.

Delphi

The Danish contributions to the study of the Sanctuary of Apollo at Delphi under the auspices of the French School have long been recognized, especially the work of Erik

Hansen. In 2013 the Danish Institute at Athens received a permit under the direction of Rune Frederiksen for Erik Hansen and Gregers Algreen-Ussing to study the infrastructure for the construction of the 4th-century temple of Apollo. The project received support from the Carlsberg Foundation and the Danish Institute at Athens.

The background for the project is the detailed study of the 4th-century BC phase of the temple of Apollo by Pierre Amandry and Erik Hansen, published in 2010 in the *Fouilles de Delphes* series.[18] This study revealed that 7500 tons of blocks were transported from the St. Elias quarry, located 6 km to the west and 300 m below the level of the sanctuary of Apollo in a mountain funnel. Some of the heaviest blocks visible in the temple foundation weigh approximately 9 tons. It has been estimated that the transport of the blocks took 1900 trips, and for this purpose an extensive network of roads was constructed. The project has identified the tracks and roads for the transportation

18   Amandry & Hansen 2010.

Fig. 11. *View of the plain of Pre-Hellenistic Sikyon towards the Corinthian Gulf (Photo: Silke Müth-Frederiksen).*

of building material for the 4th-century temple. Their report on the results in this volume of *Proceedings* testifies to a remarkably rectilinear infrastructure through the steep mountain funnels and the extraordinary skills of ancient Greek engineers.[19]

Sikyon

In 1918, Knud Friis Johansen suggested that the widely exported pottery archaeologists have come to consider of Corinthian origin since the American excavations there were actually produced at Sikyon, a famous centre for arts and crafts in ancient times.[20] The Danish Institute at Athens in collaboration with the National Museum of Denmark was granted the permit to investigate the plain of pre-Hellenistic Sikyon for the purpose of identifying the site of the city and analyzing the material remains, the specific settlement structures and urban fabric of 'Old

Sikyon'. The project is a *synergasia* between The National Museum, Copenhagen, the Ephorate of Antiquities of Corinth and the Danish Institute at Athens and is funded by the Carlsberg Foundation. It was conceived by former director of the Danish Institute Rune Frederiksen, who also co-directed the project's first season in 2015, the report of which is published in this volume.[21] The Greek co-director is Konstantinos Kissas, the Ephor of Antiquities of Corinth. In 2016, the Danish directorship of the project was taken over by Silke Müth-Frederiksen (National Museum). In two campaigns in April and June/July 2016, geoarchaeological augering, geophysical investigation, intensive survey, aerial photography and remote sensing were applied to great effect. It is now possible to define the limits of the old city in most directions and to characterize some of its quarters and buildings. Furthermore, there are some first indications for the localization of the harbour of Sikyon.

---

19   Hansen et al., this volume.
20   The French version came out in 1923.
21   Frederiksen et al., this volume.

25 years of publications: PoDIA and MoDIA

Proceedings of the Danish Institute at Athens (*PoDIA*) and *Monographs of the Danish Institute at Athens* (*MoDIA*) form the infrastructural backbone of the institute's promotion of Danish research in Greece as well as internationally.

The first volume of the scientific journal *PoDIA* appeared in 1995, and the series issue normally with an interval of two to four years. *PoDIA* is a collection of occasional papers written primarily by scholars from the Danish scholarly environment, but also by foreign scholars working on topics thematically related to the activities of the Institute. Although Greek archaeology and epigraphy dominates, the scope of *Proceedings* is geographically wide, encompassing the entire Greek world from the 3rd millennium BC to the present day. The most recent volumes include sections on ancient studies and art historical studies, as well as reports on Danish fieldwork in Greece. Articles other than field reports are peer-reviewed by at least one reviewer and with mutual anonymity. An editorial board decides on titles to publish and control the review process. *PoDIA* is available online (http://ojs.statsbiblioteket.dk/index.php/pdia/issue/archive).

The present volume is number 8 in the series. *Ancient Studies* consist of five articles which reflect well the geographical width of Danish research interests in the eastern Mediterranean in recent years in Greece and the islands (Barfoed; Kaninia & Schierup), in Turkey (Winther-Jacobsen & Bekker-Nielsen and Sauer) and in Cyprus (Sørensen). This section also includes an evaluation of the research into ancient polychromy by one of its main proponents (Østergaard). The section on *Art Historical Studies and Modern Greece* consists of an article on 19th century reception of the Parthenon (Kragelund). Finally, there are six preliminary reports from four Danish and Danish-Swedish-Greek field projects in Greece: the excavations of the ancient City of Kalydon in Aitolia (Vikatou & Handberg), the architectural studies at Delphi (Hansen, Algreen-Ussing & Frederiksen), the Minoan excavations in the center of the old town of Chania in Crete (Hallager & Andreadaki-Vlazaki; McGeorge), and the investigations at Ancient Sikyon in the Peloponnese (Frederiksen, Kissas, Donati, Giannakopoulos, Müth, Papathanasiou, Rabbel Stümpel, Rusch & Winther-Jacobsen).

The monograph series, *MoDIA*, publishes Danish and Danish-Greek fieldwork in Greece and Cyprus and well as conference proceedings. The generous gift from the Velux Foundation in 2000 provided the Danish Institute with a modern auditorium, which is a popular venue for international conferences. Conferences continue to be an extremely important academic tool to gain access to the most current research. As we write this, 17 volumes have appeared and an additional eight are in preparation (see list below). Ten of these volumes are dedicated to Danish and Danish-Greek field projects while the remaining volumes are conference proceedings. Many of these conferences are related to the field projects, and the Danish Institute at Athens remain grateful to all the institutions and foundations, Danish and Greek, that have made such rich opportunities and favourable conditions available to Danish Classical Archaeology. We, the authors and editors of this volume, can only look forward to the exploits of future generations.

Proceedings volume 8 is published by Aarhus University Press, and the production has become possible only by the very generous support of a Danish foundation wishing to remain anonymous. The Institute is grateful for the help received without which this volume would never have issued.

KRISTINA WINTHER-JACOBSEN
The Danish Institute at Athens
Herefondos 14, 10558 Athens
Greece
kwj@diathens.gr/kwjacobsen@hum.ku.dk

RUNE FREDERIKSEN
Ny Carlsberg Glyptotek
Dantes Plads 7, 1556 Copenhagen V
Denmark
rufr@glyptoteket.dk

SØREN HANDBERG
University of Oslo
Department of Archaeology, Conservation and History
Blindernveien 11, 0371 Oslo
Norway
soren.handberg@iakh.uio.no/shhandberg@hotmail.com

List of Monographs

E. Hallager & B. P. Hallager (eds), *Late Minoan III Pottery. Chronology and Terminology. Acts of a Meeting held at the Danish Institute at Athens, August 12-14 1994* (MoDIA 1), 1997.

Chr. Troelsgaard (ed.), *Byzantine Chant. Tradition and Reform. Acts of a Meeting held at the Danish Institute at Athens 1993* (MoDIA 2), 1997.

J. Isager (ed.), *Foundation and Destruction. Nikopolis and Northwestern Greece.The archaeological evidence for the city destructions, the foundation of Nikopolis, and the synoecism. Acts of a Meeting held at the Danish Institute at Athens, March 1999* (MoDIA 3), 2001.

I. Nielsen (ed.), *The Royal Palace Institution in the First Millennium BC. Regional Development and Cultural Interchange between East and West. Acts of a Meeting held at the Danish Institute at Athens, November 1999* (MoDIA 4), 2001.

J. Eiring & J. Lund (eds), *Transport Amphorae and Trade in the Eastern Mediterranean. Acts of the International Colloquium at the Danish Institute at Athens, September 26-29 2002* (MoDIA 5), 2004.

L. Wriedt Sørensen & K. Winther Jacobsen (eds), *Panayia Ematousa I – A rural site in south-eastern Cyprus; II – Political, cultural, ethnic and social relations in Cyprus. Approches to regional studies* (MoDIA 6.1-2), 2006.

S. Dietz & Y. Moschos (eds.) *Chalkis Aitolias I – The prehistoric periods* (MoDIA 7.1), 2006.

S. Houby Nielsen, *Chalkis Aitolias II – The Emporion. Archaic, Classical and Early Hellenistic Habitations on the Hagia Triada* (MoDIA 7.2), forthcoming.

S. Dietz & L. Kolonas (eds), *Chalkis Aitolias III – The Archaic Period* (MoDIA 7.3), 2016.

T. M. Brogan & E. Hallager (eds), *LM IB pottery – relative chronology and regional differences. Acts of a workshop held at the Danish Institute in collaboration with the INSTAP Study Center for East Crete, 27-29 June 2007* (MoDIA 11.1-2), 2011.

S. Dietz & M. Stavropoulou-Gatsi (eds), *Kalydon in Aitolia I – Reports and Studies. Danish/Greek Field Work 2001-2005; Kalydon in Aitolia; II – Catalogues. Danish/Greek Field Work 2001-2005* (MoDIA 12.1-2), 2011.

E. Hallager & D. Mulliez (eds), *The French Connection – 100 years with the Danish architects at l'École française d'Athènes. Acts of a Symposium held in Athens and Copenhagen 2008 by l'École française d'Athènes and The Danish Institute at Athens* (MoDIA 13), 2010.

G. Vavouranakis (ed.), *The seascape in Aegean Prehistory* (MoDIA 14), 2011.

B. Lovén & M. Schaldemose with contributions by B. Klejn-Christensen & M.M. Nielsen, *The Ancient Harbours of the Piraeus I.1 – The Zea Shipsheds and Slipways: Architecture and Topography; I.2 – The Zea Shipsheds and Slipways: Finds, Area 1 Shipshed Roof Reconstructions and Feature Catalogue* (MoDIA 15.1-2), 2012.

B. Lovén & I. Sapountzis, *The Ancient Harbours of the Piraeus II – Zea Harbour: the Group 1 and 2 shipsheds and slipways – architecture, topography and finds* (MoDIA 15.3), forthcoming.

N.M. Nielsen, *The Ancient Harbours of the Piraeus, III.1 – The Harbour and Coastal fortifications of the Mounichia and Zea Harbours – architecture and topography* (MoDIA 15.4), forthcoming.

B. Lovén & I. Sapountzis, *The Ancient Harbours of Piraeus III.2 – Mounichia Harbour: the shipsheds – architecture, topography and finds and finds from the fortifications at Mounichia and Zea Harbour* (MoDIA 15.5), forthcoming.

M. Tsipopoulou (ed.), *Petras, Siteia. 25 years of excavations and studies* (MoDIA 16), 2012.

R. Frederiksen, E. Gebhard and A. Sokolicek (eds), *The Architecture of the Ancient Greek Theatre: conference at the Danish Institute at Athens January 2012* (MoDIA 17), 2016.

R. Frederiksen, S. Müth, M. Schnelle & P. Schneider (eds), *Fokus on Fortifikation. Conference on the Research of Ancient Fortifications, Athens 6-9 December 2012* (MoDIA 18), 2016.

N. H. Andreasen, P. Pantzou & D. Papadopoulos, *Unfolding a mountain. An ethno-archaeological investigation of modern cave use on Mount Pelion (2006-2008)* (MoDIA 19), forthcoming.

S. Dietz et al., *Communities in Transition* (MoDIA 20), forthcoming.

M. Tsipopoulou, *Petras-Siteia. The Pre- and Proto-Palatial cemetery in Context* (MoDIA 21), 2017.

S. Handberg, A. Gadolo & C. Morgan (eds), *Material Koinai in the Greek Early Iron Age and Archaic Period* (MoDIA 22), forthcoming.

W. Friese, T. Myrup Kristensen & S. Handberg (eds), *Ascending and Descending the Acropolis. Sacred Travel in Ancient Attica and its Borders* (MoDIA 23), forthcoming.

Bibliography

Amandry, P. & E. Hansen 2010
Fouilles des Delphes II, *Le temple d'Apollon du IVe siècle*, Paris.

Blinkenberg, C. F. 1931
Lindos I – *Fouilles de l'Acropole 1902-1904. Les Petit Objects*, Berlin.

Blinkenberg, C. F. 1941
Lindos II – *Fouilles de l'Acropole 1902-1914.Inscriptions. Publiée en grande partie d'apres les copies de K.F. Kinch*, Berlin.

Dietz, S. 1984
Lindos IV.1 – *Excavations and Surveys in Southern Rhodos: The Mycenean Period.* Copenhagen.

Dietz, S. & S. Trolle 1974
Arkæologens Rhodos, Copenhagen.

Dyggve, E., F. Poulsen & K. Rhomaios 1934
Das Heroon von Kalydon, Copenhagen.

Dyggve, E. & F. Poulsen 1948
Das Laphrion, der Tempelbezirk von Kalydon 1 (*Arkæologisk-kunsthistoriske skrifter* 2), Copenhagen.

Dyggve, E. 1951
'A Second Heroon at Calydon', in *Studies Presented to David M. Robinson* 1, George E. Mylonas (ed.), St. Louis, 360-4.

Dyggve, E. 1960
Lindos II – *Fouilles de l'Acropole 1902-1914 et 1951. Le Sanctuaire d'Athena Lindia et l'architecture lindienne*, Berlin.

Frederiksen,R., K. Kissas, J. Donati, G. Giannakopoulos, S. Müth, V. Papathanasiou, W. Rabbel, H. Stümpel, K. Rusch & K. Winther-Jacobsen 2017
'Finding Old Sikyon', 2015. A preliminary report', *PoDIA* 8, 305-24.

Friis Johansen, K. 1918
Sikyoniske vaser: en arkæologisk undersøgelse, Copenhagen.

Friis Johansen, K. 1923
Les vases sicyoniens. Études archéologique, Paris.

Friis Johansen, K. 1957
'*Exochi,* ein frührhodisches Graberfeld', *Acta Archaologica* 28, 1-192.

Hallager, E. & M. Vlazakis-Andreadaki 2017a
'The Greek–Swedish–Danish Excavations 2013 – a short preliminary report', *PoDIA* 8, 265-79.

Hallager, E. & M. Vlazakis-Andreadaki 2017b
'The Greek–Swedish–Danish Excavations 2014 – a short preliminary report', *PoDIA* 8, 281-92.

Hansen, E., G. Algreen-Ussing, & R. Frederiksen 2017
'A Short Cut to Delphi: Indications of a vehicle track from a stone quarry to the Sanctuary of Apollo at Delphi', *PoDIA* 8, 209-63.

Kinch, K. F. 1914
Fouilles de Vroulia (Rhodes). Berlin.

McGeorge, P. J. P. 2017
'The Pit L Baby Burial – Hermeneutics: Implications for immigration into Kydonia in MMIII/LMI', *PoDIA* 8, 293-303.

Poulsen, F. & K. A. Rhomaios 1927
Erster vorläufiger Bericht über die dänisch-griechischen Ausgrabungen von Kalydon, Copenhagen.

Randsborg, K. 2002
Kephallenia I – II. *Archaeology and History. The Ancient Greek Cities* (Acta Archaeologica 73), Copenhagen.

Rathje, A. & J. Lund 1991
'Danes Overseas – A Short History of Danish Classical Archaeological Fieldwork', in *Recent Danish Research in Classical Archaeology: Tradition and Renewal* (Acta Hyperborea 3), T. Fischer Hansen, P. Guldager, J. Lund, M. Nielsen & A. Rathje (eds), Copenhagen, 11-56.

Sørensen, L. Wriedt & P. Pentz 1992
Lindos IV.2 *Excavations and Surveys in Southern Rhodos: The Post-Mycenean Periods until Roman Times and the Medieval Period*, Copenhagen.

Vikatou, O. & S. Handberg 2017
'The Lower Acropolis of Kalydon in Aitolia: preliminary report on the excavations carried out in 2013-15', *PoDIA* 8, 191-206.

Ancient Studies

A Late Roman building complex in the Papaz Tarlası, Vezirköprü
(ancient Neoklaudiopolis, northern Asia Minor)

KRISTINA WINTHER-JACOBSEN
& TØNNES BEKKER-NIELSEN

Cruciform structures are common in the Late Roman and Byzantine religious architecture of Asia Minor.[1] Most structures, however, have arms of unequal length; the 'Greek cross' shape with arms of equal length is quite rare. This paper discusses a building complex including a Greek cruciform structure identified by geoelectric re-

sistivity survey just north of Vezirköprü, Samsun province, Turkey, in the region known in antiquity as Pontos (Fig. 1).[2] Vezirköprü was founded as Neapolis by Pompey the Great in 64 BC and later renamed Neoklaudiopolis in honour of the emperor Claudius or Nero. The city continued, however, to be known under its indigenous

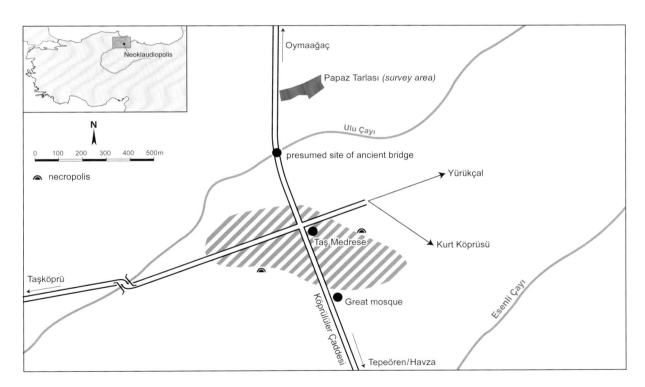

Fig. 1. *Map of ancient remains in Vezirköprü and surroundings (Map: Richard Szydlak).*

1   All dates are AD unless otherwise indicated.
2   The work was done under the auspices of the *Where East meets West Project*, investigating the Pompeian model of settlements in northern Anatolia and its trajectory from different material and historical perspectives focusing on one of its cities, Neoklaudiopolis, see Bekker-Nielsen 2013; 2014; Bekker-Nielsen et al. 2015; Winther-Jacobsen 2015.

Fig. 3. *Ploughed surface of the Papaz Tarlası (Photo: Kristina Winther-Jacobsen).*

Fig. 2. *Google image of the Papaz Tarlası on December 8, 2012.*

name, Andrapa, as well.[3] This was also the name of the Late Roman bishopric. Several bishops from Andrapa are named in the attendance lists of church councils and provincial synods. The earliest bishop mentioned in the lists is Paralios, who in 431 was unable to attend the council of Ephesus in person but sent a deacon, Eucharios, to represent him.[4]

Introduction

The field known as the Papaz Tarlası ('priest's field') is located in the Kuruçay Mahallesi on the southern edge of the plateau that stretches northward and westward from Vezirköprü towards the Kızılırmak river (ancient Halys). The shape of the field is irregular and its size approximately 8250 m². At the southeastern corner, the field drops towards the southeast, and the southern edge of the field is defined by the ravine of the river, the Ulu. To the west, the field abuts the road leading from Vezirköprü northwards to Adatepe, Oymaağaç and Türkmenköy. To the east and north, it abuts on other fields (Fig. 2).

The surface of the Papaz Tarlası is densely scattered with ceramics and the sub-surface structures are immedi-

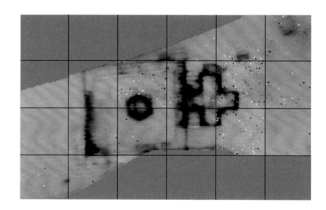

Fig. 4. *Georesistivity map of the Papaz Tarlası (Plan: Harald von der Osten-Woldenburg).*

ately visible on the ground as high density areas, as well as small elevations on the surface (Fig. 3). The finds include numerous architectural remains: fragments of roof tiles, floor tiles and bricks, as well as a stone threshold (Figs 7-8) and a broken column (Figs 9-10). In the ravine to the south, foundations are visible in the slope and according to local informants, looters have uncovered masonry and a small vaulted chamber in the field.

---

3   Ptolemy, *Geography* 4.4, *Andrapa hê kai Neoklaudiopolis*. An inscription now in the Köprülü Mehmet Paşa Parkı, Vezirköprü, commemorates a soldier on detached duty "in (the city of) the Andrapans"; Bekker-Nielsen, Høgel & Sørensen 2015, no. 3.

4   Le Quien 1740, 1.539-40; Fedalto 1988, 1.79. Paralios is also named in an inscription found at Doyran on the southern outskirts of Vezirköprü: Anderson et al. 1910, no. 68, 87-8.

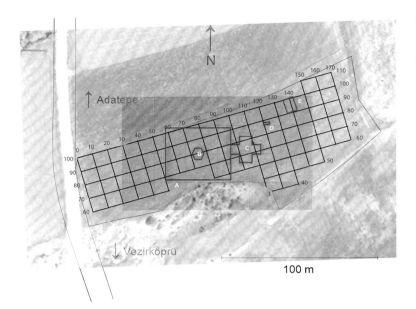

Fig. 5. *Gridded survey map of the Papaz Tarlası indicating the subsurface structures and other recorded features (Plan: Kristina Winther-Jacobsen).*

Georesistivity survey

In April 2010, a georesistivity survey of the central part of the Papaz Tarlası was carried out by a team from the Nerik excavation project under the direction of Prof. Dr. Rainer Czichon and Dr. Harald von der Osten-Woldenburg.[5] The survey, which covered a surface of 6000 m², revealed the foundations of a large building complex composed of three main elements oriented east–west (Figs 4-5): in the west was a quadrangle 42 x 42 m lined by structures on all four sides. From the georesistivity scan it is not possible to say with certainty whether the plan is completely regular or whether the northern side is slightly skewed in relation to the others. At the centre of the quadrangle, a hexagonal structure approximately 10 m in diameter can be seen. To the east lies a structure in the shape of a Greek cross, measuring 21 x 21 m; its western arm is attached to the quadrangle although its axis is not aligned with it, nor with the central structure, but shifted approximately 2 m northwards (hereafter the complex with the cruciform structure). The plans of the cruciform and hexagonal structures show up on the georesistivity plot as distinct, dark areas, indicating that their foundations remain in situ. The foundations of the quadrangle, on the other hand, appear to be best preserved on the western and eastern sides; in the north and south, its

Fig. 6. *Silver coin of the emperor Arcadius collected in 2010.*

contours show up as two parallel grey lines, suggesting that the foundations have been removed, leaving only a robber trench.

Two additional structures are visible on the map: just northeast of the cruciform structure is a small rectangular structure approximately 4 x 2 m and of a slightly different orientation. Also in the northeastern corner of the area

5   The georesistivity survey was not part of the WEmW project. See Czichon et al. 2011.

27

Fig. 7. *Threshold ploughed out of the Papaz Tarlası (Photo: Kristina Winther-Jacobsen).*

Fig. 8. *Detail of threshold ploughed out of the Papaz Tarlası (Photo: Kristina Winther-Jacobsen).*

surveyed is another rectangular structure approximately 6 x 7 m, again of a different orientation (hereafter the northeastern complex).

The main structural elements of the complex with the cruciform structure identified in the Papaz Tarlasi are quite distinctive (see below). Based on the plan, the quadrangle is tentatively identified as an open courtyard, possibly with a colonnade; the hexagonal structure in its centre as a fountain; and the cruciform structure as a *martyrion*.

Simultaneously with the resistivity survey, a grab sample was collected from the field for the purpose of a preliminary assessment of the chronology. The preliminary analysis of the pottery by Kristina Winther-Jacobsen in 2012 suggested that only Roman and post-Roman material was collected. A silver coin of the Emperor Arcadius, already known, provided a preliminary date for the assemblage (Fig. 6).

Architectural fragments

The plan produced by the resistivity survey is complemented by the evidence of multiple architectural remains recovered from the surface of the field believed to originate from the sub-surface structures; these include a stone threshold and a broken column. The grey limestone threshold of the standard Roman type (Fig. 7) measures 1.46 x 0.55 m and the door opening was 1.175 m wide. Two thirds of the surface has been cut down to a lower level, leaving a small step to shut the door against, 6 cm high. The positions of the five holes, one square hole in the

Fig. 9. *Fragmented column shaft ploughed out of the Papaz Tarlası (Photo: Kristina Winther-Jacobsen).*

middle and one square and one round hole facing each other at either end, indicate that the threshold was intended for a double door with a vertical locking bar. The

Fig. 10. *Detail of fragmented column shaft ploughed out of the Papaz Tarlası (Photo: Kristina Winther-Jacobsen).*

hinges rotated in the round holes at either end, positioned opposite the square holes which received the lower ends of the jambs. All three square holes are the same size, 7.5 cm wide, and the two round holes are also identical with a diameter of 8 cm, suggesting some level of standardization. On the side of the block, tool marks of both point and tooth chisels can be seen very clearly (Fig. 8). A fragment of a similar threshold can be seen lying in a field in the Tikenli Mahallesi on the southwestern edge of the city where tombs were reported to have been found in the spring of 1900.[6] A complete threshold was found in 2012 during construction work in the 517 Sokak.[7]

A broken monolithic column of polished grey limestone was also observed in the field (Fig. 9). The fragment is 1.03 m long. The diameter at the top is wider than 0.35 cm, and the shaft is 0.365 cm in diameter at the fracture. The top of the column is finished with two flat bands, each 4 cm high, of which the edges are not sharp, but slightly rounded and smooth. The shaft measures 0.95 cm and it tapers towards the bottom. On the top, tool marks of both point and tooth chisels can be seen very clearly (Fig. 10).

A fragment of a grave stele was also found (Fig. 11). The top had been cut off and the surface worked with a point chisel. The bottom is broken, leaving the shape of the block irregular. It measures approximately 0.50 x 0.28 m. There is an irregular, rounded hole in the back which points toward its secondary use as a threshold. Remains of mortar with small pebbles on the back indicate that

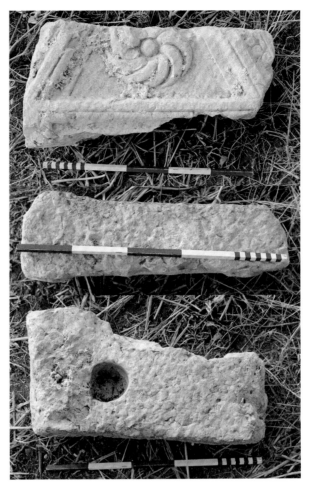

Fig. 11. *Grave stele ploughed out of the Papaz Tarlası: front, top section and back (Photo: Kristina Winther-Jacobsen).*

it was fitted into some kind of architecture, presumably the structure in the Papaz Tarlasi. Preserved on the front of the block is the top of the double-framed main panel and the lower part of the double-framed pediment flanked with acroteria. At the centre of the pediment is a rosette with curved pointy leaves. The acroteria appear to consist of at least three leaves pointing downwards and ending in three spirals resembling 'comma' locks. A stele from Pompeiopolis in the Museum of Kastamonu may have been produced by the same workshop or artist. Although the decoration of the pediment is different (a

6   Cumont & Cumont 1906, 132.
7   Nerik database, photo no. 000020938.

Fig. 12. *Foundation exposed in the south slope (Fig. 5.2) (Photo: Kristina Winther-Jacobsen).*

Fig. 13. *Foundation exposed in the south slope (Fig. 5.1) (Photo: Kristina Winther-Jacobsen).*

pine cone resting on acanthus leaves), the proportions and details of the double frame and acroteria are similar and quite distinctive. The inscription on this stele does not mention the era, but based on the Antonine name it can be dated to the 2nd century.[8] Another stele photographed by Professor E. Olshausen in 1990 in Karkucak (6 km south of Vezirköprü) is decorated in the same fashion as the stele from Pompeiopolis, but the relief appears to be deeper.[9] In 1988 Olshausen photographed a well-preserved stele with a similar but apparently unfinished double frame in Kocaoğlu, c. 5 km southeast of Kayabaşı, formerly Tahna, near the bridge known as the Kurt Köprüsü ('wolf bridge').[10] The pediment is decorated with a rosette similar to the one found in the Papaz Tarlası, but the panel with the inscription is also decorated with a mirror and a comb. This stele was inscribed with the era of the city, dating it in the year 192 of the era, i.e. 186/7, providing an approximate *terminus post quem* for the structure in the Papaz Tarlası. To the non-epigraphist the lettering seems to indicate three different hands, but such conclusions await the publication by Olshausen. Indeed some inscriptions give evidence of multiple hands on the same monument and there

need not be any connection between the artist and the stonecutter who carves the inscription.[11] From the distribution of the four pieces and the seemingly unfinished state of the stele from Kocaoğlu, it seems most likely that the workshop was located in Vezirköprü, but the pieces could also have been produced by an itinerant artist. The existence of itinerant artists is widely assumed, but there appears to be little research into the phenomenon.[12] An inscription from Havza/Thermai tôn Phazemonitôn set up by a Proklos from Sinope mentions at the bottom the name of the artist, Chresstos.[13] The word following the artist's name is not complete but based on the preserved letters and the parallel with the first line mentioning the dedicator, the word may be reconstructed as an ethnic reference to his home town Sinope. Multiple scenarios can be reconstructed from this information. Was Chresstos a famous artist in Sinope, who made the stele at his workshop there? Did he travel to Thermai specifically to make the stele? Was he an itinerant artist? The case certainly testifies to the mobility of people and/or artefacts as Proklos himself seems to have come from Sinope to be healed in the springs of Thermai, about 125 km away as the crow flies but over difficult terrain.

8   Marek 1993; Pompeiopolis 38, 147.

9   Personal communication by Professor Eckart Olshausen and Dr. Vera Sauer, for which we are very grateful. The stele will be published in the volume of the inscriptions of Neoklaudiopolis, which is in preparation for the series *Inschriften griechischer Städte aus Kleinasien*.

10   See n. 6.

11   Bekker-Nielsen & Høgel 2012, 153, no. 1. Studies of the craftsmen cutting the inscriptions focus mainly on Athens, e.g. Tracy & Dow 1975.

12   Jennifer Trimble (2011, 121, 144) mentions itinerant artists but cites no references. Boon 1989, 248.

13   Anderson, Cumont & Grégoire 1910, 38-40. We're grateful to Søren Lund Sørensen for drawing our attention to this inscription and explaining the epigraphical context.

Fig. 14. *Water channel exposed in the south slope (Fig. 5.3) (Photo: Kristina Winther-Jacobsen).*

Many fragments of tiles and bricks, as well as some cut stone blocks bonded with mortar were found in rubbish heaps on the southern edge of the field. In 2013 a foundation matching the southeastern corner of the quadrangle on the geoelectric map had become visible in the slope. The foundation consists of stratified layers of field stones bound by mortar tempered with small pebbles (Figs 5.2, 12). It is at least 80 cm deep.

Another foundation was identified in the slope southwest of the quadrangle, which from its location is not immediately associable with the complex with the cruciform structure (Figs 5.1, 13). This foundation seems to be of a different quality, including cut stone blocks and brick, and it appears to be at least 2.5 m wide.

Furthermore, a water channel constructed from field stones and mortar tempered with small pebbles and lined with pink mortar was identified protruding from the slope further to the east (Fig. 5.3): however, its location at a much lower level suggests that it is either not in situ or not associated with the structures in the field (Fig. 14).

The intensive systematic survey

Based on the preliminary survey carried out in 2010 under the auspices of the Nerik project and the analysis of the data carried out in 2012, it was decided to apply an inten-

sive, systematic survey strategy to the field to analyze the distribution of finds in order to confirm the relationship between surface and sub-surface structures identified by the resistivity survey, and to reach a better understanding of the chronology and function of the sub-surface structures and their interrelationship.[14]

Methodology

The field was divided into geomorphologically homogeneous units in a grid of 10 x 10 m squares (73 in total, as well as sub-sized ones along the edge of the field laid out using a total station and marked with flags at the corners of each square; Fig. 5). A total collection of 10% of the surface material was achieved by total count/collection of all finds in 1 m transects spaced at 9 m intervals (81 in total). Total collection included anything from the size of a thumbnail and bigger – smaller objects were only collected if they were diagnostic or recognizable by a distinctive feature. The vast majority of sherds were architectural fragments. Subsequently, the pottery collected was sorted into use-categories, counted and weighed in the field; only a diagnostic sample was collected for full registration in the inventory. The survey of the transect lines was followed up by an intensive, systematic (nine field-walkers shoulder to shoulder) survey of the squares between the transect lines. The sample collected from the squares was random, aiming at specifically diagnostic pieces for the inventory.

We operated with three levels of recording: 1) sherds per transect line (number and weight); 2) finds groups per transect line (number and weight); and 3) inventory (individual sherds). Since the total sum is unknown, the validity of our data rests on our ability to control and compare them. The different levels of recording provide us with different data sets for different purposes:

Recording of sherds allows us to map their distribution across the survey area.

Recording of finds groups allows us to detect differentiation in the distribution of different functions of finds across the survey area.

---

14   The survey was carried out under permit number 94949537-161.02-174996, issued on September 9, 2013, by the Ministry of Tourism and Culture, General Directorate of Cultural Heritage and Museums of the Turkish Republic. The representative of the Turkish government was Mustafa Kolağasıoğlu from the Directorate of Samsun Museum. We are grateful to the director and staff of the Museum and to the local authorities of Vezirköprü for their cooperation.

Fig. 15. *Tiles collected from WEmW13:090-100/080-090.*

Fig. 16. *Tile collected from WEmW13:060/090.*

Recording individual finds allows us to study differentiation in temporal patterns and provenance.

The initial sorting of the finds into use groups was done in the field by the field-walkers, but checked by the ceramics expert before recording. The definitions of the use categories were established based on the results of the analysis of the pottery from the preliminary survey in 2010, when a random sample was collected. The use-categories were: architectural fragments, tableware, kitchen ware, cooking ware, transport amphorae and 'other'. The individual finds were categorized based on shape, fabric, decoration, firing technology, style and size. Two of the groups – cooking wares and transport amphorae – were rarely recognized as such in the field, where they were categorized as kitchen ware. Consequently, the quantified distribution maps which are based on the statistically valid, systematic, total collection in the transect lines only include the categories architectural fragments, tableware, kitchen ware (including cooking wares and transport amphorae) and other.

In accordance with the guidelines set out by the Turkish authorities, all inventoried finds of the inventory were photographed, drawn and described, then re-deposited back in the field from which they came. The results of the three levels of registration were recorded into an Access database.

The finds

Based on their visual similarity with the fabrics of Iron Age ceramics from Nerik/Oymaağaç, the vast majority of ceramics collected appear to be of regional production for which no *comparanda* have been published. The only contexts in the Nerik excavations dated to the Roman or Early Byzantine period are the graves, which included no pottery.[15] The nearest published site to Vezirköprü is Taşköprü (ancient Pompeiopolis), where the ceramics are currently undergoing analysis and only preliminary studies of the tablewares and selected coarse wares have been published.[16] KWJ was kindly allowed to study some of the Pompeiopolis material for reference.[17] Consequently, the chronology for the Papaz Tarlası is based almost exclusively on the tableware and coins, as well as parallels with the Pompeiopolis material and general typo-morphology and technology. The tableware is almost exclusively Pontic Red Slip ware, a type of pottery studied by Dr. K.

15   Personal communication by Dr. Pavol Hnila, who is studying the Nerik tile graves, for which we are very grateful.

16   Domżalski 2011; Zhuravlev 2011.

17   KWJ is very grateful to the director of the Pompeiopolis project, Professor Lâtife Summerer and to the director of the Late Roman villa project, Dr. Luisa Musso for allowing her to study their material and refer to it here, and to Drs M. Brizzi, K. Domżalski, and M. Gwiazda for sharing their thoughts on the matter.

Fig. 17. *Ceramics collected from WEmW13:090-100/060-070.*

Fig. 18. *Ceramics collected from WEmW13:120-130/030-040.*

Domżalski.[18] The 2002 article by Arsen'eva and Domżalski is the most detailed publication to date, but this material includes little of the Pontic Red Slip form 7, which is the most common Pontic Red Slip form found in the Papaz Tarlası. 504 ceramics sherds were inventoried, including the material collected in 2010: 37 architectural fragments, 40 cooking ware fragments, 313 kitchen ware fragments, 110 tableware fragments, four transport amphora fragments and one lamp nozzle. The inventory is not proportionally representative, but selected for its chronological significance and morphological range.

Architectural fragments

The vast majority of ceramics collected belonged in the architectural category: flat square floor tiles/bricks and Corinthian-style pan tiles/tegulae combined with curved cover tiles/imbrices (so-called Sicilian style) (Pl. 1 nos. 060/090.2, 090-100/080-090.1, 120-130/030-040.2, 110-120/060-070.5). Although the curved cover tiles can be difficult to distinguish from the traditional pre-modern tiles of which many had been dumped among the rubbish along the slope, their sheer number and the fact that no

other types of cover tiles were identified suggests the association with the pan tiles. None of the fragments preserve the complete profile, but they were probably V-shaped rather than U-shaped.[19] All the different types of tiles are smoothed on the upper side and rough on the underside from being made in a mould. The flat part of the pan tiles ranges in thickness from 1.6 to 2.3 cm. The cover tiles range from 1.4 to 1.8 cm in thickness, and the two possible ridge tiles are both 2.7 cm thick (Pl. 1 nos. 110-120/060-070.5 and 150-160/090-100.1). Unlike the tiles from the Nerik tile graves, the outer edges are smoothed.[20] Some of the tiles testify to a more mechanical production with sharper lines (Fig. 15 above left), while others appear more "handmade", with curved and smoothed transitions (Figs 15 below right, 16 and 17 right). One sub-type of tile has raised edges with a smoothed surface running straight to the edge (Fig. 15 below right), another has curved corners (Fig. 17 right), while a third type with a more mechanical appearance has a raised band along the short end (Figs 15 above left and 18 left). The lower corners are narrower to allow insertion into the next layer on the roof and the transition is angular (Figs 15 below left and 16). No fragments preserve both ends, and all styles appear in the same transect lines. In

---

18   We are very grateful to Dr. Domżalski for his personal comments on the Pontic Red Slip fragments from the Papaz Tarlası. For his publications on Pontic Red Slip see Domżalski 2000; 2007; 2011 and Arsen'eva & Domżalski 2002.

19   Similar to Özyiğit 1990, fig. 5g–h.

20   The Nerik tiles are yet unpublished, but in 2012 KWJ was allowed to study the material, for which we are very grateful.

33

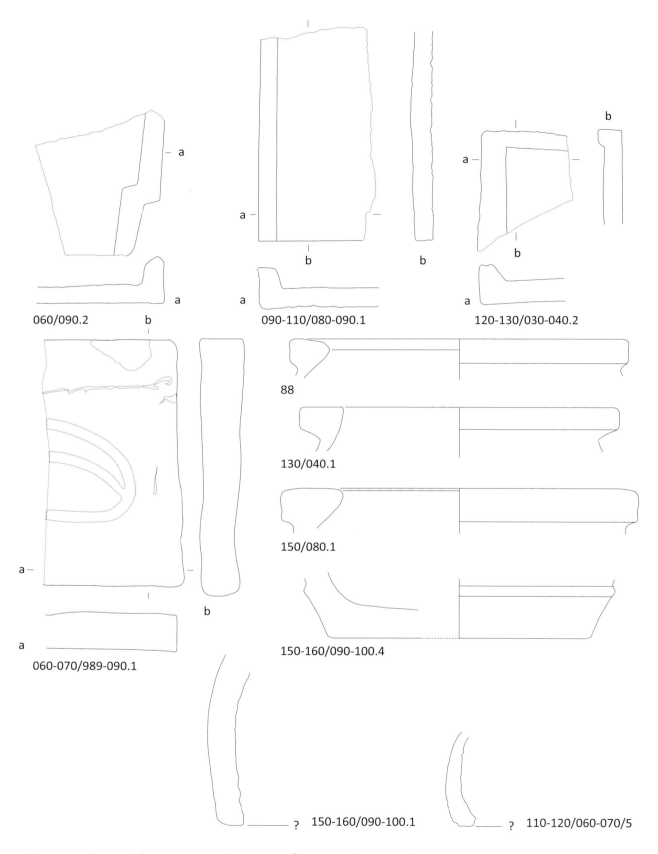

060/090.2   b

090-110/080-090.1

120-130/030-040.2

060-070/989-090.1

88

130/040.1

150/080.1

150-160/090-100.4

? 150-160/090-100.1

? 110-120/060-070/5

34

Plate 1. *Architectural fragments and pithoi, scale 1:4 (Drawings: Christina Hildebrandt & Kristina Winther-Jacobsen).*

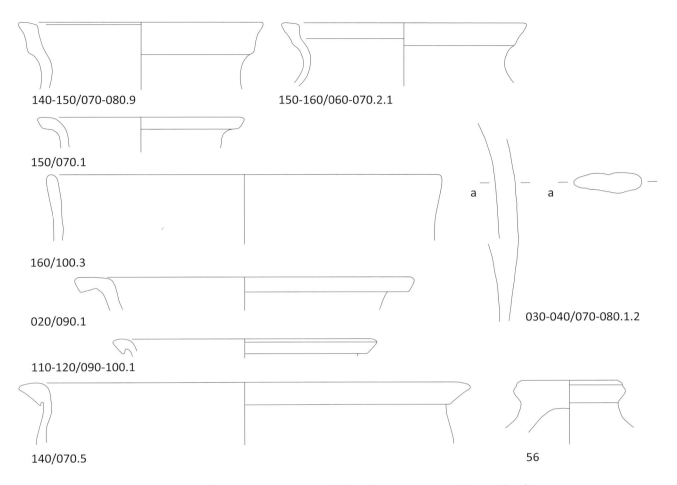

140-150/070-080.9

150-160/060-070.2.1

150/070.1

160/100.3

020/090.1

030-040/070-080.1.2

110-120/090-100.1

140/070.5

56

Plate 2. *Cooking wares. Scale 1:2 (Drawings: Christina Hildebrandt & Kristina Winther-Jacobsen).*

terms of production, the variety of composition of temper suggests multiple phases, workshops or batches. A range of misfired tiles were recorded, with everything from discoloured to malformed and vitrified, suggesting the tiles were produced close by (Figs 15 right and 19). A few distinctive tiles were inventoried including the two possible ridge tiles, interpreted according to their greater width (Fig. 20, pl. 1, no. 150-160/090-100.1). One fragment is decorated with shallow grooves traced with the fingers. Another one appears to have undergone a secondary use (Fig. 21). The raised edge has been chipped away slanting towards the flat part, possibly for a drain. In the preliminary report we tentatively concluded that the types of tile found in the Papaz Tarlası are different from the tiles used in the tile graves at Nerik, which may suggest a different chronology, but also denote a different workshop. The difference is confirmed by the material collected in the intensive survey.

Many floor tiles/bricks were recorded, sometimes decorated with finger marks (Fig. 22, pl. 1 no. 060-070/080-090.1). They are approximately 3-5 cm in thickness, often preserving a thick layer of mortar up to 4 cm on at least one side (Fig. 23). Two complete floor tiles found on the steep slope measured 29.5 x 30 cm, being 3-3.5 cm thick. Stone tiles in a similar range of thicknesses were also used for floors, as indicated by their shape and the mortar attached to them (Fig. 24).

In the preliminary survey, fragments of water pipes were collected, but in the 2013 season it became obvious from their occurrence in the rubbish heaps on the slope south of the field that they are not ancient.

Additionally, three small fragments of marble decoration, probably architectural, were recorded during the survey (Figs 25-6). The first is a 1.34 cm-thick white marble tile, probably from *opus sectile* decoration of a vertical

Fig. 19. *Tile collected from WEmW13:090-100/070-080.*

Fig. 20. *Ridge tile collected from WEmW13:150-160/090-100.*

Fig. 21. *Chipped tile collected in 2010.*

Fig. 22. *Floor tile/brick collected from WEmW13:160-170/080-090.*

Fig. 23. *Floor tile/brick collected from WEmW13:040/060.*

Fig. 24. *Stone floor tile(?) collected from WEmW13:150-160/110-120.*

Fig. 25. *Decorative fragments of marble collected from the Papaz Tarlası (front).*

Fig. 26. *Decorative fragments of marble collected from the Papaz Tarlası (back).*

37

Fig. 27.
Ceramics collected from
WEmW13:140-150/070-080.

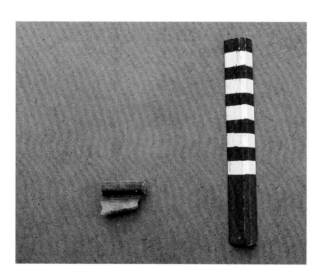

Fig. 28. Cooking pot fragment collected from
WEmW13:150/070.

Fig. 29. Ceramics collected from WEmW13:160/100.

Fig. 30. Ceramics of phyllite-rich fabric collected from
WEmW13:010/090.

surface. On the back there are traces made with a pointed chisel, but the location of these tool marks along the edge suggests that these may have been made when prying the tile off a wall. The second fragment resembles a Doric hawk's beak on a plain flat band. The fragment is too small to be sure, but the front also appears to be curved like a rosette or a clipeus. Only the hawk's beak part is polished. The third marble fragment has a decorated front and a flat rear face: it consists of a straight band with two curved stems abutting, and on their convex side the remains of a small knob. This fragment must come from some sort of shallow, openwork relief.

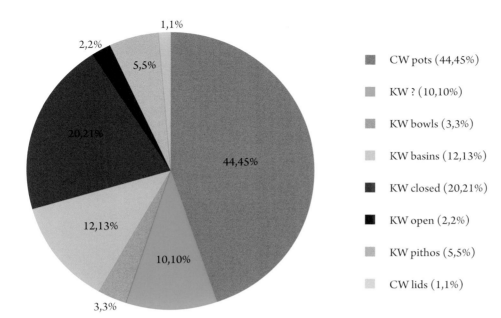

- ■ CW pots (44,45%)
- ■ KW ? (10,10%)
- ■ KW bowls (3,3%)
- ■ KW basins (12,13%)
- ■ KW closed (20,21%)
- ■ KW open (2,2%)
- ■ KW pithos (5,5%)
- ■ CW lids (1,1%)

Table 1 *Form and functional distribution of vessels in phyllite-rich fabric (Graph: Kristina Winther-Jacobsen)*

Other finds

Apart from the architectural fragments, the finds include pottery, a lamp, glass, two coins and slag. The pottery consists mainly of kitchen ware, some tableware and cooking wares and a few, rare fragments of transport amphorae. Initially, it was difficult to distinguish the cooking wares as the types otherwise widely produced and imported across the Roman Empire appear not to have been used regularly in this area. A single thin strap-handle of quartz-rich fabric collected in the preliminary survey in 2010 and less than a handful of rim fragments collected during the intensive survey come from types of cooking vessel typical of the Roman period, suggesting that the type appeared irregularly here. Furthermore, soot, which would assist in the identification of local/regional cooking wares, is relatively rare. The three sooted fragments all belong to a type of vessel which we, based on its distinctive shape and fabric and its similarity with Late Roman cooking wares at Pompeiopolis,[21] interpret as local/regional cooking ware (Figs 27-9, pl. 2 nos. 140-150/070-080.9, 150/070.1, 160/100.3). The fabric is highly distinctive because it is dominated by a characteristic inclusion: although this mineral changes colour in the firing process, its large grain size, angular,

thin, flat shape, slate-like surface and its predominance makes it distinctive (Fig. 30). Based on a sample kept by the Nerik project, we believe the mineral to be phyllite, which occurs in the region.[22] Among the sherds from the Papaz Tarlası, ninety-eight are made from phyllite-rich fabrics. The cooking wares represent almost half of these vessels, but the phyllite-rich fabrics are not exclusive to cooking wares (Table 1). The range of pottery made from the phyllite-rich fabrics, including rather heavy vessels such as pithoi, suggests that much of this pottery was produced in the area. The phyllite does not, however, appear in the same combination in the tile fabrics, another type of ceramics assumed to have been produced in the area given the presence of many misfired pieces. This is probably the result of some sort of functional differentiation in the production. Our knowledge of ancient ceramics production suggests that none of the fabrics are 'natural'.[23] They have all undergone the process of purification including some selection of inclusions. In the case of the phyllite-rich fabrics, the angular shape, large grain size and number of these specific inclusions indicate that they were produced by crushing rock fragments specifically for

---

21   The pottery from Pompeiopolis is unpublished except for Domżalski 2011, 168. See n. 2.
22   Personal communication by Dr. Rainer Czichon, for which we are very grateful.
23   E.g. Rice 1987, 52; Winther-Jacobsen 2010, 51-2.

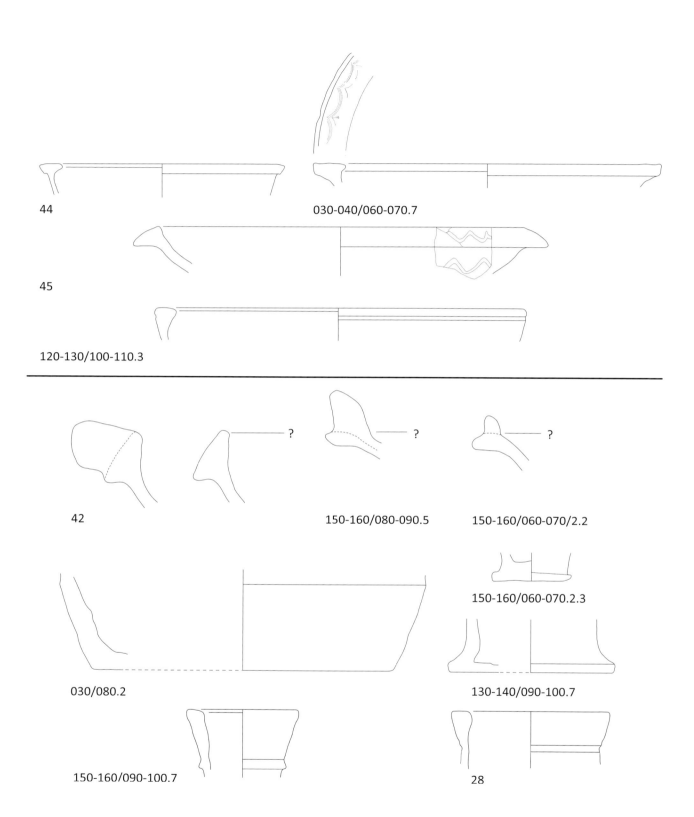

Plate 3. *Kitchen wares, above scale 1:4; below scale 1:2 (Drawings: Christina Hildebrandt & Kristina Winther-Jacobsen).*

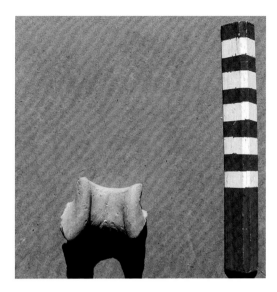

Fig. 31. *Spout of basin collected from WEmW13:150-160/060-070.*

Fig. 32. *Fragment of pithos collected from WEmW13:160-170/080-090.*

the purpose of providing the fabric with certain qualities, real or imagined.[24] The mineral also appears in a wide range of shapes and types of pottery at Pompeiopolis.

The kitchen wares consist of mostly open and some closed vessels as well as pithoi (Pl. 1 nos. 88, 130/040.1, 150/080.1/ 150-160/090-100.4 and pl. 3). The most common type of kitchen ware is the basin, often with a spout attached to the rim (Fig. 31). This type of vessel is also common in the late Roman contexts at Pompeiopolis.[25] Two types occur in the Papaz Tarlası: the type with the spout inserted into the section of the rim (Pl. 3 no. 42) and the apparently more popular type where a spout is attached like a gutter on top of the rim (e.g. pl. 3 nos. 150-160/80-90.5 and 150-160/060-070.2.2). Among the kitchen wares are fragments of large thick-walled pithoi (Figs 32-3, pl. 1, nos. 88, 130/040.1, 150/080.1, 150-160/090-100.4). Although the kitchen wares are very difficult to date, certain stylistic features indicate a symbiotic relationship to the Late Roman Pontic Red Slip. Firstly, a distinctive type of hollow stemmed base

which is known from the closed vessels in the Pontic Red Slip production occur among the kitchen wares, although a similar design is also known from lids (Pl. 3 nos. 150-160/060-070.2.3 and 10-140/090-100.7).[26] Secondly, the type of combed decoration popular on Pontic Red Slip form 3 is found on a kitchen ware basin (Fig. 34, pl. 3 no. 030-040/060/070.7).[27]

One handle attachment of a Sinopean amphora was identified by the volcanic sand, but the fragment is too poorly preserved to reveal any information about the shape and type (Fig. 35).

The lamp, of which only the spout was found, was originally slipped, but the surface is very poorly preserved (Fig. 36). The proximity of the hole for the wick and the filling hole, both of which are surrounded by an exterior offset rim, is very unusual and no close parallels have been found. Overall, the range of pottery types and styles is restricted, suggesting that the different structures belong within the same period and that the structures were relatively intensely used within a fairly short time span.

---

24 Several articles in the recent volume on ancient cooking wares edited by Spataro & Villing (2015), e.g. Whitbread 2015, discuss the significance of inclusions.

25 Domżalski 2011, 168, pl. 7.2.

26 Arsen'eva & Domżalski 2002, fig. 13.581-2; Ferrazzoli & Ricci 2007, 686, fig. 16.79; Pellegrino 2007, 665, figs 2.20 and 22.

27 Domżalski 2001, pl. 3.2.

Fig. 34. *Ceramics collected from WEmW13:030-040/060-070.*

Fig. 33. *Fragment of pithos lid(?) collected from WEmW13:150/100.*

Fig. 35. *Sinopean amphora handle attachment collected from WEmW13:130-140/100-110.*

The only pottery that can be dated within a narrow chronological bracket is the red slipped tableware (Table 2). The most popular tableware by far is Pontic Red Slip form 7, produced in the second half of the 5th and first quarter of the 6th century. Form 7 appears in several variants at the Papaz Tarlası (Pl. 4 nos. 5-6, 090-090.2, 140/080.1, 080-090/100-110.1).[28] Interestingly, this large dish with false ring-base and everted angular rim is not a common form at Pompeiopolis, the closest neighbouring city to have been excavated. The second half of the 5th century is a period in time when the repertory of forms changed and Pontic Red Slip ware lost its predominance to LRD tablewares from Western Asia Minor, even if only a single base fragment of LRD was identified in the Papaz Tarlası.[29] The identified Pontic Red Slip also includes fragments of form 3 (Fig. 37), as well as an unclassified form dated from the mid 4th to the mid 5th century (Pl. 4 no. 080-090/100-110.1).[30] A few of the tableware sherds appear to be Pontic Sigillata, which was the predecessor of Pontic Red Slip; these include two possible rims of Pontic Sigillata forms 14-16 dated in the 2nd or 3w century (Pl. 4 no. 090-100/060-070.1).[31] Due to their small size and poor preservation, it is possible that these early sherds are residual.

The glass is too fragmented for any definite conclusions to be drawn, except that all the fragments are made from monochrome, clear, blue-green glass and that vessels

---

28 Personal communication by K. Domżalski for which we are very grateful.

29 Arsen'eva & Domżalski 2002, 424-5.

30 Arsen'eva & Domżalski 2002, 424-5, figs 10-3; Domżalski 2011, pl. 2.7-11.

31 Zhuravlev 2011, 151, pl. 1.17-9. Less likely, but also possible is Pontic Red Slip from 4 (Arsen'eva & Domżalski 2002, fig. 13).

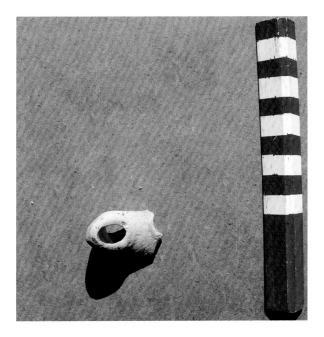

Fig. 36. *Nozzle of lamp collected from WEmW13:110-120/080-090.*

Fig. 37. *Base fragment of Pontic Red Slip form 3 collected from WEmW13:110-120/070-080.*

appear to be have been small and very thin-walled. The two coins, one of which had been minted on a clipped elder one, are poorly preserved, but have been identified as Byzantine *folles* by Vera Sauer. The clipped coin was minted between 652 and 656 and the other coin can only be dated between 539 and 717.[32]

Finally the slag, which appears to be from the production of iron, was found in the northeastern corner of the grid near the structure there, indicating the possibility of a complex combining domestic and productive activities (Fig. 38). However, as a roughly round object, it has high mobility and could be intrusive.

The Post-Roman periods are represented by, for instance, green glazed table and utility wares common of the Ottoman period. An amphora handle stamped with four incuse asterisks finds its closest parallel in a fragment

Type	Date
Pontic Red Slip form 1?	Mid 4th-mid 5th century?
Pontic Red Slip form 3	late 4th/5th -mid 5th century
Pontic Red Slip form 4	late 4th-mid 5th century
Pontic Red Slip unclassified form	second half of 4th-first half of 5th century
Pontic Red Slip form 7 variants	second half of 5th-first quarter of the 6th century
Phocaean Red Slip	mid 5th century onwards

Table 2. *Tableware chronology based on Domżalski 2000 and Arsen'eva & Domżalski 2002.*

---

32   For reconstruction of dates see appendix by Vera Sauer.

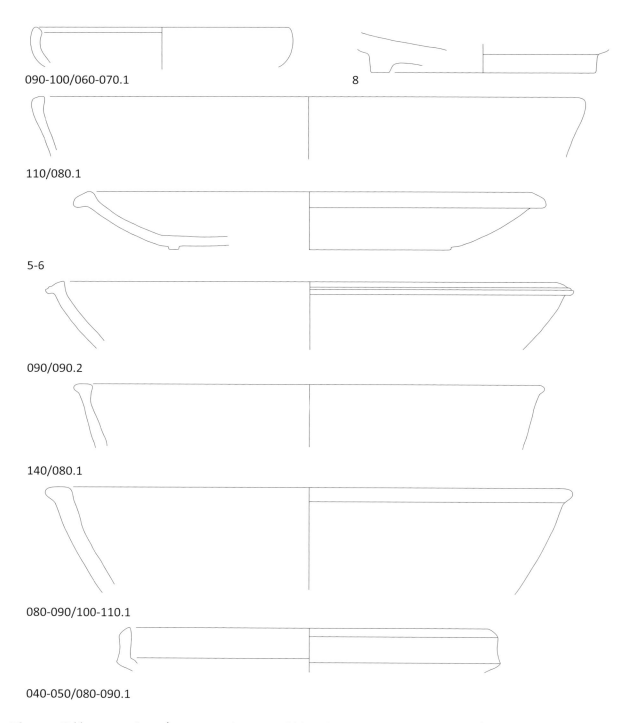

090-100/060-070.1

8

110/080.1

5-6

090/090.2

140/080.1

080-090/100-110.1

040-050/080-090.1

Plate 4. *Tablewares, scale 1:2 (Drawings: Christina Hildebrandt & Kristina Winther-Jacobsen)*

from Saraçhane dated to the late 10th/early 11th century, although it was found with earlier material (Fig. 40).[33] A similar stamp also occurs on Saraçhane amphora type 54 of the 10th or 11th century.[34] However, the majority of fragments belong to plain domestic types of pottery, jars, bowls and basins, which cannot be securely dated at the moment. Consequently it is not currently possible to estimate how much of the kitchen and cooking wares are

Fig. 38. *Iron slag collected from WEmW13:170/090.*

Fig. 39. *Amphora handle collected from WEmW13:140-150/090-100.*

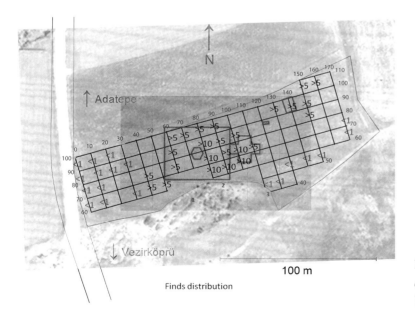

Fig. 40. *Finds distribution recorded across the Papaz Tarlası (Plan: Kristina Winther-Jacobsen).*

33   Hayes 1992, 78, no. 19, fig. 27, pl. 14.
34   Vroom 2005, 95, fig. MBYZ 13.1.

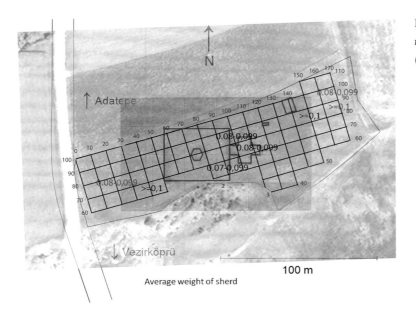

Fig. 41. *Average weight of sherds recorded across the Papaz Tarlası (Plan: Kristina Winther-Jacobsen).*

post-Roman. As for tablewares, small glazed fragments were collected in the squares, but none in the transect lines; consequently there is no statistical material. By comparison, 29 fragments of Roman red slipped tableware were collected in the transect lines.

The distribution pattern

The distribution of ceramics across the field confirms the expectations concerning the state of preservation of the sub-surface structures as suggested in the preliminary investigations of 2012. The state of preservation of the pottery ranges from poor to medium, with a few well-preserved fragments indicating that new material is ploughed up in every new agricultural episode. This is supported by the emergence in 2013 of the broken column, which was not on the surface in 2010, and the reused stele. Consequently, the sub-surface material should be in a good state of preservation. Additional evidence is the discreteness of the densities – the fact that surface finds are closely related to sub-surface structures, e.g. the large number of architectural fragments over the cruciform structure. The areas immediately over the sub-surface structures, especially the hexagonal and the cruciform structures and the southeastern corner of the quadrangle, reveal high densities of up to 1.4 kg of ceramics per square metre (Fig. 40). The highest densities were recorded along the southern edge of the quadrangle, where its edge has been eroded and become

visible in the steep slope (see above). The small rectangular structure just northeast of the cruciform structure almost disappears in the high densities on its immediate southwest and northeast sides, but it can be traced in the ceramics distribution map as an increase in finds of approximately 80% in the transect line cutting across it, compared to the transect lines left and right. The structure approximately 20 m further to the northeast is visible as a discrete, high density cluster of about 800 m². This cluster extends outside the area of the resistivity survey, and it is highly likely that there were additional structures in this part of the Papaz Tarlası, aside from the one revealed by the resistivity survey. Although the chronological range appears to be similar, there is a clear functional differentiation between this northeastern complex and the complex with the cruciform structure (see below).

The total range of the average weight of individual sherds is 1 to 134 g, but in 49 of the 81 transect lines, the average weight ranges between 0.015 and 0.034 g. Only in eight transect lines is the average weight of sherds between 75 and 134 g (Fig. 41). A partial correlation between density and average weight (average weights of minimum 0.08 kg per sherd) can be observed in the area of the complex with the cruciform structure and the northeastern complex, but there are also deviances from this pattern – for instance the high average weight in transect 170 at the northeastern edge of the field, where there is evidence for less ploughing and consequently less destruction. The explanation for the high average weight of sherds in transect line 020/070 can be explained by the occurrence of a single, very large tile fragment, a type of find which behaves differently on the surface as it gets caught very easily in the agricultural equipment.[35] In all the transect lines except 150/080 the non-architectural fragments make up only a tiny proportion of the finds, especially by weight, which was to be expected given the original size of the complete artefacts.

The ratio of architectural ceramics to other types of ceramics/pottery is 271:16 kg or 17:1, suggesting that the structures were coved by tile roofs when they collapsed. The category includes both roof and floor tiles/bricks as these are indistinguishable when very fragmented. The ratio is of course not constant across the field, but a particularly interesting variation is observed in the cluster overlying the northeastern complex. Here the ratio is only 16:4 kg or 4:1 because of 3.59 kg of pithos fragments recorded in transect line 150/080, a type of kitchen ware rarely recorded in other parts of the field; this suggests a domestic function for this complex. None of the other transect lines produced more than 700 g of pottery per 10 m². If we subtract the 3.59 kg of pithos fragments, the ratio becomes 16:1, which is very close to the average of the field.

Several observations can be made based on the overall distribution of the different use-categories (Figs 42-3). Fig. 42 includes the data from both the transects and the squares, whereas Fig. 43 only includes the quantifiable data from the transects. Consequently, patterns observed in Fig. 42 should be consistently checked against Fig. 43. Tiles and kitchen wares are not included as they are found all over the field, although clearly concentrated over the structures (see above). Fig. 40 can be viewed as a tile distribution map due to the size and predominance of this type of ceramic (17:1) when weighed. As mentioned before, the distribution of pithoi appears to be highly significant, especially when correlating the pattern with that of the basins (Figs 42-3). The majority of fragments of pithoi and all the fragments of spouted basins came from the northeastern part of the field where the combination of tiles, pithoi, kitchen, cooking and tablewares with iron slag suggests a combination of domestic and productive activities for the northeastern complex. Some function-

al differentiation may be implied by the distribution of pithoi, which seem to concentrate in the northeast, and cooking wares, which seem to concentrate to the south, but the collection in the squares was not systematic and consequently this pattern should not be over-emphasized. The field boundary system favours ploughing longitudinally, which affects the displacement of the surface, making it more likely to move east–west than north–south. The pithos fragments found in the central south corner of the field are explained by the topography. The field slopes down quite steeply in this corner, and these large fragments have probably rolled to the lowest part of the field. In the area of the complex with the cruciform structure mainly kitchen ware and tableware were found, which may be another indication of functional differentiation suggesting that cooking and storing took place mainly in the northeastern complex. However, there seems to be a concentration of cooking and tableware west of the square structure, either originating from the complex with the cruciform structure or indicating the existence of further, unknown structures in this area. As deeper foundations have been identified in the slope (Fig. 5.1), this is not impossible, but it seems more likely that these finds originate in the complex with the cruciform structure and have been displaced by ploughing.

In general, the types of ceramics found are very homogeneous, suggesting a relatively short period of activity. The finds from the northeastern complex appear to belong to the same chronological period, but the slag may be an indication of other than domestic activities. An obvious interpretation of the finds in the northeastern complex is that it served as domestic quarters for the activities associated with the complex with the cruciform structure, and possibly also as a farmhouse.

Interpretation

The cruciform structure is tentatively identified as an early Christian *martyrion*-complex. A *martyrion* was not a church in the strict sense of the word but a shrine to a martyr, often located at the site of the martyr's death or burial.[36] However, the distinction between the *martyrion* and church tended to disappear towards the end of the

---

35   Baker 1978; Dunnell 1990, 592.
36   Grabar 1972, 152-61; Syndicus 1962, 72-89.

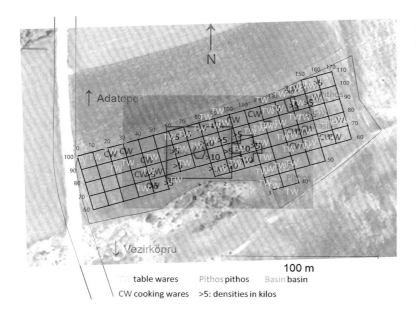

Fig. 42. *Functional categories recorded across the Papaz Tarlası (Plan: Kristina Winther-Jacobsen).*

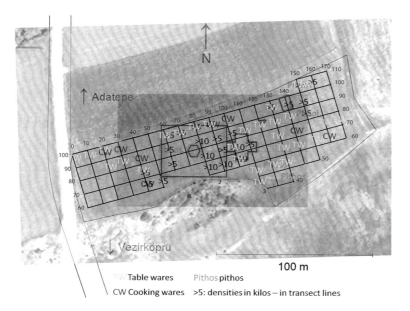

Fig. 43. *Functional categories recorded in transect lines only (Plan: Kristina Winther-Jacobsen).*

4th century, when the practice of depositing relics or the body of a saint near the altar became more widespread.[37] Several writers of the early church mention *martyria* in Pontos. Thus in the *Passion* of St Athenogenes, we are told that the saint built an octagonal chapel in the village of Pêdachthoê to house the remains of five martyrs executed during the persecutions of Diocletian. The same text also mentions a *martyrion* of St Rheginos which in the writer's time (the 4th or 5th century) could be seen in Neokaisareia (modern Niksar).[38] Gregory of Nyssa (4th century) describes a *martyrion* on his family's estate near Ibora and another probably located in Euchaita (modern Avkat).[39]

---

37 Spieser 2001, ch. 7, 1-12.

38 *Passion of St Athenogenes*, Maraval 1990, 13, 27. The exact location of Pêdachthoê is unknown. For the date of the *Passion*, see 11-2.

39 Gregory of Nyssa, *In XL Martyres*, PG 46.784C; *De S. Theodoro Martyre*, PG 46.738D-740A

The cruciform plan is typical of early Christian architecture,[40] although the Latin cross is predominant and in fact the free-standing Greek cross which we find in the Papaz Tarlası is relatively rare. Both types are believed to have been modelled on the Church of the Holy Apostles in Constantinople, also known as the imperial Polyándreion, where the Byzantine emperors were buried.[41] According to Procopius this church was shaped like a Greek cross with a dome in the centre, though this is a description of the Justinian reconstruction of c. 540.[42] Preserved examples of the free-standing Greek cross with a central dome include the much larger *martyrion* of St. Babylas at Antioch (c. 379)[43] and the Church of St. Simeon Stylites in Syria (c. 475). A number of Greek cruciform structures at Chersonesos (Sevastopol) are much more similar in scale.[44] Several of the cruciform structures at Chersonesos have been excavated and were found to be associated with tombs confirming the interpretation of the structures as *martyria*. In 1897, in the so-called Reliquary Church built inside the ancient theatre, a tomb was excavated containing a reliquary shrine with skeletal material wrapped in silk.[45] This cruciform structure in the shape of a Greek cross is traditionally dated to the 6th century based on the date of the reliquary, but based on the context the church could not have been built before than the end of the 10th century.[46] Finds from a cruciform church outside the city walls on the western side of town date to the 8th to 9th centuries, but the church was still standing in the 10th century.[47] Furthermore stratigraphy, ceramics and coins dated the rebuilding of a Greek cruciform church excavated near Mangup Kale in 1981 at the end of the 9th or the early 10th century.[48] Consequently, a 10th-century date has also been suggested for the other cruciform structures within the city.

Outside the city walls of Chersonesos to the south in Quarantine Bay is yet another *martyrion* identified by multiple tombs and located in one of the city's necropoleis. According to the excavator a small chapel was built over tomb D in the 6th century, which was replaced in the 10th century by the cruciform *martyrion* which received a mosaic floor during the 12th century.[49] The 6th-century phase is dated by thirteen coins of Justinian I found in the fill under the basin of the Diakonikon/the wall of the baptismal font. Although the images and plans available are not of the best quality, the mosaic floor seems consistent with a 6th-century date, and according to L.G. Khrushkova, the glazed sherds responsible for the late date came from 12th-century repairs to the floor.[50] Furthermore, Khrushkova argues that since the lid was already removed when the cruciform church was built, a coin of Arcadius found in the upper layer of the filling of Tomb D could have found its way there during the construction of the cruciform *martyrion*, thereby dating this as early as the turn of the 5th century. The date suggested by Khrushkova correlates better with the finds from the Papaz Tarlası, but her attractive hypothesis concerning the Arcadian coin in the fill of Tomb D rests on an assumption that is difficult to prove. A re-examination of the finds from the other three excavated contexts of 8th- to 10th-century date appears to be called for.

Closer to Pontos, in central southern Turkey many churches have been preserved in the area known as Binbirkilise ('1001 churches'), and a survey of the published material (and the numerous churches in the so-called dead cities in Syria) confirms the rarity of the free-standing Greek cross design. Only two of these structures are designed as Greek crosses: an antechamber to a

---

40   Schäfer 1978, 13-6.

41   Heisenberg 1908; Freely & Çakmak 2004, 145-6.

42   Procopius (De Aedificiis 1.9-24).

43   Sodini 1986, 236.

44   The churches are published in various places in Russian, but all are discussed by Romančuk 2005, 83-6, fig. 18: 11-5, figs 24 and 27.

45   Kostsyushko-Valuzhinich 1897.

46   Romančuk 2005, 83--4.

47   Romančuk 2005, 85.

48   Мыс 1990, 226 in Russian. Discussed by Romančuk 2005, 84, n. 12.

49   The chronology of the phases of this site was reconstructed by the excavator O.I. Dombrovskij, cited by Romančuk 2005, 84 and Khrushkova 2006 (a conference paper only published on the internet).

50   Khrushkova 2006.

church and an attached "side-chapel".[51] The antechamber at Karadagh-Mahaletch is very interesting because of a funerary inscription reading "Through the vow of Kallinikos? … to Leo" on the outer wall of the apse, interpreted as a possible reference to the Bishop of Barata in the 5th or early 6th century. The inscription suggests that the cruciform antechamber was a memorial to Leo, supporting the use of this particular design for memorial purposes. Several of the Greek cruciform structures in Chersonesos were also attached to churches, although they appear to be "side-chapels" rather than antechambers.[52]

According to Krautheimer there are many cross-shaped *martyria* and chapels at Binbirkilise, in Cappadocia and in Lycaonia.[53] In the latter two regions the type appears as early as the 6th century, but none of the examples from Binbirkilise antedate the 8th century. It is not clear from the text what type of cross-shape Krautheimer is discussing. Although the design of the church at Viranşehir resembles a Greek cross, one arm is extended with a deep apse; the church at Helvadere has three different types of arms, one short, two longer (next to each other) and one in the shape of a deep apse; and the church at Kurşuncu is designed as a Latin cross.[54] In fact, the more common free-standing cruciform design is the Latin cross as known from the Church of St John in Ephesos (c. 565), which also had an atrium.[55] Numerous small churches also in Asia Minor follow this design, e.g. the Church of the Panayia in Tomarza of the late 5th or early 6th century, and Sivrihisar at Kizil Kilise, possibly dating around 600.[56] A well-dated 5th-century example

of a similar design is the so-called Mausoleum of Galla Placidia in Ravenna.[57] A small church in Klissé-Keui in Bulgaria, 7 km northwest of Pirdope in the Sofia District, combining the Latin cross with a narthex and an atrium in front appears to be an intermediary between the design of St. John in Ephesos and the complex with the cruciform structure in the Papaz Tarlası.[58] This building is dated stylistically to the 6th century. There is however at least one Greek cruciform church (although the main arm is extended with an apse) with a courtyard in front of it in the Balkans, in Justiniana Prima in Serbia.[59] This structure is securely dated since the entire town had only a brief existence between 535 and 615.

This interpretation of the complex with the cruciform structure in the Papaz Tarlası is also consistent with the orientation of the cruciform structure along an east–west axis. On this hypothesis, the large quadrangle formed the *atrium* or forecourt of the shrine and the central structure would have been a fountain. Such forecourts are a familiar feature of early Christian shrines and churches; the first Basilica of St. Peter in Rome (c. 320), for instance, had an *atrium* with a fountain, as did the Church of St John mentioned above.[60] A much closer parallel has come from Komana, where a hexagonal basin 10.5 m across was excavated by Prof. Dr. Burcu Erciyas.[61] In their article from 2010 Erciyas and Çinici cite Late Antique parallels from church *atria* in Cyprus (Kourion) and Jordan (Pella), although these are much smaller, as well as a hexagonal basin, 9.25 m across, in the Roman bath in Kourion.[62]

Martyria are often associated with burial grounds, which according to Roman law had to be placed outside

51 Karadagh no. 12 (Ramsay & Bell 1909, 122-5). Karadagh-Mahaletch (Ramsay & Bell 1909, 249, 556-7). Additionally, Karadagh-Tchet Dagh (Ramsay & Bell 1909, 268-73) appears to be either a Greek or a Latin cross, and Karadagh no. 44 (Ramsay & Bell 1909, 221-9) is not strictly speaking free-standing and all the arms end in apses.

52 E.g. Khrushkova 2006, figs 11 and 14.

53 Krautheimer 1986, 166 on the 5th century but without references or examples, 395 on the 6th and 7th centuries referring to Halvedere (Rott 1908, 265-7), Kurşuncu (Ramsay & Bell 1909, 353), and Viranşehir (Ramsay & Bell 1909, 363-70).

54 See n. 42.

55 Krautheimer 1986, fig. 196. Also Ramsay & Bell 1909, 340-428.

56 Krautheimer 1986, 164-6. Also Doğan 2008.

57 Krautheimer 1986, 181-2, figs 144-6. Another parallel possibly worth mentioning is the originally 4th-century basilica of San Nazaro in Brolo in Milan (Krautheimer 1986, 81-2, fig. 38).

58 Moutaftchiew 1915, 110-1 (abstract in French).

59 Krautheimer 1986, 274, fig. 236B, again mentioning the frequency of this type of building all over the Roman world. We're grateful to Max Ritter for bringing this church to our attention.

60 Krautheimer 2000, 26-7, figs 21-2.

61 Erciyas & Çinici 2010.

62 Megaw et al. 2007, fig. 1.Z; McNicoll, Smith & Hennessy 1982; McNicoll 1992; Erciyas & Çinici 2010, 293.

the *pomerium* or city limit and are often found along the streets leading out of a city. This is the case with the Chersonesean cruciform *martyrion* in Quarantine Bay discussed above. It would not be surprising to find a necropolis along the road leading north from Neoklaudiopolis. As indicated above, the pottery in the field is domestic in character, suggesting that the structures (or as yet unidentified structures nearby) were used for habitation. However, the reworked grave stele found in the field could have come from such a necropolis in the 2nd century. The few fragments of Pontic Sigillata forms 14-16 dated in the 2nd or 3rd century, which we have suggested above may be residual due to their small size and poor preservation, may also have come from a necropolis.

However, not all our findings are consistent with this hypothesis. For instance, one might expect the western side of the quadrangle to follow the line of the ancient road, but the georesistivity survey did not reveal any traces of a roadway, nor of a pipeline to supply the presumed fountain. Likewise, so far no blocks or artefacts carrying specifically Christian symbols or imagery (e.g. fish, the *chi-rho* monogram or a cross) have turned up.

Conclusion and perspectives

On the basis of our present knowledge, the structures in the Papaz Tarlası can be conjecturally interpreted as parts of an early Christian complex dating to the second half of the 5th century and presumably associated with the cult of a local martyr of whom nothing else is known. This person was important enough to require a monument directly inspired by the imperial church of the Holy Apostles in Constantinople. Based on the date, the complex with the cruciform structure is likely to have functioned as a church, possibly dedicated at the site of a martyr's tomb. The church may have been built by someone intending it for his own burial, as was the case with the *martyrion* of St. Babylas and that on Gregory's family estate.

The alignment of the cruciform building and the atrium is not perfect, begging the question of different phases. The chronology of the pottery on the surface seems to suggest the complex was the centre of formal activities for a rather brief period of time just before the middle and in the second half of the 5th century. This is consistent with our knowledge of the problems of maintaining the numerous small Early Christian shrines.[63] The finds associated with the northeastern complex are domestic with a possible element of production. It is tempting to interpret this as a small farmstead associated with and providing for the staff of the *martyrion*-complex, a presbyter/paramonarios/oikonomos.[64] There is nothing in the finds to suggest a differentiation in the chronology between the northeastern complex and the *martyrion*-complex, however the coins seem to suggest a longer period of activities. Of course the necropolis could have continued to have been used, and although it seems unlikely this is the only source, the ancient custom of being buried with a coin is known to have been adopted by Christians.[65] Two possible scenarios suggest themselves: 1) The collapse of the production of Pontic Red Slip tablewares was followed by a period with no imported ceramic tablewares and the other categories of pottery cannot be dated very precisely; consequently the period of activities should be extended beyond the 5th century. 2) Although the activities associated with pottery – habitation in the northeastern complex and rituals involving food consumption in the *martyrion*-complex – were associated with the 5th century, activities of an archaeologically more transient nature continued to take place, visible on the surface from coins and a few ceramics. A shrine or monastery being erected at the initiative of a local landowner or group of monks, then falling into disuse and neglect after the death of the founder or the departure of the monks, was a familiar phenomenon in Late Antiquity. Indeed, the problem of neglected or half-finished sanctuaries was so widespread that it prompted the Emperor Justinian to issue an edict laying down that "those who would build churches must

---

63   Spieser 2001, ch. 7, 9.

64   We're grateful to Max Ritter, for his thoughts on *martyrion* staff.

65   Stevens 1991, 226; Snoek 1995, 103, n. 8; MacMullen 1997, 218, n. 20.

in advance provide the revenues required for their maintenance … for there are many churches in this capital as well as in the provinces which, instead of being properly maintained, are in danger of being ruined by age".[66]

In some areas of Turkey, religious architecture of the Early Christian and Byzantine periods is still highly visible either as ruins or reused as mosques. In Pontos, religious architecture of the early Christian and Byzantine periods is relatively rare,[67] but the finds from the Papaz Tarlası have shown that the deep soils of the fertile farmlands still hold monuments for archaeologists to discover. However, farming is rapidly being modernized and intensified, and the window of opportunity may soon be closing on this part of Turkey's heritage.

KRISTINA WINTHER-JACOBSEN
The Danish Institute at Athens
Herefondos 14, 10558 Athens
Greece
kwj@diathens.gr/kwjacobsen@hum.ku.dk

TØNNES BEKKER-NIELSEN
University of Southern Denmark
Department of History
Campusvej 55, 5230 Odense M
Denmark
tonnes@sdu.dk

---

66 Justinian, *Novels* 67.2. The issue evidently persisted, for in the ninth century, Emperor Leo VI 'the Sage' issued an edict (Leo, *Novel* 14) addressing the problem of unfinished monasteries.

67 E.g. Bryer & Winfield 1985.

Appendix: Two Byzantine Coins from the Papaz Tarlası

BY VERA SAUER

In the course of the survey two coins were collected. Though all in all poorly preserved, due to the value mark M (*My*, meaning 40; that is 40 *nummi*) on the reverse which is clearly visible, they can be definitely identified as *folles* dated between 498, the year of implementation of the *follis* in the reign of Anastasius I (491-518), and the reign of Theophilus (829-842), when this value mark went out of use.[68] According to the observations and considerations discussed below in all probability the time span within which they were struck can be narrowed down to 653/4-655/6 for coin WEmW13:050-060/080-090 and at least to 539-717 for coin WEmW13:150/100.

WEmW13:050-060/080-090

This coin was produced by clipping and overstriking an older one, a technique which was very common during the reigns of Heraclius (610-641) and Constans II (641-668), when coinage declined and the weight of coins was reduced dramatically.[69] After 668 coinage recovered – with respect both to weight and to technical/artistic quality.

On the reverse, to the right of the M, no number (that is: no year of reign of the emperor) is to be detected but there are parts of a different legend (Fig. 44). On the *folles* of Heraclius the year of the reign is always written here,[70] so this indicates that the coin was struck during the reign of Constans II. The letters can be read as €O (vertically), followed by an abbreviation mark which looks like a C with an additional "hook" fixed at the bottom of it. These three signs fit perfectly with the legend ANAN€O plus abbreviation mark which is common on *folles* of Constans II, ἀνανέω(σις) meaning *renovatio*, renewal.[71]

Coins with this legend (and a square rather than round M) were minted only between the eleventh and fifteenth years of the reign of Constans II, corresponding to 651/2-655/6 AD.[72] Year 11 can be excluded, as there is a star on top of the M (not a cross). Underneath the horizontal line below the M are traces of signs which certainly belong to one of the Roman numerals XII, XIII, XIIII or XV, indicating the years of the reign of Constans II in the period 652/3-655/6.

Apparently coins with the described features were struck without exception at the mint of Constantinople. The letter A which is inscribed into the M marks the first *officina* of the mint.

For this *officina* coins with the reverse features are recorded only for years XIII, XIIII and XV.[73] Consequently, the coin was most likely issued between 653/3 and 655/6. (With all due caution: year XV seems most probable as where the year was written the remnants of only two signs can be detected – and the second one looks round. This fits well with the fact that the sign V on coins of this epoch was round in shape, looking like ꝯ.[74])

The obverse is so encrusted that nothing of what should be seen there – the emperor with long beard, standing, holding a long cross (or Chi-Rho), the legend €N TOYTO NIKA, "in this (sign) gain victory" – can be discerned reliably.[75]

---

68   Cf. Grierson 1982, 43, 59, 172. Unfortunately we had no scale fine enough for weighing the coins. The maximum preserved diameter is 21 mm (coin WEmW13:050-060/080-090), respectively 31 mm (coin WEmW13:150/100).

69   Grierson 1982, 90, 92, 105-7, 110-1.

70   Grierson 1982, 108.

71   Grierson 1982, 111-3.

72   For this and the following: Grierson 1982, 111-3; DOC 450-1, nos 69-74.

73   Sear 1987, 210, no. 1007.

74   Cf. DOC 451, no. 73a.

75   Cf. Grierson 1982, 111-2; DOC pl. 26 nos 69a, 70a, pl. 27 no. 72a.

Fig. 44. *Coin collected from WEmW13:050-060/080-090.*

WEmW13:150/100

The *terminus post quem* for the production of this coin is the year 539, because it was not until this year that the reverse legend ANNO plus year of the reign of the emperor came into use (Fig. 45).[76] The *terminus ante quem* is the beginning of the reign of Leo III (717-741): from 717 onwards this formula was no longer used to provide the actual year of minting, but served only as an ornament, the letters being reduced to ANN XX or AA XX – and later on even to XXX NNN or XN.[77] On the coin from the Papaz Tarlası, however, ANNO (with the O) is clearly legible. The year, on the other hand, is not, though at the bottom right of the M there is a character that looks like an X. Furthermore during the reign of Leo III the number of *officinae* in Constantinople was reduced first to three then to two.[78] The coin in question, however, has Δ (inscribed in the M) indicating a fourth *officina*.

In reality only poor traces of the mint mark can be detected: it may be the upper part of the letter O, which would fit well with the expected mark CON, for Constantinople. Due to the find spot of the coin and, more importantly, to the composition of the different elements of the reverse, all in all (M, cross above the M, *officina* mark, mint mark, legend ANNO plus year) and not least due to the large *officina* number, it is extremely improbable that the coin was struck at a different mint. Should the coin have been issued somewhere else, this would not affect the *terminus ante quem* as the formula ANNO plus year was given up at all mints before 717.

On the obverse, only the letter N can be read clearly. The small structure immediately to the right of the N is most probably a cross. Further traces of the coin image, though extremely poorly preserved, make it plausible that it depicted the bust of the emperor in frontal view, hold-

---

76   Grierson 1982, 60.

77   Grierson 1982, 154.

78   Grierson 1982, 162-3.

Fig. 45. *Coin collected from WEmW13:150/100.*

ing a globe topped by a cross in his right hand.[79] Supposing that this is true, the letter N is one of the first letters of the legend; it may therefore belong to the abbreviation DN, *dominus noster*, and should have been followed by the name of the emperor. Such an obverse composition is not distinctive enough for closer dating, however, as it is attested for different emperors – even combined with the reverse described.

VERA SAUER
Mühlweg 6, 72414 Rangendingen
Germany
vera.sauer@gmx.de

Abbreviations

DOC: *Catalogue of the Byzantine coins in the Dumbarton Oaks Collection and in the Whittemore Collection* ed. by Alfred R. Bellinger and Philip Grierson. Vol. 2, *Phocas to Theodosius III (602-717)* by Philip Grierson. Part 2, *Heraclius Constantine to Theodosius III (641-717)*, Washington 1968 (second printing 1993).

---

79 For this obverse type see for example Grierson 1982, pl. 5 nos 80-2 (*folles* of Iustinianus I).

Bibliography

Anderson, J. G. C., F. Cumont & H. Grégoire 1910
Recueil des inscriptions grecques et latines du Pont et de l'Arménie I (*Studia Pontica* 3.1), Brussels.

Arsen'eva, T. M. & K. Domżalski 2002
'Late Roman Red Slip pottery from Tanais', *Eurasia Antiqua* 8, 415-91.

Arslan, A., N. İğci & B. Kivrak (eds) 2008
Geçmisten Günümüze Vezirköprü, Vezirköprü.

Baker, C. M. 1978
'The size-effect: an explanation of variability in surface assemblage content', *American Antiquity* 43, 288-93.

Bekker-Nielsen, T. 2013
'350 years of research on Neapolis (Vezirköprü)', *Orbis Terrarum* 11, 3-31.

Bekker-Nielsen, T. 2014
'To be or not to be Paphlagonian? A question of identity', in *Space, Place and Identity in Northern Anatolia* (Geographica Historica 29), T. Bekker-Nielsen (ed.), Stuttgart, 63-74.

Bekker-Nielsen, T. & C. Høgel 2012
'Three epitaphs from the Vezirköprü region', *Epigraphica Anatolica* 45, 153-60.

Bekker-Nielsen, T., R. Czichon, C. Høgel, B. Kivrak, J. M. Madsen, V. Sauer, S. L. Sørensen & K. Winther-Jacobsen 2015
Ancient Neoklaudiopolis (Vezirköprü in Samsun Province): A Historical and Archaeological Guide. Istanbul: Arkeoloji ve Sanat Yayınları; Turkish

edition: *Neoklaudiopolis Antik Kenti (Vezirköprü, Samsun): Tarihsel ve Arkeolojik Rehber*.

Bekker-Nielsen, T., C. Høgel & S.L. Sørensen 2015
'Inscriptions from Neoklaudiopolis/Andrapa (Vezirköprü, Turkey)', *Epigraphica Anatolica* 48 [2016], 115-36.

Bryer, A. & D. Winfield 1985
The Byzantine monuments and topography of the Pontos, Washington.

Cumont, F. & E. Cumont 1906
Voyage d'exploration archéologique dans le Pont et la Petite-Armenie (Studia Pontica 2), Brussels.

Czichon, R. M., J. Klinger, P. Breuer, J. Eerbeek, S. Fox-Leonard, H. Marquardt, H. von der Osten-Woldenburg, S. Reichmuth, S. Riehl & Th. Johannsen 2011
'Vorbericht über die archäologischen Forschungen am Oymaağaç Höyük/Nerik (?) in den Jahren 2007-2010', *Mitteilungen der Deutschen Orient-Gesellschaft zu Berlin* 143, 169-250.

Doğan, S. 2008
Kappadokia Bölgesi Sivrihisar'daki Kızıl Kilise (Arkeoloji ve Sanat Yayınları. Araştırma, İnceleme ve Belgeleme Dizisi), Istanbul.

Domżalski, K. 2000
'Notes on Late Roman Red Slip wares in the Bosporan Kingdom', *Rei Cretariae Romanae Fautorum Acta* 36, 161-8.

Domżalski, K. 2007
'La céramique sigillée romaine tardive en Abkhazie', in *Tsibilium: la nécropole apsile de Tsibilium. L'étude du site 2* (BAR International Series S1721), M.

Kazanski & A. Mastykova (eds), Oxford, 75-7.

Domżalski, K. 2011
'Late Roman pottery from Pompeiopolis', in *Pompeiopolis 1, Eine Zwischenbilanz aus der Metropole Paphlagoniens nach fünf Kampagnen (2006-2010)* (Schriften des Zentrums für Archäologie und Kulturgeschichte des Schwarzmeerraumes 21), L. Summerer (ed.), Langenweissbach, 163-78.

Dunnell, R. C. 1990
'Artifact size and lateral displacement under tillage: comments on the Odell & Cowan experiment', *American Antiquity* 55, 592-4.

Erciyas, B. & A. Çinici 2010
The hexagonal basin at Komana: a preliminary architectural study', *Middle East Technical University Journal of Field Archaeology* 27:1, 281-96.

Ferrazzoli, A. F. & M. Ricci 2007
'Elaiussa Sebaste: produzioni e consume di una città della Cilicia tra V e VII secolo', in *LRCW 2, Late Roman Coarse Wares, Cooking Wares and Amphorae in the Mediterranean, Archaeology and Archaeometry* (BAR International Series 1662 (II)), M. Bonifay & J.-C. Treglia (eds), Oxford, 670-88.

Fedalto, G. 1988
Hierarchia Ecclesiatica Orientalis: Series episcoporum ecclesiarum Christianarum orientalium 1: Patriarchatus Constantinopolitanus, Padova.

Freely, J. & A. S. Çakmak 2004
Byzantine Monuments of Istanbul, New York, 145-6.

Gönendik, H. & B. Kivrak 2012
Vezirköprü: Rehber kitap, Vezirköprü.

Grabar, A. 1946 (repr. 1972)
Martyrium: Recherches sur le culte des reliques et l'art premier chrétien 1, Architecture, Paris, 152-61.

Grabar, A. 1948
'Les monuments de Tzaritchingrad', *Cahiers archéologiques. Fin de l'antiquité et moyen âge 3*, 49-63.

Grierson, P. 1982
Byzantine Coins, Berkeley/Los Angeles.

Hayes, J. 1992
Excavations at Saraçhane in Istanbul II: *The pottery*, Princeton.

Heisenberg, A. 1908
Grabeskirche und Apostelkirche. Zwei Basiliken Konstantins. Untersuchungen zur Kunst und Literatur des ausgehenden Altertums 2, Die Apostelkirche in Konstantinopel, Leipzig.

Khrushkova, L. G. 2006
'Tauric Chersonesus (Crimea) in the 4th–5th centuries: suburban *martyria*' in *Report to 21st International Congress of Byzantine Studies*, Kesha Gelbak (trans.), London.

Kostsyushko-Valuzhinich, K. K. 1897
Reports for the Imperial Archaeological Commission. http://www.kostsyushko.chersonesos.org/1897/1897_en.php?year=1897 Accessed November 13, 2013.

Krautheimer, R. 1986
Early Christian and Byzantine Architecture (4th ed.), R. Krautheimer & S. Ćurčić (rev.), London.

Krautheimer, R. 2000
Rome: profile of a city, 312-1308 (2nd ed. with a new foreword by Marvin Trachtenberg), Princeton.

Le Quien, M. 1740.
Oriens Christianus, in quatuor patriarchatus digestus, Paris.

MacMullen, R. 1997
Christianity and Paganism in the Fourth to Eighth Centuries, Princeton.

Maraval, P. (ed. and transl.) 1990
La Passion inédite de S. Athénogène de Pédachthoè en Cappadoce (BHG 197b) (Subsidia Hagipographica 75), Brussels: Société des Bollandistes.

Marek, Ch. 1993
Stadt, Ära und Territorium in Pontus-Bithynia und Nord-Galatia (Istanbuler Forschungen 39), Tübingen: Ernst Wasmuth Verlag GmbH & Co.

McNicoll A. W., R. H. Smith & B. Hennessy 1982
Pella in Jordan 1, An interim report on the joint University of Sydney and the College of Wooster excavations at Pella, 1979-1981, Canberra.

McNicoll, A. W. (ed.) 1992
Pella in Jordan: the second interim report of the joint University of Sydney and College of Wooster excavations at Pella, 1982-1985, Sydney.

Megaw, A. H. S. (ed.) 2007
Kourion: Excavations in the Episcopal Precinct (Dumbarton Oaks Studies 38), Washington D.C.

Moutaftchiew, P./Мутафчиевъ. П. 1915
'Кръстовидната църква въ Клисе-кьой', *Bulletin de la Société Archéologique Bulgare/Izvěstija na Bălgarskoto Archeologičesko Družestvo 5*, 85-111.

Мyc, V. L. 1990
'Krestoobraznyj chram Mangupa', *Sovetskaja Archeologija* H. 1, 226.

Özyiğit, Ö. 1990
'Alaturka Keremidin oluşumu', *Arkeoloji – Sanat Tarihi Dergisi* 5, 149-79.

Pellegrino, E. 2007
'Les céramiques de la maison du nord-est de l'acropole lycienne de Xanthos: un ensemble original de la fin du VIe-début du VIIe s. apr. J.-C.', in *LRCW 2, Late Roman Coarse Wares, Cooking Wares and Amphorae in the Mediterranean, Archaeology and Archaeometry* (BAR International Series 1662 (II)), M. Bonifay & J.-C. Treglia (eds), Oxford, 659-70.

Ramsay, W. M. & G. L. Bell 1909
The thousand and one churches, London.

Romančuk, A. I. 2005
Studien zur Geschichte und Archäologie des byzantinischen Cherson (Colloquia Pontica 11), Leiden.

Schwartz, E. (ed.) 1927
Concilium Universale Ephesenum 1, Acta Graeca (Acta Conciliorum Oecumenicorum 1.1.1). Berlin.

Schäfer, H. 1978
Byzantinische Architektur, Munich.

57

Sear, D. R. 1987
Byzantine Coins and their values (2nd ed.), London.

Snoek, G. J. C. 1995
Medieval Piety from Relics to the Eucharist: A Process of Mutual Interaction, Leiden.

Sodini, J. P. 1986
'Les tombes privilégiées dans l'Orient Chrétien (à l'exception du diocèse d'Égypte)', in *L'inhumation privilégiée du IVe au VIIe siècle en Occident, Colloque de Créteil 1984*, Y. Duval & J.-Ch. Picard (eds), 233-46.

Spataro, M. & A. Villing (eds) 2015
Ceramics, Cuisine and Culture: The Archaeology and Science of Kitchen Pottery in the Ancient Mediterranean World, Oxford.

Spieser, J.-M. 2001
Urban and religious spaces in Late Antiquity and Early Byzantium (Variorum collected studies series), Aldershot.

Stevens, S. T. 1991
'Charon's Obol and Other Coins in Ancient Funerary Practice', *Phoenix* 45:3, 215-29.

Syndicus, E. 1962
Early Christian Art, London.

Tchalenko, G. & E. Baccache 1979-80
Églises de village de la Syrie du nord, Paris.

Tchalenko, G. 1990
Églises syriennes à bêma, Paris.

Tracy, S. V. & S. Dow 1975
The Lettering of an Athenian Mason (Hesperia Supplements 15), Princeton.

Trimble, J. 2011
Women and Visual Replication in Roman Imperial Art and Culture, Cambridge.

Vroom, J. 2005
Byzantine to Modern pottery in the Aegean: An Introduction and Field Guide, Utrecht.

Whitbread, I. 2015
'Materials choices in utilitarian pottery: kitchen wares in the Berbati valley, Greece', in *Ceramics, Cuisine and Culture: The Archaeology and Science of Kitchen Pottery in the Ancient Mediterranean World*, M. Spataro & A. Villing (eds), Oxford, 28-36.

Winther-Jacobsen, K. 2010
From pots to people: A ceramic approach to the archaeological interpretation of ploughsoil assemblages in Late Roman Cyprus (BABESCH Supplement 17), Leuven.

Winther-Jacobsen, K. 2015
'Contextualising Neoklaudiopolis: a glimpse at settlement dynamics in the city's hinterland', in *Landscape and settlement dynamics in Northern Anatolia in the Roman and Byzantine period* (Geographica Historica 32), K. Winther-Jacobsen & L. Summerer (eds), Stuttgart, 83-100.

Zhuravlev, D. 2011
'Early Roman fine ware from Pompeiopolis, in *Pompeiopolis I. Eine Zwischenbilanz aus der Metropole Paphlagoniens nach fünf Kampagnen (2006-2010)* (Schriften des Zentrums für Archäologie und Kulturgeschichte des Schwarzmeerraumes 21), L. Summerer (ed.), Langenweissbach, 149-62.

True to type?
Archaic Cypriot male statues made of limestone[1]

LONE WRIEDT SØRENSEN

During the Cypro-Archaic period (750-450 BC), a large number of statues and figurines were dedicated in sanctuaries throughout the island. These images are made of terracotta and the local limestone, which is easily cut to shape, and they range in size from colossal dimensions to small figurines. Briefly characterized, Cypriot limestone statues are standing, usually with only the front carefully worked; they have a square build; and sculptors often concentrated their technical ability and energy on a meticulous rendering of facial features, hair and beard – and in some cases also the clothing.

Many of the statues were retrieved during uncontrolled excavations during the 19th century, and as a result important information, for instance concerning their contexts, was lost. The Swedish Cyprus Excavations conducted from 1927 to 1931enabled the director Einar Gjerstad to provide a more systematic frame for the material development of the island during the first millennium BC.

Where sculpture is concerned, Gjerstad used the results from his stratigraphic excavations in the sanctuary at A. Irini in northwestern Cyprus and Cypriot sculptures found abroad.[2] Today his chronology has been challenged based in particular on Cypriot sculpture found in the sanctuary of Hera on Samos,[3] and a higher chronology is generally preferred.[4] Furthermore, Gjerstad's stratigraphy at A. Irini has been questioned, and it has been suggested that his Proto-Cypriot and Neo-Cypriot styles are contemporary productions located respectively at Soloi and Salamis.[5]

Apart from chronology other issues such as stylistic development and social, cultural and political influences have been discussed. Due to its geographical location Cyprus was an important stepping stone in the communication between Egypt, the Levant and the Mediterranean, and people from many different backgrounds frequented the island and most likely lived there. According to Gjerstad and Pryce, for instance, the political situation

Gjerstad's chronology: Cyprus	Schmidt's chronology: Samos	Schmidt's chronology: Cyprus
1st Proto-Cypriot: 650-560 BC	Proto-Cypriot: 670/660-610/600 BC	1st Proto-Cypriot: 650-560 BC
2nd Proto-Cypriot: c. 600-540 BC		2nd Proto-Cypriot: 600-540 BC
Neo-Cypriot: c. 560-520 BC	Neo-Cypriot: 610/600-560/550 BC	Neo-Cypriot: 560-520 BC
Cypro-Greek: 540-450 BC		

1   I wish to thank the Danish Institute at Athens for granting me a stay, during which this article was begun. I also wish to thank my colleague, Jane Fejfer, for constructive discussions and my reviewers for well-deserved critique.
2   Gjerstad 1948, 207, 318.
3   Schmidt 1968, 94.
4   Fourrier 2007, 103. However, see also Hermary & Mertens 2014, 24.
5   Fourrier 2007, 104; Hermary & Mertens 2014, 23.

of the island during the Cypro-Archaic period had an important impact on the local sculpture.[6] According to Assyrian inscriptions at Khorsabad and the stele erected by Sargon II at Kition, seven Cypriot kings submitted to him in 707 BC, and the later prism of Esarhaddon mentions by name ten Cypriot kings and their kingdoms as tribute payers.[7] Based upon Herodotus, Gjerstad likewise believed in a conquest of Cyprus by the Egyptian pharaoh Amasis shortly after 570 BC,[8] and in 545 BC Cyprus became part of the 5th Persian satrapy; from then on it was involved in the Greco-Persian conflict.[9] Others, like Vermeule, held the opposite view that different garments did not reflect shifting foreign political dominations of the island.[10] Furthermore, discussions pertaining to a possible Mycenaean influx at the end of the Bronze Age and a Phoenician colonization at Kition on the southeast coast of the island have had and still have an indirect bearing on the interpretation of Cypriot culture.[11] Other contributions have focused on the significance of sculpture as social or religious markers,[12] and efforts aimed at identifying specific regional styles have recently been sketched by Counts in his examination of some stone sculptures from the area of Athienou-Malloura.[13]

Archaic Cypriot male statues are interesting because they are dressed in different garments, unlike, for instance, free-standing sculpture produced in the Greek area. The assumption that different messages were embedded in the different outfits and probably denoted specific tasks suggests that the Cypriots found it important to communicate and underline various societal obligations or events through the sculpture dedicated in the sanctuaries. Traditionally, Archaic Cypriot stone sculpture has been classified according to style, attire and foreign influences, and as only the heads of the majority of the large statues survive, headdresses have been used as important criteria for establishing typological groups.[14] However, the present analysis focuses primarily on the garments of three main statue types: statues dressed in a tunic and a mantle/chiton and himation, statues dressed in the so-called Cypriot pants, and statues wearing an Egyptianizing kilt. A point of departure is taken in the garments and their combination with the various types of head-gear, hair and beard styles, and in the statement made by Counts that "Variations exist among the types of male votaries, suggesting that sculptors mixed and matched attributes and dress to procure more 'individual' pieces. The overwhelming majority, however, conform to a set typology."[15] The intention here is to examine how "true to type" the statues actually are, and therefore statues and larger statuettes preserved well enough to form an opinion of the statues in toto are primarily addressed, assuming that they are more trustworthy as to details than many of the 'mass-produced' small statuettes.

Subsequently the paper addresses other relevant issues currently discussed in other fora, such as material, size, appearance and context, from a local as well as a Mediterranean perspective. During the Archaic period only the local limestone was used by the Cypriot sculptors to produce stone statues. This is interesting considering the island's geographical proximity to the marble-rich islands of Naxos and Paros and the Greek enthusiasm for this particular material. In both Greece and Cyprus statuary was produced in different sizes, but while the Greeks more or less stuck to the naked kouros formula, the Cypriots engaged different types of statues in connection with dedications of images of males in the Cypriot communities. According to the present knowledge, Cypriot stone statues were produced to act as votives, or images of their donators, in the local sanctuaries; as such they seem to have played an important role in the religious and cultural life of the communities.

---

6   Gjerstad 1948, 339; Pryce 1931, 5.

7   Gjerstad 1948, 449

8   Gjerstad 1948, 466.

9   Gjerstad 1948, 471-78.

10   Vermeule 1974, 290.

11   For recent contributions cf. Jacovou 2008, 650; Hermary 2005; Sommer 2010, 118.

12   Cf. for instance Counts 2001; Faegersten 2003; Senff 2005, 100.

13   Counts 2012, 151. For regional productions of Cypriot terracottas cf. Fourrier 2007.

14   For instance Hermary 1989; Senff 1993; Sørensen 1994; Counts 2001.

15   Counts 2001, 157.

Fig. 1. *Bearded male statue in tunic and mantle, H: 166 cm. The Metropolitan Museum of Art (74.51.2468).*

Fig. 2. *Bearded male statue in tunic and mantle from the sanctuary of Golgoi-A. Photios. H: 191.8 cm. The Metropolitan Museum of Art (74.51.2460).*

Statues wearing a tunic and a mantle/chiton and himation

During the Cypro-Archaic period the standard Cypriot male statue, bearded as well as unbearded, is dressed in a long tunic and a mantle, and wears a pointed cap atop a bag-shaped hairdo. The tunic is plain and the mantle is tight-fitting and draped over the left shoulder, carried across the back to cover the right shoulder and arm and leaving the left arm free. The right arm is bent in front of the body with a clenched fist resting on the chest (Fig. 1),[16] and in some cases the end of the mantle carried from behind is visible on the left shoulder.[17] The vertical edge of the mantle may be incised, raised or raised with

indentations,[18] probably indications of a special fabric or fringes, which are also seen on statuettes and early terracotta statues and probably betray Near Eastern influences.[19] The early stone sculptures wear a wig-like haircut of Egyptian inspiration and a large beard, which is either plain or divided into vertical tresses sometimes terminating in snail curls.[20] A later statue (Fig. 2) wears the same narrow mantle with a raised indented border and an additional row of incised zigzags, which suggests a double row of fringes.[21] The mantle is now provided with softly modelled folds following the curved edge of

---

16   Cesnola 1885, pls 44, 281; 60, 407; Hermary 1989, 22; Senff 1993, 26.

17   Cesnola 1885, pl. 47, 284. Fringes are prominent on some small terracottas, but only few of the large the terracottas from A. Irini carry the mantle draped in this particular manner. Karageorghis 1993, figs 9-12, pl. 12.

18   Karageorghis 1969, fig. 39; Hermary & Mertens 2014, cat. 3.

19   Senff 1993, pl. 51, d; Karageorghis 1993, nos. 35, 37, 47-8, 73; Hermary 1989, 22.

20   A row of curls may likewise appear above the forehead, cf. Hermary 1989, nos 1-5; Karageorghis et al. 2000, no. 171. Large beards are also seen on early terracottas, cf. Karageorghis 1993, nos 34, 46, 62, 66, 68-9; Buchholz & Untiedt 1996, pl. 67; Fourrier 2007, pl. 3, 1. Early terracottas demonstrate that this type of statue is sometimes provided with a short plain beard, and limestone heads with similar beards probably also belong to the type, cf. Karageorghis 1993, nos 5, 7, 23, 44; Hermary 1989, nos 23-4, 50.

21   Cesnola 1885, pl. 60, 407; Karageorghis et al 2003, no. 173; Hermary & Mertens 2014, cat. 12.

Fig. 3. *Beard-less male in tunic and mantle, H: 61 cm. From the sanctuary of Golgoi-A. Photios. The Metropolitan Museum of Art (74.51.2646).*

Fig. 4. *The so-called priest with dove, H: 217.2 cm. From the sanctuary of Golgoi-A. Photios. The Metropolitan Museum of Art (74.51.2466).*

the mantle, and the pointed cap is more ornate. The large beard and the hair at the nape of the neck are divided into rows of snail curls and a single row of curls run across the forehead. Markoe, following the conventional date, suggested that the row of curls above the forehead is inspired by Achaemenid art and he referred to Ridgeway for a similar suggestion concerning Greek sculpture.[22] On the other hand, Markoe suggested an Ionian influence in the short moustache and the low-cut beard line with clean-shaven under-lip (above the chin) also seen on heads with an Egytianizing crown.[23] However, although Markoe is right that Assyrian and Achaemenid beards cover a larger part of the cheeks it should be mentioned that the low-cut beard-line is seen even on the earliest

Cypriot stone sculpture, like the colossal head from Golgoi-A. Photios, and a short moustache is seen on the early terracottas.[24]

The tight-fitting mantle continued to be used throughout the 6th century BC. In some cases the vertical edge is provided with parallel folds, which terminate in Greek zigzag folds, and the long locks falling to the chest show inspiration from Greek kouros statues (Fig. 3).[25] However, the wreath around the head is not a familiar trait of Greek kouroi. In other cases shorter "kouros-locks" are combined with the tight mantle without folds,[26] or mantles with folds are combined with a hairdo consisting of a row of curls above the forehead, plain transversal locks across the skull and incised locks on the front of the wig-like hair

---

22 Markoe 1987, 120, note 14.

23 Markoe 1987, pl. 41, 3-4.

24 Hermary & Mertens 2014, cat. 1; Karageorghis 1993, nos. 1, 57, 68, 73-4, 76-9.

25 Karageorghis et al. 2000, no. 187; Hermary & Mertens 2014, cat. 11.

26 Hermary & Mertens 2014, cat. 62.

Fig. 5. *Bearded male in tunic and mantle, H: 162 cm. The Collection of George and Nefeli Giabra Pierides, Nicosia (without inv. no.)*

falling behind the ears.[27] Yet other statues wear a mantle with a broad central fold along the vertical edge, which is familiar from East Greek statues[28] and seems to have been very popular in Cyprus, where it was used into the 5th century BC combined with short hair and a wreath/diadem.[29]

Concerning garments, the so-called 'Priest with dove' dated to the late 6th century BC is an interesting statue (Fig. 4).[30] He seems to wear a pleated chiton below a plain chiton with a horizontal relief-decorated border below the knees and a conical cap, richly decorated and surmounted by a small bull's head. His mantle is an enigma calling to mind the mantle of some of the Acropolis korai. Like some of the korai, he carries the mantle over the right shoulder and the broad diagonal central fold and the arrangement of the drapery below the right arm looks like one system,[31] while the draping of the mantle over the left arm seems to belong to another system,[32] or perhaps it should be read as a separate piece of cloth.[33] His curly beard resembles that of the statue with a pointed cap discussed above (Fig. 2). In this case it is combined with a moustache and long "kouros locks" falling to the chest. A strange arrangement of folds is repeated on another statue which carries it over a chiton adorned with a border like the chiton worn by the 'Priest with dove'. The mantle is comparatively tight-fitting, but it is provided with a rather artful drapery on the left shoulder; a bundle of folds falling from the left shoulder and enveloping the right forearm is difficult to explain and looks like a folded shawl (Fig. 5).[34] One suspects that these mantles were used to express a certain degree of individuality. At first glance they look Greek, but they are actually more or less artful, and if not for the fine technical quality of the statues it could be argued that the sculptors had simply misunderstood the details. This may still be the case, but it seems rather that the correct arrangement of the mantles was not an issue as long as the effect was striking. These

27 Hermary & Mertens 2014, cat. 65.

28 Bernhard-Walcher et al.1999, no. 77; Freier-Schauenburg 1974, no.72, pls 59-60; Hermary 2005, fig. 6.

29 Hermary 1989, no. 246; Hermary & Mertens 2014, cat. 109.

30 Karageorghis et al., 2000, no. 172. For a discussion of the statue cf. Masson & Hermary 1993; Hermary & Mertens 2014, cat. 22.

31 Karakasi 2001, pls 144-5, 174-5.

32 Karakasi 2001, pl. 200.

33 Hermary & Mertens 2014, cat. 22.

34 Karageorghis et al. 2002, 186. To judge from the photograph the head probably does not belong to the statue.

Fig. 7. *Bearded male statue in mantle, H: 201cm. From Pyla. Kunsthistorisches Museum, Vienna, inv. ANSA I 341.*

Fig. 6. *Bearded male statue in chiton and himation, H: 164.5 cm. From the sanctuary of Golgoi-A. Photios. The Metropolitan Museum of Art (74.51.2461).*

statues were still meant to be seen from the front, and it seems that an effort was made to push the material of the mantle to the front of the statues and to add realistic as well as unrealistic details in order to underscore the volume of the garment.

From about 500 BC less flamboyant himatia, but still indicating volume, and also combined with a Greek-look-ing chiton, are seen on bearded as well as unbearded statues with short hair and a wreath around the head. Their himatia cover the left arm and are carried below the right arm, covering most of the body like himatia worn by Greek sculpture.[35] In some cases the mantle provided with narrow parallel folds along the vertical edge is combined with short hair and the old large curly beard.[36] On another statue with a similarly draped himation the narrow folds terminate in what looks like fringes (Fig. 6).[37] However, the somewhat strange arrangement of folds below his left arm suggests that the intention was to reproduce under-cut folds like the ones seen on the mantle of the Antenor kore from the Acropolis.[38] The beard of these statues is still provided with snail curls but now they terminate in separate vertical corkscrew locks evidently inspired by bronze sculptures like the Cap Artemision statue and the hair of the so-called Chatsworth Apollo.[39] Thus two different beard systems are apparently blended.

35   Hermary 2005, figs 1-3; Karageorghis et al. 2000, no. 335; Hermary & Mertens 2014, cat. 103.
36   Hermary & Mertens 2014, cat. 80.
37   Karageorghis et al. 2000, no. 336; Hermary & Mertens 2014, cat. 85.
38   Stewart 1990, fig. 154.
39   Hermary 2005, 101; Neer 2010, pl. 1; Bouquillon et al. 2006, figs 1-2.

Although the tunic and mantle and the later chiton and himation remained standard garments for Cypriot males the different details of these garments and their combinations with different hair- and beard styles suggest that particular combinations of old and new elements were often the result of individual choices. An exceptional male statue dated to about 500 BC underlines this eclectic attitude (Fig. 7).[40] He is taller than life-size and with his stance he looks very much like a Greek kouros, and yet not. He is naked except for the old tight-fitting mantle, which leaves his left side uncovered and actually clings to his muscular (Greek) body, revealing it rather than covering it up. The mantle is provided with the old raised or perhaps folded border, but the out-curving lower end reflects his dynamic stride, diagonal folds run across his body, and the end of the mantle resting on the left shoulder terminates in Greek-looking zigzag folds. Like the 'Priest with dove' he has a large curly beard and a tiny moustache combined with long "kouros locks", but around his head he wears a wreath, unfamiliar from Greek kouroi. Although this statue is unique it displays the same interest in playing with details as the statues mentioned above; one could say that he epitomizes the Cypriot eclectic attitude to sculptural representations and that an affluent look was an important aspect of the statues.

Statues wearing "Cypriot pants"

The other discrete but smaller group of statues and statuettes is usually considered to be the Cypriot version of the Greek kouros. The statues are dressed in what has been called a perizoma – Badehosen or "Cypriot pants" or shorts combined with a short, tightly fitting garment with short sleeves akin to a modern T-shirt, a diadem and sometimes also armlets and earrings. As a detailed study

Fig. 8. *Beardless male wearing "Cypriot trousers" and diadem, H: 73 cm. Istanbul Museum, inv. No. 3329.*

of this group has been presented by Hurschmann,[41] the following is confined to some brief comments. The diadems are painted red and decorated with rosettes, which are incised or carried out in relief, and it has been suggested that the incisions sometimes seen on the surface of the diadem indicate that they were made of cloth or leather.[42] Red paint is also preserved on some of the pants. However, as also pointed out by Hurschmann, a closer look at the pants reveals that at least the rendering of them shows a lack of consistency, sometimes prompting the question of whether the same dress is actually rendered. Some pieces wear what looks like short modern pants with a fly, which seem to be cut to shape and sewn, but again they are rendered in different ways.[43] Others look more like a diaper system with loose flaps meeting on the front of the figure where they are tied together above another flap carried between the legs, or the flaps meet over short pants.[44] It has been suggested that they represent a pants and belt system related to the other

---

40 Bernhard-Walcher et al. 1999, no. 76.

41 Hurschmann 2003.

42 Hurschmann 2003, 174.

43 Hurschmann 2003, 179. On some the rosette decorates a lozenge-shaped fly (Cesnola 1885, pl. 25, 63; Hermary 1989, no. 57). another has a vertical relief line below the rosette (Ergülec 1972, pl. 17, 3), or one above and below the rosette with no indication of a fly (Cesnola 1885, pls 25, 65: 25, 285. Yet another has a fly shaped like an inverted U and an additional rosette placed above the fly (Cesnola 1885, pl. 62). On a single statue the upper part of the pants seems to be bent over, forming an inverted U line in the centre (Karageorghis 1969, fig. 35), and on some other pieces the pants are only indicated by incised lines (Cesnola 1885, pl. 25, 60; Hermary 1989, no. 61).

44 It is known in a short version (Ergülec 1972, pl. 23, 7), as well as a longer version (Ergülec 1972, pl. 18; Hermary 1989, no. 62). One of these, a torso dated to the middle of the 5th century BC, actually looks as if it is wearing baggy pants, perhaps indicating that the original garment had been changed or forgotten.

Fig. 10. *Bearded male wearing Egyptianizing outfit, H: 130.2 cm. From the sanctuary of Golgoi-A. Photios. The Metropolitan Museum of Art (74.51.2472).*

Fig. 9. *Beardless male wearing "Cypriot pants" and diadem, H: 73 cm. From the sanctuary of Golgoi-A. Photios. The Metropolitan Museum of Art (74.51.2479).*

pants.[45] Although the T-shirt decoration is only preserved in a few cases we are informed that it was far from uniform. While one is decorated with vertical red borders,[46] (Fig. 8) another has a central red border with reserved rosettes,[47] and the decoration of others are incised or carried out in relief. One has incised decoration on the front consisting of sections of vertical twigs (Fig. 9),[48] and the most elaborate T-shirt with a chiton-like surface is decorated with a central broad vertical relief band with superimposed stylized sacred trees.[49] Perhaps the T-shirts

indicate differences as to rank and status, but otherwise the images are fairly homogenous despite the different details. Most of the statues and statuettes are unbearded and have a bag-shaped hairdo, indicating a young age group, although some of them do have a row of curls above the forehead[50] or short plain beard combined with a Greek curly hairstyle.[51] Perhaps more interestingly, other pieces demonstrate that the pants could be matched with a pointed cap or an Egyptian looking double crown[52] and that at least one statue with the rosette diadem is dressed in an Egyptian-looking kilt.[53] It should furthermore be noticed that only a few terracottas are shown wearing "Cypriot pants", a diadem and a T-shirt.[54]

Statues wearing an Egyptianized kilt

Statues dressed in an Egyptian-looking outfit have attracted much attention over the years, and the hybridity displayed by this group has been underlined in particular by Faegersten in her seminal work on the subject.[55] The statues usually wear a bag-shaped hair-do, and they are dressed in an Egyptianized kilt, sometimes a large Egyp-

---

45 Schurmann 2003, 181.

46 Ergülec 1972, pls 17. 2; Hermary & Mertens 2014, cat. 29, 30.

47 Ergülec 1972, pls 23.

48 Karageorghis et al. 2000, no. 169.

49 Ergülec 1972, pl. 18. The upper part of a statue with lotus flowers decorating the T-shirt may belong to a similar type, cf. Hermary 1989, no. 54.

50 Karageorghis et al. 2000, no. 170; Cesnola 1885, no. 65.

51 Cesnola 1885, pl. 25, 62; Hermary & Mertens 2014, cat. 39.

52 Pryce 1931, C7, 20.

53 Faegersten 2003, cat. 13.

54 Karageorghis 1993, fig. 17; Karageorghis 1995, figs 1-2, pl. 2, 3.

55 Faegersten 2003.

Fig. 11. *Beardless male statue wearing Egyptianizing outfit, H: 104.8 cm. From the sanctuary of Golgoi-A. Photios. The Metropolitan Museum of Art (74.51.2471).*

tianized necklace – an usekh – and a local version of an Egyptian crown, which in some cases has been replaced by a diadem or a wreath (Fig. 10).[56] Most of them also wear a T-shirt with short sleeves, while a small number of statues seem to have a naked upper body.[57] Earlier terracottas demonstrate that short tunics or skirts, sometimes combined with a broad belt, were used in Cyprus in the 7th century BC, although they show no Egyptian influ-

ence.[58] According to Faegersten, the Cypriot kilt is based on a mixture of two different Egyptian kilt types.[59] One is the wrap-around shenti, and the other is the New Kingdom-type kilt. What is particularly interesting, however, is Faegersten's observation that only a couple of Cypriot figures dated to the early 6th century BC reproduce the standard Egyptian shenti with vertical ends covering the abdomen,[60] and that just a single piece from the middle of the century reproduces faithfully the New Kingdom Egyptian kilt with a devanteau,[61] although a small handful are closely related (Fig. 11).[62] The rest displays a mixture of the two garments, and the adornment of the kilts does not ascribe to any fixed formula, although Uraeus snakes rendered in different ways are constant figural elements. Another small group shows a more elaborate decoration depicting frontal heads on the centre-piece of the kilt like the panther heads on the original Egyptian devanteaux.[63] But even these differ from one another, showing the heads of Hathor and Bes, a Gorgoneion, a smiling or grimacing head and a bearded head, Bes or a satyr.[64] Thus, some of the heads refer to a Phoenician-Egyptian sphere while others have Greek connotations, leaving a confused message – to us, that is. A similar blending was noticed by Counts in connection with images of the so-called Herakles and Bes.[65] In the case of the kilt decoration, confusion may at least partly be overcome if the heads are perceived as apotropaic images.[66] Some of the belts also carry a figural decoration which is not an Egyptian trait and seems to be a Cypriot invention.[67] Again different motifs are rendered: a disc-like object between X-shaped pattern, perhaps the remains of originally seated sphinxes; a winged sun disc with facial features of perhaps Bes or a Gorgo; a lion slayer, perhaps Herakles, flanked by paradise flowers; a frieze of crouching sphinxes and a

---

56 Karageorghis et al. 2000, no. 182; Faegersten 2003, no. 21.

57 Faegersten 2003, nos 20, 21, 30, 59, 61.

58 Karageorghis 1993, nos 26-9, 34. The overlapping side borders on no. 43 and the two central snakes on no. 72 are probably inspired by the Egyptianizing kilts.

59 Faegersten 2003, fig. 2.

60 Faegersten 2003, 34, nos 16, 21.

61 Faegersten 2003, no. 3.

62 Faegersten 2003, nos 29, 52-3, 57.

63 Faegersten 2003, fig. 11.

64 Faegersten 2003, nos 22, 30, 12, 15, 31, 50.

65 Counts 2008, 12.

66 Sørensen 2014, 42.

67 Faegersten 2003, 65.

four-winged scarab set in an animal frieze with a lion and a goat preserved to its left.[68] A single belt is decorated with rosettes and others are adorned with a bead-like pattern or an Egyptian block-border pattern, while others again are provided with a belt buckle.[69]

The adornment of the T-shirts also varies. One is decorated with a central vertical border in relief showing so-called Phoenician cup palmettes, double vertical lines perhaps indicating stripes adorn two of the T-shirt and a fourth is provided with vertical and horizontal borders filled with hanging lilies and buds linked with loops.[70] As noted by Faegersten the Egyptian collar, the usekh, is worn both by statues dressed in a T-shirt and those who seem to have a naked upper body, and most of the collars which are made in relief or incised or painted show two decorated registers of stylized floral and vegetal designs with a bottom row of hanging drops.[71] However, although painted colours may have worn off over the years it was apparently not imperative that the kilt was combined with an Egyptian collar, as demonstrated by a statue from Golgoi, and in a couple of cases the collar even seems to be converted into a neck border of the T-shirt.[72]

The rendering of the hair and the beard also shows that no strict formula was observed, which is demonstrated by the two statues with striped T-shirts from Golgoi dated to the early 6th century BC.[73] Both have a bag-shaped hairdo and a short plain beard but only one of them has a feathered moustache and feathered eyebrows. Another two statues from Golgoi of the late 6th century with long kouros-like locks falling behind the ears onto the back provide another example. One of them is beardless and a row of upturned locks runs across the forehead, while the other has a plain beard, curls across the forehead and the long locks subdivided by horizontal incisions.[74] If the heads ascribed to this type of statue are also taken into consideration, it appears that the combination of different hair and beard types is actually quite varied,[75] and that variety is also displayed by beardless males.[76] According to Faegersten, none of the statues wear the crown placed on top of an Egyptian-type headdress, in the Egyptian manner.[77] The shape of the crowns varies, and in some cases they even look like a mixture between the crown and the conical cap.[78] The more ornate crowns carry an individual relief decoration.[79] Yet other kilt statues are bare-headed, or they wear a rosette diadem, a wreath or a helmet; a single figure with a Horus head/mask poses as a scribe.[80] The outfit is also worn by males carrying weapons[81] or an animal under the arm.[82]

Summary and further discussions

In the Archaic Cypriot communities it seems to have been important that free-standing stone statues of males dedicated in the sanctuaries conveyed different messages

---

68 Faegersten 2003,66 nos 30-3, 60; Idem 2005, 45-58.

69 Faegersten 2003, 40, nos 27, 12 and 29, 21 and 47, 24, 34, 43-4, 59.

70 Faegersten 2003, nos 12, 23-4, 34.

71 Faegersten 2003, 48.

72 Faegersten 2003, nos 24, 23, 34.

73 Faegersten 2003, nos 23-4.

74 Faegersten 2003, nos 29, 31.

75 Faegersten 2003, no. 7: An Egyptian wig with horizontal sections, a short curly beard, moustache partly cut and painted black; Idem nos 26-8: a bag-wig, plain beard and eyebrows; Idem no. 9: A plain beard and moustache; Idem no. 24: a bag-wig, plain beard, incised moustache and eyebrows; Idem no. 20: A bag-wig, a row of curls above the forehead plain beard and incised eyebrows; Idem no. 8: A bag-wig, beard finely tooled; Idem no. 2, 58: what looks like a reduced curly bag-wig, curls above the forehead, incised moustache and eyebrows; Idem no. 21: Short curly hair, curls above the forehead, curly beard and plain eyebrows.

76 Cf. Faegersten 2003, no. 49: A bag-wig divided vertically and horizontally: Idem nos 52, 61: A bag-wig and incised eyebrows; Idem nos 34, 67-8: A bag-wig and curls above the forehead; Idem nos. 29, 45: long "kouros locks" and short hair with curls above the forehead.

77 Faegersten 2003, 57.

78 Faegersten 2003, no. 20.

79 Faegersten 2003, nos 20, 21, 30, 58, 66; Brönner, 1994, 48.

80 Faegersten 2003, nos 13, 31, 35; Faegersten 2003, no. 1. Similar representations are not seen in Egypt, but are known from Phoenician ivories (Faegersten 2003, 228); the figure is also unique in a Cypriot context, although it blends in with other Cypriot figures wearing other types of masks (Karageorghis et al. 2000, nos 222-6).

81 Faegersten 2003, cat. 30, 37.

82 Faegarsten 2003, cat. 39, 45, 62.

expressed by different attire, and, although the majority of stone statues were dedicated in sanctuaries located in the Mesaoria plain, it was apparently an island-wide phenomenon and not confined to kingdoms of eastern Cyprus.[83] The above discussions of the three typological groups were primarily based on dress types because the garments are so distinct and different from one another, and it showed that heads with different headgear do not necessarily appear together with only one type of garment; this, however, is far from saying that headdresses were unimportant. As in other Mediterranean societies, the tunic and mantle were standard garments worn by males with short and long beards as well as unbearded males, and this is supported by the numerous stone statuettes and terracotta figurines dedicated in the sanctuaries. Foreign elements such as the fringed mantle and Greek types of drapery were assimilated, and old and new elements blended in different ways. For instance, the old tight mantle was not given up at a time when more voluminous Greek himatia were introduced. In re-shaped forms it was combined with long "kouros locks" and a wreath around the head worn by unbearded men (Fig. 3) and mature men with large curly beards (Fig. 7). The pointed cap familiar from the earliest stone sculpture was also used later and even combined with statues wearing Greek-looking garments, "kouros locks" and curly beards (Fig. 4), while the large beard of a group of statues with wreaths around the head is a mixture of two different beard styles (Fig. 6). Statues dressed in "Cypriot pants" and a T-shirt apparently form the most homogenous group, although different shapes of pants, each revealing different details, may be noticed. Almost all of them are beardless and have a bag-shaped hairdo, with a few exceptions.[84] In comparison, statues dressed in Egyptianizing kilts show greater diversity, partly because their outfit is more complicated. Still, it is noteworthy that the Cypriots chose to blend two different Egyptian kilt types in a vari-

ety of ways and to mix non-Egyptian decorative elements and Egyptian elements, with the Uraeus snakes being the most permanent elements.[85] Moreover, it appears that the two other spectacular elements, the Egyptian collar and crown, were not imperative; the kilt is also worn by bare-headed statues or combined with a mask or a helmet, and perhaps a rosette diadem. Some are unbearded like the statues dressed in "Cypriot pants", but about the same number carry a short plain beard sometimes combined with a moustache, or a short beard provided with snail curls. If other crowned heads belong to this statue type, males with larger curly beards and moustache could also wear this particular outfit, although their number appears to be small judged by the extant sculpture.[86]

Not only the shape of garments but also their fabric and colour are important elements in conveying messages, but unfortunately the ancient Mediterranean world offers few remains of actual garments, and textual information about textiles in Cyprus is similarly scarce. However, traces of different colours are preserved on Cypriot stone sculpture and in particular on terracottas,[87] for instance the decorative elements of the cap of the "Priest with dove" are enhanced by black, red and yellow paint.[88] Otherwise, red is the colour that seems to have been used most on the various garments. The red traces on the mantle of the same statue may indicate that the entire mantle was originally red, while other statues and statuettes illustrate that mantles and tunics could be decorated with red fringes and borders.[89] The diadems, T-shirts and pants worn by the statues dressed in "Cypriot pants" also show traces of red colour, as do the T-shirts and naked upper body and details of the kilt, the collar and the crown of the statues wearing an Egyptianizing kilt. It also appears that some of the T-shirts of statues wearing "Cypriot pants" and kilts were decorated in the same way, for instance with red vertical borders (Fig. 8),[90] while the relief decoration of others document that T-shirts in both groups

---

83   Hurschmann 2003, fig. 1; Faegersten 2003, 109.
84   If a head with a rosette diadem in the Louvre once belonged to this type of statue, this outfit could also be combined with long locks, a short curly beard and a moustache. Cf. Hermary 1989, no. 60.
85   Faegersten 2003, table 1.
86   Faegersten 2003, nos 2, 58, 66, 69.
87   Pryce, 1931, 4; Senff 1993, 24; Counts 2001, 155.
88   Karageorghis et al. 2000, no. 172.
89   For instance Karageorghis et al. 2000, nos 190, 196-7.
90   Faegersten 2003, no. 24.

could be more elaborate, with a central border showing superimposed stylized sacred trees.[91]

If it is not that red is simply more resistant than other colours,[92] there seems to have been a preference for this particular colour, perhaps because it connoted wealth and or prestige. This may be supported by the red garments worn by figures painted on Cypro-Archaic pottery, although it should be kept in mind that we are dealing with bichrome pottery decorated with black and red paint.[93] Generally speaking, traces of paint are better preserved on terracotta sculpture, and the cuirasses from Salamis and Kazaphani decorated with patterns and panels with figures in bichrome technique are good examples of how ornate an outfit could be.[94] Yon, however – drawing attention to fragments of another large terracotta statue with traces of red, black, yellow, white and green paint now in the Musée de Toulouse – has proposed that this dress item is not a cuirass but an embroidered chiton with fringes which the Persians, according to Herodotus, wore on top of the cuirass.[95] If this is correct we get a glimpse of vividly patterned tunics somewhat like renderings of Assyrian textiles and garments painted on Attic Black Figure vases,[96] and such tunics would seem to be a better match for the decorated T-shirts and pants or kilts worn by the other Cypriot statues treated here. This is not to say that all tunics were this ornate, as also indicated by the tunics with painted borders worn by the statuettes mentioned above; elsewhere, undecorated or white garments may have held specific connotations, for instance of purity.[97]

The body

Generally speaking, Cypriot sculptors did not invest much attention and workmanship in the execution of the body and the physical details of the statues, and this may be part of the reason why Cypriot sculpture has been considered inferior to Greek sculpture. Not even at the turn of the 20th century, when modernist circles praised Archaic Greek sculpture and embraced it for being anti-academic and produced by master craftsmen, was Cypriot sculpture part of the picture, perhaps because soft limestone is easily worked compared to hard marble.[98] In particular the Greek kouros has received much attention and much praise; but Snodgrass, although acknowledging its social importance, saw the kouros as a tiresomely inhibiting and conventional medium.[99] Recent and still ongoing discussions address issues such as the message(s) embedded in this particular type of statue and its agency. Some of the viewpoints are mentioned here partly to illustrate the different perceptions of modern viewers and to put into perspective the lack of attention given to contemporary Cypriot statues, which share the same frontal pose and the same frontal stare. For Tanner the kouros is "a hieratic image distanced from and eschewing interaction with the viewer",[100] and Neer finds that "type is disengaged, aloof from those addressees who actually stop to read, look and mourn", in the case of the Anavysos kouros.[101] Other, very different viewpoints emphasize the interaction between the kouros and the viewer by means of the kouros' return of the viewer's gaze, and thus it "establishes a relationship with the viewer", as Elsner puts it.[102] The interaction between the Cypriot statues and their spectators has not been an issue of debate, and one may wonder if this is because, unlike the Greek kouroi, they are clothed and thus do not have an eroticized effect. As succinctly described by Neer, "kouroi are all about bodies",[103] not least to a viewer in the present-day Western world, where trim males, epitomized by shiny oil-anointed body builders,

---

91   Ergülec 1972, pl. 18; Faegersten 2003, cat. 12.

92   Faegersten 2003, 43.

93   Karageorghis & des Gagniers 1974, 56, VI.7

94   Karageorghis & des Gagniers 1974, 12.a.7 and b.13; Karageorghis 1993, nos 80-2.

95   Yon 2005, 43.

96   For instance Dalley 1991, figs 5-11; Hirmer & Arias 1962, pl. 17.

97   Gawlinski 2008.

98   Prettejohn 2012, 204.

99   Snodgrass 1980, 179.

100 Tanner 2001, 257.

101 Neer 2010, 44.

102 Osborne 1988, 7; Stewart 1997, 66; Elsner 2005, 76.

103 Neer 2010, 50.

have become role models. The renewed interest in the kouros may in fact partly reflect this phenomenon. Seen from this perspective it is perhaps not surprising that the clothed Cypriot male statues have attracted limited interest; this is clear in Vermeule's statement that "the bodies of the limestone statues tend to be decorative vehicles, distinguished by costume or quality of carving rather than subtleties of style".[104]

Although we may trace Ionian and Attic stylistic influence in Cypriot sculpture, the Cypriot sculptors did not follow the new naturalistic trend, which has been termed "the Greek revolution" and connected with the introduction of democracy in Athens, the date of which, however, is still debated.[105] To Ridgway, on the other hand, the change in Greek sculpture from the 6th to the 5th centuries BC cannot be narrowed down to a specific time or event, but is the result of a series of consecutive developments,[106] and Neer, discarding the notion of the Greek revolution, sees the Classical style as "an ongoing adjustment of emphasis" and "a reconfiguration of the relation of image to beholder".[107] As in the case of the kouros, the changed interconnection between the early Classical statue and the viewer in Attica has received various interpretations. While some consider these statues self-absorbed and turning the spectator into a voyeur,[108] others find that "the life and movement of the Classical statues makes for more direct contact".[109]

This serves to underline the diverse interpretations of the development of Attic sculpture from which some Cypriot sculptors partly drew their inspiration, and also to emphasize that stylistic influence is only part of the picture: there are limitations to the Attic or Greek influence in Cypriot sculpture, concerning not only naturalism but also the effect of the sculpture on the viewer. Unlike the development in Attic and Greek sculpture, Cypriot

statues of the early 5th century BC perpetuate the frontal pose and the frontal gaze, and in Cyprus athletic statues did not catch on, which is another important deviation from the Attic/Greek development to be addressed below.

The general lack of interest in sub-dermal features on Cypriot sculpture is even more noteworthy as the Greeks developed an interest in such features, and earlier on neighbouring Assyrian sculptors made an effort to emphasize muscles and sinews of both humans and animals in a powerful although schematic way.[110] Turning to the Achaemenids, on the other hand, it has been recognized that the physicality of the body only features on the Bisitun relief – a victory monument, which according to Feldman, adheres to a Near Eastern tradition going back to the stele of Naram-Sin.[111] Otherwise, the Persians, like the Cypriots, tended to pay little attention to bodily details, perhaps because the meaning of the Persian relief sculpture was symbolic and meant to convey permanence – as suggested by Ridgway –[112] and perhaps a deliberate continuation of a traditional formalism may also have been instrumental where Cypriot sculpture was concerned. This may be supported by a few exceptions which, although they point in different directions, indicate that local sculptors did occasionally elaborate on the physicality of the body. The over life-size statue from Pyla mentioned above (Fig. 7) is the most impressive and powerful example, as it rushes forward in a dynamic stride.[113] His narrow mantle directs the attention of the spectator to his naked body underneath it, rather than covering it up, aspiring to share what Neer calls the erotic perspective of the kouros.[114] A statue from Potamia identified as Apollo with a lyre is another noteworthy example. He, too, is apparently naked but for the mantle, which is also draped over the left shoulder and carried under the right arm. But it is draped very low, almost

---

104 Vermeule 1974, 288.

105 Stewart 1997, 70; Tanner 2001, 272. For a discussion of the date cf. Osborne 2006, 10.

106 Ridgway 1985, 6, 14.

107 Neer 2010, 4.

108 Elsner 2005, 76, 85.

109 Tanner 2001, 270.

110 Aker 2007, 230.

111 Feldman 2007, 281.

112 Ridgway 1985, 11.

113 Bernhard-Walcher et al. 1999, no. 76.

114 Neer 2010, 49.

below the hip. Again the mantle is not voluminous, but it is draped in a way that reveals the soft body structure and the genitals beneath it.[115] Again the drapery is part of the play.[116] Some of the Egyptianizing statues present another and quite different approach to the rendering of the body, which is provided with a somewhat floppy belly[117] that brings to mind Egyptian statues from the New Kingdom period, rather than the contemporary Egyptian/ Phoenician look. Although the slender waist may result from cutting away the stone between the arms and the body as suggested by Faegersten,[118] this does not account for the floppy belly.

The material

The materials used for statuary are also important elements of their visual expression and the messages embedded in them. The production of stone sculpture started more or less at the same time in Cyprus and the Greek world. The beginning of the Cretan series of limestone statues of the so-called Daidalic style is dated to the early 7th century BC.[119] The style is also represented by stone statuary outside Crete as for instance the Nikandra statue, which was erected to Artemis on Delos by the middle of the 7th century BC and represents the first statue made of marble, which became the famed material for Greek sculpture. The production of Cypriot limestone statues also began in the 7th century BC, but like their Near Eastern and Egyptian neighbours the Cypriots used local stone material. According to Counts "The lack of an indigenous source of marble and an *apparent* lack of desire or economic ability to import it resulted in the

widespread use of local limestone for Cypriot sculpture".[120] As to the latter suggestion, it should be taken into consideration that during the Cypro-Archaic period Cyprus was hardly impoverished, and as just mentioned marble was available and exploited on the islands of Paros and Naxos, located not far away.[121] It rather seems that marble was not an issue in Cyprus at this point in time. Greek marble is praised for its radiance, its wonder and its whiteness,[122] while Cypriot limestone shares only the whitish colour and perhaps sometimes the shine.[123] The choice of local material may actually be one of the reasons why Cypriot sculpture has been considered inferior by modern spectators. However, such an attitude may not have prevailed during the late 7th and early part of the 6th century BC, as indicated by the series of limestone statuettes of Cypro-Ionian style found in the Levant, at Naucratis in Egypt and in Greek sanctuaries in particular on Rhodes, Samos, Cnidos and at Miletus.[124] Although the series raises a number of other interesting questions, the few comments here address only the material. Scientific analyses indicate that at least the examined statuettes from Samos and Lindos and Vroulia on Rhodes are most likely made of Cypriot limestone. However, the variety of limestone in Cyprus is a complicating factor, and it cannot be excluded that some of the other statuettes were made of limestone from sources outside of Cyprus.[125] Jenkins has pointed out that a group of similar statuettes found at Naucratis are made of Cypriot gypsum and not Egyptian alabaster, as previously believed.[126] According to him "The gypsum statuettes seem to have been a de luxe alternative to limestone, intended to simulate the white marble of the Greek sculptures they copy".[127] Both materials may also

---

115 Karageorghis 1979, fig. 4; 1998, no. 72.

116 The concentration of the elaborate folds along the left side together with the block-like right side and the strange position of the abdomen seen from the front indicate that the statue was not made to be seen from a strictly frontal viewpoint. The statue seems to be restored, but it is difficult to pinpoint the extent of the restoration.

117 Karageorghis et al. 2000, no. 176; Faegersten 2003, nos 30, 44.

118 Faegersten 2003, 84.

119 Stewart 1990, 107.

120 Counts 2001, 153.

121 Stewart 1990, 38.

122 Stewart 1990, 36; Neer 2010, 73.

123 For the different hues cf. Kourou et al. 2002, 2.

124 Kourou et al. 2002.

125 Kourou et al. 2002, 3, 75.

126 Jenkins 2001, 167.

127 Jenkins 2001, 177.

have a shiny quality like marble and thus support Jenkin's suggestion. Still, they too carry painted decoration. The use of colour was commented on above in connection with the dress types, and in Cyprus colouring continued as an important element used to enhance dress and ornamental details during the 5th century BC, as documented by one of the Hathor capitals and sarcophagi found at Amathus and Kouklia-Palaipaphos.[128] Furthermore, painted sculpture was not confined to Greece and Cyprus. In other neighbouring societies such as Egypt and the Assyrian and Achaemenid empires, paint was used for instance on architectural reliefs made of yet other sorts of stone material, which is likewise being analyzed and debated.[129] Considering the geographical location of Cyprus, these areas are likewise important when it comes to understanding the use of colours on Cypriot sculpture.

Discussions of materials should also include other materials such as metals, wood and ivory. Here it may be useful to draw attention to Neer's discussion of "shining stone", i.e. marble.[130] According to Neer, marble not considered shiny enough could be improved with bright tin or silver foil, as in the case of the "Ballplayer Base", a statue base from Kerameikos in Athens named after its relief decoration showing ball players and athletes. But this statement would seem to contradict Neer's praise of the radiance of marble itself and could even speak in favour of a preference for play with colours produced by combining different materials. The application of foil may also reflect influence from bronze statuary, where metals were similarly used in colourful combinations and in combination with other materials.[131] Taking the Cypriot natural resources of copper into consideration, it is hard to believe that bronze – another shiny material, with which the verb *marmairo* (to glitter or shine) was often associated –[132] was apparently not used for statues

during the Archaic period; if it was, it is usually assumed that such statues have disappeared because they were vulnerable and prone to re-melting. The 7th-century BC sphyrelata from Krete and Olympia, the latter produced from a combination of Greek and re-used Near Eastern relief plaques, document that bronze was indeed used for larger statuary in the Mediterranean during the Archaic period,[133] and not just for small figures, which are also known from Cyprus.[134] As it stands, the so-called Chatsworth head found at Tamassos (which belongs together with a leg in the Louvre) is the earliest evidence of local large-scale cast bronze statuary.[135] However, it is dated to the second quarter of the 5th century BC, and it is noteworthy that, pace a single kouros from Marion, the earliest and similarly scarce evidence of marble statuary appeared at the same time or later.[136]

We know that wood and ivory was used for Greek sculpture – wood for xoana – and the remains of the two 6th-century BC statues found at Delphi testify to a combination of ivory and other precious materials such as gilded bronze sheets, gold foil and silver and bronze nails, and in the latter case Stewart rightly emphasizes their colourful effect.[137] Here it should be mentioned that paint along with gold, was applied on Achaemenid sculpture as a colouring device.[138] The ivory and some of the woods used in Greece derive from the Levant, and one would expect that the nearby island of Cyprus, itself densely forested at the time, would have used the same materials for sculpture, although not a shred of evidence is available. The possibility has therefore largely been ignored, but in her meticulous study of the Cypriot Egyptianizing statues Faegersten argues for Phoenician models made of wood, which were either brightly painted or embellished with ivory and coloured glass inlays.[139] Considering the local characteristic rendering of the bodies and faces of the

128 Hermary 1985, fig. 7; Hendrix 2001, pl. 1; Flourentzos 2007, figs 13-7.
129 Nagel 2013, 1-19.
130 Neer 2010, 75.
131 Wünsche 2007, 153; Brinkmann 2014, 97.
132 Neer 2010, 76.
133 Borell & Rittig 1998, 206.
134 Hermary 2001, 145-64.
135 Bouquillon et al. 2006, 234, 252.
136 Senff 1993, 48; Ridgeway 1970, 58, figs 84-7; Maier & Karageorghis 1984, fig. 170; Fontan 2007, 149.
137 Stewart 1990, 37.
138 Nagel 2013, 7.
139 Faegersten 2003, 225-43.

Cypriot statues, Faegersten specifically comments that what was being imitated was the "new and foreign, colourful pleasing attire", thus underscoring the importance of the play with colours.[140] The relief decoration of the Egyptianizing kilts brings to mind ivory carvings, and the indented borders of some of them certainly indicate that inlays were inserted or that the stone sculpture imitated products made of other materials,[141] and perhaps refer to beads applied to real kilts.[142] Other details of the stone sculpture reveal influence from techniques more at home in other materials. For instance, the incised decoration on the T-shirt of one of the statues dressed in "Cypriot pants" (Fig. 9) and the drapery of some of the tunics and mantles seem to be more at home in works of clay or bronze.[143] Like the mantle edge of some of the stone statues mentioned above (Figs. 1-2), the stippled moustache and feathered eyebrows of some stone sculpture reveal influence from work in clay,[144] thus supporting the more general comment by Hermary that stone sculpture essentially developed from terracotta sculpture.[145] It should also be mentioned that the lower part of terracotta figurines with wheel-made bodies look very much like the high feet on stemmed bowls,[146] while the loose locks of hair and beard on some of the later statues rather reveal influence from metalwork.[147] It thus seems that sometimes techniques more at home in other media were borrowed to achieve certain effects in stone statuary, and the question arises of how closely the craftsmen working in different media actually collaborated.[148]

According to Jenkins the use of marble was one of the self-defining characteristics of Greek sculpture,[149] and perhaps similar Cypriot connotations were embedded in the local limestone. The persistent use of limestone and clay for votary statues should perhaps be seen from a religious and/or local perspective. From the onset the statues were primarily produced to perform as dedications in sanctuaries, and the use of these materials, once established for this specific purpose, was by and large perpetuated until the Roman period. Marble was indeed used before, but as demonstrated by Fejfer,[150] it was systematically employed in architectural settings in Cyprus during the Roman period in order to accommodate the Roman imperial style, while bronze and limestone continued to be used for self-representations in traditional settings such as sanctuaries.

Size

Both Greeks and Cypriots produced statuary of different sizes. A 7th-century terracotta statue from Salamis originally more than 4.60 m tall and a helmeted head of limestone, more than 0.8 m tall and dated to around 600 BC,[151] demonstrate the large sizes of some of the earlier statues, and although the size seems to diminish with time statues taller than life-size, as for instance the "Priest with dove" (Fig. 7), were still being produced by the end of the 6th and the beginning of the 5th century BC. The large size would have been rather spectacular and overwhelming in the setting of the Cypriot sanctuaries, which were themselves hardly impressive architectural structures and utterly different from the large stone temples in Greece and the monumentality of Egyptian versions, as pointed out by Senff.[152] In Greek sanctuary settings the colossal kouroi would likewise have made an overwhelming impression, and in the case of the Samian Heraion these "monsters", to use Stewart's expression, may even have been one of

---

140 Faegersten 2003, 242.

141 Faegersten 2003, no. 6.

142 Faegersten 2003, nos 15, 20-2.

143 Karageorghis et al. 2000, nos 169, 336.

144 Markoe 1987, pls 40, 41, 3-4; Faegersten 2003, nos 21, 24.

145 Hermary 1991, 146.

146 For instance Karageorghis et al. 2000, nos 228, 233.

147 Hermary 1989, no. 78; Karageorghis et al. 2003, no. 336; Hermary 2005, 103.

148 Cf. Karageorghis 1993, 5.

149 Spivey 1996, 64.

150 Fejfer 2013, 192.

151 Hermary 1991, 143; Karageorghis et al 2000, no. 171.

152 Senff 1993, 6.

the reasons why the construction of the Rhoikos temple was begun.[153] The votives were first and foremost offerings to the gods, and large and even colossal sizes may of course express a wish to present the deity with the best one could afford, but simultaneously they also conveyed messages concerning economic and social power.[154] As stated by Miller, "power is, among other things, a property of materiality",[155] and investigations of Achaemenid art, for instance, have shown that hierarchical proportions were used as a means to convey information on social stratification.[156] Following this line of thought one would expect the large statues also to be the most ornate, but the group of the Egyptianizing statues for instance contradicts this assumption. They, too, appear in different sizes from statuettes to colossal dimensions. While three of the six pieces with ornate kilt aprons decorated with a frontal head are indeed tall, the other three are less than one metre tall,[157] and small and large statues of this particular type appeared together in the sanctuaries at Idalion and Golgoi.

Interpretations

The Egyptianizing outfit looks rather impractical and could hardly have been used in a daily context; one wonders what materials it was made of in real life. It is and was flashy and eye-catching, and was probably reserved for particular segments of the Cypriot kingdom societies, who clearly wished to display themselves in an ostentatious way. The decorative elements suggest that it was used within a religious sphere, and at the same time the variety of details and the inconsistent use of the crown and broad collar indicate that a donator and his sculptor were free to choose the exact

details, which probably held specific meanings. This outfit, or parts of it, is worn by bearded as well as unbearded males, and so it seems to have little to do with a specific age group or age-related rituals. The statues have been interpreted as images of the local aristocracy, kings and princes, perhaps also presiding as priests.[158] Having traced the inter-dependency between Cyprus and Phoenicia concerning this type of statue as well as other media, Faegersten suggested that "this particular figure type was connected to a Phoenician royal and/or divine sphere, where a (foreign) royal reference was one preferred means for attracting the attention of the divine powers".[159] A sacral aspect seems to be supported by a colossal statue of the so-called Cypriot Herakles, also named Master of the Lion by Counts, dressed in a kilt-like skirt combined with a T-shirt.[160] The Egyptianizing garment was probably worn by priests, royal or not, but this does not exclude that a wider range of officials attached to the sanctuaries were entitled to wear it. This would account for the falcon-headed scribe and the figures with weapons and carrying animals mentioned above, as well as the different sizes of the statues.

Statues dressed in "Cypriot pants" are usually interpreted as princes or members of the royal families. Senff emphasizes the display of luxury items such as the jewellery.[161] According to Hermary, diadems with rosettes were reserved for kings, princes and princesses in the Near East and the Cypriot statues may represent princes in divine service,[162] while Counts is open to this dual interpretation without necessarily referring to the Near East.[163] Hurschmann agrees with Senff that the outfit would be practical and easy to move in, and he suggests that the statues represent ceremonial assistants participating in an-

---

153 Stewart 1990, 117.

154 Sørensen 1994, 88.

155 Miller 2005, 20.

156 Azarpay 1994, 178.

157 Faegersten 2003, nos 15, 30, 50.

158 Maier 1989, 377; Hermary 1989, 49; Senff 1993, 71.

159 Faegersten 2003, 205, 265.

160 Karageorghis et al. 2000, no. 190; Counts 2008, 10. Here the broad belt securing the kilt is repeated, as is the beaded edge of the kilt covering the left thigh, thus repeating a dress detail seen on other kilt statues. However, the two ends do not meet in the middle, where the vertical devanteau or apron is missing. The left hem of the kilt is provided with a Greek drapery system ending in zigzag folds, and the line of beads marking the right border of the kilt has been incorporated as the central decoration of this system. It should also be noticed that his beard is of the old-fashioned type with vertical tresses.

161 Senff 1993, 71.

162 Hermary 1989, 44.

163 Counts 2001, 158. It should be noticed, though, that the simple rosettes decorate the garments of kings as well as officials on Neo-Assyrian reliefs, cf. Guralnick 2004, 231.

75

imal sacrifices or representatives of family clans or other social groups.[164] The small terracotta group of two youths with rosette-decorated pants and diadems flanking a large bull – perhaps being led off to be sacrificed – may support a religious interpretation.[165] However, this does not exclude an athletic aspect, and it is interesting that similar pants are used by Mongolian wrestlers competing at the Naadam festival, which has its roots in ritual sacrificial ceremonies.[166] In Mongolia wrestling is one of the three games of men, which are instrumental in restructuring traditions, values and identities, and in Cyprus the similar outfit may have embodied comparable notions and were perhaps connected with rites of passage. Compared with the extant corpus of sculpture dressed in tunic and mantle, statues and statuettes wearing "Cypriot pants" and Egyptianizing kilts are comparatively few and hardly appear in terracotta, which may also indicate that these garments were reserved for specific occasions and members of the Cypriot societies.

The tunic-–mantle and later chiton–himation combination may be considered an international garment combination of the time. In Cyprus details of these garments show influence first from the Near East, then Ionia and Attica; but as mentioned above, old traits continued and blended with new ones in an inconsistent way. This type of sculpture seems to represent older as well as younger men of different social groups, primarily based upon their size and elaboration.[167] Fringes and borders of mantles were inspired by the Near East where personalized borders and fringes could be used by the Assyrians to seal legal records,[168] and in Cyprus they may likewise have served to distinguish certain members of the societies. During the 6th century the Cypriots adopted the Greek-inspired himation with folds, which indicates that the volume of the garment became an issue. References were made above to the so-called Anakreontic revellers on Attic vase paintings produced around 500 BC. On these sympotic vessels revellers, including Anakreon whose name is written on three of the vases, are shown in lavish chitons and himatia which they adopted among other things from their Lydian aristocratic peers in order to differentiate themselves from their contemporaries.[169] Based upon literary sources, Kurke has provided a list of the elements that made up this luxurious lifestyle called habros, which includes long, flowing garments of expensive material, hair worn long and elaborately coiffured, gold ornaments, perfumes and scented oils. Kurke also pointed out that while the term carried positive connotations in the 6th century BC it took a negative turn in Greece during the 5th century, probably because of the Persian wars and the turn to democracy in Athens.[170] The adoption of the Greek-inspired chiton and himation in Cyprus may be seen as an expression of Grecophilia and/or a political manifestation against the Persians, or simply as a social manifestation of members of the upper classes leading a luxurious lifestyle like Greek and other Mediterranean aristocrats. Some of the statues dressed in chiton and himation have also been interpreted as kings or priests or both.[171] In this respect one particular group has received attention: according to Senff, statues from Idalion with a tasselled beard and a wreath around the head (Fig. 6) represent members of the local royal dynasty prior to its annexation by Phoenician Kition, and should be seen as "verstärkter Anschluss" to Greek culture.[172] Hermary, on the other hand, dating the annexation of Idalion to 470-460 BC and the statues in question to about the middle of the 5th century BC, interpreted them as images of royal members of the new Kitian dynasty of Idalion.[173] Although it is highly likely that kings and members of the royal family acted as priests during the Cypro-Archaic period it is difficult to prove.[174] The epigraphic evidence dates

---

164 Senff 1993, 46, note 369; Hurschmann 2003, 205.

165 Karageorghis 1995, pl. 52, 1.

166 Rhode 2009, 28, 99.

167 Senff 1993, 71; Sørensen 1994, 88.

168 Dalley 1991, 125.

169 Neer 2002, 19 with further references.

170 Kurke 1992, 97-8, 102.

171 Senff 1993, 71.

172 Senff 1993, 73.

173 Hermary 2005, 112.

174 Cf. Hermary 2014, 143 for a summary.

to the late 4th century BC and later, and the archaeological evidence concerning the Archaic period is inconclusive.[175]

Discussing royalty and sculpture, three sarcophagi dated to the first part of the 5th century BC should be taken into consideration not least because it has been suggested that these painted and relief-decorated sarcophagi became the new medium for manifestations of power and royalty, thus taking over the former role of statuary.[176] On the so-called Amathus sarcophagus procession scenes are seen on the long sides and figures of Astarte and Bes decorate the short sides.[177] The long sides of the slightly later sarcophagus from Golgoi are decorated with symposium and hunting scenes, while the myth of Perseus and Medusa and two persons standing in a horse-drawn chariot decorate the short sides.[178] The sarcophagus from Kouklia (Palaepaphos) carries figural scenes which may relate to Greek mythology, such as Ajax carrying the body of Achilleus, and Odysseus and his men escaping from the Cyclops Polyphemos.[179] All three sarcophagi show a mixture of details which point to Greek, Ionian, Phoenician and Persian spheres, and the sarcophagi from Golgoi and Palaepaphos relate to the so-called Greco-Persian tomb reliefs from Ionia, Lycia and Western Anatolia, areas likewise subjugated by the Achaemenid empire.[180] To Draycott, "the materials present Western Anatolian emulation of Persian nobles",[181] and she asks whether it is possible to detect variations among the areas in question,[182] topics that are likewise relevant in the case of Cyprus. It has been suggested that the sarcophagus from Amathus, which is decorated with traditional Cypriot elements based on Near Eastern iconography, was made for a local king and reflects the city's refusal to join the Ionian uprising against the Persians in 499 BC, while the sarcophagus from Golgoi may have belonged to a dignitary probably from the kingdom of Idalion.[183] The rendering of Greek myths on this sarcophagus links it with the sarcophagus from Palaepaphos; it has been suggested that the foremost intention with the scenes was to re-affirm Greek culture, and that the scene from Troy on the Palaepaphos sarcophagus referring to Teucros, son of Telamon and founder of Salamis in Cyprus, served to underline the Greek roots of the island as such.[184] Whether or not the decoration of the sarcophagi was intended to convey political statements, images of Greek gods appeared on the island at the same time and statues dressed in the "Cypriot pants" and Egyptianizing kilts were given up, suggesting changes within the religious practice. If these garments were first and foremost associated with performances of religious rites connected to the local deities, they were perhaps considered old-fashioned or incompatible with new developments and were accordingly given up. However, if the statues, and in particular those wearing Egyptian kilts, were associated with royalty it is noteworthy that they were given up while the Cypriot kingdoms prevailed. Furthermore, it does not necessarily follow that their disappearance from the sculptural realm implies that statuary ceased to be a prominent ground for manifestation of power during the 5th century BC, as proposed by Satraki.[185] The role of statues as status markers seems rather to have continued, as suggested by the statues wearing himatia and wreaths mentioned above. The continued dedication of statues in the sanctuaries demonstrates that statuary did, indeed, remain a significant social and cultural marker. In fact, the sanctuaries probably functioned as important places, which helped keep the societies together by means of ritualized behaviour. As stated by Bollmer, "Ritual is the embodied performance of history as memory. And for memory to persist in time the ritual must be maintained".[186]

175   Hermary 2014, 143.

176   Satraki 2013, 133, 137.

177   Tatton-Brown 1981, 74; Hermary & Mertens 2014, cat. 490 with further references.

178   Karageorghis et al. 2000, no. 331.

179   Raptou 2007, 316.

180   Tatton-Brown 1981, 81; Tatton-brown 1984, 169; Petit 2004, 51.

181   Draycott 2010, 1.

182   Draycott 2010, 2. Cf. also Baughan 2010, 32.

183   Hermary 2014, 361, 370.

184   Raptou 2007, 326.

185   Satraki 2013, 133.

186   Bollmer 2011, 459.

Context

The context of statues plays a vital role, and as the Cypriot stone sculptures primarily functioned as dedications to a god or gods and objects to be viewed in the sanctuaries, they belong to a category that Snodgrass has termed converted offerings, meaning offerings which have no possible use outside of a "votive" context,[187] and Whitley adds that the votives are new objects whose social lives, as dedications and custodians of social memory, are just beginning. The majority is believed to represent adorants alias donators, who were thus immortalized and meant to be exhibited forever in the sanctuaries. The sanctuary at A. Irini on the northwest coast of Cyprus was excavated by the Swedish Cyprus expedition, and the terracottas dedicated here present an interesting phenomenon.[188] Although serious questions have been raised concerning the stratigraphy and the date of Gjerstad's Proto-Cypriot and Neo-Cypriot stylistic groups the location of the majority of statuary remains unchallenged.[189] It was found in an open-air temenos, arranged in concentric semicir-

cles around an altar, almost conveying the impression of participants focusing on the altar, as suggested by Senff (Fig. 12).[190] It might even be suggested that the figures were arranged in a theatre-like setting where the smaller figures close to the altar and the large ones at the back ensured that they were all able to follow and even partake in what was being performed at the altar. Furthermore, they seem to be turned approximately towards the entrance of the temenos, which in period 5 and perhaps also the preceding period, 4, was located in the north eastern corner of the temenos. Upon entering, visitors would have been faced with this scenario of closely grouped imagery dedicated by their ancestors and possibly themselves, and thus live adorants and images of previous votaries interacted with the altar as the focal point.

The Apollo sanctuary at Idalion[191] serves as another example (Fig. 13). The statues were erected within an architectural setting apparently belonging to different phases, which the excavators recorded together with the location of the statue bases. Although it cannot be proved, Senff sug-

---

187 Quoted Whitley 2003/04, 190.

188 Gjerstad 1935, 808, figs 263; 277-9.

189 Stylianou 2003, 47; Fourrier 2007, 104.

190 Senff 1993, 14.

191 According to Gaber 1994, 162; 2008, 59; Gaber & Dever 1996, 105, the exact location of the sanctuary was not recorded on a map by the excavator and based upon her investigations she has proposed another area than that indicated by Ohnefalsch-Richter in his work, Kypros, die Bibel und Homer, Berlin 1893 pl. 2. Instead of a temple a temenos with utilitarian buildings is proposed.

Fig. 13. *Model of the Apollon sanctuary at Idalion (Senff 1993).*

gests that the different statue types were placed in groups according to their attire, based on the notes left by the excavator Hamilton Lang.[192] The statues dedicated in the earlier eastern part of the sanctuary probably also focused on an altar, while the statues in the late Archaic western section of the sanctuary were aligned in rows both under shelter and in the large courtyard, apparently without an altar as a focal point, but facing the procession entering the court from the west as past spectators, or "Vertreter der Festteilnehmer" to use Senff's expression.[193] However, supposing Lang's information is reliable, a slightly different scenario may be proposed. If the two stone basins on an axis running north–south in the centre of the courtyard were focal points in some kind of ceremony, participants could have entered through both entrances and lined up along the three sides of the basins, while the rows of statues would have formed the southern part of the audience and participated along with the living adorants in a way more similar to the situation at A. Irini. The interplay between statues and adorants is repeated at the palace at Vouni,

where statues placed in the temenos before the entrance to the cult room flanked the approaching visitors.[194] The bases recorded on the plan of the sanctuary at Achna indicate that here statues were raised partly in line and partly in small clusters,[195] and according to Cesnola's perhaps not reliable observations of the sanctuary at Golgoi-A. Photios, the statues were arranged in lines along the walls and in the centre of the sanctuary,[196] recalling the situation at Idalion. On the other hand the statuary in the Apollo sanctuary at Tamassos was apparently placed in a separate temenos, which gives the impression of being a storage area.[197]

Although votives were removed periodically as witnessed by depositions in bothroi, the find circumstances at A. Irini and Idalion for example suggest that this did not happen on a regular basis, since both older and more recent statues were found together by the excavators. The statues, which were dedicated at different times within the sanctuaries, presented different pasts in a continuously forward-moving present, and so they were instrumental for upholding links with the past and for marking out a

192 Senff 1993, 17; Senff 2005, 103.

193 Senff 1993, 13-4.

194 Senff 1993, 14.

195 Gjerstad 1948, fig. 1.3.

196 Hermary & Mertens 2014, 14.

197 Gjerstad 1948, 9, fig. 1.4; Buchholz & Untiedt 1996, 47, fig. 66.

79

sanctuary as a place of memory. The importance of the past in the present is indeed underlined by the fact that some Cypriot sanctuaries of the Iron Age like A. Irini, Maroni and Enkomi were located at places with earlier Late Bronze Age activities.[198]

The statues were probably also invigorating a sense of community in the Cypriot societies – which was especially important because neither the 6th nor the following centuries were peaceful times on the island. We do not know whether the statues in question were personal or collective dedications, but according to Guggenheim "objects outside the remembering persons or collectives may act as catalysts for the production and interpersonal adjustment of memory".[199] Furthermore, as stated by Bollmer, "For a collective to exist over any extended period of time, memory has to be performed repeatedly, as rituals" and "it is in embodied action that the collective is united, in spite of the plurality of individual affects, beliefs and interpretations of history and policy".[200] This was not a local Cypriot phenomenon, as witnessed for instance by the situation in the sanctuary at Olympia in Greece. According to Hölscher, interaction between various types of free-standing statues and the visitors to this sanctuary was played out from the 6th century BC onwards, and the statues acted not only as votive monuments but also as spectators to successive celebrations.[201] Still, our comparatively slight knowledge of the physical appearance of the Cypriot sanctuaries makes it difficult to imagine the impression the structures together with the votives, and the statuary in particular, made on the visitors. The experience would also have been influenced by what time of the year they were there, and whether the visit took place during broad daylight or by torch-light. Although it is problematic to ascertain in this case, the effect of light and lightning on sensual perception is an important issue, which should be addressed along with materials, colours and sizes employed, as demonstrated by a number of other studies.[202]

Many of the Cypriot sanctuaries were located outside the city centres, and, largely based upon studies of Cypriot terracottas and pottery, Fourrier has suggested that the location of extra-urban sanctuaries defined spheres of influence and were used as a means to legitimize the claim of a territory by an urban centre.[203] According to Fourrier the use of the names Golgia and Paphia for the "Great Goddess" of the island written on dedications found in sanctuaries located in the Mesaoria reflects political negotiations between certain kings,[204] and Golgia and images of the "Cypriot Heracles", alias "the Master of the Lion", may have been promoted in order to unify Mesaoria as a homogeneous cultural region.[205] If this is correct, it demonstrates that sanctuaries were involved in political tensions of the area during the 5th century BC, and it is quite likely that they played a similar role during the previous centuries. Sanctuaries provided permanent loci for meetings of many kinds of people, and the traditional settings as well as the votives and in particular the statues were probably important signifiers not only in respect to religion but also in political and cultural negotiations. Although new elements such as sarcophagi were introduced as markers of social superiority, statues dedicated in sanctuaries did indeed remain important for the duration of the Cypriot kingdoms and beyond.

Conclusions

The analysis above suggests that although Count's remark about Cypriot statues being true to type seems convincing, we cannot be absolutely sure that heads with certain headdresses belong to specific statue types. Furthermore, the variety concerning details indicates that statue-making was not governed by strict formulae and that the Cypriots appreciated the ability to provide their dedications with an individual touch. Some details may also have been used to convey specific messages unreadable to us today. The details and the combination of various

---

198 Fourrier 2007, 122.
199 Guggenheim 2009, 41.
200 Bollmer 2011, 458.
201 Hölscher 2002, 338.
202 Bille & Sørensen 2007.
203 Fourrier 2013, 107.
204 Fourrier 2013, 110.
205 Fourrier 2013, 113.

elements are actually quite impressive, in particular in the case of the statues wearing the Egyptianizing kilt, but also where statues dressed in a tunic and mantle/chiton and himation are concerned. Even the Cypriot pants are rendered in a number of different ways, although they are basically a simple dress item. Traces of paint furthermore indicate that the statues were once more colourful and painted details were probably also used to enhance the individual look of a statue. Hathor capitals and sarcophagi demonstrate how brightly coloured relief sculpture in stone could be, and the local terracottas underline the importance of paint as a communicative device. Comparative studies not only of Cypriot stone and terracotta sculpture but also of Greek, Near Eastern and Egyptian sculpture may provide us with a better understanding of how the use and perception of colour in Cyprus relates to the practices in neighbouring, usually considered dominant cultures. Analyses of how the details were made, for instance carved in relief, incised or painted, may also provide a better insight into the interrelation between craftsmen working in different media. The continuation of the foursquare build of the Cypriot statues and the general lack of interest in physical details sets Cypriot sculpture apart from the development in Greece during the late 6th to 5th centuries BC. Perhaps Cypriot sculpture along with Persian sculpture was meant to convey permanence, and seen through political lenses, it could be argued that if the disappearance of the kouros and kore statues is linked to the abolition of well-known aristocratic emblems in the Greek area, a similar impetus for change was not present in Cyprus, where the kingdom-based societies prevailed. Additional comparative analyses of sculptural expressions in Cyprus and the various societies in western Anatolia as well as the Levant likewise subjected to Persia offer possibilities of providing a deeper insight into how areas, each with their different backgrounds, reacted to Persian political domination. Such studies would also put the reception of 'Perseria' in Athens into perspective.[206]

The persistent use of the local limestone for all types and sizes of local statues and statuettes is also noteworthy. Apparently the assimilation of Greek stylistic traits in Cypriot sculpture was not accompanied by the use of Greek marble, and according to the present evidence the Cypriots did not acquire Archaic Greek marble statues in great numbers. It seems that like the Persians the Cypriots preferred local stone material, perhaps because it was part of their identity- building and maintenance. The size of the Cypriot statues is another interesting aspect, which deserves further deliberation. As mentioned above the wide range of sizes in particular of statues wearing an Egyptianizing outfit makes it difficult to interpret them all as images of kings and princes. If so, materiality was of little consequence to Cypriot royalty, which is hard to believe considering that we are dealing with hierarchic societies in which the elite was presumably keen on outshining subordinate classes. The ornamentation of the kilts carries religious connotations and suggests that these garments were used first and foremost by persons functioning as priests and as sanctuary dignitaries, however not necessarily to the exclusion of royalty. Otherwise we might have to argue that the inconspicuous statuettes were dedicated by humble citizens trying to please their sovereign, and thus open up a discussion of the relation between donator and dedicated statue.

Concerning size, the naked kouros figure represents another interesting phenomenon in Cyprus. A single marble kouros was found in a tomb at Marion,[207] but only a few small local statuettes are known,[208] indicating an indifference to this particular type of statue. One may therefore wonder what prompted the making and dedication of what could be called the colossal semi-kouros from Pyla (Fig. 7). On the one hand the sculptor of this statue clearly paid attention to bodily details like those seen on Greek kouroi, and on the other hand it could be argued that the statue with its large beard, mantle and wreath not only stands apart from the Greek kouroi but actually ignores the concept of the kouros statue.

From what we know Cypriot stone statues were produced to be dedicated in the local sanctuaries where they functioned not only as gifts to the gods but also as links to the past, and they may even have been perceived as representatives of past generations participating in ongoing ceremonies at the sanctuaries. As such, they sustained the role of the sanctuaries as places of memory throughout

---

206 Miller 1997.
207 Richter 1970, no. 179, figs 527-9.
208 Senff 1993, 48.

the duration of the Cypriot kingdoms and later. Apparently Cypriot free-standing male and female statues were not used for other purposes, for instance grave markers, as were the Greek kouros and kore statues in some Aegean areas.[209] This single function seems to underline a very close connection between statues and sanctuaries in Cyprus, and it raises the question of whether the statues were by themselves somehow perceived as belonging to the divine realm.[210] Whether this is accepted or not, the

dedication of different Cypro-Archaic statue types suggests that it was important that different functions and/or events meaningful to the local societies were put on display and commemorated. As stated by Entwistle, "human bodies are dressed bodies", "dress is a basic fact of social life", and "conventions of dress attempt to transform flesh into something recognizable and meaningful to a culture".[211]

---

209 Meyer and Brüggemann 2007, maps 4-5.
210 Unfortunately none of the 6th-century BC Cypriot grave stelai crowned with lions or sphinxes are preserved well enough to ascertain whether their shafts carried an image of the deceased like Attic grave stelai; cf. Tatton-Brown 1986, 439; Hermary 1985, 668, 676, 681; Pogiatzi 2007, 4-8, 30.
211 Entwistle 2000, 6, 8.

Bibliography

Aker, J. 2007
'Workmanship as Ideological Tool in the Monumental Hunt Reliefs of Assurbanipal', in *Ancient Near Eastern Art in Context, Studies in Honour of I. Winter by her Students*, J. Cheng & M.H. Feldman (eds.), 229-263.

Azarpay, G. 1994
'Designing the body: Human Proportions in Achaemenid Arts', *IrAnt* XXIX, 2-19.

Bernhard-Walcher, A. et al.1999
Bernhard-Walcher, A., G. Dembsky, K. Gschwantler & V. Karageorghis, *Die Sammlung zyprischer Antiken im Kunsthistorischen Museum. The Collection of Cypriote Antiquities in the Kunsthistorisches Museum*, W. Seipel (ed.), Vienna.

Bille, M. & T.F. Sørensen 2007
'An Anthropology of Luminosity: The Agency of Light', *Journal of Material Culture* 12, 263-84.

Bollmer, G.D. 2011
'Virtuality in systems of memory: Toward an ontology of collective memory, ritual, and technological', *Memory Studies* 4, 450-64.

Borell, B. & D. Rittig 1998.
'Orientalische und griechische Bronzereliefs aus Olympia. Der Fundkomplex aus Brunnen 17', *OlForsch* 26. Berlin & New York.

Bouquillon, A. et al. 2006
Bouquillon A., S. Descamps, A. Hermary & B. Mille, 'Une nouvelle Étude de l'Apollon Chatsworthy', *RA*, 227-61.

Brinkmann, V. 2014
'Arkaisk og klassisk polykromi', in *Som forvandlet. Antik skulptur i farver*, J. Stubbe Østergaard & A.M. Nielsen (eds.), København, 80-109.

Brönner, M. 1994
'Heads with Double Crowns', in *Cypriote Stone Sculpture*, F. Vandenabeele & R. Laffineur (eds.), Brussels-Liege, 47-53.

Buchholz, H,-G. & K. Untiedt, 1996
Tamassos. Ein antikes Köningreich auf Zypern, Jonsered.

Cesnola, L.P. di 1885
A desriptive Atlas of the Cesnola Collection of Cypriote Antiquities in the Metropolitan Museum of Art New York, Vol.1, Boston.

Counts, D.B. 2001
'Prolegomena to the study of Cypriote Sculpture', *CCEC* 31, 129-81.

Counts, D.B. 2008
'Master of the Lion: Representation and Hybridity in Cypriot Sanctuaries', *AJA* 112, 3-27.

Counts, D.B. 2012
'Local Styles and Regional Trends in Cypriot Limestone Sculpture, in Crossroads and Boundaries; The Archaeology of Past and Present in the Malloura Valley, Cyprus', M.K. Toumazou, P.N. Kardulias & D.B. Counts (eds.), (*AASOR*) 65, 149-62.

Dalley, S. 1991
'Ancient Assyrian Textiles and the Origins of Carpet Design', *IRAN* 29, 117-35.

Draycott, C.M. 2008
'What does "being "Greco-Persian" mean? An introduction to the papers', *Bolletino di Archeologia on line* I 2010 volume special G/ G1 / 1 www.aecologia. Beniculturali.it, 1-6. Accessed 10.05.2015.

Elsner, J. 2005
'Reflections on the 'Greek Revolution' in art: from changes in viewing to the tranformtation of subjectivity', in *Rethinking Revolutions through Ancient Greece*, S. Goldhill & R. Osborne (eds.), Cambridge, 68-95.

Entwistle, J. 2000
The Fashioned Body. Fashion, Dress and Modern Social Theory, Cambridge.

Ergülec, H. 1972
'Large-Sized Cypriot Sculpture in the Archaeological Museums of Istanbul', *SIMA* 20. 4, Gothenburg.

Faegersten, F. 2003
The Egyptianizing Male Limestone Statuary from Cyprus, Lund.

Faegersten, F, 2005
'A Cypriot Limestone Torso in the National Museum, Stockholm – Approaching the so-called Egyptianizing Group in Cypriote Sculpture', in *Medelhavsmuseet. Focus on the Mediterranean*, S. Houby Nielsen (ed.), Stockholm, 45-68.

Fejfer, J. 2013
'Marble Mania: Code-switcing in Roman Cyprus', in *Artefact Variebility, Assembage Differentiation, and Identity Negotiation: Debating Code-Switching in Material Culture*, J. Poblome, D. Maalfitania & J. Lund (eds.) (HEROM 2), Belgium, 169-97.

Feldman, M.H. 2007
'Darius I and the Heroes of Akkad', in *Ancient Near Eastern Art in Context. Studies in Honour of Irene J. Winter by Her Students*, J. Cheng & M.H. Feldman (eds.), Leiden & Boston, 265-93.

Flourentzos, P. 2007
The Sarcophagos of Palaepaphos, Nicosia.

Fontan, E. 2007
'La sculpture en Phénicie', in. XX La Méditeranée des Phéniciens de Tyr à Carthage. Paris, 149-55.

Fourrier, S. 2007
La coroplastique chypriote archaïque. Identités culturelles et politiques à l'époque des royaumes, Lyon.

Fourrier, S. 2013
'Constructing the Peripheries: Extra-Urban Sanctuaries and Peer-Polity Interaction in Iron Age Cyprus', *BASOR* 370, 103-22.

Freyer-Schauenburg, B. 1974
'Bildweke der archaischen Zeit und des Strengen Stils', *SAMOS* XI, Bonn.

Gaber, P. 1994
'In Search of Adonis', in *Cypriot Stone Sculpture. Proceedings of the Second International Conference of Cypriote Stone Studies Brussels-Liège 1993* F. Vandenabeele & R. Laffineur (eds.), Brussels-Liège, 161-5.

Gaber, P. 2008
'Excavations at Idalion and the Changing History of a City-Kingdom', *Near Eastern Archaeology* 71: 1-2, 52-63.

Gaber, P. & W.G. Dever, 1996
'Idalion, Cyprus. Conquest and Community', in *Preliminary Excavation Reports Sardis, Idalion and Tell el-Handaquq North*, W.G. Dever (ed.), *ASOR* 53, 85-113.

Gawlinski, L. 2008
'"Fashioning" Initiates: Dress at the Mysteries', in *Reading a Dynamic Canvas: Adornment in the Ancient Mediterranean World*, C.S. Colburn & M.K. Heyn (eds.), Cambridge, 146-69.

Gjerstad, E. 1935
'Ajia Irini', *The Sweedish Cyprus Expedition. Finds and Results of the Excavations in Cyprus 1927 – 1931, Vol II*, Stockholm, 642-824.

Gjerstad, E. 1948
The Sweedish Cyprus Expedition IV.2. The Cypro-Geometric, Cypro-Archaic and Cypro-Classical Periods. Stockholm.

Guggenheim, M. 2009
'Building Memory: Architecture, networks and users', *Memory Studies* 2 (1), 39-53.

Guralnick, E. 2004
'Neo-Assyrian Patterned Fabrics', *Iraq* 66, 221-32.

Hendrix, E.A. 2001
'Polycromy on the Amathus Sarcophagos, a "Rare Gem of Art"', *Metropolitan Museum Journal* 36, 43-58.

Hermary, A. 1985
'Un nouveau chapiteau Hathorique trouvé à Amathonte', *BCH* 109, 657-99.

Hermary A. 1989
Catalogue des antiquités de Chypre. Sculptures. Musée du Louvre. Département des antiquités orientales, Paris.

Hermary, A. 1991
'Les débuts de la grande plastique chypriote en terra quite', in *Cypriote Terracottas*, Proceedings of the First International Conference of Cypriote Studies, Brussels-Liège-Amsterdam, 29 May – 1 June, 1989, F. Vandenabeele and R. Laffineur (eds.), Brussels-Liège, 139-47.

Hermary, A. 2001
'Les statuettes en bronze à Chypre à l'époque de royaumes', *Archaeologia Cypria* IV, 145-64.

Hermary, A. 2005
'Les derniers temps du royaume d'Idalion et son annexion par Kition', *CCEC* 35, 99-126.

Hermary, A. 2014
'Les fonctions sacerdotales des souverains Cypriotes', *CCEC* 44, 137-52.

Hermary, A. & J.R. Mertens 2014
The Cesnola Collection of Cypriote Art. Stone Sculpture, New York.

Hirmer, M. & Arias, P.E. 1962
A History of Greek Vase Painting, London.

Hurschmann, R. 2003
'Archaisch-kyprische Kouroi mit Hosen', *CCEC* 33, 169-209.

Hölscher, T. 2002
'Rituelle Räume und politische Denkmäler im Heiligtum von Olympia', in *Olympia 1875 – 2000. 125 Jahre Deutsche Ausgrabungen*, Mainz am Rhein, 331-45.

Jacovou, M. 2008
'Cultural and Political Configurations in Iron Age Cyprus: The Sequel to a Protohistoric Episode', *AJA* 112, 625-57.

Jenkins, I. 2001
'Archaic Kouroi in Naucratis: The Case for Cypriot Origin', *AJA* 105, 2, 163-79.

Karageorghis, V. 1969
'Chronique des fouilles et découvertes archéologiques a Chypre en 1968', *BCH* 93, 431-569.

Karageorghis, V. 1979
'Material from a Sanctuary at Potamia', *RDAC*, 289-320.

Karageorghis, V. 1993
The Coroplastic Art of Ancient Cyprus III. The Cypro-Archaic Period. Large and Medium Size Sculpture, Nicosia.

Karageorghis, V, 1995
The Coroplastic Art of Ancient Cyprus IV. The Cypro-Archaic Period. Small Male Figurines, Nicosia.

Karageorghis, V. 1998
Greek Gods and Heroes in Ancient Cyprus, Athens.

Karageorghis, V. & J. des Gagniers 1974
La céramique chypriote de style figuré. Âge du Fer (1050-500 Av. J.-C.). Biblioteca di antichità cipriote 2, Rome.

Karageorghis, V. et al. 2000
Karageorghis,V., J.R. Mertens & M.E. Rose, *Ancient Art from Cyprus. The Cesnola Collection in the Metropolitan Museum of Art*, New York.

Karageorghis, V. et al. 2002
Ancient Art from Cyprus in the collection of George and Nefeli Giabra Pierides, Athens.

Karakasi, K. 2001
Archaische Koren, Munich.

Kourou, N. et al. 2002
Kourou,N., V. Karageorghis, Y. Maniatis, K. Polikreti, Y. Basiakos & C. Xenophontos, *Limestone Statuettes of Cypriote Type found in the Aegean*, Nicosia.

Kurke, L. 1992
'The Politics of habrosyne in Archaic Greece', *ClAnt* 11, 91-120.

Maier, F.G. 1989
'Priest Kings in Cyprus', in *Early Society in Cyprus*, E. Peltenburg (ed.), Edinburgh, 376-91.

Maier, F.G. & V. Karageorghis 1984
Paphos. History and Archaeology, Nicosia.

Markoe, G. 1987
'A Bearded head with a conical cap from Lefkoniko: An Examination of a Cypro-Archaic Votary', *RDAC*, 119-25.

Masson & Hermary 1993
O. Masson & A. Hermary, 'À propos du "pretre à la colombe" de New York', *CCEC* 20, 25-34.

Meyer, M & N. Brüggemann 2007
Kore und Kouros. Weihgaben für die Götter, Vienna.

Miller, D. 2005
'Materiality: An Introduction', in *Materiality*, D. Miller (ed.), Durham & London, 1-50.

Miller, M.C. 1997
Athens and Persia in the Fifth Century BC, Cambridge.

Nagel A. 2013
'Color and Gilding in Achaemenid Architecture and Sculpture', in *The Oxford Handbook of Ancient Iran*, D.T. Potts (ed.), Oxford.

Neer, R.T. 2002
Style and Politics in Athenian Vase-Painting. The Craft of Democracy, ca. 530-460 B.C.E, Cambridge.

Neer, R.T. 2010
The Emergence of the Classical Style in Greek Sculpture, Chicago & London.

Osborne, R. 1988
'Death Revisited; Death Revised. The Death of the Artist in Archaic and Classical Greece', *Art History* 11 (1), 1-16.

Osborne, R. 2006
'When was the Athenian democratic revolution?', in *Rethinking Revolutions through Ancient Greece*, S. Goldhill & R. Osborne (eds.), Cambridge, 10-28.

Papantoniou, G. 2013
'Cypriot Autonomous Polities at the Crossroads of Empire: The Imprint of a Transformed Islandscape in the Classical and Hellenistc Periods', *BASOR* 370, 169-205.

Pogiatzi, E. 2003
Die Grabreliefs auf Zypern von der archaischen bis zur römischen Zeit, Mannheim & Möhnesee.

85

Prettejohn, E. 2012
The Modernity of Ancient Sculpture. Greek Sculpture and Modern Art from Winckelmann to Picasso. London & New York.

Pryce, F.N. 1931
A Catalogue of Sculpture in the Department of Greek and Roman Antiquities of the British Museum. Vol. I. Part II. Cypriote and Etruscan, London.

Raptou, E. 2007
'Culture grecque et tradition orientale à Paphos', *CCEC* 37, 307-28.

Rhode, D. 2009
'Mongolia's Naadam Festival: past and present in the construction of national identity', *ir.canterbury.ac.nz* accessed 17.05.2016.

Richter, G.M.A. 1970
Kouroi. Archaic Greek Youths. A Study of the Development of the Kouros Type in Greek Sculpture, London & New York.

Ridgway, B.S. 1970
The Severe Style in Greek Sculpture, Princeton.

Ridgway, B.S. 1985
'Late Archaic Sculpture', in *Greek Art Archaic into Classical. A Symposium held at the University of Cincinnati April 2-3, 1982*, C.G. Boulter (ed.), Leiden, 1-17.

Satraki, A. 2013
'The Iconography of Basileis in Archaic and Classical Cyprus: Manifestations of Royal Power in the Visual Record', *BASOR* 370, 123-44.

Schmidt, G. 1968
'Kyprische Bildwerke aus dem Heraion von Samos', *Samos* VII, Bonn.

Senff, R. 1993.
'Das Apollonheiligtum von Idalion. Architektur und Statuenausstattung eines zyprischen Heiligtums', *SIMA* XCIV, Jonsered.

Senff, R. 2005.
'Dress, habit and status-symbols of Cypriote statuary from Archaic to Roman times', in *Cyprus: Religion and Society* from *the Late Bronze Age to the End of the Archaic Period*, V. Karageorghis, H. Matthäus & S. Rogge (eds.), Münster, 99-110.

Snodgrass, A. 1980
Archaic Greece. The Age of Experiment, London.

Sommer, M. 2010
'Shaping Mediterranean Economy and Trade: Phoenician Cultural Identities in the Iron Age', in *Material Culture and Social Identities in the Ancient World*, S. Hales & T. Hodos (eds.), Cambridge, 114-37.

Spivey, N. 1996
Understanding Greek Sculpture. Ancient Meanings, Modern Readings, London.

Stewart, A. 1990
Greek Sculpture. An Exploration, New Haven & London.

Stewart, A. 1997
Art, Desire and the Body in Ancient Greece, Cambridge.

Stylianou, A. 2003
'Neues zur Chronologie der frühen kyprischen Plastik', in *Junge zyprische Archäologie*, V. Karageorghis & S. Rogge (eds.), Münster.

Sørensen, L.W. 1994
'The Divine Image?', in *Cypriot Stone Sculpture*, in Proceedings of the Second International Conference of Cypriote Stone Studies Brussels-Liège 1993, F. Vandenabeele & R. Laffineur (eds.), Brussels-Liège,79-89.

Sørensen, L.W. 2014
'Creating identity or identities in Cyprus during the Archaic period', in *Attitudes towards the Past in Antiquity. Creating Identities*, Proceedings of an International Conference held at Stockholm University, 15-17 May 2009, Stockholm Studies in Classical Archaeology, B. Alroth and Ch. Scheffer (eds.), Stockholm, 33-45.

Tanner, J. 2001
'Nature, culture and the body in classical Greek religious art', *WorldArch* 33 (2), 257-76.

Tatton-Brown, V. 1981
'Le "sarcophage d'Amathonte"', in *Amathonte II. Testemonia 2: La sculpture*, A. Hermary (ed.), Paris, 74-83.

Tatton-Brown, V. 1986
'Gravestones of the Archaic and Classical Periods: Local Production and Foreign Influences', in: *Acts of the International Archaeological Symposium "Cyprus between the Orient and the Occident*, V. Karageorghis (ed.), Nicosia, 439-53.

Vermeule, C. 1974
'Cypriote Sculpture, the Late Archaic and Early Classical Periods: Towards a More Precise Understanding. Modifications in Concentration, Terms and Dating', *AJA* 78, 287-90.

Whitley, J. 2003/04
'Letting the Stones in on the Act. Statues as Social Agents in Archaic and Classical Greece', *KODAI* 13/14, 185-98.

Wünsche, R. 2007
'Zur Farbigkeit des Münchener Bronzekopfes mit der Siegerbinde', in *Bunte Götter. Die Farbigkeit antiker Skulptur*, V. Brinkmann & R. Wünche (eds.), Munich, 151-65.

Yon, M. 2005
'Peintres, potiers et coroplplathes à Salamine. À propos d'une tête de statue archaïque en terra cuite', *CCEC* 35, 35-54.

Sources for figures and credits

Fig. 1. The Cesnola Collection. The Metropolitan Museum of Art. Purchased by subscription, 1874-76 (74.51.2468). Courtecy Virginia Museum of Fine Arts, Richmond. Photo: Katherine Weizel @Virginia Museum of Fine Arts. I thank the Virginia Museum of Fine Arts for permission to reproduce the photo.

Fig. 2. The Cesnola Collection. The Metropolitan Museum of Art. Purchased by subscription, 1874-76 (74.51.2460). "http://DP263870. jpg"

Fig. 3. The Cesnola Collection. The Metropolitan Museum of Art. Purchased by subscription, 1874-76 (74.51.2646) "http://DP263919. jpg"

Fig. 4. The Cesnola Collection. The Metropolitan Museum of Art. Purchased by subscription, 1874-76 (74.51.2466) "http://DP276954. jpg"

Fig. 5. The Collection of George and Nefeli Giabra Pierides. Photo: Bank of Cyprus Cultural Foundation Collection.

Fig. 6. The Cesnola Collection. The Metropolitan Museum of Art. Purchased by subscription, 1874-76 (74.51.2461) "http://DP201085. jpg"

Fig. 7. Antikensammlung, Kunsthistorisches Museum, Vienna, inv. ANSA I 341. Purchased 1872 from Georg V. Millosicz. Photo: KHM-Museumsverband.

Fig. 8. I am grateful to Kristina Winther-Jacobsen for providing me with this photo.

Fig. 9. The Cesnola Collection. The Metropolitan Museum of Art. Purchased by subscription, 1874-76 (74.51.2479) "http://DP207675. jpg"

Fig. 10. The Cesnola Collection. The Metropolitan Museum of Art. Purchased by subscription, 1874-76 (74.51.2472) "http://DP263874. jpg"

Fig. 11. The Cesnola Collection, The Metropolitan Museum of Art. Purchased by subscription, 1874-76 (74.51.2471) "http://DP263873. jpg"

Fig. 12. Excavation photo published in Gjerstad 1935, fig. 278. I am grateful to The Medelhavs Museet, Stockholm, for providing me with a copy.

Fig. 13. Made by Reinhard Senff published Senff 1993, pl. 2a. I am grateful to Reinhard Senff for providing me with a copy.

Vroulia revisited

From K. F. Kinch's excavations in the early 20th century to the present archaeological site*

ERIPHYLE KANINIA & STINE SCHIERUP

Introduction

The Archaic settlement of Vroulia is one of the most important early settlements in the Aegean, with an organized plan but a short lifespan, most probably dating from the 7th to the 6th century BC.[1] Its strategic position at the southernmost tip of the island of Rhodes was ideal for controlling the sea-routes to and from Cyprus, Phoenicia and Egypt, as well as providing an intermediate anchorage at a time of thriving colonization and great prosperity of the three ancient city-states of Rhodes, Kamiros, Ialysos and, particularly, Lindos (Figs 1-3).

The excavation of the settlement took place in the early 20th century under the supervision of Karl Frederik Kinch (1853-1921), who, together with Christian Sørensen Blinkenberg (1863-1948), was the leading member of the Danish Archaeological Expedition in Rhodes in the years 1902-1909 and 1913-1914. The Danish Expedition carried out several excavation projects on the island.[2] The early years were mainly devoted to the excavation of the Athena Lindia Sanctuary at Lindos (1902-1905)[3], but hereafter Kinch turned his attention especially towards the southern part of the island, where, in addition to the excava-

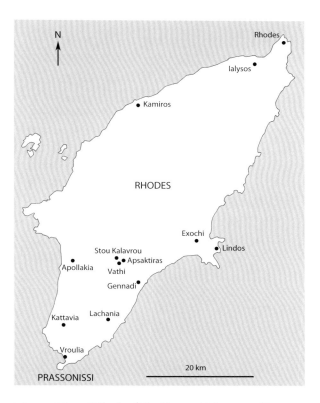

Fig. 1. *Map of Rhodes (The National Museum of Denmark).*

---

* The article has been authored by Eriphyle Kaninia (EK) and Stine Schierup (SS) as follows: Introduction (EK and SS); The Site of Vroulia (EK and SS); K.F. Kinch and the excavation of Vroulia (SS); Current work on the site (EK); Aim for future activities on the site (EK); Appendix: The Vroulia collection in the National Museum of Denmark (SS).

1 From the evidence of the pottery, Kinch considered the settlement to have been active from the beginning of the 7th century until 570/60 BC (Kinch 1914, 89), while Lang (1996, 194) argues for a settlement period between the middle of the 7th and the middle of the 6th century BC. Morris (1994, 174, n. 1) dates it to 625-575 BC.

2 For a general presentation of the Danish expedition to Rhodes, see Dietz & Trolle 1974; Rathje & Lund 1991, 22-6, 39-40; Rasmussen & Lund 2014.

3 The finds from the sanctuary in Lindos were published by Blinkenberg in two double volumes devoted to the small finds and the inscriptions respectively (Blinkenberg 1931; 1941). The architecture was published by Ejnar Dyggve (Dyggve 1960).

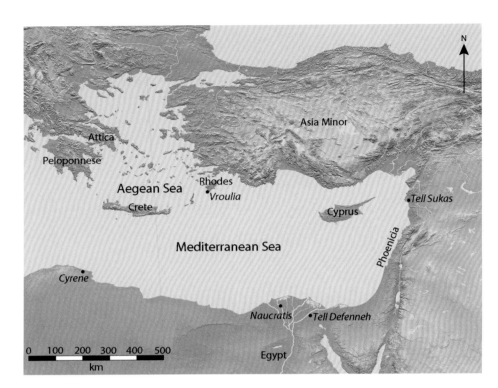

Fig. 2. *Map showing the strategic location of Vroulia in the Mediterranean network between East and West. (The National Museum of Denmark).*

Fig. 3. *Sunrise on the southern edge of the island of Rhodes, showing Vroulia and Prassonissi; aerial view from the west (The Ephorate of Antiquities for the Dodecanese).*

Fig. 4. *Aerial view from south-east; the Archaic settlement of Vroulia before the beginning of restoration project (The Ephorate of Antiquities for the Dodecanese).*

tions at Vroulia, he also investigated a number of Mycenaean tombs in Apollakia, Apsaktiras, Stou Kalavrou and Passia near Vathi.[4] The campaigns at Vroulia were carried out during two main seasons in 1907 and 1908, but initial work did also take place on the site in 1905. The results were finally published in 1914 by Kinch in the significant volume *Fouilles de Vroulia*, which until now remains the only monograph about the settlement.[5]

For more than a century thereafter no further excavations were carried out at the site; the exposed remains of the Archaic settlement suffered serious weathering and erosion and were gradually covered with the woody phrygana vegetation of this windy place (Fig. 4). As a consequence of this critical state of the ancient ruins, in 2011 the Ephorate of the Antiquities for the Dodecanese launched the project "Consolidation and Enhancement of the Archaic Settlement of Vroulia at Southern Rhodes", which was co-financed by the European Union.[6] Apart from its practical aspect (i.e. the restoration and consolidation of the ancient remains, as well as the organization and enhancement of the archaeological site), the project has also provided an excellent opportunity to re-consider Kinch's publication of the Archaic settlement of Vroulia and enrich its scope.[7]

4   For publication of the Mycenean tombs, see Dietz 1984. Further material from the expedition has been published in Wriedt Sørensen & Pentz 1992. Another important project led by Kinch was the excavation of the geometric necropolis at Exochi in the Lindos region (Friis Johansen 1957).

5   Kinch 1914.

6   National Strategic Reference Framework (NSRF).

7   The project was carried out by a team consisting of an architect (Chryssoula Hapipi), a land surveyor (Demetres Sarantopoulos) and six to eight workers alternating periodically (Theodoros Papandreou, Vangelis Pergourakis, Elias Antiphiliotis, Leonidas Dellas, Katerina Lergou, Chryssaphina and Kyroula Kolaini and Konstantina Chatziyannaki) under the supervision of the co-writer of this article, archaeologist Eriphyle Kaninia. Since April 2011, as part of the project, a series of infrastructure works have already been completed, such as the construction of a new enclosure of the archaeological site, the installation of water supply pipes, the levelling of the parking area, the installation of two prefabricated warehouses, the construction of a paved path leading uphill and the building of a small guardhouse provided with toilets. Moreover, the Technical Department of the South Aegean Region recently approved the asphalt surfacing of the public road leading to the archaeological site of Vroulia.

The present article is the result of a collaboration between The Ephorate of Antiquities for the Dodecanese and the National Museum of Denmark; it aims to present some aspects of the history of the Vroulia excavation in the early 20th century along with a brief account of the recent restoration/enhancement project carried out by the Ephorate a century later. From the very early stages of this project, a need emerged for a better understanding of the circumstances under which Kinch lived and excavated (with remarkable efficiency) the isolated site of Vroulia, one of the most important Archaic settlements, but a place that is difficult to access (now as then) and is buffeted by strong winds even in the summer. It is noteworthy that in the nearby villages (especially Kattavia) many people have stories to tell from their great-grandfathers about "the Danish archaeologist and his painter wife who lived at Prassonissi in a stone house", part of which still exists.[8]

Kinch's personal diaries, together with the excavation journal, drawings and further documentation, now in the archives of the Collection of Classical and Near Eastern Antiquities in the National Museum of Denmark, have served as the primary source for the account of the early 20th-century excavations at Vroulia presented here.[9] A thorough study of all preserved archival records have shown that in general Kinch's observations and interpretations of the excavation work were thoroughly recorded in his publication of the site.[10] However, many of his ethnographic observations are of interest, and selected passages of his personal diaries as well as the excavation journal will be included here in order to document the environment they lived in, the people they encountered and the conditions of their work. Furthermore, this article includes an Appendix with a full list and updated bibliography of all excavated material from Vroulia that can now be found in

the collection of the National Museum of Denmark.[11] As a consequence of the political situation in the years following the Danish excavations in Rhodes, the majority of the excavated objects that were not brought back to Denmark have either been lost or possibly moved to Istanbul. Since Kinch's publication does not include any indications on what material was left behind and what was brought back to Denmark, the Appendix is a first step towards identifying the present location of the excavated material from Vroulia.

The Site of Vroulia

The excavations carried out by Kinch are thought to have revealed the most important part of the Archaic settlement of Vroulia and made the understanding of its basic plan possible (Fig. 5): the settlement is enclosed in the northeast by a fortification wall (in fact a *peribolos* wall), which borders the natural prominency of the Vroulia hill into the sea. The fortification wall, which runs NW–SE, is visible for a total length of about 300 m, most of which (about 220 m) was excavated by Kinch. The fortification wall seems to have been cut off abruptly at the brow of the steep cliffs on either side, which surround the Vroulia hill. It is obvious that a large part of the Vroulia hill (probably together with part of the settlement) has fallen into the sea. A similar geological phenomenon is in progress on the opposite coast of Prassonissi, where a piece of land has been cut off and is almost ready to fall into the sea. Although not yet fully documented, the human skeletons found very recently buried under the collapsed stones of the south cliffside of the Vroulia hill may prove to belong to residents of the Archaic settlement, who were possibly victims of a landslide (Fig. 6).[12] This natural disaster was probably the reason for the short life of the settlement, which seems to have come to a rather sudden end, as

---

8   See p. 102-103 below and Fig. 15a-b.

9   The archival records include two sketchbooks by Helvig Kinch, the excavation journal, and numerous passages in Kinch's personal diaries that he wrote consistently during his time on the island. To this can be added 23 photos taken by the expedition that can be accessed from the National Museum of Denmark's collection online webpage: http://samlinger.natmus.dk/. Furthermore, the archival records include Kinch's manuscript and correspondence concerning the publication of the excavation report, as well as additional drawings and paintings made by Helvig Kinch.

10   Kinch 1914.

11   Including material presently deposited at the Museum of Ancient Art at the University of Aarhus.

12   The short trial was undertaken in August 2015 by the co-writer of this article (EK). Two skeletons belonging to adults, seemingly fallen the one above the other, were found and partly excavated, while a third one was simply located. Further research at the spot is necessary as well as a systematic study by an anthropologist in order to specify a possible chronology of the skeletons, age, sex and death circumstances. Over the head of one of the skeletons some unpainted sherds were collected (among them a leg of a tripod vessel), possibly Archaic.

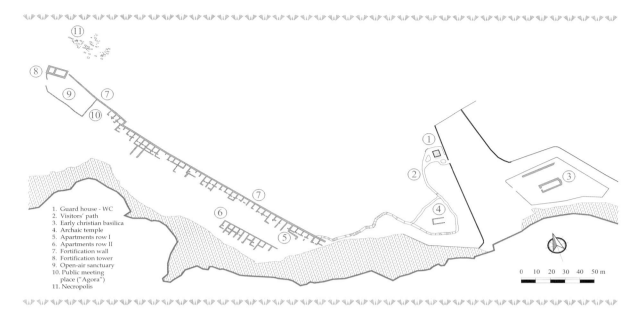

Fig. 5. *Vroulia archaeological site, general plan (The Ephorate of Antiquities for the Dodecanese).*

1. Guard house - WC
2. Visitors' path
3. Early christian basilica
4. Archaic temple
5. Apartments row I
6. Apartments row II
7. Fortification wall
8. Fortification tower
9. Open-air sanctuary
10. Public meeting place ("Agora")
11. Necropolis

Fig. 6. *Human skeletons as found on the steep south side of the Vroulia hill (The Ephorate of Antiquities for the Dodecanese).*

can be indicated by the high quantity of well-preserved pottery that came to light in the habitation rooms.[13]

The row of habitation rooms (row I; Fig. 5, no. 5), or rather apartments ("pièces d' habitation") – 43 units have been revealed – were located in contact with the inner side of the fortification wall. A second parallel row (row II; Fig. 5, no. 6) with only 10 units was revealed at a distance of about 20 m to the west of the first one. The rectilinear arrangement of this type of so-called *Reihensiedlungen*[14] can be distinguished from the settlements of the preceding phases and shows an early, tentative attempt at a planned layout of the houses, a feature otherwise mainly known from western Greek settlements at this time.[15] The individual houses appear generally to have consisted of a two- or three-room unit, possibly with an open courtyard in front, as suggested by Hoephner's reconstruction drawing (Fig. 7).[16]

On the top of the hill, a rectangular building was excavated, which was identified by Kinch as a fortification

---

13 Other explanations for the sudden end of the settlement have been put forward by e.g. Hoepfner, who suggested that "Seeräuber den Ort erobert und die Bevölkerung verkläut" (Hoepfner 1999, 198). A sudden and violent departure from the site might also be indicated by a late burial of four adults (Tomb 18). As one of only two adult inhumation tombs from a site where cremation is the common ritual associated with adult burials, it might indicate that the funeral was carried out in haste. Furthermore, it is the only tomb where a spear has been identified (Kinch 1914, 50-2).

14 Lang 1996, 193-4.

15 However, an orthogonal street layout has also been suggested for the 7th-century settlement at Halileis in Argolis (Lang 1996, 176 with further references).

16 Hoepfner 1999, 194-9.

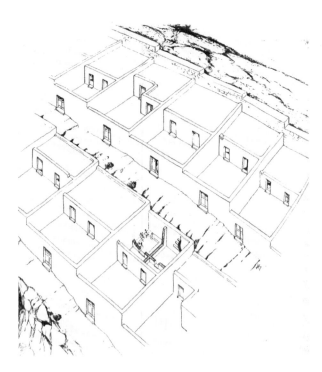

Fig. 7. *Reconstruction drawing of the houses at Vroulia (after Hoepfner 1999, 198).*

Fig. 8. *'La chapelle' at the foot of the Vroulia hill; aerial view after the restoration (The Ephorate of Antiquities for the Dodecanese).*

tower (Fig. 5, no. 8).[17] Southeast of this building was a well-defined area, where the remains of two rectangular altars were found (Fig. 5, no. 9). This was interpreted as an open-air sanctuary,[18] whereas further to the south, another extended empty space was thought to have functioned as a public meeting place, an agora (Fig. 5, no. 10).[19]

Outside the town gate (not actually located but supposedly in close proximity to the fortification tower), the cemetery of the settlement was found (Fig. 5, no. 11). The excavation of the graves gave important information about the age and sex of the inhabitants of the settlement, as well as of the burial customs.[20] Altogether Kinch estimated the burials of around 125 individuals, and of these no less than 43 were tombs of children below the age of six, usually – as the tradition prescribed – buried in large storage vessels with only a few burial gifts.[21] The rectan-

gular cremation tombs usually held several subsequent cremations, in some cases up to eight or nine (e.g. Tomb 2 and possibly 6), and only two adult inhumation tombs were identified (Tombs 18 and 30). Burial gifts consisted of various types of pottery (alabastra, aryballoi, drinking

17   Kinch 1914, 90-7; for a discussion of this structure and the suggestion of the possible existence of a funnel-shaped gate at Vroulia, see Melander 1988.

18   Kinch 1914, 97-108.

19   Kinch 1914, 108-12.

20   Kinch 1914, 34-89.

21   One exception to this is children's burial 's', which was equipped with numerous burial gifts; see description on p. 104 below.

Fig. 9a–b. *Cypriot limestone sphinx found in 'la chapelle', detail of the inscription on the wing, inv. 11328 (The National Museum of Denmark.*

cups, oinochoai and plates), including a distinct group of pottery classified as "Vroulia style pottery".[22] Among the finds were also fibulas, beads and scarabs.

On the southeast foot of the Vroulia hill, Kinch had investigated the poor remains of a small Archaic temple 'in antae' ("la chapelle"), belonging to the early 7th century BC and therefore considered to be one of the earliest temple-buildings known from the Archaic period (Fig. 5, no. 4; Fig. 8).[23] Further to the east, on the side of the opposite hill, the remains of an early Christian basilica with mosaic floor were located (Fig. 5, no. 3).[24]

Between the southeast side of the Vroulia hill and the opposite slopes, a cove protected from the north and south winds may have served as the settlement's harbour. The harbour and the access to the sea in general undoubtedly had a great significance for this otherwise isolated settlement. As is the case for all main sites on Rhodes in this period, the archaeological material from Vroulia

clearly demonstrates the island's strategic location on the sea-routes between the eastern and western Mediterranean region (Fig. 2).[25] This connection can be further emphasized by examples of the otherwise only limited distributed and produced 'Vroulia' style pottery that has been found in Naucratis and Tell Defenneh in the Nile Delta, in Cyrene in North Africa and in Tell Sukas along the Levantine coast.[26] One particular find from "la chapelle", a limestone sphinx with an inscription on the right wing (Fig. 9a–b), has furthermore led scholars to argue for the presence of Phoenicians in Vroulia.[27] Although it has proved impossible to decipher the exact meaning of the inscription it is clear that the text is of Phoenician origin, while the sphinx is of a Cypriot type.

Considering the isolated location together with the distinctive structures of the settlement at Vroulia, Kinch defined the function of the site as that of a residential military garrison, an interpretation later accepted by Me-

22   Kinch 1914, 168-90.
23   Kinch 1914, 8-26.
24   Wriedt Sørensen & Pentz 1992, 245.
25   See e.g. Coulié & Filimonos-Tsopotou 2014, 76-119 with further references.
26   Cook & Dupont 1998, 114-5; according to Herodotos (2.178), the Rhodians were involved in the foundation of Naucratis.
27   Kourou 2003; Bourogiannis 2014, 163-4, figs 4-5.

Fig. 10. *K.F. Kinch (1853-1921) (The National Museum of Denmark).*

lander, who described it as "a point of military interest as the last port of call on the territory of the city state or polis of Lindos…".[28] Ian Morris on the other hand, based on a demographic analysis of the tomb material, came to the conclusion that "the age structure of its cemeteries would fit a 'normal' agricultural population far better than a putative garrison."[29] His analysis and treatment of the archaeological evidence has subsequently been discussed and questioned by Lone Wriedt Sørensen, who among other things emphasized the fact that the landscape surrounding Vroulia is barren and thus not suitable as farmland.[30] Nota Kourou, who stresses the possible function of the site in the trading network,[31] suggests that a commercial installation might best explain the character of the Vroulia settlement.

K. F. Kinch and the excavation of Vroulia (1905, 1907-1908)

K. F. Kinch was born in 1853 in Ribe in the southern part of Jutland (Fig. 10). He was the son of the Danish historian and schoolteacher Jakob Frederik Kinch (1817-1888). As a young man he began his studies in philology at the University of Copenhagen, where he was the pupil of Professor in Philology and Archaeology, Johan Louis Ussing. Ussing at the time played an important part in the establishment of an early interest in Greek archaeology and excavations in Denmark; he published numerous important works on these subjects and visited Greece several times during his lifetime.[32] It seems reasonable to suppose that it might have been him who inspired Kinch to turn his focus towards archaeology, and soon after he received his doctorate in 1883, Kinch visited Greece for the first time. Here he developed a special interest in the ancient remains of Macedonia, the Chalcidian peninsula and Thessaloniki.[33] During several subsequent trips in the years between 1885 and 1893 he thoroughly studied the topography of this – at the time – not very well-known region. Unfortunately, he never managed to publish the results of this work in its entirety,[34] possibly because from the late 19th century he became involved in the Carlsberg Foundation's plan to establish a major Danish excavation project in the Mediterranean region.[35] This idea was

---

28 Melander 1988, 83
29 Moris 1992.
30 Sørensen 2002.
31 Kourou (2003, 257) defines the site as a "port of call for a Cypriot trade network".
32 Ussing 1906.
33 Dyggve 1943, 149-50.
34 He did publish his studies of the triumphal arch in Thessaloniki, *L'Arc de triomphe de Salonique* (Kinch 1890). A collection of his epigraphic notes has recently been published by Juhel & Νίγδελης (2015).
35 Before he was involved in this project he also worked as schoolteacher in Borgerdydskolen in Copenhagen, and functioned as administrator at Maribo School on the island of Lolland in the southern part of Denmark. He even made an unsuccessful attempt to found his own school (Juhel & Νίγδελης 2015, 20).

undoubtedly inspired by projects such as the German excavations in Olympia and Pergamon, and the Austrian excavations at Ephesus.[36]

It was Kinch's previous professor, Ussing, who, as a member of the Foundation committee, was behind the initiative of establishing a Danish excavation project, and Kinch was entrusted with the task of finding a suitable location. After several reconnaissance trips mainly in the eastern Mediterranean region, the Foundation finally decided in 1901 to support the project of an excavation of the Athena Lindia sanctuary on Rhodes.[37] After having gained the necessary permissions from the Turkish government in Constantinople, Kinch – together with the archaeologist and curator of the National Museum of Denmark, Christian Sørensen Blinkenberg – was able to begin the excavation work in Lindos in April 1902. Of these two main members of the expedition, Kinch was undoubtedly the driving force behind the fieldwork and he stayed almost continuously on the island through all the expedition years. Blinkenberg, due to his position at the National Museum, was only present on Rhodes for shorter periods of time during the early years of excavation (1902-1905).[38]

Lindos was an appropriate choice for such a prestige project, with its prominent location in the landscape and as the main sanctuary of an important Rhodian polis with significant contacts with the eastern Mediterranean region. It was highly likely that an excavation would reveal important votives, interesting architectural structures and inscriptions – as it did.[39] However, Kinch's interests clearly extended further than the excavations in Lindos, and the region of southern Rhodes was of major interest to him. This interest seems to have been encouraged by his concern to find and document the archaeological remains before they were damaged by

unauthorized excavations and the archaeological finds sold.[40] These concerns are clear from the accounts of his own diary that he meticulously wrote during all his years in Rhodes.

The excavation of Vroulia took place during two main seasons from July to September 1907 and again from May to August 1908. However, Kinch did carry out a week of preliminary investigation on the site in 1905, a few weeks after he visited Vroulia for the first time in September 1905:

With Nikolaos Karpathios from Kattavia to Vroulia. After one hour we reached H. Giorgios monastery in a valley that opens towards the Sea. Shortly hereafter at Spilia (no caves!) near Kymisala (two hills with a valley between). All over tableland with a few hills and valleys. After two and half hours the ocean was visible, a valley extends across the island and then follows a hill (Vroulia). Beyond this lies το νησί [Prassonissi] – the island with the lighthouse. This island as well as Vroulia are rocky hills where no growth can be seen except thorny plants and low thuja. The island is connected to the mainland (Rhodes) with a low isthmus. […] With Nikolaos up the hill of Vroulia. On the northeastern side and above a considerable number of walls visible. According to Nikolaos they are remains of houses, and also of terrace walls (?). Along the ridge of the hill (south–north) can be seen the remains of a wall of the same type; Nikolaos thinks, that this is the city wall. The outside of the wall is oriented towards the island of the lighthouse. The wall extends from ocean to ocean […]. The walls end on both ends towards an escarpment. Hereafter down the hill towards southeast, a building around 30-40 metres from the Sea. This building was found and excavated this year around fasting. [Kinch, September 20, 1905: personal diary, no. 36, 27]

---

36 Fellmann & Scheyhing 1972; Wiplinger & Wlach 1996.

37 Several other sites were suggested, such as Cyrene in northern Africa and Kleonai or Nemea on the Peloponnese (Dietz & Trolle 1974, 9; Wriedt Sørensen 1992, 7-8).

38 Dietz & Trolle 1974, 9.

39 Ussing published the arguments for choosing Lindos in 1906 (Ussing 1906, 228-9).

40 With the increasing interest shown in the archaeological remains of Rhodes (beginning with the first excavations by Salzmann and Biliotti in Kamiros in the 1860's), the local farmers had soon acknowledged the possible wealth to be made by selling archaeological objects. Undoubtedly it was a lucrative market at the beginning of the 20th century and the Turkish gendarmes were earnestly trying to prevent these activities (Dietz & Trolle 1974, 18-20).

The excavation of the building by the sea, 'La Chapelle', in 1905

The small building by the sea, the so-called 'chapelle', became Kinch's first excavation project on the site (Fig. 8). In early October 1905 he writes that permission has been given for him to begin the work:

Yesterday Sameg visited the governor and talked with him on my behalf about Vroulia. They had agreed that I would be given permission, in the presence of Georgaki, to excavate the building already excavated (and subsequently backfilled) by the local farmers of Kattavia and to investigate the surrounding area. [Kinch, October 6, 1914: personal diary, no. 36, 58]

Subsequently Kinch re-excavated the sanctuary between the 9th and 14th of October, and he also made some initial surveys in its surroundings, including the excavation of a few rooms in the urban area. With him were the foreman Nikolaos Vatinos and six men, as well as the local supervision chief Georgakis. During the first days of excavation Kinch soon acknowledged the problems of gaining a complete understanding of the structures of this small antae-building as it was originally found. The Kattavians had not only removed objects from the small sanctuary but also several stone slabs that had originally been placed around the altar:[41]

Diako Jani visited us today. He had tried to gain some information from people on how the stone slabs had been placed on the table in the sanctuary. Nothing definite came out of his questions, but it seems that no 'opening' was present in the table below the upper slab, but that the stones have been placed close together. [Kinch, October 15, 1905: personal diary, no. 36, 68]

Georgakis wrote to the Mudir and requested that he send Mustapha and Savvas, who took part in the excavation work during the first day. They confirmed Manolis' description. There were three layers, two stones in the lowest, laying parallel with the Sea, the two above conversely; above a thinner stone […]. At Mustapha's house more stones from the lower part can be found, now cut up. It is rough poros, carefully worked [Kinch, October 15, 1905: personal diary, no. 36, 69].

Fig. 11. *Dinos and stand in wild-goat style, from 'la chapelle', inv. 11275 (dinos) and 11276 (stand) (The National Museum of Denmark).*

During the season in 1907, Kinch was still trying to get the stones back to Vroulia in order to test the original construction of the altar:

Sunday. To Kattavia. Have made an agreement with Mustapha, that the stones from the table on the sacrificial place should be brought back to Vroulia. Christakis Kazanis should come with him and show the original location of the stones in the table. The weather for the last couple of days has been unstable. Some clouds can be seen now in the sky. Today when we returned, we drove after sunset and saw thunder and lightning [Kinch, excavation journal, August 18, 1907].

The finds made by Kinch and his men in the backfill of the building consisted mainly of smaller fine- and coarseware fragments, while the main objects found in the building had already been removed by the Kattavians. From the diaries it is clear that Kinch spend some time trying to locate these finds among the local farmers and to collect them for his documentation. According to his own

41 Kinch 1914, 7.

Fig. 12. *Cypriot limestone horse with rider, from 'la chapelle', inv. 11274. (The National Museum of Denmark).*

statement he succeeded in collecting almost everything.[42] Among these finds were a large north Ionian dinos in wild-goat style (Fig. 11), together with several Cypriot limestone figures – such as the sphinx with preserved Phoenician inscription described above (Fig. 9)[43] and a horseman (Fig. 12).[44] A significant part of these finds seems to have been brought back home with Kinch at an early time and they are now kept in the collection of the National Museum of Denmark (Appendix nos 1.1-1.8).

More than anything, this first week seems to have been marked by several conflicts with the Turkish administration and the local farmers concerning their rights to work on the site. On the very first morning of work the two sons of the local farmer claiming to own the land turned up on the site seeking to prevent them from working there:

Started with the building. The old soil was examined. Numerous fragments of coarse and finer vessels were found, among these a few fragments of the large rhodian-corinthian vase.

The two sons of the owner of the field showed up on the site around 8 ½ and tried to prohibit us from continuing the work. They brought with them a property letter. We told them that since they had carried out excavation here and sold the objects they had lost their rights and that we could inform the authorities about their activities [Kinch, October 9, 1905: personal diary, no. 36, 61].

A few days later Kinch wrote "the two brothers Christos and Savvas, the so-called owners, have gone to town to complain over our work on their property" [Kinch, personal diary, no. 36, 65]. Finally on the 14th of October Kinch, as a consequence of this situation, wrote that an appeal had been sent to the local authorities asking them to keep their promises of preventing illegal excavations and to take care that the excavated building would not suffer further destruction:

Georgaki wrote a letter to the Demogerontia (Turkish and Greek) that they had not kept their promise of preventing excavations […]. Again we commanded them to take care that the revealed building at Vroulia would not suffer any further destruction and that no one would start excavating there [Kinch, October 14, 1905: personal diary, no. 36, 68].

The whole situation however seems to be more complicated than this and the relationship with the Mudir appears to have been quite tense at this point. The Mudir apparently travelled to Vroulia in order to inspect their work or even stop it – his intentions are unclear. Kinch clearly felt that he was trying to stop their work and he even suggests that it was he who had encouraged the owners of the land to try to stop them on their first day. A meeting between the supervision chief, Georgakis, and the Mudir appears to clear up the matter, and the Mudir claimed to have an interest in protecting their work while at the same time wanting to inspect what exactly was going on. Miscommunication seems to be a general problem here and though the Mudir told Georgakis that he was not interested in stopping the work, Kinch still continued to hear from several other people that the Mudir was trying to stop them:

---

42   Kinch 1914, 12-26.

43   See n. 27 above.

44   He also received two further examples of Cypriot limestone figures (Copenhagen, National Museum, inv. 11326-11327, Appendix nos. 1.6-1.7; Kinch 1914, 15, pls 13-4, 2-3).

Fig. 13a–b. *a) Pencil drawing showing the view from the Oros hill towards Prassonissi (Kinch, personal diary, book 39, September 22, 1907); b) Painting by Helvig Kinch with the view from the excavation house on Prassonissi towards the Vroulia hill (The National Museum of Denmark).*

100

Fig. 14a–b. *Excavation photo: the lighthouse on Prassonissi and the lighthouse guard, Halil (The National Museum of Denmark).*

[during a visit to the H. Giorgios monastery] When we arrived at the exit a Zaptich [policeman] was standing with a shotgun at the hole, looking after us. When we came out, we found the Mudir sitting by our clothes with a boy from the monastery. He said hello and some words indicating that he didn't knew that it was me who was here. A man had told him, that a Frenchman was excavating here. I asked him: What are you doing here? Briefly hereafter he left and we didn't exchange a word.

[…] The Mudir is trying from all sides to get information on our work at Vroulia, and what has been going on there [Kinch, October 14, 1905: personal diary, no. 36, 68].

The Mudir has sent for Georgakis, who stayed with him for some hours and then gave me the following message. The Mudir is worried and seeks our understanding. He has arrived here because he received a message from the Pasha. Maarif has written to the Pasha and informed him that excavations without permission were taking place in Kattavia and Lachania; the Maarif therefore asked the Pasha to give the Mudir orders

on making the necessary precautions, to go there himself and make a record of previously excavated locations, prevent further unauthorized excavations and place Zaptichs everywhere to protect the sites, while I intend to carry out excavations in the name of the museum. This apparently should be the real reason for the arrival of the Mudir. The Mudir also has an order from the Pasha to inspect the place where we are working. Yesterday he wanted to go to Vroulia, when we met him at H. Giorgos. [Kinch, October 15, 1905: personal diary, no. 36, 69]

In Gennadi Leonidas told me that the other day when the Mudir came to Gennadi, he had told him that he was going to Vroulia in order to stop our work. The same they had heard in Vati both from the people in Gennadi and Lachania [Kinch, October 15, 1905: personal diary, no. 36, 69]

On their return to Lindos, Kinch seeks explanation for these incidents:

101

Fig. 15a–b. *a) Excavation photo: the excavation house on Prassonissi, with Mrs. Kinch and their daughter, Gunhild; the lower building at the back of the house still survives today (The National Museum of Denmark); b) The present remains of the Danish excavation house on Prassonissi (The Ephorate of Antiquities for the Dodecanese).*

In Lindos the Gendarme Ali claims, at Stephanos' Coffee House, that the Mudir really intended to stop our work, and, if we had not already finished the work he would have forced us to do so [Kinch, October 17, 1905: personal diary, no. 36, 71].

In the afternoon, I went with Sameg to the Pasha in order to thank him for the permission and to complain about the Mudir. Sameg thinks: that the governor has sent someone for our protection and help, but also to make sure that nothing illegal was going on. While the governor does not have the necessary authority to give me such a permission that I had received through Sameg. The governor has told Sameg that it was him who instructed the Mudir – however Sameg thinks that the Mudir has exceeded his instructions. [Kinch, October 21, 1905: personal diary, no. 36, 71]

The excavations at Vroulia in 1907-1908

In July 1907 Kinch arrived in Vroulia again to begin the first of the two main excavation seasons. This time his wife, the artist Helvig Kinch (1872-1956), and their 3-year-old daughter, Gunhild (1904-1998), stayed with him during the excavation. Helvig Kinch was responsible for all the drawings included in the publication of the site, and from the diaries it seems that she spent most days working in their home, a house that was built for them on Prasso-nissi, the island with the lighthouse (Figs 13-15). In several passages during the first month of work, Kinch is clearly concerned about the quality of this house:

At night Kyriakos turned over the house to me. The work was poor or mediocre as Lysandros said during his inspection of the house. The wall towards the north is inwardly curved. It is doubtful whether the roof can withstand the rain. No corner is regular, no line straight. The woodwork is miserable; the wood in the windows is too thin. The lime cover on the interior walls is impossible, very irregular. The floor (irregular slabs with clay in between) of no use – payed for the house and the barracks 50; 4 held back for reparations and improvements. There I was right in the contract ("no payment before the work has been approved"). [Kinch, July 31, 1907, personal diary no. 37, 70-71]

The diaries do not reveal why Kinch decided to build his house on Prassonissi instead of closer to the site of the excavation. The location, however, undoubtedly had an amazing view of the surrounding landscape and the fact that it must have been an inspiring place for his wife to settle down as a painter might serve as the most reason-able explanation:

Absolutely quiet in the morning. The coast opposite our house quite dark and sharply outlined. The outermost point (to the west) seems quite near. Karpathos can be seen quite clearly. The mountains of Crete behind. [Kinch, May 28, 1908: personal diary, no. 39, 81-2].

On July 21, 1907, the excavation work started. Usually there were between 10 and 20 workers active and dis-tributed in groups around the area. Some were responsi-ble for the necropolis and others for the urban area, the sanctuary, tower, city wall and houses. Altogether they excavated and surveyed a significant area during only a few months' work, and although Kinch was very thorough in his documentation of the excavation work, the general impression is undoubtedly that the excavations seem to have been carried out in a rather hasty manner by the standards of today.

During the previous days, the terrain (mainly on the hill) was divided into the system of a square net through pile driving (with 10 m² distance in between the piles).

Seven workers. Lysandros (from Monolithos), who has been entrusted with the task to find and excavate the necropolis, spent most of the day searching for it in the area east of the city, beyond the valley. The other workers were partly cleaning the well and raising the stone work around it, and partly mak-ing a test excavation in and around the rectangular building (a rectangular temenos wall with a building inside?) east of the valley, here among other things was found a base fragment, seems Roman. A part of the wall exposed. The thickness of the walls c. 0.75. Stones – small or medium-sized; no lime. While the number of workers was inadequate for a building of this size, it was decided to postpone the work here. [Kinch, excavation journal, July 21, 1907].

Through both seasons a number of experienced work-ers were connected to the project and several of these are well-known from Kinch's activities elsewhere on the island, as documented in his diaries. One of these is the worker Lysandros (from Monolithos), who was entrusted with finding and excavating the necropolis, as described in the quotation above. Kinch reports in the excavation journal on their agreement that "Lysandros should have 1 medsch for the first tomb found. 5 piastre for every later tomb and 3 piastre for every children's tomb" [excavation journal, August 3, 1907].[45] From day one of the 1907 sea-son a systematic search for the tombs in the area east of the city plateau was begun. And after one week's work, on July 31, the first tomb was revealed:

At 9 o'clock in the morning Lysandros reported that he had found an Archaic tomb. Tomb 1, on the slope around 50 m. outside the city gate, approximately out of the tower. A crema-tion tomb carved in the soft bedrock, no stone enclosure. […]. All tombs had in every corner an elongated circular depression

---

45   The medsch coinage that Kinch is referring to here is probably a mecidiye or mecit. This is a silver coin of approximately 23 gr. in weight, in use during the late 19th and early 20th centuries.

Fig. 16. *Excavation photo: Lysandros during the excavation of the children's tomb 's' on August 31, 1907 (The National Museum of Denmark).*

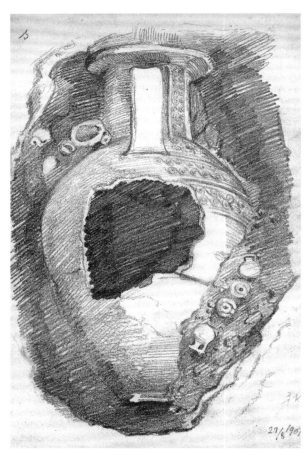

Fig. 17. *"Child tomb 's': drawing by Mrs. K. Large decorated amphora, high up towards the gate, lying on one side with the mouth of the vessel towards NW, a little upwards" [Kinch, excavation journal, 36] (The National Museum of Denmark).*

(λάκκος). In tomb 1 the burned layer (charcoal, bones and some pebbles) was located around 70-80 cm below the present surface and was around 12 cm deep.

Lysandros thinks that the burial took place in the following way: the tombs with its four λάκκοι were dug. In the holes small vases (alabastra etc.) were deposited. On the bottom wood and above the corpse of the deceased was laid. Ignited, the body burned. After the burning, the other vases were placed in the glowing mass. Hereafter the tomb is filled with earth. Often the tomb was reopened and a new cremation took place... Later, burial gifts (vases) were placed above the tomb, unburned. [Kinch, excavation journal, July 31, 1907][46]

Throughout the first season new tombs were found almost every day. Tomb 's' was found on August 23, 1907

(Figs 16-17), an extraordinary tomb due to the significant number of burial gifts, which was not common in the tombs of young children.[47] Among the finds were a ring-shaped aryballos decorated with geometric patterns, now in Copenhagen (Fig. 18, Appendix no. 2.1).

Kinch often seems to have relied upon the experience of his workers, and he always describes them in a respectful manner. In several cases he chooses to include the interpretations of Lysandros and other workers in the final publication, for instance in the following example where the construction of Tomb 23 is explained:

---

46 This interpretation of the tomb ritual is also given by Kinch (1914).
47 Kinch 1914, 44-8, pl. 31.

Fig. 19. *Bowl of north Ionian type found in room I, 25, inv. 11278 (The National Museum of Denmark).*

Fig. 18. *Ring-shaped aryballos from tomb 's', inv. 11318 (The National Museum of Denmark).*

Tomb 23 opened; close to tomb 22. Conspicuously many pebbles (flat – or sea stones) below the surface, covering the complete extent of the tomb. Opened by Manolis Furtukas: he thinks because of the stones that the buried person must have been a κακούργος [bandit] and that he was stoned. [Kinch, excavation journal, August 31, 1907][48]

At the end of the first season, the necropolis appeared to have been completely excavated and attempts were made to locate additional tombs in other areas as well:

An attempt is made to find out whether the necropolis is larger or whether another burial place can be found. Excavation has been without any success. It seems as if the burial place is not larger (or at least not much larger). Nothing in the terrain towards V to the Sea. [Kinch, excavation journal, September 6, 1907]

A few more tombs did turn up in 1908 in the area closer to the urban area, but after less than one month's work the search for more tombs was stopped. Kinch finally concluded in his publication: "La recherché de tombeaux dans d'autres parties de Vroulia, hors de la cité et dans la cité même, étant restée infructueuse, nous sommes presque certains que la nécropole découverte par nous est la seule; c'est celle d'une petite cité et d'une cité qui, encore, n'a duré que peu de temps".[49]

While Lysandros and usually a couple of other workers were concerned with the excavation of the necropolis, the leading worker Nikolaos (from Karpathos), together with his men, were focused on the excavation of the houses and the area of the urban sanctuary. However, it seems clear that in several cases, when a more experienced excavator was needed, Lysandros was called in to carry out the work:

---

48   Interpretation repeated in Kinch's description of this tomb, Kinch 1914, 82.
49   Kinch 1914, 34.

Fig. 20. *Female terracotta figurine from the open-air sanctuary, inv. 11273 (The National Museum of Denmark).*

House h (the upper part of the wall could be recognized in the surface before excavation). Finds: a bronze plate (with suspension holes), broken into many pieces. A proto-corinthian alabastron, without rim. A proto-corinthian alabastron or aryballos in small pieces. A well-preserved aryballos – since the house seems to be exceptionally rich it was decided that it should be excavated by Lysandros, with a small knife and pickaxe, and most of the workers were moved to house i. [Kinch, excavation journal, August 6, 1907].

Actually the excavation of the first rooms in row I was begun in 1905, but these rooms were reopened at the beginning of the 1907 season. The majority of the objects found in the houses were various types of pottery (e.g. Fig. 19 found in house I 25). Another distinctive object from the area is the female terracotta figure found in the open-air sanctuary (Fig. 20). The figurine was found close to the small structure placed against the wall of the tower, which Kinch interpreted as an altar (Figs 26-27):[50]

Near the south side of the tower a larger fragment of a female terracotta figurine was found. Another fragment (of a head) found on the same spot a couple of days ago belongs to the same figurine. Still missing is the backside and one arm. Is the building a temple? What does the throne mean, which is leaning against the southern wall? [Kinch, excavation journal, August 21, 1907]

Fig. 21. *Aerial view from the southeast: the successive apartments of row I following the slope of the Vroulia hill (The Ephorate of Antiquities for the Dodecanese).*

50   Kinch 1914, 98-108.

Close to the throne/altar mentioned yesterday was found a recess, hollowed in the earth. We have here a sacrificial place on the south–southwestern side of the building. The altar seems old (older than the building?). [Kinch, excavation journal, August 22, 1907].

As was the case during the initial surveys on the site in 1905, the communication with the local Turkish administrators was not always easy for Kinch and during these two seasons he often reported difficulties in communication with the supervisors who stayed with them through the excavation period. The chief of supervision in 1907, Begen, seems occasionally to have been suspicious of the work of the expedition and Kinch's priorities:

Begen suspicious at night. Examined before our departure from Vroulia my sketchbook where he found tomb 's' [Kinch, excavation journal, August 27, 1907].

Difficult scene at night between Begen and I. Begen claims: 1) that I have hidden excavated objects from him; 2) that he was being kind, when he left things for us to draw and study; 3) that I should have finished the museum in our house before I finished the bedroom. I told him that when talking like that he was an *imbicile et un impertinent*. – Helvig then arrived. We managed to get him to admit that he was wrong – we have the impression that he is unhappy, has weak lungs and therefore is irritable and not able to control his temper. [Kinch, personal diary, August 28, 1907]

A quite different problem appears in 1908 when the new chief of supervision, Husni Effenti, seemed to be bored with the work carried on at the site and wanted to leave:

Hussni had already the other day talked about having to leave soon for town, but that he would be back in 3-4 days (?). Today he repeated that he has to leave for 6 days, and that he assumed that I would stop the excavation work during his absence. I declared that this was impossible. Soliman (gendarme) informed me that Hussni wants to leave, he has no understanding of this type of excavation and he thinks we are finding gold. He wants to return to Rhodes [Kinch, personal diary, May 27, 1908]

Guests in Vroulia

That the excavations at Vroulia were of interest to several of the important archaeologists working in Greece at the time can be emphasized by Kinch's description of such visits in the diaries.

On August 8, 1907 Kinch reported that a number of guests from the German Archaeological Institute had arrived, among these Dr. Georg Karo, Dr. Walter Müller, Dr. Karl Müller and Dr. Frickenhaus. He also describes how Tomb 6 was opened in their presence and how they subsequently spent some days together during which they visited a number of sites on their trip to Lindos:[51]

August 8 […] Dr. Georg Karo, Dr. Walter Müller and Dr. Frickenhaus, all from the German Archaeological Institute in Athens, arrived here in the morning. Tomb 6 was opened in their presence, only 3 disques and a few proto-corinthian fragments.

August 9 […] At 3 o'clock in the afternoon Kinch together with Karo and the rest of the visitors to Lachania and the monastery H. Georgios. Spent the night here.

August 10 […] Kinch with the German company to Lindos. [Kinch, excavation journal, 21]

In 1908 Kinch writes in a note from July 19 that "Wace and Thompson arrived here in the evening". These are undoubtedly Alan Wace and Maurice S. Thompson from the British School in Athens, who at the time were working on several important excavations in Thessaly.[52] Kinch does not describe this visit in detail, but Wace has left some notes on a page in Kinch's diary and drawings of two prehistoric vessels that he asks Kinch to look for in the Rhodian material [Kinch, July 20, personal diary no. 40, 11].

The end of the expedition and Kinch's return to Rhodes in 1913-1914

Kinch's diaries clearly document the conflicting interests in Rhodes at this time: the local farmers and owners of the land, the Turkish administration trying to control and

51 Kinch 1914, 66-9, pl. 38.
52 Thompson and Wace worked on prehistoric sites in Thessaly in the years 1907-1909 (Thompson & Wace 1912).

prevent illegal activities and then the Danish expedition. Finally, shortly after the work in Vroulia had ended, a group of local Lindians wrote a petition to the Turkish government in Constantinople to ask them to stop the Danish activities on the island. In January 1909 Kinch received the message in Lindos that the permission to work on the island had ended, due to a wish not to excite the local population further:

Today yet again at the Mudir's; he had received a letter from the Pasha as an answer to my inquiry. He had presented my case for the council. The Lindians maintain that my permission to excavate has expired, that I have sent most of the finds to foreign countries; and that my permission to make new excavations on private ground would lead to excitement among the local population. [Kinch, January 1, 1909, personal diary, no. 41, 1]

By the beginning of February 1909 Kinch had left the island. During his return to Denmark he tried to negotiate in Constantinople for the extradition of excavated material, but the process failed.

When Kinch finally returned to Rhodes again in December 1913, the political situation had undergone dramatic changes. In 1912 the island had been seized by the Italians in the Italo-Turkish War,[53] and during this period of instability the Lindian acropolis had served as a garrison for the Italian troops. The storerooms (Kinch's museum) had been partly destroyed and the majority of the excavated material, including the finds from Vroulia, were no longer to be found. The few objects that remained when Kinch returned had been stacked around the windows to prevent them from falling out.[54] Today the material in the National Museum of Denmark (see Appendix) is the only securely identified material from the excavations in Vroulia. It is probably safe to say that these finds would also have been lost if they had remained in Rhodes.

In the spring of 1914 Kinch paid a final visit to Vroulia:[55]

From Kattavia to Vroulia. The rain and the times have gradually ruined more and more of the lower sanctuary and the houses. However we did find everything almost how we left it, including also the pottery sherds on the wall where we had placed them […]. We visited the lighthouse. Here lives Mehemet Ali with his wife and their two married sons Chukri and Hussein. With Chukri to our house. In the large room the people had placed a boat and planks. In a few places around the doorway the plaster has loosened and is about to fall down. [Kinch, May 11, 1914, personal diary, no. 44, 74]

Kinch seems to have been very thorough in his archaeological work but the Vroulia publication – for its time a very valuable excavation report –was unfortunately the only one that he managed to finish himself.[56] After he returned to Copenhagen in 1914 he continued his work on the publication of the Lindos excavation, but in 1917 he suffered from a brain haemorrhage and subsequent strokes that in the end made it impossible for him to continue his work.[57] He died in 1921.

In the period between the Danish expedition and launch of the project *Consolidation and Enhancement of the Archaic Settlement of Vroulia at Southern Rhodes* by the Ephorate of the Dodecanese in 2011, no excavation activities have been carried out at the site. In the following the current work and aims for the future will be outlined.

Current work on the site

The consolidation of the row I apartments and the adjacent fortification wall, as well as the restoration of the tower, are the major operations being carried out under the co-financed project for the *Consolidation and Enhancement of the Archaic Settlement of Vroulia*; in addition, the consolidation of the small Archaic temple on the

---

53   After the end of World War I, according to the Treaty of Lausanne, Rhodes officially became part of Italy together with the rest of the Dodecanese.

54   Kinch's diaries clearly reveal how upset he was about this; see Wriedt Sørensen 1992, 64-5, who gives an account of several passages from Kinch's diary in January 1914 where he questions various people about the incidents on the acropolis in the years of his absence.

55   Only a few months after he had completed the manuscript for the field report *Fouilles de Vroulia* (Kinch 1914).

56   See n. 3-4 above. That the Vroulia publication was an important one at the time can be seen in the reviews in *JHS* 34 (1914), 332, and *Revue Archéologique. Quatrieme Série* 24 (1914), 154-5.

57   Juhel & Νίγδελης 2015, 22.

Fig. 22. *The door opening of apartment I, 13, view from the southwest. (The Ephorate of Antiquities for the Dodecanese).*

southeast foot of the Vroulia hill is also taking place together with a reconstruction of its internal partition and altar.

The preliminary clearing of vegetation revealed the apparently chaotic state of the ancient ruins: however, careful examination made possible the successful identification of the "pièces d' habitation" as numbered in Kinch's initial plan.

Kinch provides a general but comprehensive description of the row I apartments, which are adjacent to the inner face of the fortification wall, and laid directly on the natural soft bedrock following the slope of the hill (Fig. 21). Only the lower part of the walls is preserved (to a height of about 0.40-0.90 m and 0.40-0.55 m wide), built with irregular stones that supported their superstructure,

which was made of mud bricks. The dividing walls of the series of apartments on the hillside are usually set on rough steps cut into the bedrock. A large proportion of the dividing walls still maintain a degree of consistency, which made the work of their restoration easier through the use of the stones fallen in front of them and obviously belonging to the masonry. In several cases (apartments row I 3, 6, 12, 13, 18, 21, 23, 28, 33, 34, 35, 36) it became possible to identify door openings, which were of varying widths and, occasionally, to locate and restore the sill and the lower part of the jambs (Fig. 22).

According to a theoretical reconstruction proposed by Wolfram Hoepfner (Fig. 7),[58] in front of each house lay a courtyard for the outdoor activities of the occupants. Unfortunately, within the co-financed project it was not

58 Hoepfner 1999, 194-9.

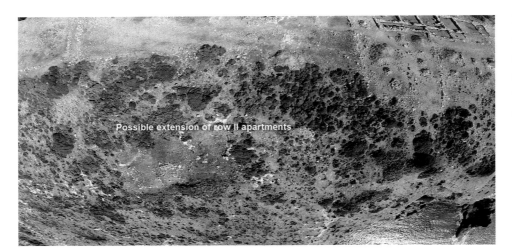

Possible extension of row II apartments

Fig. 23. *Aerial view of the assumed extension of row II apartments (The Ephorate of Antiquities for the Dodecanese).*

possible to undertake large-scale excavations to properly explore the walls partly visible to the west of the row I apartments. However, an extension of the row II apartments was clearly traced west of the empty space of the agora (Fig. 23).[59]

Of particular interest is the location of a cistern at the northeast corner of apartment I 40, and another one at the northeast corner of apartment I 38, which are shown in the small text drawings of Kinch.[60] Other possible cisterns (or rather their openings) are located west of the row I apartments, at the space supposed to have been occupied by the courtyards of the houses.

A major problem was the establishment of the original floor level of the apartments. According to Kinch, in most cases the levelled rock functioned as a floor, any hollows being filled with earth. Also, in apartments I 23, 32, 34 and II 4, limestone slabs are reported to have been laid over the surface of the levelled rock. In apartment I 15, Kinch observed floor remnants consisting of compacted earth incorporating small flat stones near the door. Rationally, the floor level of the apartments should coincide with the threshold level (where it survives). Moreover, the slightly raised surface of the rough step-like cutting of the

natural rock, where the dividing walls of the successive apartments are laid, provides an additional indication, particularly at the point where the walls join the inner side of the fortification wall.[61]

The cleaning of the dividing walls of the row I apartments showed that the walls interlocked firmly with the inner face of the fortification wall at their eastern ends. The part of the fortification wall excavated by Kinch (from apartment I 2 to the tower) has a total length of approximately 220 metres. Its 1.00-1.20 metre-wide substructure is thought to survive today to about the same height as in antiquity (1-1.25 m). It was built with large or medium-sized unworked stones, which, according to the excavator, were available locally. The upper part of the fortification wall was built with mud bricks, like the walls of the houses.

At a distance of about 175 metres from its southeast end, the fortification wall bends at an angle before continuing further to the northwest: in the recess thus formed, the three last apartments of row I (i.e. room 41, 42 and 43) were accommodated. Kinch thought they functioned as guard-shelters rather than proper houses. The cleaning of the unnaturally wide south wall of apartment I

---

59   The poor remnants of a supposed third row of apartments, apparently fallen into the sea, were located west of the second one, at the brow of the steep cliff.

60   Kinch 1914, 117-8, fig. 37.

61   In several cases, the rock is by no means level and in places obviously protruded from the supposed floor level. Most likely, the ground floor of the apartments was used for storage or as stables, whereas a low upper floor or a mezzanine (of mud bricks and, possibly, wood) served as living quarters. Before the beginning of the excavation, Kinch observed that masses of broken and fallen mud bricks were found inside the apartments, covering the lower part of the walls (Kinch 1914, 112).

Fig. 24. *Aerial view of the assumed gate at the bending of the fortification wall (The Ephorate of Antiquities for the Dodecanese).*

Fig. 25. *Aerial view of the fortification tower before its consolidation (The Ephorate of Antiquities for the Dodecanese).*

111

Fig. 26. *The 'altar' as it has survived, following the clearing of vegetation and the restoration (The Ephorate of Antiquities for the Dodecanese).*

FORTIFICATION TOWER - SOUTH ELEVATION

FORTIFICATION TOWER - SOUTH ELEVATION (with Kinch's photograph of the 'altar')

Fig. 27. *Fortification tower, south elevation (The Ephorate of Antiquities for the Dodecanese).*

41 revealed the remains of what may have been a gate controlling the entrance to the settlement: this gate, apparently of the so-called overlapping type, was blocked with stones at a later phase; it consists of two parallel walls in a slanting arrangement with a threshold of green limestone between them.[62] No pottery was found except for a few unidentifiable potsherds; further exploration at this point is currently taking place (Fig. 24). Moreover, a complex of unidentified walls, visible to the north of apartment I 40 and west of the successive apartments I 41, 42 and 43, are indicative of an intermediate phase of the settlement's development, in spite of its short lifespan. Beyond the assumed gate, the fortification wall extends without a break as far as the tower at the highest point of the Vroulia hill, forming the northeast boundary of the public meeting area (agora) and the open-air sanctuary.

The tower was a rectangular edifice oriented east–west; according to Kinch, access to it was by means of an external staircase (probably situated at its eastern side), which led to an upper floor made of mud bricks (Fig. 25). The preserved lower part of the tower was built of rough or half-dressed blocks with mud as binder and was externally clad with limestone slabs, dark grey-blue in colour: this gives the edifice an almost monumental character. The tower was built on uneven ground, which rises towards the southeast. A dividing wall of rough stones splits the lower part of the building into two unequal parts which do not communicate with each other, the eastern being the larger. This part was probably not used at all, perhaps because of its relatively low height due to the elevation of the terrain to the east. In the smaller western part, Kinch found some indications of its use as a possible storage space. In contact with the southern, long face of the tower and somewhat off-centre to the east, a structure (possibly an offering table) has survived; Kinch thought it to have been an "altar".[63] Although its present state of preservation

---

62 In Kinch's town plan, a detail of an upright stone has been drawn in a position parallel to the south wall of apartment I 41.

63 The identification was not accepted by Yavis (1949, 100-1), who believes that it is probably an open-air hearth. Taking into account the findings from the adjacent deposit, we believe that the construction was probably intended for offerings by those who entered the sanctuary, perhaps newly arrived foreigners.

Fig. 28. *The south side of the fortification tower with the adjacent "altar", after its restoration; view from the southeast. The wall west of the altar, supposedly the western limit of the open-air sanctuary, which was at right angles to the south side of the tower, had to be reconstructed almost entirely (The Ephorate of Antiquities for the Dodecanese).*

was very poor, its western upright side slab remained in situ and a restoration was feasible, with the assistance of a photograph in Kinch's publication which shows the central part of the tower's south side with the "altar" almost intact (Figs 26-27).[64] In addition, the wall west of the altar, supposedly the western limit of the open-air sanctuary, which was at right angles to the south side of the tower, had to be reconstructed almost entirely, since only a few remnants were preserved at its southern edge (Fig. 28).

At a distance of approximately 5 m from the southwest corner of the tower, a large accumulation of sherds was found in the soft soil, which was removed to reveal the foundation level of the western part of the south wall.[65] Many sherds of relief pithoi, the handles of an oversized pithos and sherds with painted decoration were found.

It is worth noting that Kinch remarked on large-scale collapse and degradation of the external cladding at the northern side of the tower (especially at the northwest

corner), possibly due to poor support by its substructure: "L'angle NO, probablement insuffisamment assis, s'était écroulé entraînant, des parties du bâtiment attenant à l'angle, les pierres carrées qui constituaient le revêtement des murs". There, in order to prevent further collapse of the wall, Kinch used ancient material to build a retaining wall ("mur de soutènement") which contained the degraded west part of the north side of the tower to a (maximum) length of 5.60 m and a (maximum) height of 1.65 m. This reinforcement, out of line with the horizontal east–west axis of the tower, was a cause of considerable puzzlement, speculation and frustration for the unfortunate archaeologist and the architect responsible for the restoration project, until the simple truth was discovered hidden in a tiny footnote in Kinch's publication.[66] Eventually, this wall was dismantled in order to reveal and clean the inner rough masonry of the northern side of the tower as well as the poros block foundations (Fig. 29).

---

64 Kinch 1914, pl. 19. The upright slab of its east side had collapsed but was easily identified among the scattered material.

65 This sherd accumulation does not coincide with Kinch's cited "fosse à offrandes" near and to the left of the "altar" still visible today. The collected pottery has not yet been examined thoroughly but it seems typical of the 7th and 6th centuries BC.

66 Kinch 1914, 92, n. 1.

Fig. 29. *View of the northwest corner of the tower, before and after dismantling Kinch's retaining wall (The Ephorate of Antiquities for the Dodecanese).*

115

FORTIFICATION TOWER - NORTH ELEVATION

FORTIFICATION TOWER - NORTH ELEVATION (after dismantling Kinch's retaining wall and the NE corner)

drawn by Chrysoula M. Hapipi

Fig. 30. *Fortification tower, north elevation (The Ephorate of Antiquities for the Dodecanese).*

After clearing the tower's interior of rubble, it was discovered that the inner faces of the tower's masonry, which remained in place, were fortunately quite solid. It was also observed that the grey-blue limestone slabs of the outer cladding were laid on poros block foundations; poros blocks were also partially used at the lower part of the outer cladding, often interlocked with the grey-blue limestone slabs. On the northern side of the building, the level of the foundations changes significantly: on the eastern part of the wall the foundation's poros blocks are set on the rising conglomerate bedrock, while on the western part the foundation's level slopes downwards, so that the lower row of poros blocks and the cornerstone sink into the soft poros rock (Figs 29-30).

The main entrance gate to the settlement seems to have been in close proximity to the fortification tower; its plan and precise position are not yet known, although the existence of a funnel-shaped gate has already been suggested.[67] It is possible that the northwest corner of the tower, laid deep into the soft bedrock, also functioned as part of the adjacent gateway.

The erosion of the foundation poros blocks, particularly on the north side of the building, led to the collapse of the overlying cladding slabs and caused considerable problems for the restoration. In order to provide adequate support for the restored cladding slabs, it was decided to reinforce the eroded foundations by the addition of new pieces of poros blocks with solid grey-blue limestone slabs inserted underneath them (Fig. 31).

Aim for future activities at the site

A century after Kinch's original publication, there is still much scope for research on the Vroulia Archaic settle-

67 Melander 1988, 83-6.

Fig. 31. *View of the northeast corner of the tower, showing the foundation reinforcements (The Ephorate of Antiquities for the Dodecanese).*

ment and the present joint publication will, hopefully, set a useful precedent for it. The rather practical approach under the current co-financed project, concerning mainly the consolidation of the ancient ruins, at the moment does not permit conclusions relating to chronology or interpretation of the site. However, it seems that the Vroulia Archaic settlement had a more sophisticated urban design than was initially thought, with a possible intermediate phase of development.

Further investigation of the site ought to complete the layout of the surviving part of the settlement as recorded by Kinch. It also ought to reveal new finds that will throw light upon its chronology and function.

Future research on the site should not neglect to do the following:

a) Reveal the terraces extending in front of the "pièces d' habitation" series I.

b) Investigate the extension of the row II apartments or other settlement remains.

c) Further investigate the assumed gate revealed at the bending of the fortification wall.

d) Further investigate the unidentified walls partly visible in the southeast section of the agora area, to the north of apartment I 40 and west of apartments I 41, I 42 and I 43.

e) Investigate the main gate complex, the part of the fortification wall which flanks the empty (?) area west of the tower,[68] as well as the ruins of an unidentified rectangular building outside the fortification wall at a distance of about 30 m from the northwest corner of the tower.

---

68   Kinch noted that the site was called Λέσχα.

117

Fig. 32. *Vroulia and Prassonissi, aerial view from the north (The Ephorate of Antiquities for the Dodecanese).*

f) In addition, future activity on the site might also include the excavation of the early Christian basilica on the opposite slope and the conservation of its mosaic floor.

However, apart from the consolidation/restoration work and the reassessment of the archaeological evidence, the enhancement of the site as a whole should also be continued. Minor discreet interventions are feasible as, for example, the construction of a visitors' path along the external side of the fortification wall, or a route between Kinch's house, partially preserved on Prassonissi, and the Vroulia archaeological site, either along the coast or by sea. Such interventions could be incorporated into a major research project (financed either by the next NSRF or other programme), so that the Vroulia settlement, isolated within its exceptional surrounding seascape, may emerge as an elite destination and emotional experience for the visitor (Fig. 32).

ERIPHYLE KANINIA
Ephorate of Antiquities for the Dodecanese
Odos Ippoton,
851 00 Rhodes
Greece
ekaninia@otenet.gr

STINE SCHIERUP
National Museum of Denmark
Ancient Cultures of Denmark and the Mediterranean
Frederiksholms Kanal 12,
1220 København K
Denmark
stine.schierup@natmus.dk

Appendix:
The Vroulia collection in the National Museum of Denmark

The appendix includes all the objects that Kinch brought home from the excavations in Vroulia except for a few sherds that were given to the Museum of Classical Archaeology in Cambridge in 1958.[69] After his death in 1921 Kinch's private collection was donated to the Collection of Classical and Near Eastern Antiquities at the National Museum of Denmark. Some of these finds are presently deposited in Museum of Ancient Art at the University of Aarhus. The appendix has been organized as far as possible in accordance with Kinch's publication, *Fouilles de Vroulia*, from 1914.

1   La Chapelle

1.1

Dinos and stand (Fig. 11)
Dinos: H: 31 cm, D: 37,5 cm
Stand: H: 25 cm
Provenance: Vroulia, suburban sanctuary, 'la chapelle'
Production: North Ionian, Late Wild Goat style
600-575 BC
On the neck four relief imitations of metal handles. The vessel is decorated on the rim and exterior parts with a dull black to brown slip with added colours in purple and white. On the mouth a cable ornament; on the neck in the zone between the handles a lotus-sprout ornament. The shoulder is dark-slipped and decorated with a floral frieze executed in incised lines and added colours. The body of the vessel is decorated with three animal friezes. On the upper one, the following figure groups can be seen: a) two lions attacking a deer; b) two goats around a large rosette; c) two griffins around a large rosette; d) two lions attacking a deer; and finally, e) two geese around two small rosettes. In the central frieze there are goats in grazing posture with their heads turning towards the right and in the final one a similar frieze of grazing goats, now turning towards the left. In the lower part of the body a

frieze decorated with a lotus-sprout ornament. On the bottom: concentric circles in two groups with a reserved zone in the middle. The vessel has been reconstructed from several fragments. Significant parts of the handles, body and bottom of the vessel are missing. A fragment belonging to this dinos is also known from Tübingen, Antikensammlung.
The National Museum of Denmark
Inv. 11275 (dinos) and 11276 (stand)
BIBLIOGRAPHY: Kinch 1914, 11, 18-9, no. 1, pl. 15, 1, 3-4; Pfuhl 1923, 147; Friis Johansen 1942, 11, n. 15, figs 13-4; Walter-Karydi 1973, 144, no. 941, pl. 115; Cook & Dupont 1998, 53, fig. 8.19; *CVA* TÜBINGEN, band 1, 25-6, taf. 10.5; Coulié 2013, 175, fig. 169.

1.2

Stemmed dish
H: 6.0 cm; D: 34.5 cm
Provenance: Vroulia, suburban sanctuary, 'la chapelle'
Production: Milet
Late Wild Goat Style
Brown to greyish-brown clay with dark particles and mica. Light greyish-yellow slip, only preserved in areas below decorated parts covered by a dull to blackish-brown slip. Where no slip survives the decoration can be identified from incisions made in the clay. In the centre of the bowl a large incised rosette, and a meander pattern. Hereafter follows a metope-frieze with various figures: 1) the head of a goose; 2) the head of a goat; 3) a rosette ornament; 4) as 2, 5) as 3; 6) as 2, 7) as 3.
The National Museum of Denmark (deposited in The Museum of Ancient Art, Aarhus University).
Inv. 11280
BIBLIOGRAPHY: Kinch 1914, 21, no. 36, 193, 207, 252, pl. 17.3a–b; for parallels, see e.g. Coulié & Filimonos-Tsopotou 2014, cat.no. 88, 250 (Cécile Colonna); for the head of the goose, see e.g. Coulié 2014, no. 28, 142-3.

---

69   The material can be found on the museum webpage: http://museum.classics.cam.ac.uk/collections/sherds. Accessed January 21, 2017.

1.3

Stemmed dish

L rim fragment: 26.5 cm; L foot fragment: 13.5 cm

Provenance: Vroulia, suburban sanctuary, 'la chapelle'

Production: Milet

Late 7th to early 6th century BC

Body, rim and foot fragment of a stemmed dish. Dark reddish-yellow to light reddish-brown clay with numerous mica. Light yellowish slip. Decoration in dull reddish-brown to dark brown slip. In the centre of the bowl wide concentric bands and a meander pattern. Followed by a wide zone with rays and metopes with: 1) large S-volute ornament; 2) fallow. Framing this zone a wide band and rays.

The National Museum of Denmark

Inv. 11290

BIBLIOGRAPHY: Kinch 1914, 21, no. 3e, 193, 199, 207, 252, pl. 17.2a–b. For parallels of the large S-volute ornament, see e.g. Coulié 2014, no. 31, 146.

1.4

Alabastron

H: 8.4 cm

Provenance: Vroulia, suburban sanctuary, 'la chapelle'

Production: Transitional-Early Corinthian

Late 7th to early 6th century BC

Light green-greyish clay. Decoration in brownish-grey to black, glossy slip with incisions and red slip. On the neck a tongue ornament, band on the handle, lion and rosettes on the widest part of the vessel, below the vessel an incised rosette. Upper part of the handle and rim not preserved.

The National Museum of Denmark

Inv. 11322

BIBLIOGRAPHY: Kinch 1914, 26, no. 9, pl. 14.8; for parallels, see e.g. Amyx 1988, pl. 19.1a–b, 19.2a–b, 33.4 and 33.6.

1.5

Sphinx, limestone (Figs 9a–b)

H: 18.5 cm

Provenance: Vroulia, suburban sanctuary, 'la chapelle'

Production: Cypriot

600-575 BC

Sphinx seated on a plinth. Head and chest are missing, as is the tail. Incised Phoenician inscription on the right wing, read as: "t(or: š) s m z (or: g). g (or: n) h (or: t) q k š" [reading by Professor B. Otzen, University of Aarhus].

The National Museum of Denmark

Inv. 11328

BIBLIOGRAPHY: Kinch 1914, 11, 16, no. 3, pl. 14.4; Blinkenberg 1931, 402, 446; Kourou 2003, 255, fig. 4; Karageorghis & Rasmussen 2001, 87, cat. 165 (Lone Wriedt Sørensen); Bourogiannis 2014, 163-4.

1.6

Statuette, limestone

H: 9.8 cm

Provenance: Vroulia, suburban sanctuary, 'la chapelle', near altar

Production: Cypriot

600-575 BC

Upper part of a standing woman. Right hand has been placed in front of her breast; the left one is lowered. The hair falls in a large and wide braid down her back. She wears a chiton with kolpos, squared neck and long 'sleeves'. On the left shoulder and the hips faint traces of red paint. Nose is missing, some chips on surface.

The National Museum of Denmark

Inv. 11326

BIBLIOGRAPHY: Kinch 1914, 11, 15, no. 1, pls 13.2, 14.2; Mylonas 1999, 285, n. 1140.

1.7

Statuette, limestone

H: 9.4 cm

Provenance: Vroulia, suburban sanctuary, 'la chapelle', near altar

Production: Cypriot

600-575 BC

Upper part of a limestone statuette, a flute player. On the mouth and the flute faint traces of red paint. Left arm and shoulder as well as part of the back of the figure missing.

The National Museum of Denmark

Inv. 11327

BIBLIOGRAPHY: Kinch 1914, 11, 15-6, no. 2, pls 13.3, 14.3; Riis et al. 1989, no. 15; Mylonas 1999, 285, n. 1140; Karageorghis & Rasmussen 2001, no. 150, 81 (Lone Wriedt Sørensen). Similar limestone flute-players of Cypriot origin are also known from the Archaic deposit in Lindos: Blinkenberg 1931, 425-7. Generally on this type, see Mylonas 1999, 159-61.

1.8

Bird (falcon?), limestone
H: 5.5 cm; L: 6.8 cm.
Provenance: Vroulia, suburban sanctuary, 'la chapelle', near altar
Production: Cypriot
600-575 BC
The National Museum of Denmark
Inv. 11329
BIBLIOGRAPHY: Kinch 1914, 11, 16-7, no. 4, pl. 14.5; for parallels, see bird votives from Lindos: Blinkenberg 1931, 455-7.

2   Nécropole

2.1

Ring-shaped aryballos (Fig. 18)
H: 13 cm
Provenance: Vroulia, children's tomb 's'
Production: Rhodian
700-675 BC
Light brown micaceous clay. On the ring transverse, close parallel lines in a zig-zag pattern and on the neck horizontal bands. Handle decorated with a simple meander pattern.
The National Museum of Denmark
Inv. 11318
BIBLIOGRAPHY: Kinch 1914, 45-7, no. 3, pl. 31.3; Friis Johansen 1923, 28, n. 3 (Exochi, tomb A); Blinkenberg 1931, 308; Dietz & Trolle 1974, 57, fig. 56.

2.2

Stemmed dish.
H: 12.3 cm; D: 24.7 cm.
Provenance: Vroulia, tomb 17
Production: North Ionia?
Late 7th to early 6th century BC

Light brown clay with small dark inclusions and mica. On the interior covered by a light brown-yellowish slip. Decoration in dull brown to black slip and yellowish-white and added red. In the centre of the bowl a lotus ornament of four flowers and four buds. The central lotus ornament is encircled by a braided band between wide concentric bands. Restored from numerous fragments.
The National Museum of Denmark
Inv. 11277
BIBLIOGRAPHY: Kinch 1914, 77, no. 3, 194, 262, pls 6.1, 6.1a. For similar examples, see no. 2.3 below; Copenhagen, National Museum, inv. 5178 (from Kenchraki, Rhodes): *CVA* Copenhague 2, pl. 75.4; Coulié 2014, no. 42, 168-9.

2.3

Stemmed dish
H: 11.4 cm; D: 23.8 cm
Provenance: Vroulia, tomb 11
Production: North Ionia?
Late 7th to early 6th century BC
Light brown clay with small dark inclusions and mica. Decorated in black, partly brown slip with added yellowish-white and red paint. In the centre of the bowl a lotus ornament of four flowers and four buds. This motif is encircled by a meander between concentric wide bands. On the exterior of the bowl and the foot several concentric shallow bands.
The National Museum of Denmark
Inv. 11279
BIBLIOGRAPHY: Kinch 1914, 71-2, no. 5, 194, 262, pl. 8.1a–b. For similar examples, see no. 2.2 above with further references.

2.4

Plate
D: 27 cm
Provenance: Vroulia, tomb 2
Production: Cos?
Early 6th century BC
Brownish-grey clay with small dark inclusions. Decorated in dull greyish black slip. The plate has been exposed to secondary firing. Centre of the plate divided into two parts. The upper one decorated with a large ibex jumping towards the right; the lower one decorated with two

121

antithetical birds with cross-hatched bodies. On the back of the plate two suspension holes around 2.9 cm apart. Restored from numerous fragments.
The National Museum of Denmark
Inv. 11284
BIBLIOGRAPHY: Kinch 1914, 60-1, no. 21, 222, pl. 35; PAYNE 1931, 312, n. 4. Plates of this type are known in numerous examples from Rhodes and especially from Kamiros; clay analysis seems to suggest the origin of this group to be Cos: Cook & Dupont 1998, 61-3; Couliè 2014, nos 50-55, 182-91.

2.5

Globular oinochoe with short, narrow neck
H: 18.3 cm
Provenance: Vroulia, tomb 12
Production: Cypriot, White Painted V Ware
Early 6th century BC
Greyish to light brownish clay with mica. Decoration in dull, dark brown to black-grey slip. Trefoil mouth, visible interior parts and rim covered by slip, on the neck a wide wavy line between two concentric horizontal bands. On the twin handle a wide band. The globular belly decorated in front and back with a large three-part palm-leaf ornament. On each side of the belly four concentric circles, two large with two smaller inside. Restored from several fragments. The vessel has been exposed to secondary firing.
The National Museum of Denmark
Inv. 11285
BIBLIOGRAPHY: Kinch 1914, 73, no. 2, pl. 40.12:2; another example of this type was found in house I,12: Kinch 1914, 156, pl. 26.3; similarities in shape and decoration can be found in Gjerstad 1948, fig. XLVI, 9b; fig. XLIX, no. 7c and with the 'palm-leaf workshop' (Morris 1987).

2.6

Oinochoe, shoulder and neck fragment
L: 18.2 cm
Provenance: Vroulia, tomb 18
Production: Wild Goat Style, North Ionia?
Late 7th to early 6th century BC
Light brown clay with dark inclusions and mica. Shoulder covered by a dull brownish to greyish black slip. Incised

goat running towards the right (preserved parts include the head, neck, parts of a foreleg and the back). Added details in red paint. Only this small fragment of the oenochoe can be found in the Vroulia collection in Copenhagen, although the description in the publication testifies that the whole vessel was originally found.
The National Museum of Denmark
Inv. 11286
BIBLIOGRAPHY: Kinch 1914, 51, no. 5, 190, pl. 11.1.

2.7

Bird Vase
H: 9.5 cm
Provenance: Vroulia, tomb 1
Production: Rhodian?
Early 7th century BC
Greyish clay with mica. The details of the head, wings and feet are made with greyish black to dark brown slip. Restored from several fragments.
The National Museum of Denmark
Inv. 11317
BIBLIOGRAPHY: Kinch 1914, 43, 56-7, pl. 34.1.3; Blinkenberg 1931, 297-8, pl. 48, nos 1026 and 1027.

2.8

Alabastron, conical
H: 9.9 cm
Provenance: Vroulia, tomb 2
Production: Rhodian
Early 7th century BC
Light yellowish clay with mica.
The National Museum of Denmark
Inv. 11319
BIBLIOGRAPHY: Kinch 1914, 59, no. 5, pl. 34.2:5. Similar examples are known from Vroulia, Kinch 1914, 47, no. 13; from Exochi (tomb A), Friis Johansen 1957, 15, 155-61, no. A12, pls 22-3; Coldstream 2008, 276.

2.9

Globular aryballos
H: 4.8 cm
Provenance: Vroulia, children's tomb 'bb'
Greyish clay caused by secondary firing. Decorated with vertical ribs.
The National Museum of Denmark
Inv. 11320
BIBLIOGRAPHY: Kinch 1914, 48, pl. 32, bb3.

2.10

Alabastron
H: 8.7 cm
Provenance: Vroulia, children's tomb 'p'
Light brownish clay. Decoration in shiny black to brownish slip.
The National Museum of Denmark
Inv. 11321
BIBLIOGRAPHY: Kinch 1914, 43, no. 2, pl. 33.p2; Payne 1931, 56.

2.11

Ovoid aryballos
H: 9.5 cm
Provenance: Vroulia, children's tomb 'p'
Light yellowish clay. Decoration in brown to black slip.
The National Museum of Denmark
Inv. 11323
BIBLIOGRAPHY: Kinch 1914, 43, no. 1, pl. 33.p1; Payne 1931, 56.

2.12

Skyphos, miniature
H: 4.8 cm; D rim: 10 cm.
Provenance: Vroulia, children's tomb 'bb'
Light brown clay with mica. Geometric decoration in a dull, greyish-brown slip.
The National Museum of Denmark.
Inv. 11324.
BIBLIOGRAPHY: Kinch 1914, 48, no. 2, 163-4, pl. 32, bb2; Payne 1931, 294 note 1.

3. *Sanctuaire principal*

3.1

Terracotta figurine (Fig. 20)
H: 18.4 cm
Provenance: Vroulia, main sanctuary, near altar
Early 7th century BC
Dark brownish clay with small dark inclusions and mica. Modelled female figure with a solid block-shaped lower body. Breast and eyes made of attached pellets, nostrils and hair on forehead with incisions. Nose and chin protruding. The hair falls in five thick locks down the back and two on the front falling down each shoulder. Arms outreached. Hands indicated by incised lines marking the separated fingers. Restored from three fragments, the original parts of the lower part of the neck, hair locks and fragments of the back side missing.
The National Museum of Denmark
Inv. 11273
BIBLIOGRAPHY: Kinch 1914, 102, no. 1, pl. 19.1; Poulsen 1912, 140; Müller 1929, 66, 188, 211, pls 20.274, 33.351. Similarities in the style and execution of this distinctive figurine can be found in Cypro-Archaic examples (note particularly the rendering of the lower body, the pellets used for eyes and breasts as well as the protruding nose and chin), see e.g. Karageorghis 1998.

4. *Place publique, Quartier de Maisons*

4.1.

Cup with narrow conical foot (Fig. 19)
H: 11.0; D 24.4 cm
Provenance: Vroulia, room I, 25
Production: North Ionia?
600-575 BC
Decorated with added colours in black, brown, yellowish white and purple. The centre of the cup is decorated with a sixteen-leaved rosette followed by a wide zone of concentric circles, a cable ornament and towards the rim another zone of concentric circles. Exterior decorated with numerous, narrow concentric bands.
The National Museum of Denmark
Inv. 11278
BIBLIOGRAPHY: Kinch 1914, 120, 131, no. 9, pp. 194, 262, pl. 7.1a–b; Walter-Karydi 1973, 146, no. 990, taf. 122; Dietz & Trolle 1974, 56, fig. 55.

4.2

Kylix

H: 9.4 cm

Provenance: Vroulia, room I, 32

Production: Rhodes, 'Vroulia' style

610-580 BC

Light brown to reddish yellow clay with mica. Dull, dark brown to black slip. Further decoration has been added with a combination of incisions and added red. On the interior a large seven-leaved rosette. Below the exterior everted rim an incised tooth pattern. Between handles a frieze decorated with vertical lines and a double triangle pattern. On the lower part of the vessel circular floral ornaments and palmettos. Restored from several fragments. Preserved are nine ancient repair holes.

The National Museum of Denmark

Inv. 11281

BIBLIOGRAPHY: Kinch 1914, 124, 144, no 5, 163, 178, pl. 10.1.

4.3

Kylix

Provenance: Vroulia, room I, 6

Production: Rhodes, 'Vroulia' style

610-580 BC

15 rim and body fragments, a few joining. Brown to greyish clay. Decoration of the bowl can be assumed as follows: below the rim incised tooth-pattern, frieze between handles with vertical lines and below incised palmetto with added red paint on fronds.

The National Museum of Denmark (deposited in the Museum of Ancient Art, University of Aarhus)

Inv. 11288

BIBLIOGRAPHY: Kinch 1914, 182, no. 24, pls 10.2 and 2a–b.

4.4

Kylix

H: 8.5 cm; D: 15.3 cm

Provenance: Vroulia, room I, 18

Light brown clay with mica. Decorated with black to reddish brown slip. On the rim and upper handle zone a thin concentric line in added dull red paint. One of the handles

as well as small fragments of rim and body missing, but has been restored.

The National Museum of Denmark

Inv. 11283

BIBLIOGRAPHY: Kinch 1914, 145-6, no. 2, pl. 5.2.

4.5

Stemmed dish, rim and body fragment

L: 12.7 cm; W: 11.1 cm; estimated D: 27 cm

Provenance: Vroulia, room I, 18

Reddish brown clay with numerous mica. Surface covered by pale yellow coating. Decorated with dark reddish brown to red slip and added red paint: on the surface wide concentric lines, thin red ones in combination with three zones of hooked meanders. Below the dish narrow concentric lines. Restored from two fragments.

The National Museum of Denmark

Inv. 11287

BIBLIOGRAPHY: Kinch 1914, 130, no. 5, p. 193, pl. 4.2a–b (the centre rosette has not been preserved and the drawing in fig. 2a is therefore partly hypothetical).

4.6

Stemmed dish

L: 11.3 (rim); 8.9 (rim); 6.3 cm (body).

Provenance: Vroulia, room I, 29

Two rim fragments and one body fragment. Light brownish clay with numerous mica. On the surface a white-yellowish coating. Decorated in dull black to brown slip and added red. In the centre of the bowl a rosette (?) encircled by thin concentric lines. Around the central decoration, sprouts and three-leaved palmetto, followed by concentric lines and a hooked meander zone. On the rim short oblique lines.

The National Museum of Denmark (deposited in the Museum of Ancient Art, University of Aarhus)

Inv. 11291

BIBLIOGRAPHY: Kinch 1914, 130, no. 7, pp. 193, 204, pl. 9.1a–b.

4.7

Chalice fragment

W: (incl. handle) 7.1 cm; H: 4.0 cm

Provenance: Vroulia, room I, 32

Production: Chios

Three joining fragments of body and vertical handle. Light brown clay with mica. Surface covered by a white-chalky slip and decoration in added orange-red paint: in the handle zone a frieze of vertical lines framed by horizontal bands. On the upper band a partly preserved leg and foot, presumably of a human figure.

The National Museum of Denmark

Inv. 11325

BIBLIOGRAPHY: Kinch 1914, 149-50, no. 4.2, pl. 46.4. Appendix nos 4.7-4.9 belong to Kinch's group 4 "coupes naukratiéenes", now commonly recognized as having been produced in Chios. Kourouniotis' excavations on Chios in 1914-15 – after the publication of the Vroulia material – revealed significant examples of this pottery, which led to the conclusion that they might have been produced in Chios, not Naucratis (Williams 2006, 127 with further references).

4.8

Chalice fragment

1: W: 2 cm; H: 2.8 cm. 2: W: 1.9 cm; H: 1.7 cm.

Provenance: Vroulia, room I, 28

Production: Chios

Three small rim fragments (two joining). Light brown clay with mica. Decorated on the interior with a lotus flower ornament in added white and red paint. Exterior covered by a white-chalky slip.

The National Museum of Denmark

Inv. 11325

BIBLIOGRAPHY: Kinch 1914, 149-50, no. 4.5, pls 46.2-3. The lotus flower ornamentation is typical for the interior decoration of the chalices; see e.g. Lemos 1991, 121-2, figs 65-6.

4.9

Chalice fragment

Provenance: Vroulia, room I, 19

Production: Chios

Body fragment with handle attachment. Light brown clay

with mica. Surface covered by a white-chalky slip. Decoration in handle zone in added orange-red paint: a frieze of vertical lines framed by horizontal bands.

The National Museum of Denmark (deposited in the Museum of Ancient Art, University of Aarhus)

Inv. 11325

BIBLIOGRAPHY: Kinch 1914, 149-50, no. 4.4, pl. 28.4.

4.10

Dinos

Provenance: Vroulia, room I, 18

North Ionian, Late Wild Goat style

600-575 BC

39 fragments of a dinos similar to no. 1.1 found in 'la chapelle'. Light brownish clay with dark inclusions and mica. On the exterior covered by a light greyish-yellow coating with decoration in dull black to brown slip and added red and white. On the upper part of the shoulder a tongue ornament and below four zones of animals and ornaments: a) large volute ornament, griffins and geese; b) griffins, a large rosette and two lion pairs attacking a deer; c) goats in grazing posture towards the left; d) goats in grazing posture towards right. Below a frieze of lotus flowers and sprouts.

The National Museum of Denmark (partly deposited in the Museum of Ancient Art, University of Aarhus)

Inv. 11292

BIBLIOGRAPHY: Kinch 1914, 132-3, p. 194-5, pl. 24.61-c; Pfuhl 1923, 147; Friis Johansen 1942, 12, fig. 5.

4.11

Lamp, limestone

L: 14.2 cm; W: 10.8 cm; H: 5.5 cm.

Provenance: Vroulia, room I, 43.

The National Museum of Denmark

Inv. 11330

BIBLIOGRAPHY: Kinch 1914, 111, no. 4, pl. 23.13a–b.

5.   *Unknown context*

The objects included in this group have no known find context other than 'Vroulia'. They cannot be identified with certainty from the descriptions in either the diaries or the publication, but they are well-known types from the published material. Some of the objects have been exposed to secondary firing and it seems reasonable to suggest that they were found in the cremation tombs. Also included are a number of smaller fragments of iron, bones and glass.

5.1

Kylix, fragments
Light brown to greyish clay with mica
23 fragments (several joining). Decorated in a dull to brownish-black slip. The exterior covered with slip except in a wide band in the handle zone and on the interior part of the handles. The handle zone is decorated with black palmettos and between these a vertical 'tongue-shaped' line in added reddish-brown color. The interior of the vessel is similarly covered by a slip except for a narrow band on the rim and a round zone at the bottom of the bowl, decorated with two concentric circles.
The National Museum of Denmark
Inv. 11293

5.2

Kylix, fragments
Light brownish clay with mica
13 fragments (several joining). Decoration similar to no. 6.1.
The National Museum of Denmark
Inv. 11294

5.3

Ring-shaped aryballos
Light brown clay with mica
H: 13.7 cm
Production: Rhodian
700-675 BC
Restored from several fragments. Traces of secondary firing seems to suggest that it comes from one of the cremation tombs.
The National Museum of Denmark (deposited in the Museum of Ancient Art, University of Aarhus)
Inv. 11305

BIBLIOGRAPHY: similar to ring-shaped aryballoi from Vroulia, tomb 's' (appendix no. 2.1): Kinch 1914, 45-7, no. 3, pl. 31.3; and from Exochi, tomb A: Friis Johansen 1923, 28, n. 3.

5.4

Ovoid ayballos, fragment
H: 3.0 (neck and handle); H: 8.9 (body).
Joined from several fragments. Missing are small fragments between neck and shoulder. Grey-brownish clay with mica. Decorated with a dull greyish slip. On the rim concentric circles, and below wide bands. On the neck a zig-zag pattern. On the shoulder a tongue ornament and below a frieze of silhouette birds. On the lower part of the vessel rays.
The National Museum of Denmark
Inv. 11306

5.5

Ovoid aryballos, fragment
H: 6.8 cm; D (foot): 1.6 cm
Production: Middle Protocorinthian
Greyish clay. Body fragment; neck, rim and handle missing. Decorated in reddish-brown to black slip. Incised shell pattern and tongue ornaments on shoulder and lower body. The vessel has been exposed to secondary firing.
The National Museum of Denmark (deposited in the Museum of Ancient Art, University of Aarhus)
Inv. 11307
BIBLIOGRAPHY: Similar in shape and decoration to an aryballos found in Tomb 9 (Kinch 1914, 70, pls 39, 9.2).

5.6

Aryballos, fragment
H: 6.0 cm
Light brown to greyish clay. Only part of the body preserved (rim, handle and foot missing). Decorated in a greyish-black to brownish slip: four bands and between them a double row of dots, below partly preserved tongue ornament. The vessel has been exposed to secondary firing.
The National Museum of Denmark
Inv. 11308

5.7

Ovoid aryballos

H: 9.0 cm

Greyish clay. Decoration in black slip, partly worn off: on the shoulder a tongue ornament and below concentric bands; on the body a wide zone with seven incised rows of a shell pattern, below two concentric bands. Lower part of the body decorated with a tongue pattern. Neck, handle and significant parts of the shoulder and body are missing. The vessel has been exposed to secondary firing.

The National Museum of Denmark (deposited in the Museum of Ancient Art, University of Aarhus)

Inv. 11311

BIBLIOGRAPHY: similar in shape and decoration to an aryballos found in Tomb 9 (Kinch 1914, 70, pls 39, 9.2)

5.8

Alabastron

H: 6.7 cm

Light brown to greyish clay. Decoration in reddish-brown to black slip, partly worn off. On the rim concentric circles and narrow bands, on the shoulder a tongue ornament. The body decorated with four wide bands and in between them dots. In the lower part of the body a tongue ornament. Small fragment of the body missing. The vessel has been exposed to secondary firing.

The National Museum of Denmark (deposited in the Museum of Ancient Art, University of Aarhus)

Inv. 11310

BIBLIOGRAPHY: Similar to the following examples from tombs in Vroulia: Kinch 1914, pl. 33.p2, pl. 34.2,11.

5.9

Alabastron, fragment

H: 5.5 cm

Preserved are body and foot, joined from several fragments. Light yellow to greyish clay. Decorated in black slip, only partly preserved: on the body a figure-decorated frieze with four incised animals walking towards the left, on the foot a tongue-rosette ornament. A few traces of added red paint can be seen on the animals. The vessel has been exposed to secondary firing.

The National Museum of Denmark (deposited in the Museum of Ancient Art, University of Aarhus)

Inv. 11312

5.10

Small glass fragments:

a) 6 ring-shaped and globular beads in dark greenish and brownish glass. Four of the green beads are adorned with inlaid white bands. D: 1.0-1.1 cm.

b) Three white glass beads, two double conical in shape. D: 1.2-1.3 cm.

c) Ring-shaped foot of a small glass vessel. D: 2.1 cm.

The National Museum of Denmark

Inv. 11299

5.11

Small iron fragments:

a) Iron fragment. L: 3.2 cm.

b) Iron needle with preserved eye and ring-shaped attachment. L: 3.3 cm.

The National Museum of Denmark

Inv. 11300

5.12

Small bone fragments:

a) Five joining fragments of a decorated ivory plate from a fibula. The surface of the fragment has been damaged presumably due to high temperatures during firing. L: 5.4 cm. Similar examples are known from Lindos, see Blinkenberg 1931, 90-1, no. 133.

b) Tapered bone fragment with an iron pin inside. The fragment damaged presumably from strong heat during firing. L: 2.6 cm.

c) Claw, possibly from a crayfish. L: 2.8 cm.

The National Museum of Denmark

Inv. 11301

127

Bibliography

Amyx, D. A. 1988
Corinthian vase-painting of the Archaic period, Berkeley.

Blinkenberg, C. 1931
Lindos 1, Fouilles d'Acropole 1902-1914. Les petits objets, Berlin.

Blinkenberg, C. 1941
Lindos 2, Fouilles d'Acropole 1902-1914. Inscriptions, Berlin.

Bourogiannis, G. 2013
'Who hides behind the pots? A Reassessment of the Phoenician Presence in Early Iron Age Cos and Rhodes', *ANES* 50, 139-89.

Bourogiannis, G. 2014
'Instances of Semitic Writing from Geometric and Archaic Greek Contexts: An Unintelligible Way to Literacy?', in *Transformations and Crisis in the Meditterranean. "Identity" and Interculturality in the Levant and Phoenician West during the 12th–8th Centuries BCE*, G. Garbati & T. Pedrazzi (eds), Rome, 159-70.

Coldstream, J. N. 2008
Greek Geometric Pottery. A Survey of Ten Local Styles and their Chronology, Bristol.

Cook, R. M. & P. Dupont 1998
East Greek Pottery, London.

Coulié, A. 2013
La Céramique Grecque aux Époques Géométrique et Orientalisante (XIe–Vie Siécle AV J.-C.), Musée du Louvre, Paris.

Coulié, A. 2014
La Céramique Grecque de l'Est: le style de chévres sauvages, Paris.

Coulié, A. & M. Filimonos-Tsopotou (eds) 2014
Rhodes. Une île grecque aux portes de l'Orient. XVe–Ve Siècle Avant J.C., Paris.

Dietz, S. 1984
Lindos 4, 1 Excavations and Surveys in Southern Rhodes: The Mycenean Period, Copenhagen.

Dietz, S. & S. Trolle 1974
Arkæologens Rhodos, København.

Dyggve, E. 1943
'Recherches et explorations archéologiques danoises dans la peninsula des Balkans, en Égypte et dans le Proche Orient', *Le Nord* 6, 133-64.

Dyggve, E. 1960
Lindos III. Fouille de l'Acropole 1901-1914 et 1951. Le sanctuaire d'Athena Lindia et l'architecture lindienne, Berlin.

Fellmann, B. & H. Scheyhing (eds) 1972
100 Jahre Deutsche Ausgrabung in Olympia, München.

Friis Johansen, K. 1923
Les Vases Sicyoniens: Etude archéologique, Paris.

Friis Johansen, K. 1942
'Clazomenian Sarcophagus Studies. The Earliest Sarcophagi', *Acta Archaeologica* 13, 1-64.

Friis Johansen, K. 1957
'Exochi. Ein Frührhodisches Gräberfeld', *Acta Archaeologica* 28.

Gjerstad, E. 1948
The Swedish Cyprus Expedition 4, 2 The Cypro-Geometric, Cypro-Archaic and Cypro-Classical Periods, Stockholm.

Hoepfner, W. 1999
Geschichte des Wohnens. Bd. 1: 5000 v.Chr. – 500 n.Chr. Vorgeschichte, Frühgeschichte, Antike, Stuttgart.

Juhel, P. O. & Π. Μ. Νίγδελης 2015
Un danois en Macédoine à la fin du 19e siécle. Karl Frederik Kinch et ses notes epigraphiques, Thessaloniki.

Karageorghis, V. 1998
The Coroplastic Art of Ancient Cyprus 5, The Cypro-Archaic Period Small Female Figurines. A. Handmade/Wheelmade Figurines, Nicosia.

Karageorghis, V. & B. B. Rasmussen 2001
Ancient Cypriote Art in Copenhagen. The Collection of the National Museum of Denmark and the Ny Carlsberg Glyptotek, Nicosia.

Kinch, K. F. 1890
L'Arc de triomphe de Salonique publié sous les auspices de la foundation Carlsberg, Paris.

Kinch, K. F. 1914
Fouilles de Vroulia (Rhodes), Berlin.

Kourou, N. 2003
'Rhodes: the Phoenician Issue Revisited. Phoenicians at Vroulia?', in *Sea Routes… Interconnections in the Mediterranean 16th – 6th c. BC. Proceedings of the International Symposion held at Rethymnon, Crete on September 29th – October 2nd 2002*, N. Chr. Stampolidis & V. Karageorghis (eds), Athens, 249-62.

Lemos, A. A. 1991
Archaic pottery of Chios: The decorated styles, Oxford.

Lang, F. 1996
Archaische Siedlungen in Griechenland. Struktur und Entwicklung, Berlin.

Melander, T. 1988
'Vroulia: Town Plan and Gate', in *Archaeology in the Dodecanese*, S. Dietz & I. Papachristodoulou (eds), Copenhagen, 82-7.

Morris, I. 1992
Death-Ritual and Social Structure in Classical Antiquity, Cambridge.

Morris, R. S. 1985
'The Palm Leaf Workshop', *RDAC*, 127-35.

Müller, V. 1929.
Frühe Plastik in Griechenland und Kleinasien, Augsburg.

Mylonas, D. G. 1999
Archaische Kalksteinsplastik Zyperns. Unterzuchungen zur Ikonographie, Typologie und formgeschichtlichen Entwicklung der kyprischen Rundplastik der archaischen Zeit, Universität Mannheim. http://www.uni-mannheim.de/mateo/verlag/diss/mylonas/mylonas.pdf. Accessed January 16, 2017.

Payne, H. 1931
Necrocorinthia; a study of Corinthian Art in the Archaic period, Oxford.

Pfuhl, E. 1923
Malerei und Zeichung der Griechen 1-3, München.

Poulsen, F. 1912
Der Orient und die Frühgriechische Kunst, Leipzig.

Rasmussen, B. B. & Lund, J. 2014
'Fouilles et explorations danoises à Rhodes', in *Rhodes. Une île grecque aux portes de l'Orient. XVe–Ve Siècle Avant J.C.*, A. Coulié & M. Filimonos-Tsopotou (eds), Paris, 42-7.

Rathje, A. & Lund, J. 1991
'Danes Overseas – A Short History', *Acta Hyperborea* 3, 11-56.

Riis, P. J., M. Moltesen & P. Guldager Bilde 1989
Catalogue of Ancient Sculptures 1, 1 Aegean, Cypriote and Graeco-Phoenician (The National Museum of Denmark), Copenhagen.

Thompson, M. S. & A. J. B. Wace 1912
Prehistoric Thessaly. Being some account of recent excavations and explorations in north-eastern Greece fom Lake Kopaios to the borders of Macedonia, Cambridge.

Ussing, J. L. 1906
At mit Levned, København.

Walter-Karydi, E. 1973
Samos VI.1. Samische Gefässe des 6. Jahrhunderts v. Chr: Landschaftsstile ostgriechischer Gefässe, Bonn.

Williams, D. 2006
'The Chian Pottery from Naukratis', in *Naukratis: Greek Diversity in Egypt. Studies on East Greek Pottery and Exchange in the Eastern Mediterranean*, A.Villing & U. Schlotzhauer (eds), London, 127-33.

Wiplinger, G. & G. Wlach 1996
Ephesos. 100 Jahre österreichische Forschung, Vienna.

Wriedt Sørensen, L. 2002
'The Archaic Settlement at Vroulia on Rhodes and Ian Morris', *Acta Hyperborea* 9, 243-53.

Yavis, C. 1949
Greek altars, Saint Louis, Missouri.

129

The cults of Kalydon
*Reassessing the miniaturised votive objects**

SIGNE BARFOED

The past 15 years has witnessed renewed and intensive archaeological fieldwork at the ancient Greek city of Kalydon in Aitolia. In the years 2001-5, Drs Søren Dietz and Maria Stavropoulou-Gatsi directed excavations in several areas of the city, and the results were published in two volumes in 2011.[1] In the period 2011-6, Drs Rune Frederiksen and Søren Handberg carried out excavations in collaboration with the Ephorate of Antiquities of Aetolia-Acarnania and Lefkada in Kalydon's Theatre, and on the Lower Acropolis plateau.[2] These renewed excavations have produced much new information about the ancient city, including its religious cults.

The purpose of this article is to cast further light on the religious cults of the city and Kalydonian ritual behaviour. The renewed excavations have produced a substantial amount of miniature votive pottery, and in drawing attention to this hitherto rather overlooked aspect of material culture, I will argue that it must play an important role in our understanding of religious practice in ancient Kalydon. Within the last decade miniature pottery has attracted considerable scholarly attention, which has produced insight that may be applied to the evidence from Kalydon. The author has been involved in the work at Kalydon since 2011 and has been able to study both published and unpublished miniature pottery

found since 2001. Meticulous searches through the finds in the storerooms have led to the identification of more than 200 fragments of miniature pottery. Both published and unpublished miniature pottery is contextualized, and the cult related to the miniature votives is re-examined.[3] Kalydon's most famous cult is to Artemis Laphria, but two additional cults have been identified during the recent excavations: a shrine on the central Acropolis, and the cult in the Peristyle House in the Lower Town.

Research History

A brief research history of miniature pottery

The 7th century BC marks a considerable change in the use of miniature pottery in the ancient Greek world. From this period onwards miniatures were dedicated on a larger scale in Greek sanctuaries, and their introduction as a form of votive offering was a fundamental change in the material culture of the early Greek sanctuaries during the Archaic period.[4] It has been suggested that this change was caused by the fact that the authority to dedicate in the sanctuaries had been handed down from the aristocracy to the common people, and that the sanctuaries thus experienced a growth in clientele. The abundant miniature

* I would like to thank Drs Søren Dietz and Rune Frederiksen for kindly granting me permission to work with the pottery from their excavations. I am grateful to the anonymous reviewers for their helpful suggestions.

1 Dietz & Stavropoulou-Gatsi 2011.
2 The publication of Kalydon's theatre is currently underway. For a preliminary report, see Vikatou et al. 2014. For a preliminary report on the excavations on the Lower Acropolis, see Vikatou & Handberg, this volume.
3 Some of the Kalydon material is also discussed in the author's unpublished PhD dissertation, see Barfoed 2015b.
4 Gimatzidis 2011, 81; Foley 1988, 69.

Fig. 1. *Miniature bowls from Phlius (a-b) and from the Argive Heraion (c) (after: Biers 1971, nos. 49-50, pl. 90; Caskey & Amandry 1952, no. 262, pl. 57).*

pottery from the Archaic period onwards consequently reflects wide participation in the rituals.[5]

Miniature pottery is still a relatively neglected group within material studies, and in the past it was often disposed of in excavations and not recorded in any detail. In those cases where miniature pottery was recorded and published, for example, in the early excavations of the sites of Perachora and the Argive Heraion, it was generally described as useless, non-important and cheap.[6] Many scholars have accepted this interpretation, despite its simplicity.[7] Even in literature from the 1990s some scholars share this elementary idea of miniatures being a cheap, poorly produced product; one even calls them "decayed versions" of regular pottery or fancier votives.[8] Most frequently no interpretations or discussions are offered for miniature pottery, and when they are, it is considered as the offerings of people who could not afford dedications in metal or regular-sized pottery vessels.

However, some newer and more persuasive interpretations exist: Gunnel Ekroth has convincingly argued that since miniature pottery could be transported more easily than normal-sized pottery, it had value in itself, and perhaps it was more suited for foreign visitors making dedications when visiting different sanctuaries. In a deposit

from Phlius in modern Corinthia, near Nemea, miniature bowls with particular handles are found, and examples of this local miniature type have also shown up at both Perachora and the Argive Heraion (Fig. 1).[9] Similarly, Corinthian miniature pottery has been discovered at many sanctuary sites throughout Greece – Nemea, Kalapodi, Olympia and Sane, to mention a few examples.[10] Another suggestion is that the small scale of the object demanded closer scrutiny compared to a larger object and, as Ekroth framed it, miniature pottery therefore expressed a more personal mode of dedication.[11]

Exactly how the miniature pottery was used in the rituals is still debated, but some miniature bowls from Corinth, the Argive Heraion, Tiryns and Tegea, for instance, have suspension holes near the rim, indicating that they could be hung, perhaps in the temple/ritual buildings within a sanctuary, or on a nearby tree or bush.[12] It is also possible that the suspension holes were used to attach one or two miniatures to one's belt when travelling, or perhaps for exhibition in suspension at sales booths (in the sanctuary). Miniature pottery is also found on and next to altars at Kalapodi, Nemea and the Artemis Altar in the Sanctuary of Zeus in Olympia, and must therefore have been used in the rituals performed around the altar.[13]

5   Gimatzidis 2011, 85-6; Kiernan 2009, 1.

6   Waldstein et al. 1905, 96; Payne et al. 1962, 290.

7   E.g. Caskey and Amandry 1952, 211; Payne et al. 1962, 290; Dickens 1906-7, 172; Foley 1988, 76, 165; Strøm 2009, 84-5.

8   Sparkes 1991, 78; see also Hammond (1998, 20) and Barfoed (2015b, 9-11, 44-55) for an evaluation of previous scholarship and terminology.

9   Ekroth 2003, 36.

10   Barfoed 2009; 2015a; Felsch & Jacob-Felsch 1996; Felsch et al. 1980; Gimatzidis 2011, 80-2.

11   Ekroth 2003, 36.

12   Hammond 1998, 218-9; Ekroth 2003, 36. For examples in Corinth see e.g. cat. nos 581, pl. 52, Pemberton et al. 1989, 176; and cat. nos 1916, 1923, 1927, 1936-7, pl. 71, Stillwell & Benson 1984, 328-30.

13   Felsch et al. 1980, 89-99, figs 71-89; Birge et al. 26, fig. 35; Heiden 2012.

Another interpretation is that miniature pottery served a commemorative function in rituals.[14] Miniature vessels may, for instance, be seen as commemorating ritual dining events when miniature cups and kraters are present – shapes that in a regular size are connected to dining. Thus, miniature pottery can be perceived to epitomize, in a dynamic manner, a ritual action in regular size.[15] Additionally, it must be kept in mind that despite the miniatures' sometimes very small size, the vessels were often still capable of containing a small quantity of offerings, for instance liquids that could be used for a 'mini' libation in the rituals.[16] Lastly, Gina Salapata has introduced the idea of votives being dedicated in sets, an idea that is certainly also applicable to miniature pottery.[17] One can imagine these small votives being piled up on the altar; perhaps some people dedicated them in sets for greater impact, believing that quantitative dedications mattered.

The precise definition of 'miniature pottery' remains to be firmly established.[18] Elizabeth G. Pemberton was probably the first to suggest an accurate definition in her publication of the Vrysoula deposit in Corinth from 1970. She states that miniatures are: "vases which reproduce a shape in reduced size without the original function, to serve as votive or funerary offerings".[19] Pemberton's definition is very applicable and also includes consideration of the function of miniatures. However, it must be kept in mind that miniatures other than scaled down models do exist; some miniatures do not have regular-sized equivalents.[20] One example is a miniature bowl with female protomes dating to the Archaic period which has been found exclusively in the Argolid.[21] Most common, however, are miniature vessels with a regular-sized pottery counterpart. The small size of the miniature pottery and the fact that it

is sometimes found in children's graves have occasionally led to the conclusion that it was a children's toy. However, since this type of pottery is so extensively found in sanctuary contexts, and is also common in adult graves in, for instance, the North Cemetery at Corinth, it must have been deemed suitable for both funerary and dedicatory purposes, and could not exclusively have been the property of children.[22] Lastly, the definition of the votive offering is important to keep in mind when discussing miniatures. Votives can be defined as objects removed from the secular world, e.g. when they are found in funerary and/or ritual deposits.[23] Alternatively, they may be produced specifically for dedications; this category includes terracotta figurines and, in some cases, such as the discussion presented below, miniature pottery.[24]

Research history of the miniature pottery from Kalydon

The research history of Kalydon's miniature pottery is relatively short. Elizabeth Bollen, who published most of the ceramic finds from the 2001-5 excavations in 2011, also worked with the miniature pottery.[25] She presented the miniature pottery in a separate chapter, and 35 complete and fragmented vessels of different shapes were included in the publication (6 of them represented with drawings).[26] Photos of the miniature pottery were presented together with the remaining (regular-sized) pottery in the main pottery catalogue, containing the pottery from the Central Acropolis (11 photos in total).[27] Bollen showed that most miniatures were found in Area XI on the Central Acropolis. She also analysed the fabric and placed the prevailing part of the miniature pottery in two Archaic

---

14 Barfoed 2015a.
15 Barfoed 2015b, 56-9; Foxhall 2013, 151.
16 Barfoed 2015a, 174, 183-4.
17 Salapata 2011; Ekroth 2003, 36.
18 Barfoed 2015a, 9-11; Kiernan 2009, 1-2; Hammond 1998, 14-22.
19 Pemberton 1970, 293, n. 49.
20 Hammond 1998, 16; Ekroth 2013; Rice 1987, 452.
21 Ekroth 2013, fig. 7.
22 Barfoed 2015b, 9-11, 44-54; Luce 2011, 61; Blegen et al. 1964, 169-300.
23 Kiernan 2009, 1.
24 Osborne 2004, 2.
25 Bollen 2011b; 2011b.
26 Bollen 2011c, pl. 23.
27 Bollen 2011d, 455-518.

fabric groups, suggesting that some of the vessels were imported from Corinth.[28] Bollen does not provide any further interpretations related to the miniature pottery and how they were used in the rituals at Kalydon.

It is possible that miniature pottery was discovered in the early explorations of the city. The earliest organized excavations in Kalydon took place in 1926, 1928, 1932 and 1935 and were carried out by a Danish–Greek collaboration consisting of Frederik Poulsen (director of Ny Carlsberg Glyptotek from 1926-43), the archaeologist Konstantinos Rhomaios and the architect Ejnar Dyggve. Four publications appeared as a result of these Danish–Greek explorations at Kalydon: a preliminary publication; a publication of the architecture and some of the architectonical terracottas of the Artemis Laphria sanctuary; a publication of the architecture of the so-called Hellenistic Heroon (located c. 250 m east of the sanctuary); and Rhomaios' study of architectural terracottas and tiles from the Artemis sanctuary.[29] Poulsen was supposed to publish the pottery from the excavations in a separate volume, but did not finish the work before his death in 1950.[30] In a few instances pottery is mentioned in the publications, but no catalogue or depictions (drawings and/or photos) of the pottery was included.[31] The only exception is a rim fragment of an Attic column krater with an inscription to Artemis (see below). Furthermore, there is no mention of miniature pottery in any of the publications from the early excavations.[32] These publications have provided valuable information about the Artemis Laphria sanctuary and the Heroon, but the unfortunate circumstances of a missing pottery publication are part of the reason that Kalydonian and Aitolian pottery production is relatively unknown and unexplored, although the publication from 2011 is a valuable contribution.[33]

Fig. 2. *Rim fragment of Attic Column-Krater with Artemis inscription (after: Poulsen & Rhomaios 1927, fig. 3).*

The Cults of Kalydon

In the following section, the different cults in Kalydon will be presented and the votives (miniature pottery and figurines) will be used as an analytical tool in an attempt to enhance our knowledge of the different cults within and outside the city walls. I include solely the cults that are archaeologically attested, and none of the as-yet unidentified cults mentioned in inscriptions and literary sources.[34] The examination will be done chronologically, thus the starting point is the most ancient cult we know of in Kalydon, the cult of Artemis Laphria.

The extra-mural sanctuary of Artemis Laphria

The goddess Artemis Laphria is attested in inscriptions, as well as Pausanias' later account. One example of a preserved inscription is the graffito on the Attic column-krater rim fragment previously mentioned. It was found south of the Artemis Laphria temple, and carries a dedication to Artemis that Poulsen and Rhomaios dated to the 5th century BC on the basis of the style of the incised letters: [ΑΡΤΕ]ΜΙΔΟΣ ΗΙΑΡΟΣ (Fig. 2).[35]

---

28   Bollen 2011c, 355.

29   Poulsen & Rhomaios 1927; Poulsen et al. 1934; Dyggve & Poulsen 1948; Rhomaios 1951.

30   Dyggve & Poulsen 1948, 2.

31   A rhyton, a fragment of a Corinthian pinakion and a base fragment of a terra sigillata vase with an inscription are mentioned as "die wichtigeren Keramik" in a footnote, Poulsen & Rhomaios 1927, 43 n. 1. Additionally, "Roman lamps and coins" are said to have been found in the Artemis Laphria sanctuary, Poulsen & Rhomaios 1927, 42-3.

32   Poulsen & Rhomaios 1927, fig. 3; Dyggve & Poulsen 1948, fig. 308.

33   Permission to study the pottery and terracotta figurines from the Artemis Laphria sanctuary, which are being kept in the National Archaeological Museum, Athens, has recently been obtained by the author. I am very grateful to the Greek Ministry of Culture and Sport and the Ephorate of Antiquities of Aetolia-Acarnania and Lefkada, as well as my collaborators in the National Archaeological Museum of Athens for being very accommodating, and for kindly granting me the permission.

34   For instance, Strabo mentioned a sanctuary to Apollo in Kalydon that remains to be discovered, Strabo, 10.22.

35   Poulsen & Rhomaios 1927, 9, fig. 3.

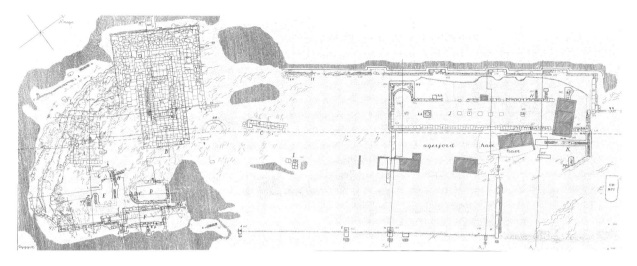

Fig. 3. *Plan of the Artemis Laphria sanctuary (after: Dyggve & Poulsen 1948, pl. 1; reproduced with courtesy of the Royal Danish Academy of Sciences and Letters).*

Poulsen and Rhomaios also described an unpublished inscription on stone mentioning Artemis Laphria:]ΑΠΕΔΟΤΟ ΑΓΕΜΑΧΑ...]ΤΑΙ ΑΡΤΕΜΙΤΙ ΤΑΙ ΛΑΦΡΙΑΙ[...]ΣΤΕΦΑΝΟΥΤΩ ΔΕ ΦΙΛΙΝΟΣ ΤΑΝ ΕΙΚΟΝΑ ΤΑΝ ΑΝΔΡΟΝΙΚΟΥ ΤΑΝ ΕΝ ΤΟΙ ΛΑΦΡΙΑΙΟΙ[. It was found built into the stone altar of a church in the nearby village of Old-Bochori.[36] Poulsen and Rhomaios stated that the inscription was transferred to the museum in Thermos.[37] Despite the inscription not being found in situ, it most likely originated from the sanctuary. Concerning the ancient literary evidence, Homer mentions Kalydon and Artemis together, but does not specifically mention the epithet Laphria or any other specifics of her cult.[38] Pausanias is the only source to mention Artemis Laphria; he does so when he describes how the Emperor Augustus laid the land of Aitolia to waste, and moved the population to his new city Nikopolis. At that time the people of Patras "secured the image of Laphria".[39]

The Artemis Laphria sanctuary includes a temple to Artemis (Temple B), a smaller temple, perhaps to Dionysus (Temple A), and several auxiliary buildings; one is a large stoa located along the processional road leading to the temples (designated 'J' on the plan, Fig. 3).[40] The earliest phase of the two temples can be dated to the 7th century BC. These early temples were presumably made of wood, and had painted terracotta roof tiles and decorated pediments.[41] The best preserved architectural terracotta is the famous Kalydon sphinx, now on display in the National Archaeological Museum in Athens.[42] Other remarkable examples are fragments of painted metopes with bordering dot rosettes and gorgons, and an example of a painted metope with a man and a wild boar, probably depicting the famous myth of the Kalydonian boar hunt.[43] The metopes have been compared to the extraordinary painted metopes from the Apollo Sanctuary in Thermon (about 50 km NE of Kalydon), and it is interesting that the gorgon metope also finds parallels at the island of

---

36 Modern-day Evinochori, the village closest to the site of Kalydon.

37 Poulsen & Rhomaios 1927, 8-9.

38 Homer called Artemis "golden throned", χρυσόθρονος Ἄρτεμις, Homer, *Il.* 9.530-5; Dyggve & Poulsen 1948, 336.

39 Paus. 7.18.8-13 and 4.31.7; Dietz 2009.

40 The suggestion of Dionysus is mainly based on Pausanias, see Paus. 7.21.1; a boundary stone dating to the 6th century BCE attests to the undiscovered sanctuary of Apollo Laphrios, see Dyggve & Poulsen 1948, 295-7, fig. 296; Freitag et al. 2004, 384.

41 Dyggve & Poulsen 1948, 138-212.

42 Dyggve & Poulsen 1948, 176-84, figs 182-5, 191-3, pls 22-3.

43 Dyggve & Poulsen 1948, 152-6, 160-1, fig. 164; Barringer 2001, 147-61.

135

Fig. 4. *'Artemis' terracotta figurine from the Artemis Laphria sanctuary, Kalydon (after: Dyggve & Poulsen 1948, 342, fig. 310; reproduced with courtesy of the Royal Danish Academy of Sciences and Letters).*

Kerkyra, in the Mon Repos sanctuary to Hera.[44] It is particularly interesting to note that Dyggve and Poulsen believed that a close connection to Corinth could be observed in the architectonical terracottas.[45] Temple A, possibly dedicated to Dionysus, has been reconstructed with a central running gorgon akroterion on its roof surrounded by lions, which Dyggve and Poulsen believed were also imported Corinthian terracottas. The architectural terracottas suggest a date in the early 6th century BC.[46] The first monumental temple to Artemis (Temple B) was enlarged in the 4th century BC to have 6 x 13 columns and a marble roof.[47] According to Pausanias, a chryselephantine statue of the huntress Artemis was on display inside the temple, but later the cult statue was moved to Patras.[48]

As mentioned above, miniature pottery is not referenced in the publications from the excavations of the sanctuary of Artemis Laphria and the Heroon. However, there is some comment on another type of votive: figurines in both terracotta and metal. Terracotta figurines depicting a standing female holding a bow and a deer are mentioned to be "zahlreiche" and interpreted as representing Artemis in her role as huntress (Fig. 4).[49]

Females carrying hydriai or kana (trays; the so-called hydrophoren and kanephoren terracotta figurines) were also found, as well as terracotta animal figurines of lions, deer, horses, bulls, pigs, doves and even an example of a grasshopper.[50] Additionally, numerous terracotta protomes depicting women are known from the sanctuary and Dyggve and Poulsen stated that these could have been "for hanging on walls". Terracotta apples, a pomegranate and two fragmented figurines of naked females, one with a swollen abdomen, were also found.[51] The fruit cannot be so easily explained but the terracotta figurines and protomes show the cult's emphasis on women. Some of the metal votives mentioned in the publications are on display at the National Archaeological Museum in Athens, including bronze figurines of a deer, goats and a cock, as well as some bronze fittings, probably for a wooden box.[52] In the publications fibulae, iron spear- and arrowheads are also briefly mentioned.[53] Other interesting votives are antlers, and teeth of boar and horses.[54] Despite the lack of a full publication, based on the existing publications, a preference for objects related to a cult of both women and hunting seems to prevail in the votives, which is indeed very suitable for Artemis, the huntress. The stoa northeast of the Artemis temple might have housed stalls for selling votives for dedication in the sanctuary, so the visitors did not need to bring dedications with them.[55] A deposit dating to the 3rd century BC from Corinth attests

---

44 Sapirstein 2012, 50.

45 Dyggve & Poulsen 1948, 201-2; Antonetti 1990, 253.

46 Dyggve & Poulsen 1948, 222-5.

47 Dyggve & Poulsen 1948, 123-34, for the marble tiles, see fig. 145; Rathje & Lund 1991, 40.

48 Paus. 7.18.9.

49 Dyggve & Poulsen 1948, 342, fig. 310.

50 Dyggve & Poulsen 1948, 344-5, 48.

51 Dyggve & Poulsen 1948, 345-8, figs 316-7.

52 Dyggve & Poulsen 1948, 344-5, figs 313-5. The metals are on display in the National Archaeological Museum in Athens' bronze collection, in a case named 'Aitolian Sanctuaries'.

53 Poulsen & Rhomaios 1927, 43; Dyggve & Poulsen 1948, 345.

54 Dyggve & Poulsen 1948, 344-5.

55 Brandt 2012, 172; Bookidis & Stroud 1997, 201, 214.

to the practice of buying figurines at the South Stoa for dedications at the Demeter and Kore sanctuary.[56] Albeit publication of such deposits are rare, when stoas are found in sanctuaries they may have served as a convenient place to sell votives and other goods that the visitors/dedicators needed. When comparing the votives from the Artemis Laphria sanctuary to the votives from the Central Acropolis, some similarities in the preference for certain votive objects can be seen.

The Archaic shrine on the Central Acropolis

During the years 2002-4, excavations on the Central Acropolis (Areas X–XIII) yielded the remains of a possible shrine. A concentration of figurines and miniature pottery, predominantly coming from a votive deposit in the southern part of Area XI, attests to a late Archaic shrine located where the later Hellenistic wall foundations can be seen today (Fig. 5).[57] Through an examination of the pottery from the deposit which is kept in the excavation storerooms, many more fragments or complete examples of miniature pottery have been identified: in total 213 unpublished examples can be added to the 35 published examples (amounting to 248 in total). A large amount of the miniature pottery is of Corinthian production, which can be related to the possible Corinthian architectural terracottas from the Artemis Laphria sanctuary mentioned above. This presence of Corinthian miniature pottery and other Corinthian votives such as terracotta figurines can perhaps be explained by the ease of shipment by sea. Transporting vessels (and other items and goods) over long distances was not difficult, but it is noteworthy that such a large amount of Corinthian miniature pottery ended up in Kalydon. The remaining miniature pottery could not be assigned to any known production centre and it is therefore possible that it was locally produced in either Kalydon or elsewhere in the region. Both tile and pottery kilns have been attested in the city of Kalydon, thus it is possible that the locally produced miniature pottery was made within the city.[58]

Cups dominate the assemblage of miniature pottery in Kalydon: they comprise 152 out of 248 registered ex-

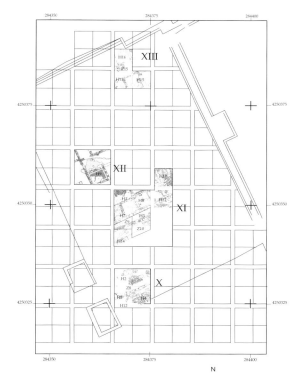

Fig. 5. *Plan of the Central Acropolis, Area XI (after: Dietz 2011e, 214, fig. 146; reproduced with courtesy of Aarhus University Press).*

amples (Table 1). This count includes kotylai, skyphoi and kanthariskoi. The second largest shape group consists of krateriskoi with 49 examples (Fig. 6a), and the third largest shape group is bowls with 15 examples (Fig. 6c). Other shape groups are jugs, saucers, phialai, pyxis and a single exaleiptron (Fig. 6d–e). Only one miniature hydria fragment has so far been registered (Fig. 6b).

Regarding the fabric, 112 examples are Corinthian and 125 are of presumed local manufacture (10 unknown and one possible Elean). The Corinthian and local clays can be difficult to discern from one another; a very light, slightly pinkish fabric is especially difficult to distinguish from Corinthian at first. However, Corinthian fabrics can have small black inclusions, whereas the possible local "Kaly-

---

56 Merker 2000, 326.
57 Dietz 2011f, 239-40. For the general stratigraphy of the excavated areas, see Dietz 2011b, 87-109; 2011e, 213-36.
58 Ljung 2011, 157-209.

Shapes	Amount	%
Cups (kotyle/skyphos/ kanthariskos)	152	61%
Krateriskoi	49	20%
Bowls	15	6%
Jugs	10	4%
Saucers	8	3%
Phialai	6	3%
Hydria	1	< 1%
Pyxis	1	< 1%
Exaleiptron	1	< 1%
Open vessel	1	< 1%
Closed vessel	1	< 1%
Unknown	3	1.5%
Total	**248**	**100%**

Table 1. *Shape distribution of published and unpublished miniature vessels from Kalydon.*

donian" fabric has some small white or reddish inclusions and often has the Munsell colour 10YR 7/4 (very pale brown) or 7.5YR 7/4 (pink). Despite the similar fabric, many examples stand out as certainly being Corinthian imports, which is interesting in that Corinthian regular-sized pottery was not found in large amounts at Kalydon. Most regular sized pottery is locally (or regionally) produced; Corinthian samples amount to just eight entries in the recent Kalydon publication, Attic to 11 entries, and Elean to two entries out of the 461 catalogue entries.[59] Overall, Corinth dominates the imports compared to Attic, Lakonian, Elean and pottery from other known production centres, which might explain the presence of the Corinthian miniatures, and no Attic miniatures have been found in Kalydon so far. However, Athens did not have the same extensive production of miniature pottery, at least not in the Archaic period, a fact that might explain the absence of these vessels (Chart 1).[60]

It is possible that the Corinthian votives were a source of inspiration for the Kalydonian votive production. This seems the most likely interpretation given the strong presence of Corinthian votives in Kalydon, but it is also possible that the preference for miniatures was related to the

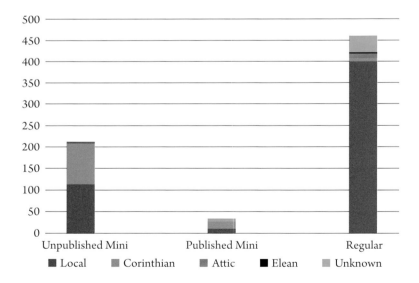

Table 2. *Published and unpublished miniatures and published regular-sized pottery from Kalydon by fabric group.*

---

59 Numbers are based on the catalogue in Bollen 2011b, 313-33.

60 From the Athenian Agora miniature pottery votives are mostly found in 4th- and 3rd-century BCE contexts, Sparkes & Talcott 1970, 185-6; Rotroff 1997, 206-10.

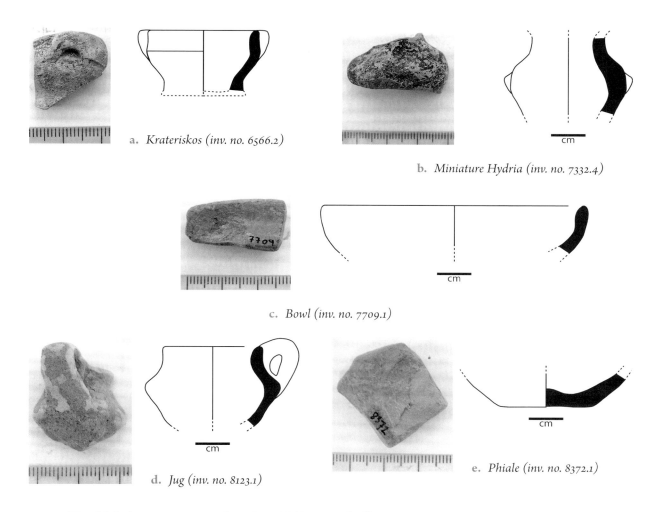

a. *Krateriskos (inv. no. 6566.2)*

b. *Miniature Hydria (inv. no. 7332.4)*

c. *Bowl (inv. no. 7709.1)*

d. *Jug (inv. no. 8123.1)*

e. *Phiale (inv. no. 8372.1)*

Fig. 6. *Unpublished miniature pottery from Area XI (Signe Barfoed).*

rituals themselves. Many of the Kalydonian miniatures are indeed very small, but the open shapes (e.g. cups, krateriskoi and bowls) could certainly still have contained a tiny offering, such as seeds, a lock of hair or incense or liquids. The closed shapes like the jugs and hydriai could have held a tiny portion of scented oil or other liquids for a 'mini' libation.

The Corinthian miniature pottery shape repertoire differs from the regular-sized Corinthian pottery. The total Corinthian miniature shape distribution (both published and unpublished miniatures) is dominated by cups at 68%, krateriskoi are at 25% and there is a large jump down to number three, jugs, at just 2%. The remaining shape groups (phiale, bowls, saucers, hydria, open vessel) constitute 1% each. The shape distribution of the sparse Corinthian regular-sized vessels in (all of) Kalydon, amounting to eight catalogue entries, consists of kotylai (two examples) and oinochoai (also two examples). Other shapes are an aryballos, an echinus bowl, a pyxis and a fragment of an undetermined shape.[61] The most popular miniature cup type is the kotyle. It has a flat base, two horizontal handles, typically with vertical black bands in the handle zones, and broader horizontal bands on the lower body (Fig. 7). However, a marked difference is that in Kalydon regular-sized kraters (of any production) are not as popular as the miniature kraters. It appears

---

61   All of the Corinthian pottery has been determined as belonging to the fabric group called 'AR1', Bollen 2011b, 338. The Corinthian pottery is not separated in the publication. The Corinthian regular-sized fragments have the following cat. nos: 224, 232, 234, 247, 254, 268, 318 and 437, see Bollen 2011d, 459-60, 462, 464, 470, 472, 481, 504.

139

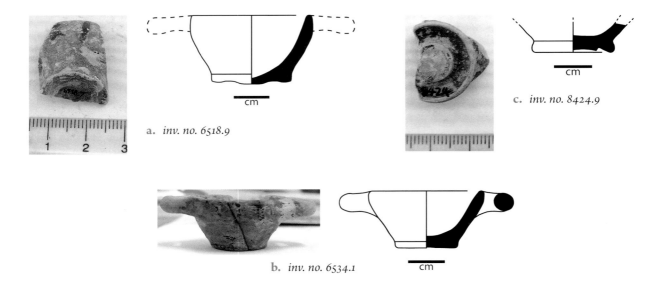

a. *inv. no. 6518.9*

c. *inv. no. 8424.9*

b. *inv. no. 6534.1*

Fig. 7a, b, c. *Unpublished miniature kotylai from Area XI (Signe Barfoed).*

that there was a form of conspicuous consumption of Corinthian miniature vessels, since the substantial interest in miniature cups is not reflected in the regular-sized Corinthian pottery.

Apart from miniature pottery, fragments of terracotta figurines were also found in Kalydon. Area XI on the Central Acropolis yielded 53 examples of females, children and animals.[62] Especially interesting are the several examples of the Corinthian 'standing kore' type, which dates to the early 5th century BC. This type of mould-made terracotta figurine is especially common in Corinth, but most of the examples from Kalydon appear to be locally produced (Fig. 8).[63]

Gloria Merker suggested that the figurine represents either Aphrodite or Kore, and that it is a lingering Archaic type, which is a convincing interpretation.[64] In addition to the Corinthian miniature pottery, these terracotta figurines emphasize the connection between Corinth and Kalydon. This type of mould-made figurine was a standing female wearing a *peplos* and a *polos* on her head.

The goddess is typically standing on some sort of platform and holds different objects in her hands: fruits or flowers.[65] A similar type of standing female carrying a bow on one arm was found in the Laphria excavations, commonly interpreted as representing Artemis the huntress (see above).[66] As mentioned above, the number of examples they recovered in the excavations is unclear. Poulsen suggested they were of Corinthian production.[67] This type is especially popular in Kalydon and was also locally produced (imitated) as mentioned above.

This type of figurine does not necessarily represent a specific goddess, but seems to be a generic type that could have been dedicated to various female deities, an idea also emphasized by Bollen.[68] A characteristic seated female type figurine found throughout the northeast Peloponnese mirrors this idea. The type appears to have been a selected dedication for Hera, but at a time during the late Archaic period began to be used in sanctuaries to other deities.[69] Additionally, Merker argues that by the Classical period the 'standing kore' type of figurine de-

---

62   Mayerhofer Hemmi & Dietz 2011, 531-43.

63   Mayerhofer Hemmi & Dietz 2011, 531.

64   Merker 2000, 23-37, 326.

65   Mayerhofer Hemmi & Dietz 2011, 530-5.

66   Dyggve & Poulsen 1948, 342, fig. 310.

67   Dyggve & Poulsen 1948, 343.

68   Mayerhofer Hemmi & Dietz 2011, 530-1; Barfoed 2013.

69   Barfoed 2013, 97-100.

Fig. 8. *Terracotta figurine of 'the Standing Kore' type, from Area XI (after: Mayerhofer Hemmi & Dietz 2011, no. 26, 529, fig. 264).*

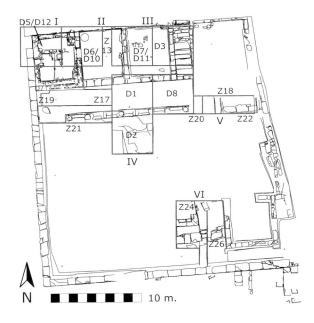

Fig. 9. *Plan of the Peristyle House, Kalydon (after: Dietz 2011b, 86, fig. 56).*

picted mortal subjects and represented votaries carrying offerings to the goddess.[70]

Other types of figurines were found in Area XI, for instance the very popular type of Classical Corinthian figurine recognized by its hairstyle, called 'melon-coiffure'. This type dates to the 4th century BC.[71] Moreover, Hellenistic terracotta figurines were discovered in Area XI. Dating to the late 3rd century BC, or a little later, are two female terracotta heads depicting a veiled lady.[72] An example of a female terracotta figurine head with the so-called 'Knidian' hairstyle dates to the 3rd century BC.[73] Four fragmented pieces of terracotta figurines have also been roughly dated to the Hellenistic period. The latest published examples of terracotta figurines from Kalydon's Area XI are thus from the late 3rd century BC.[74] Metal votive offerings from the 2001-5 excavations, such as figurines, pins and jewellery, were not found in great numbers, and only two bronze figurines are published: a bird

and the head of a wolf.[75] The sparse metal objects do not add much to our interpretations.

To summarize, no inscriptions or graffiti/dipinti attest to the name of the deity of the Archaic-Classical shrine on the Central Acropolis. As Dietz stated, the deposit and the architectural terracottas support the idea of a shrine in the area.[76] The suggestion that the shrine was for a female deity is mainly based on the presence of the many female terracotta figurines. Some of the 'standing kore' figurines are similar to the examples from the Artemis Laphria sanctuary discussed above, some are Corinthian and some are presumably local imitations. Similarly, the miniature pottery was both imported and imitated at the presumed local/regional (Kalydonian?) production centre. It is possible that further excavation in the area may clarify the situation in Area XI, but the architectural remains from the Hellenistic period would in that case have to be removed, which would be difficult.

---

70 Merker 2000, 24.

71 E.g. nos H215-H228, Merker 2000, 163-6, pl. 43.

72 Mayerhofer Hemmi & Dietz 2011, 537, cat. nos 46-7, fig. 266.

73 Mayerhofer Hemmi & Dietz 2011, 537-8, cat. nos 52, 54, 64-6, fig. 267-8.

74 Mayerhofer Hemmi & Dietz 2011, 530-45.

75 Mayerhofer Hemmi & Dietz 2011, 545, cat. nos 76-7, fig. 269.

76 Dietz 2011f, 240.

141

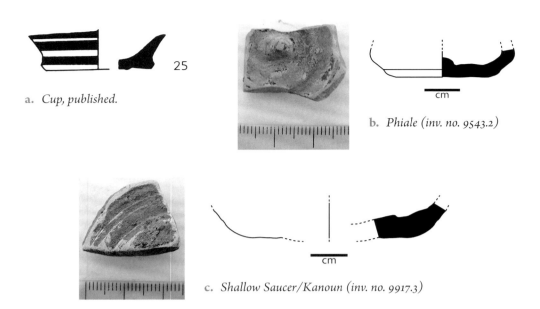

a. *Cup, published.*

b. *Phiale (inv. no. 9543.2)*

c. *Shallow Saucer/Kanoun (inv. no. 9917.3)*

Fig. 10. *Miniature pottery from the Peristyle House, Kalydon: a: miniature cup (published; after: Bollen 2011b, 356, no. 25, pl. 23; reproduced with courtesy of Aarhus University Press); b-c: phiale, and shallow bowl/kanoun (unpublished) (Signe Barfoed).*

Kybele and Artemis in the Peristyle House in the Lower Town

The excavation in 2003-5 in the Lower Town revealed a Hellenistic-Roman peristyle house destroyed sometime in the course of the 1st century BC (Fig. 9).[77] The house consists of six rooms with plastered walls, and a stylobate with traces of a pebble floor.[78] In the different rooms of the house significant discoveries were made, for instance, of a larger than life-size acrolith statue of Kybele. A herm, a small altar, and a reused sundial are also notable finds, as well as a fragmented marble offering-table.[79] Additionally, there was a small inscribed altar with Artemis' name dating to the 2nd century BC found in the so-called 'cult room' (Room 1).[80] Dietz suggested that, based on the mixed evidence of cults to both Kybele and Artemis and

the building's layout, the Peristyle House was a private and not public property, possibly a clubhouse.[81] Only four miniature vessels were found in the excavations of the Peristyle House: a cup (published, Fig. 10a),[82] a phiale, a shallow bowl or kanoun (unpublished, Fig. 10b–c)[83] and one additional unpublished miniature vessel of unknown (open) shape.[84] Some uncertainties exist about the date of the miniature pottery from the Peristyle House. The cup (Fig. 10a) was found in context DS2a/1 in Room 1, which, among other finds, yielded a kernos, a thin-walled pot in Hellenistic/Roman ware (no. 28), a plate with grooved rim (no. 24) and a lamp with red glaze (no. 29), all of which, according to the authors, can be dated to the Hellenistic period.[85] Even so, the particular decoration of reserved bands on the lower wall and in the central zone

---

77   Dietz 2011b, 85.

78   Dietz, Mayerhofer Hemmi & Lund Pedersen 2011, 111-25.

79   The offering table has the find number F03-2230.

80   See e.g. Dyggve & Poulsen 1948, 295-6, fig. 275; the altar was found in a public building inside the city walls, see Mejer 2009, 80-1.

81   Dietz 2011d, 153.

82   Bollen 2011c, no. 25, pl. 23.

83   Barfoed 2015b, 236-7, 241, nos KA45, KA59, pls 6, 8.

84   Bag. no. 9953. The open shape remains unpublished but was examined by the author in the storeroom.

85   Bollen & Eiring 2011, 400, 405-6, pl. 33.

of the underside the cup led the authors to date it to the Archaic period, and Bollen suggested that it should be regarded as a residual find that originally belonged to an Archaic deposit in a well that was found below the Hellenistic house.[86] The unpublished phiale and the shallow bowl/kanoun (Fig. 10b–c) were found in Room 3, in contexts that can be dated to the Hellenistic period on the basis of the pottery: two hemiobols of the Aitolian League dating to 220-205 BC and a tribol of the Achaean League dating to the 2nd century BC.[87] The last miniature vessels found in the Peristyle House (the unpublished miniature vessels of an open shape) was found in context DS5/5, also in Room 3, which contained pottery from the Classical-Roman period, and a coin, hemiobol, of the Aitolian League dating to 220-205 BC. Thus, based on this contextual reevaluation, it appears that at least three of the four miniature vessels from the Peristyle House can securely be dated to the Hellenistic period.

When comparing the miniatures from the Peristyle House to the assemblage on the Central Acropolis, there is certainly not a large amount. The scarcity of miniature vessels in the Peristyle House compared to the Central Acropolis area may be explained by the chronological distinction. In the Archaic and into the Classical period miniature pottery was a very popular type of dedication. In the Demeter and Kore Sanctuary at Acrocorinth the shift is especially clear; in the Archaic period miniature pottery was dedicated in the thousands, but this trend phased out in the 4th century BC, when terracotta figurines became the preferred dedication of choice.[88] In the Hellenistic period miniature pottery is no longer being dedicated in the sanctuary on Acrocorinth.[89]

In the Sanctuary of Artemis Limnatis in Kombothekra (in the region of Elis) a similar shift in dedicatory practices can be observed. The life of the sanctuary spans the Geometric to the Hellenistic period, and 113 restored examples of miniature pottery have been found dating to the Archaic-Classical period.[90] However, the shift seen in the assemblage from Kombothekra is most clearly seen in the type of figurines: in the Geometric period terracotta animal figurines were most popular (83 out of 117 examples); in the Archaic period it shifted to human figurines, mostly female terracotta figurines and protomes (26 out of 36 examples); the number went down again in the Classical period (16 examples, 14 female and 2 male figurines), and in the Hellenistic period mould-made bowls become the preferred dedication at the Artemis Limnatis sanctuary; finally, the production of terracotta figurines come to a halt and miniature pottery ceased to be dedicated at Kombothekra in the Hellenistic period.[91] Perhaps the scarcity of miniature pottery in the Peristyle House in Kalydon is due a general shift in dedicatory practice throughout Greece? At the time when the Peristyle House was in use the preferred votive offering was certainly not miniature pottery.

The six published terracotta figurines found in the 'cult room' are varied: one is an Eros playing a lyre, and four are fragments of females.[92] One example is a fragment of a hand holding a tympanon; based on a parallel from the Louvre of a terracotta figurine of a seated Kybele on a throne holding a patera and a tympanon, a date of c. 350 BC may be suggested.[93] Additional terracotta objects are: a fragment of a throne, a fragmented terracotta mask, and a fragment of a relief plate.[94] Furthermore, seven terracotta lamps and eight thymiateria were also discovered in the room, which also supports the idea of it being a 'cult room'.[95]

If the Peristyle House indeed was a clubhouse and a forum where the public and private spheres intermingled, then perhaps the civic setting meant that miniature pot-

---

86 Bollen 2011c, 355; Bollen & Eiring 2011, 406.

87 Contexts DS7/2, Z11 and DS5/4. For the Aitolian coins, see Alexopoulou & Sidiropoulos 2011, no. 7, 551-2, pl. 54 and no. 53, 556-7, pl. 56; for the Achaean coin, see Alexopoulou & Sidiropoulos 2011, no. 6, 551, pl. 54.

88 Merker 2000, 3.

89 Edwards 1975, 2.

90 Unpublished, but see Barfoed 2015b, 101-1.

91 Barfoed 2015b, 81-3; Sinn 1981, 64-9; Gregarek 1998, 76, 100-1.

92 Mayerhofer Hemmi & Dietz 2011, 521-4, cat. nos 1, 2, 5-7.

93 Mayerhofer Hemmi & Dietz 2011, 524-6, cat. no. 10. Musée du Louvre, Accession Number: CA 1797.

94 Mayerhofer Hemmi & Dietz 2011, 524-6, cat. nos 8, 9 and 11.

95 Dietz 2011c, 134.

tery and terracotta figurines were not suitable offerings. A cult room in a clubhouse must have been intended to impress its visitors, and the civic nature of the cult perhaps called for a different dedicatory behaviour. A similar idea is expressed regarding the civic nature of the Pan-Hellenic cult at Olympia, where very few miniature vessels were found compared to metal offerings of weaponry and figurines.[96] It is likely that the preferences seen for certain votive offerings is a combination of the Peristyle House's civic nature and the fact that in the Hellenistic period dedicatory patterns had changed since the Archaic-Classical period.

Concluding Remarks

The aim of this article has been two-fold: to cast further light on the cults in Kalydon and to discuss the miniaturised votives in the hope of expanding our knowledge of Kalydonian cult and ritual behaviour. In sum, three sanctuary sites have been identified in the ancient city of Kalydon: the extramural sanctuary of Artemis Laphria, which was in use from the Geometric to the Roman period; the Archaic-Classical shrine to a female goddess at the Central Acropolis; and a 'cult room' in the Peristyle House in the Lower Town, where both Kybele and Artemis were worshipped during the Hellenistic period.

The votives showed that rituals connected to women and hunting were the focus of the main sanctuary in the city, that of Artemis Laphria. It is possible that the miniature pottery from the Central Acropolis was meant to commemorate ritual dining in or near the shrine, or had an active role in the rituals devoted to a female deity. Additionally, the idea that miniature pottery was suitable for trade is supported by the large amount of Corinthian miniature pottery from the Central Acropolis. A shift in dedicatory practice seen elsewhere in the Greek world

can also been seen in Kalydon: first in the Archaic period, when the popularity of miniature pottery votives appears to have been connected to a greater influx of dedications made by the 'common' people; and second in the Hellenistic period, when miniature pottery was no longer the preferred votive as it was in the Archaic period, following the patterns seen at sites in the northern Peloponnese. The fact that around half of all the miniature vessels found in Kalydon are Corinthian imports suggests that there were close ties to Corinth. Such close ties are furthermore traceable in the import and imitation of Corinthian terracotta figurines, a trend that continued after the disappearance of the miniature pottery.

The tentative interpretations presented here have also intended to prove that miniature pottery is an important material group that can be used to differentiate between different religious practices, and should therefore not be overlooked. This material can occasionally provide new interpretations, especially in contextual and comparative analyses, which in this case show us that religious practice in Kalydon can more easily be compared to that at Corinth than was previously believed. Future studies and publications of the Hellenistic theatre and the excavations on the Lower Acropolis will without doubt cast further light on Kalydon's cultural history, and add to the tentative interpretations presented in this article.

SIGNE BARFOED
Honorary Research Fellow
University of Kent
School of European Culture and Languages
Department of Classical & Archaeological Studies
Canterbury, Kent, CT2 7NF
United Kingdom
sb711@kentforlife.net / barfoed.signe@gmail.com

96 Barfoed 2015a.

Bibliography

Alexopoulou, G. & K. Sidiropoulos 2011
'The Coins', in *Kalydon in Aitolia I. Reports and Studies: Danish/Greek fieldwork 2001-2005*, S. Dietz & M. Stavropoulou-Gatsi (eds), Aarhus, 549-78.

Antonetti, C. 1990
Les Etoliens: image et religion, Paris.

Barfoed, S. 2015a
'The Significant Few. Miniature Pottery from the Sanctuary of Zeus at Olympia', *WorldArch* 47, 170-88.

Barfoed, S. 2015b
Cult in context. The ritual significance of miniature pottery votives in ancient Greek sanctuaries from the Archaic to the Hellenistic period, PhD Dissertation, University of Kent, Canterbury.

Barfoed, S. 2013
'The Mystery of the Seated Goddess – Archaic Terracotta Figurines of the North-Eastern Peloponnese', in *Vessels and variety. New aspects of Danish research in Ancient pottery* (Acta Hyperborea 13), K. Bøggild Johannsen, A. Rathje & H. Thomasen (eds), Copenhagen, 85-105.

Barfoed, S. 2009
An Archaic votive deposit from Nemea – ritual behavior in a sacred landscape, MA Thesis, University of Cincinnati.

Barringer, J. M. 2001
The hunt in ancient Greece, Baltimore.

Biers, W. R. 1971
'Excavations at Phlius, 1924, the Votive Deposit', *Hesperia: The Journal of the American School of Classical Studies at Athens* 40, 397-423.

Birge, D. E., L. H. Kraynak, & S. G. Miller 1992
Excavations at Nemea, Volume 1. Topographical and architectural studies: the sacred square, the xenon and the bath, Berkeley.

Blegen, C. W., H. Palmer, & R.S. Young 1964
Corinth 13, The North Cemetery, Princeton, NJ.

Bollen, E. 2011a
'The Kiln Pottery', in *Kalydon in Aitolia I. Reports and Studies: Danish/Greek fieldwork 2001-2005*, S. Dietz & M. Stavropoulou-Gatsi (eds), Aarhus, 199-200.

Bollen, E. 2011b
'The Pottery of Kalydon', in *Kalydon in Aitolia I, Reports and Studies: Danish/Greek fieldwork 2001-2005*, S. Dietz & M. Stavropoulou-Gatsi (eds), Aarhus, 313-48.

Bollen, E. 2011c
'Miniature Vessels of Kalydon' in *Kalydon in Aitolia I. Reports and Studies: Danish/Greek fieldwork 2001-2005*, S. Dietz & M. Stavropoulou-Gatsi (eds), Aarhus, 355-7.

Bollen, E. 2011d
'Pottery, Lamps and Miniatures from the Central Acropolis', in *Kalydon in Aitolia I, Reports and Studies: Danish/Greek fieldwork 2001-2005*, S. Dietz & M. Stavropoulou-Gatsi (eds), Aarhus, 455-518.

Bollen, E. & J. Eiring 2011
'Pottery, Lamps and Thymiateria from the Lower Town', in *Kalydon in Aitolia I, Reports and Studies: Danish/Greek fieldwork 2001-2005*, S. Dietz & M. Stavropoulou-Gatsi (eds), Aarhus, 399-453.

Bookidis, N. & R. S. Stroud 1997
Corinth 18, 3 *The Sanctuary of Demeter and Kore: Topography and Architecture*, Princeton, NJ.

Caskey, J. L. & P. Amandry 1952
'Investigations at the Heraion of Argos, 1949', *Hesperia: The Journal of the American School of Classical Studies at Athens* 21, 165-221.

Dickens, G. 1906-07
'Laconia I. Excavations at Sparta, 1907. § 9. A Sanctuary on the Megalopolis Road', *BSA* 13, 169-73.

Dietz, S. 2009
'Kalydon and Pausanias', *PoDIA* 6, 217-221.

Dietz, S. 2011a
'The city – inside and outside the walls', in *Kalydon in Aitolia I. Reports and Studies: Danish/Greek fieldwork 2001-2005*, S. Dietz & M. Stavropoulou-Gatsi (eds), Aarhus, 77-81.

Dietz, S. 2011b
'General stratigraphy', in *Kalydon in Aitolia I. Reports and Studies: Danish/Greek fieldwork 2001-2005*, S. Dietz & M. Stavropoulou-Gatsi (eds), Aarhus, 85-109.

Dietz, S. 2011c
'The Cult-Room in its Context', in *Kalydon in Aitolia I. Reports and Studies: Danish/Greek fieldwork 2001-2005*, S. Dietz & M. Stavropoulou-Gatsi (eds), Aarhus, 133-6.

Dietz, S. 2011d
'The Peristyle Building – Function and Chronology,' in *Kalydon in Aitolia I. Reports and Studies: Danish/Greek fieldwork 2001-2005*, S. Dietz & M. Stavropoulou-Gatsi (eds), Aarhus, 153-6.

Dietz, S. 2011e
'General Stratigraphy', in *Kalydon in Aitolia I. Reports and Studies: Danish/Greek fieldwork 2001-2005*, S. Dietz & M. Stavropoulou-Gatsi (eds), Aarhus, 213-36.

Dietz, S. 2011f
'The Archaic and Classical Occupation on the Central Acropolis', in *Kalydon in Aitolia I. Reports and Studies: Danish/Greek fieldwork 2001-2005*, S. Dietz & M. Stavropoulou-Gatsi (eds), Aarhus, 239-40.

Dietz, S., S. Mayerhofer Hemmi & R. Lund Pedersen 2011
'Description of the Peristyle Building', in *Kalydon in Aitolia I. Reports and Studies: Danish/Greek fieldwork 2001-2005*, S. Dietz & M. Stavropoulou-Gatsi (eds), Aarhus, 111-25.

Dietz, S. & M. Stavropoulou-Gatsi 2011
Kalydon in Aitolia I-II. Reports and Studies: Danish/Greek fieldwork 2001-2005 (Monographs of the Danish institute at Athens 12.1-2), Aarhus.

Dyggve, E. & F. Poulsen 1948
Das Laphrion, der Tempelbezirk von Kalydon, Copenhagen.

Edwards, R. G. 1975
Corinth 7, 3 Corinthian Hellenistic Pottery, Princeton, NJ.

Ekroth, G. 2013
'Between Bronze and Clay. The Origin of an Argive, Archaic Votive Shape', in *Forgerons, élites et voyageurs d'Homère à nos jours. Hommages en mémoire d'Isabelle Ratinaud-Lachkar*, M.-C. Ferriès, M. P. Castiglioni & F. Létoublon (eds), Grenoble, 63-77.

Ekroth, G. 2003
'Small Pots, Poor People? The Use and Function of Miniature Pottery as Votive Offerings in Archaic Sanctuaries in the Argolid and the Corinthia', in *Griechische Keramik im kulturellen Kontext: Akten des Internationalen Vasen-Symposions in Kiel vom 24.-28.9.2001 veranstaltet durch das Archäologische Institut der Christian-Albrechts-Universität zu Kiel*, B. Schmaltz & M. Söldner (eds), Münster, 35-7.

Felsch, R. C. S. & M. Jacob-Felsch 1996
Kalapodi: Ergebnisse der Ausgrabungen im Heiligtum der Artemis und des Apollon von Hyampolis in der antiken Phokis, Mainz am Rhein.

Felsch, R. C. S., H. J. Kienast & H. Schuler 1980
'Apollon und Artemis oder Artemis und Apollon? Bericht von den Grabungen im neu entdecken Heiligtum bei Kalapodi, 1973-1977', *AA* 1980, 38-118.

Foley, A. 1988
The Argolid 800-600 B.C.: an archaeological survey, Gothenburg.

Foxhall, L. 2013
Studying gender in Classical Antiquity, Cambridge.

Freitag, K., P. Funke, & N. Moustakis 2004
'Aitolia', in *An inventory of Archaic and Classical poleis*, M. Herman Hansen & T. Heine Nielsen (eds), Oxford, 379-90.

Gimatzidis, S. 2011
'Feasting and Offering to the Gods in Early Greek Sanctuaries: Monumentalisation and Miniaturisation in Pottery', in *The Gods of Small Things* (Pallas 86), A. Smith & M. Bergeron (eds), Toulouse, 73-93.

Gregarek, H. 1998
'Das Heiligtum der Artemis Limnatis bei Kombothekra. IV. Die Terrakotten der archaischen und klassischen Zeit', *AM* 113, 75-102.

Hammond, L.A. 1998
The miniature votive vessels from the Sanctuary of Athena Alea at Tegea, Ph.D. dissertation, University of Missouri, Columbia.

Heiden, J. 2012
'Artemis-Altäre', in *Mythos Olympia: Kult und Spiele*, S. Bocher, H.-J. Gehrke, G. E. Hatzi, W.-D. Heilmeyer & N. E. Kaltsas (eds), Munich, 145-8.

Kiernan, P. 2009
Miniature Votive Offerings in the North-West Provinces of the Roman Empire. Wiesbaden, Rühpolding.

Ljung, E. 2011
'The Kiln. Excavations in Area VII', in *Kalydon in Aitolia I. Reports and Studies: Danish/Greek fieldwork 2001-2005*, S. Dietz & M. Stavropoulou-Gatsi (eds), Aarhus, 157-209.

Luce, J.-M. 2011
'From Miniature Objects to Giant Ones: The Process of Defunctional-isation in Sanctuaries and Graves in Iron Age Greece', in *The Gods of Small Things* (Pallas 86), A. Smith & M. Bergeron (eds), Toulouse, 53-74.

Mayerhofer Hemmi, S. & S. Dietz 2011
'Terracotta Figurines,' in *Kalydon in Aitolia I. Reports and Studies: Danish/Greek fieldwork 2001-2005*, S. Dietz & M. Stavropoulou-Gatsi (eds), Aarhus, 519-48.

Mejer, J. 2009
'A Note on a Dedication to Artemis in Kalydon', in *From Artemis to Diana: the goddess of man and beast*, T. Fischer-Hansen & B. Poulsen (eds), Copenhagen, 79-81.

Merker, G. S. 2000
Corinth, Vol. 18.4. *The Sanctuary of Demeter and Kore: terracotta figurines of the Classical, Hellenistic, and Roman periods*, Princeton, NJ.

Osborne, R. 2004
'Hoards, Votives, Offerings: The Archaeology of the Dedicated Object', *WorldArch* 36, 1-10.

Payne, H., T. J. Dunbabin & A. A. A. Blakeway 1962
Perachora 2, The sanctuaries of Hera Akraia and Limenia: excavations of the British School of Archaeology at Athens 1930-1933. Pottery, ivories, scarabs, and other objects from the votive deposit of Hera Limenia, Oxford.

Pemberton, E. G., K. W. Slane & C. K. Williams II 1989
Corinth 18, 1 The Sanctuary of Demeter and Kore: The Greek Pottery, Princeton, NJ.

Pemberton, E. G. 1970
'The Vrysoula Classical Deposit from Ancient Corinth', *Hesperia: The Journal of the American School of Classical Studies at Athens* 39, 26--307.

Poulsen, F. & K. A. Rhomaios 1927
Erster vorläufiger Bericht über die dänisch-griechischen Ausgrabungen von Kalydon, Copenhagen.

Poulsen, F., E. Dyggve & K. A. Rhomaios 1934
Das Heroon von Kalydon, Copenhagen.

Rathje, A. & J. Lund 1991
'Danes Overseas. A Short History of Danish Classical Archaeological Fieldwork', in *Recent Danish research in Classical Archaeology: tradition and renewal* (Acta Hyperborea 3), T. Fischer-Hansen (ed.), Copenhagen, 11-56.

Rhomaios, K. A. 1951
Keramoi tes Kalydonos. Symbole eis akribesteran theoresun tes hellenikes technes, Athens.

Rice, P. M. 1987
Pottery Analysis. A Sourcebook, Chicago.

Rotroff, S. I. 1997
The Athenian Agora 29, Hellenistic Pottery Athenian and Imported Wheel-made Table Ware and Related Material, Princeton, NJ.

Salapata, G. 2011
'The More the Better? Votive Offerings in Sets', *Australasian Society for Classical Studies Proceedings* 32, 1-10.

Sapirstein, P. 2012
'The Monumental Archaic Roof of the Temple of Hera at Mon Repos, Corfu', *Hesperia: The Journal of the American School of Classical Studies at Athens* (som feks Caskey & Amandry 1952) 81, 31-91.

Sinn, U. 1981
'Das Heiligtum der Artemis Limnatis bei Kombothekra. II. Der Kult', *AM* 96, 25-71.

Sparkes, B. A. 1991
Greek Pottery: an introduction, Manchester.

Sparkes, B. A. & L. Talcott 1970
The Athenian Agora 12, Black and Plain Pottery of the 6th, 5th and 4th Centuries B.C., Princeton, NJ.

Stillwell, A. N. & J. L. Benson 1984
Corinth 15, 3 The Potters' Quarter: The Pottery, Princeton, NJ.

Strøm, I. 2009
'The Early Sanctuary of the Argive Heraion and its External Relations (8th–early 6th century BC). Conclusions', *PoDIA* 6, 73-159.

147

Vikatou, O., R. Frederiksen & S. Handberg 2014
'The Danish–Greek Excavations at Kalydon, Aitolia. The Theatre: preliminary report from the 2011 and 2012 campaigns', *PoDIA* 7, 221-34.

Waldstein, C., G. H. Chase, H. Fletcher de Cou, T. W. Heermance, J. C. Hoppin, A. M. Lythgoe, R. Norton et al. 1905
The Argive Heraeum, Volume II. Terra-cotta figurines, terra-cotta reliefs, vases, vase fragments, bronzes, engraved stones, gems and ivories, coins, Egyptian or Graeco-Egyptian objects, Boston.

Colour shifts

On methodologies in research on the polychromy of Greek and Roman sculpture

JAN STUBBE ØSTERGAARD [1]

This article offers a partial overview of methodologies of research on the polychromy of Greek and Roman sculpture. The character of the evidence requires an interdisciplinary approach. This evidence is briefly presented, after which aspects of the actual investigation are considered, the section on analytical methods dealing only cursorily with invasive techniques. Attention is drawn to the importance of research-based experimental reconstruction of polychrome sculptures. Finally, some interdisciplinary research scenarios are described. The article is based on work done within the framework of the 'Tracking Colour' project of the Ny Carlsberg Glyptotek and the Copenhagen Polychromy Network, 2009-13, with the support of the Carlsberg Foundation.

Key words: Sculpture, Greek Sculpture, Roman Sculpture, Polychromy, Colour, Research Methodology, Experimental Reconstructions, Tracking Colour, Ny Carlsberg Glyptotek

The term 'colour shift' means 'a change in colour quality'. This concept is particularly, and dramatically, applicable to the case of colour on Greek and Roman sculptures as it originally appeared and as it is seen today: in fact, rather than having undergone a shift, their colours have in most cases almost entirely disappeared. In the title of this article, the 'shift' becomes a plural, in an attempt to indicate the complex character of the change which the polychromy of ancient sculpture has undergone. But, at the same time, the word also becomes a verb with the meaning 'to change position', reflecting the fact that the re-emergence of colour must fundamentally shift our approach to classical sculpture. That kind of shift is not the subject of this contribution; it deals rather with the means by which the shift may be brought about.

Interdisciplinary collaboration lies at the root of the present phase of research on polychromy, one which has been characterized as a "break-through phase".[2] Disciplines within the humanities, objects conservation, conservation science and the natural sciences have joined forces to become a *sine qua non* for future discoveries.

Writing about methodology with the ambition of reaching readers from the several disciplines involved is correspondingly challenging.[3] It is a particularly daunting task to write about the decisive contribution made by conservation science and the natural sciences in a way which is accessible to scholars from the humanities. Similarly – but requiring perhaps relatively less of an effort of 'translation' – the methodologies employed by the humanities must be described with due consideration of readers from the sciences. Promoting mutual understanding is perhaps the most important aim of this contribution.

1   Research curator, Ny Carlsberg Glyptotek. jso@glyptoteket.dk. The article is based on work done by a team in the Tracking Colour project (www.trackingcolour.com). The contribution made by project conservators Maria Louise Sargent, BA and MSc, and Rikke H. Therkildsen, BA and MSc, was vital; the support offered by external partners in the Copenhagen Polychromy Network is gratefully recognized. Generous grants from the Carlsberg Foundation made this research possible.
2   Østergaard 2010a, 86 – 7.
3   Briefly on methodology: Abbe 2015, 173-4.

We turn first to the factor which determines the need for an interdisciplinary approach, namely the character of the evidence.

The character of the evidence

Evidence of the polychromy of Greek and Roman sculpture is found in two fundamentally different classes of ancient sources: the written and the material.

Written evidence

The ancient written evidence is predominantly literary, and to a lesser extent epigraphical, i.e. provided by inscriptions. The literary evidence has survived thanks to the transmission of manuscripts; the earliest preserved manuscripts are from Antiquity, while the great majority are much later, dating mainly from the medieval period. Epigraphical evidence, on the other hand, has by its very nature come down to us from Classical Antiquity itself.

The survival of epigraphical sources has been determined mostly by chance, but to a certain extent also by strategies of archaeological exploration with their tendency to focus on famous historical sites. Ancient literature has come down to us by a process in which chance has also played a decisive part; to a certain degree, value judgements and other filters of reception (i.e. Christianity) have determined the transmission of texts as well. The study of both categories of written evidence is the province of classical philology, epigraphy and ancient history, with classical archaeology being involved more closely in epigraphy.[4] The common feature of the two categories of written evidence is that the quantity that has survived to the present day represents a minute percentage of what was originally produced. The little that remains is, however, uniquely valuable in throwing light on aspects of ancient sculpture which the works themselves cannot communicate.

The literary evidence[5]

The literary evidence for polychromy in Greek and Roman sculpture was first extensively collected and used by Antoine-Chrysostôme Quatremère de Quincy in his seminal work *n* (1814).[6] Recently this evidence has for the first time been the subject of a comprehensive study, by Felix Henke, dealing with several hundred ancient texts.[7] Henke's work was inspired and guided by earlier contributions by Oliver Primavesi on Greek sources.[8] From a perspective that includes sculpture, Latin texts have been studied in recent years by Mark Bradley,[9] Ursula Mandel[10] and Fabio Barry.[11]

Chronologically, these texts cover almost the complete span of the history of Greek and Roman polychrome sculpture. Geographically, they are less representative, having a decided emphasis on the great centres of Classical civilization. The texts are found in all ancient literary genres, poetry, philosophy, history and encyclopaedic works; and they deal with sculpture in a wide range of materials and contexts, as well as with technical aspects such as gilding and maintenance.

What, then, is the specific importance of the literary evidence; on what aspects of sculptural polychromy does it shed a light not provided by other sources? Henke deals in some detail with the question of how the evidence has been used hitherto and what its particular value is today. In a situation where investigation of the archaeological evidence is providing a mass of detailed knowledge on the 'how' of sculptural polychromy, Henke rightly concludes that the literary evidence is particularly impor-

---

4   An example is the pioneering publication of Greek and Latin inscriptions from Aphrodisias, cf. *IAph2007* at http://insaph.kcl.ac.uk/iaph2007/. See also Rouché, Holdenried & Scholz 2014.

5   It should be noted that, in principle, the evidence of ancient papyri belongs in this category. However, the papyrological evidence has not been systematically investigated. Cf. Henke 2014, 12. Evidence may possibly also be found in post-antique sources, cf. for example Baroni et al. 2014.

6   Quatremère de Quincy 1814. The 1814 edition published by Firmin Didot was followed in 1815 by an edition published by De Bure frères.

7   Henke 2014. This PhD dissertation is being prepared for publication.

8   Primavesi 2010; Primavesi 2014. See also Mandel 2010, 306 n. 21.

9   Bradley 2009.

10 Mandel 2010. Her contribution is not limited to literary evidence.

11 Barry 2011.

tant in two respects.[12] First, the texts provide access to levels of interpretation not to be found in the material evidence – namely, beyond the 'how', also the 'why', and furthermore, access to information on the reaction of ancient viewers to the sculptures.[13] Secondly, the texts help close some of the multitude of gaps existing in the material, archaeological record.

Against this background, close collaboration with classical philologists and ancient historians is an obvious necessity in polychromy research, keeping alive the synergy of investigation of the monuments and interpretation of the texts. In this respect, one may recall the fact that only as late as 1969 was the word "ágalma" in the famous passage in Euripides' tragedy *Helena* finally translated as "statue", not just "image".[14]

The epigraphical evidence

A comprehensive study of the evidence for polychromy provided by Greek and Latin inscriptions is yet to be carried out.[15] How necessary and promising such a study would be is demonstrated by the work of a more limited scope done so far, not least the in-depth research published on one period in particular, namely the Hellenistic.[16] Unlike the literary evidence, the inscriptions are not only themselves ancient but often also have an archaeological context. The inscriptions from Delos are the most prominent example of this.

The information on polychromy offered so far by inscriptions covers a narrow field in comparison to that provided by the literary evidence. Their context is almost exclusively that of sanctuaries – above all that of Apollo on Delos –[17] and their content limited to circumstances concerning the upkeep of statues: accounts and regulations specifying which statues to take care of, when, how, by whom and at what cost. The importance of this evidence lies above all in the fact that it is of a kind not provided by the literary sources. Epigraphy is therefore

Fig. 1. *A statue of Heracles being painted in the encaustic technique. Apulian red-figure column krater, c. 360-350 BCE, H: 51.5 cm. New York, Metropolitan Museum of Art, inv. no. 50.11.4. Rogers Fund, 1950. (Credit New York MMA).*

a discipline with which polychromy studies must be in close contact.

The material evidence

The term 'material', rather than 'monumental' or 'archaeological', has been chosen in order to reflect the breadth of this category of evidence, encompassing as it does not only the sculptures themselves, but also other classes of objects not easily subsumed under the heading 'monumental', as well as objects which have no archaeological context but nonetheless provide important evidence. The material evidence may be grouped under two headings, as follows.

---

12 Henke 2014, 7-8. Cf. also Leka 2014, 61 on the words and expressions used for the protection, maintenance and repair of sculpture as reflections of the value ascribed to the works.

13 On ancient viewers: Zanker 2000; Elsner 2007 (not limited to the Roman world); Marconi 2011, 145.

14 Eur. Hel. 260-66. Kannicht 1969.

15 Publication of corpora of inscriptions in digital form opens new possibilities. Cf. the Greek and Latin inscriptions from Aphrodisias, *IAph2007* at http://insaph.kcl.ac.uk/iaph2007/.

16 Leka 2014, dealing with literary and epigraphical sources; Bourgeois 2014; Blume 2015, 127-31, with a heavy emphasis on Delos.

17 The sanctuary of Apollo at Ptoion in Boeotia being another, cf. Leka 2014, 62.

151

Fig. 2. *Wall painting from the House of the Golden Bracelet, Pompeii (VI 17, 42): garden scene (detail) with fully poly-chrome satyr's heads carrying more discretely coloured reliefs. Mid 1ˢᵗ century CE, c. 200 x 375 cm. Pompeii, Antiquarium, inv. no. SAP 40690. (Credit SAP).*

Evidence from categories of material other than sculptures

This type of evidence falls into two groups, one showing the actual act of painting sculpture, the other with representations of polychrome sculptures. The classes of material concerned are – with a few notable exceptions – vase-painting and wall-painting.

Representations of the act of painting

Only four representations of sculptures being painted have come down to us from Antiquity.[18] Two are red-figure vase-paintings of the 4ᵗʰ century BCE (Fig. 1), one a wall-painting and one a ring-stone – the latter two being of Roman Early Imperial date. This is a very small number when one considers the fact that Greek and Ro-

man sculpture in (monochrome) stone material seems throughout its history of a thousand years always to have had some element of applied colour. This extreme paucity of visual evidence of something which must have been an everyday occurrence for centuries all over the ancient world is probably due to the very banality of the act; similarly, representations of sculptors at work are just as rare.

Representations of polychrome sculpture

Depictions of polychrome statuary are mostly, but not exclusively, from the Roman Imperial period – though the sculptures depicted do not necessarily have to be Roman, but may in principle be earlier, i.e. Greek. The great majority of them are to be seen in wall paintings,

---

18 Østergaard & Nielsen 2014, 319 cat. nos 3-6 (checklist text only).

19 Statues on Greek vases: Reuterswärd 1960, 88-102; De Cesare 1997; Marconi 2011 with bibliography, 145 n. 1 (add Bourgeois 2014c, 71 n. 7). Roman wall paintings: Moorman 1988; Moorman 2008; Moorman 2015, 638, 649. Cf. also Mandel 2010, 306 for possible interpretations. In principle, sculptures depicted on (monumental) reliefs, as for example those on set on the triumphal arch figuring in the Spoils Relief on the Arch of Titus, might, if properly examined, also provide information on polychromy.

Fig. 3. *Head of a youth with inlaid eyes. Marble and diorite. Roman, 2nd century BCE, H: 23 cm. Copenhagen, Ny Carlsberg Glyptotek, inv. no. IN 455.*

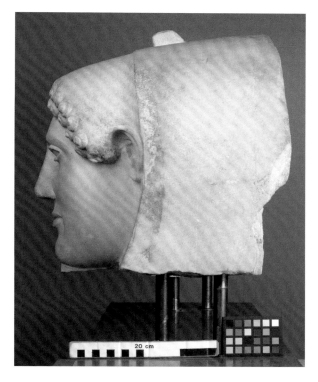

Fig. 4. *Visible remains of Egyptian blue on a lid head fragment of an anthropoid sarcophagus from Sidon. Marble. Mid 5th century BCE, H: 43 cm. Copenhagen, Ny Carlsberg Glyptotek, inv. no. IN 471.*

and far fewer in mosaics.[19] Interestingly, a study focusing on depictions of polychrome sculptures has not yet been carried out. This is probably mainly due to the absence of publications illustrated in colour.[20]

The types of sculptures shown in the two-dimensional media involved are in the main free- standing; they appear in a variety of figural contexts, or as part of an architectural setting (Fig. 2). Interpretation of these representations, with Eric Moorman as a leading exponent, seems largely unaffected by developments in research on the polychromy of Greek and Roman sculpture: here, there is work to be done.

The evidence from the sculptures themselves

A very simple distinction may be made between direct evidence on the one hand, and indirect on the other.[21] In both cases, the evidence is found on the surface of the sculpture, a surface which is the end product of the

sculpture's life history. Dealing with, and understanding, such a surface may be described as an "archaeology of the history of the surface".[22]

Direct evidence

The term 'direct evidence of polychromy' indicates the physical presence of a polychrome element on the sculpture, in whatever form and however minute. Besides remains of pigments this may also have to do with inlays – such as for the eyes (Fig. 3)[23] – leaf metals and preserved

---

20 Moorman 1988, the most complete publication of statuary in Roman wall-painting, has a great number of (small) illustrations, but all in b/w. Illustrations in Moorman 2008 are also in b/w. An online edition of Moorman 1988 with high resolution colour illustrations would be a valuable contribution; an example of obvious interest is constituted by the three depictions of the Hermes of Olympia (Moorman 2008, 207).

21 A brief introduction: Brinkmann 2003, 27-8 ('Die materiellen Spuren').

22 Bourgeois 2014b, 3.

23 Hoft 2014. A dissertation on the subject is under preparation by Verena Hoft.

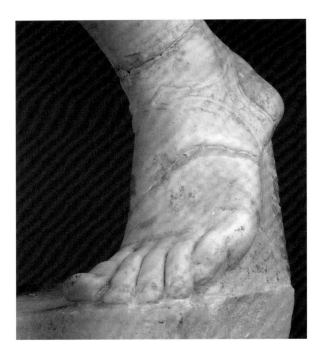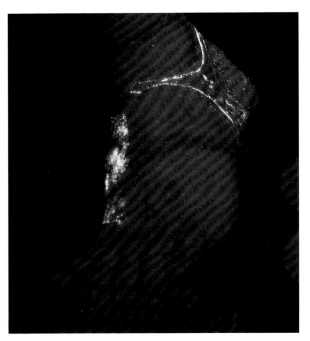

Fig. 5 a–b. *Left foot of the statue of a wounded Amazon ('Sciarra Amazon') in tungsten light (a) and in VIL image (b). The VIL image reveals the Egyptian blue used for a painted-on sandal strap. Marble. Roman, mid 2nd century BCE, H of statue: 197 cm. Copenhagen, Ny Carlsberg Glyptotek, inv. no. IN 1568.*

additions in the form of accessories or attributes, for example earrings or diadems. In the case of pigments, the evidence may at one end of the scale be so well preserved as to be immediately visible to the naked eye (Fig. 4), and at the other be of submicroscopic size and hence quite invisible (Fig. 5a–b). Tracking down and documenting this evidence is one of the main aims of the visual examination protocol dealt with below.

Indirect evidence

Even when no polychrome element is preserved, indirect evidence may be found which proves with absolute certainty that colour was once present on a sculpture – in many cases also just how and where the polychromy was once applied. This kind of evidence may usefully be divided into the following six categories:

Incision of very fine lines was used in the Archaic period to guide the subsequent painting of the sculpture. Both figurative and ornamental motifs were indicated in outline, often quite detailed. The best means of finding and documenting such incisions is by means of extreme raking light for visual examination and photography conducted under darkened conditions (Fig. 6). The development and refinement of raking light photography since the 1980s is due to the pioneering work of Vinzenz Brinkmann.[24]

Weathering relief is another surface feature for which raking light photography is the ideal method of investigation. The term describes the results of the use of pigments of varying durability. Less durable pigments will wear away the quickest and consequently expose the stone surface underneath to weathering for a longer period of time than surfaces covered by relatively durable pigments. This will result in a more or less pronounced relief effect (Fig. 7), revealing the motif of the originally applied polychromy.

'Colour shadows' is an expression used to describe a surface phenomenon closely related to weathering re-

24 Brinkmann 2010, 23. See Brinkmann 2003 for a wide selection of raking light images of incisions and weathering reliefs (as Fig. 7).

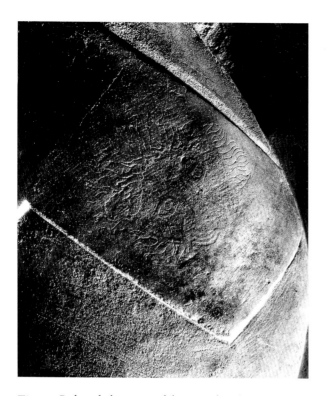

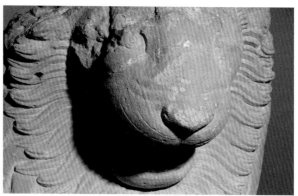

Fig. 7. *Raking light image of differential weathering of a meander border on a palmette anthemion of Classical Cypriote grave stele. Limestone. 5ᵗʰ century BCE, H (of anthemion): 46.0 cm. Copenhagen, Ny Carlsberg Glyptotek, inv. no. IN 431.*

Fig. 6. *Raking light image of the incised outline of a lion's head on the cuirass shoulder clasp of Aristion. Stele of Aristion. From Athens. Marble. Late 6ᵗʰ century BCE, H (of stele): 204 cm. National Archaeological Museum, Athens, inv. 29. (Credit Städelstiftung).*

liefs, being due also to the differences in durability of the pigments employed. The two types of indirect evidence may therefore be observed together on one and the same monument; and they may be subsumed under the common heading of 'differential weathering'.

In the case of 'colour shadows', the difference in pigment durability is evident from the tone of the stone surface: the better protected surfaces are less weathered and consequently lighter in tone than areas once covered by pigment of lower durability.

Iconographic evidence lies in the absence of something which must once have been present in colour. It is the logic of the scene or object represented which reveals what is now no longer there, but was once shown in colour. The most commonly occurring instance of this type

of evidence is undoubtedly that of sandals being shown without straps; similar finicky details are missing on a Late Classical Attic relief fragment in the Ny Carlsberg Glyptotek (Fig. 9) where the sculptor left the rein and bridle to be painted in.

Inlays and other additions form a wide-ranging category of indirect evidence of polychromy. Whether inlaid eyes, jewelry (Fig. 10), divine attributes or the equipment and weapons of mortals, the sure indirect evidence of their erstwhile presence is in the form of a preparation for their insertion in the stone surface. The signs of the former presence of inlays and/or other additions are of course evidence of the presence of the colour of the material they were made of; but they are also evidence of polychromy of other parts of the sculpture: would the skin surfaces of the marble head of a youth with inlaid eyes (Fig. 3) have been left white?

The character of the surface finish and the choice of marble must be viewed as potentially determined by the intended polychrome finish and therefore indirect evidence of it. The surface is the interface between the craftsmanship, the *technè*, of the sculptor and the painter; or it may be thought of as the result of a dialogue between the two.[25] We may take the case of the rendering of dress

25   As Bourgeois 2012, 37; Heilmeyer & Maasmann 2014, 121; Skovmøller 2016.

Fig. 8. *UV image enhancing the polychromy of the Late Classical Attic grave lekythos of Paramython. Marble. C. 370 BCE. W. of stele 33,4 cm. Munich, Staatliche Antikensammlung und Glyptothek inv. no. Gl 483. (Courtesy Städelstiftung).*

Fig. 9. *Stable boy with horse. The reins were painted in. Fragment of the side panel (parastasis) of a Late Classical Attic funerary monument. Marble. Mid to late 4ᵗʰ century BCE, H: 88 cm. Copenhagen, Ny Carlsberg Glyptotek, inv. no. IN 2807.*

in the widest sense, where we find the sculptor providing the painter with a surface texture in accordance with the material to be represented, be it a leather belt or the texture of a toga.[26]

Seeing the finished surface of the marble as a canvas for subsequent application of paint implies that the material itself was, or may have been, chosen in the light of what polychromy was to be applied and the chromatic value of the marble. An investigation of the potential value of the marble itself as indirect evidence of polychromy requires an effort to describe, identify and locate the stone.

Petrographic and isotopic analysis is therefore to be integrated whenever possible in the investigation protocol, just as the interdisciplinary network should include the competences needed.[27]

Investigating polychromy

When investigating an ancient sculpture for remains of its polychromy, autopsy is of course a basic prerequisite.[28] What meets the eye is the surface in its three-dimensionality; it is the interface between the sculpture and the physical

26 The picked surface of the leather belt of the wounded Amazon ('Sciarra Amazon') NCG IN 1568, Østergaard, Sargent & Therkildsen 2014, 55, fig. 5; the toga of Fundilius NCG IN 707, Skovmøller 2014, 289. This aspect has led to collaboration with research on ancient textiles such as that conducted by the Centre for Textile Research at the University of Copenhagen, http://ctr.hum.ku.dk/. For related work, see Drinkler 2009.

27 Therkildsen 2012, 3.

28 See Bourgeois 2012, 38 for a precise formulation of what investigating polychromy is about.

be exaggerated: the extent of ongoing deterioration of the remains of polychromy on ancient sculpture[31] means that the results we obtain today may one day be the only documentation available.

Archaeological context and the post-antique 'biography' of the sculpture

The study of Greek and Roman sculpture is the province of classical archaeologists. Consequently, the decision to investigate a given sculpture is taken because it fits a set of criteria set up within the framework of a project primarily devised by the archaeological curatorial staff responsible for it. The individual decisions will, however, in the best of worlds be the result of an informed dialogue between archaeology and conservation: win-win initiatives will always take the day. On this view, the methodology of research in our field requires that all available archaeological information on the sculpture is assembled and made accessible. It will also be a curatorial contribution to write up a 'biography' of the work, from the time of its discovery until its present position. Without this information, the state of preservation of the sculpture cannot be understood, and the 'excavation' – non-invasive and/or invasive – cannot be allowed.

Fig. 10. Female funerary relief portrait. From the Qasr Abjad tomb, Palmyra. Limestone. C. 200 BCE, H: 55 cm. Copenhagen, Ny Carlsberg Glyptotek, inv. no. IN2795.

environments it has passed through since it left the ancient workshop. As Brigitte Bourgeois has recently written, we are faced with "an archaeology of the surface" whose physical and historical depth must be probed and scientifically documented – keeping in mind the multiplicity of mostly anonymous hands which have handled and treated the surfaces over centuries, from Antiquity until today.[29] Included in this aspect is the biography of the possible maintenance and repainting of the sculpture in Antiquity.[30]

The importance of conducting such investigations with the highest possible degree of precision can hardly

Organization of work and data

In the course of the last 40 years or so, research on Greek and Roman sculptural polychromy has increasingly acquired an international character. It is still a relatively small field, but activity has increased considerably over this period, resulting in a growing quantity of primary data. To allow the essential, comparative studies of data acquired and of their interpretation, methods of data acquisition, data presentation and data organization/storage specific to polychromy should ideally conform to some agreed protocols and standards within the larger framework of established methodologies of the disciplines involved. Immediately related to these points is

29 Bourgeois 2014b, 3-5; cf. Romualdi et al. 2005; Bourgeois 2012 with an excellent bibliography for post-antique restoration of Greek sculpture, applicable in many respects also to Roman sculpture.
30 Bourgeois 2014c.
31 The factors chiefly responsible for the degradation of polychromy – humidity, temperature and light – are rarely controlled in galleries of ancient sculpture.

the matter of access to data, data sharing and intellectual property rights. In the present context, these complex issues cannot be dealt with in any detail. I shall confine myself to some general observations.

Protocols and standards

Contributing to the development of protocols and standards has from the outset been one of the principal aims of the work done by the Copenhagen Polychromy Network (CPN) and the Tracking Colour project.[32] A pilot study published in 2009 laid the foundations of the CPN protocol.[33] It noted the relatively limited literature on the technical examination of the polychromy of Greek and Roman sculpture and at the same time the apparent similarities between ancient and later European practices. The examination techniques chosen were therefore based on an existing tradition of studying polychromy on European medieval wooden polychrome sculpture and panel paintings.[34]

Within the framework of the Tracking Colour project, it was soon realized that two protocols were needed: a survey protocol and an in-depth protocol for qualitative research in the form of case studies, characterized by the application of a broader suite of analytical, non-invasive and invasive methods. [35]

Fortunately quite a number of publications with results from investigations following well-described protocols and standards are now available.[36] What is rarely made clear in these publications is the fundamentally

iterative character of working according to such protocols; observations made at a certain stage of the investigation will frequently make it necessary to return to a procedure already carried out.[37]

Data management: organization of data; data access; data sharing

Arguably the most important objective at the present time in this field of research is well-considered (rather than random) acquisition of primary data conducted according to the protocols and standards now available, and their rapid publication – including archaeological comment connecting the data with the status of our knowledge.

The data thus acquired are entirely digital in form, whether written, graphic or visual. These data must therefore be organized, stored and made accessible on digital platforms. The challenges this presents are of considerable proportions; meeting them is an ongoing, multifaceted process further complicated by the interdisciplinary character of the field.[38] The Tracking Colour project decided to set up a low-budget project website as a front-end outlet for a back-end 'keep-it-simple' database to which project members and professional users had access.[39] To my knowledge, this example has not yet been followed by other polychromy research websites.[40]

Both on its website and in preliminary reports for free download, the Tracking Colour project gave access to and shared primary data before publication in peer review

---

32 Østergaard 2009b, 69; Østergaard 2010a, 11; Sargent & Therkildsen 2010, 11-3.

33 Scharff et al. 2009; Therkildsen 2011, 31-2.

34 Scharff et al. 2009, 14-5; Scharff 2013, 80. For an overview of techniques in medieval sculptural polychromy see Theiss 2010.

35 Therkildsen 2011.

36 A selection: Sargent et al. 2009; Verri, Opper & Deviese 2010; Sargent & Therkildsen 2010; Sargent 2011a; Abbe, Borromeo & Pike 2012; Sargent 2012; Bourgeois 2014c; Santamaria et al. 2014; Donati 2014 (more programmatical); Verri, Opper & Lazzarini 2014; Verri et al. 2014; Brecoulaki et al. 2014; Iannaccone et al. 2015. Bottini & Setari 2007, 120-66 deals with two-dimensional painting on stone, not sculptural polychromy, but is exemplary. Kakoulli 2009 is equally rewarding, including a technical study of the painting on the marble throne from the tomb of Eurydice at Vergina on 87-92; the book increases awareness of the interface between techniques in marble polychromy and wall paintings.

37 This adds to the difficulty of assessing the man hours needed for investigations.

38 For the complexity of the matter, cf. for example the Getty Conservation Institute Expert's Meeting September 10-2, 2013: "Integrating Imaging and Analytical Technologies for Conservation Practice". A report is available at http://www.getty.edu/conservation/our_projects/integrating_imaging. html; on p. 16, this aspect of Graham 2012a is summarized.

39 Skovmøller2011.

40 For example: Frankfurt am Main, Stiftung Archäologie (ceased operations in 2016), http://www.stiftung-archaeologie.de/; Firenze, Dipartimento di Antichità Classica, Galleria degli Uffizi http://www.goldunveiled.it/; Athens, Georgia (US), University of Georgia http://www.ancientpolychromynetwork.com/menu-2/; London, The British Museum http://www.britishmuseum.org/research/research_projects/all_current_projects/ancient_polychromy.aspx.

Fig. 11a–c. Head of a female deity ('Treu Head'). a) Present state, tungsten light; b) UIL image showing orange red luminescence of organic pigments; c) VIL image with the white luminescence of Egyptian blue. Mid 2nd century CE. London, The British Museum, inv. no. GR 1884, 0617.1. (Credit The British Museum).

fora. Open access to data and publications related to research funded by public sources has been discussed with increasing intensity in recent years, in close connection with the modalities of intellectual property rights and publisher's copyrights.[41]

Visual investigation, technical imaging and non-invasive analysis

These three phases of the protocol have in common the fact that they are directed at the sculpture itself, either in situ wherever the work is kept, or, preferably, in a work space.[42] If the object is a large sculpture, the procedures which can take place in situ are usually restricted to all-round macroscopy, and, for accessibility reasons, imaging and analysis of only the front of the statue. In cases where the sculpture is still in its original position the situation is obviously difficult, but integrated, multi-methodological approaches are now being developed.[43] In the following, it is assumed that a work space is available.

Tungsten light photography and macroscopy

The initial step in an investigation is photographic documentation and systematic macroscopy under tungsten light.[44] Macroscopy takes place with the naked eye, assisted by magnification glasses and a binocular magnifier and/or a small video microscope.[45] Macroscopy and pho-

---

41 For access to research data see, for example, the Registry of Research Data Repositories and the thinking behind it: http://service.re3data.org/ about; for access to publications see, for example, the plan implemented by the Smithsonian Institution http://interdisciplinary.si.edu/collaboration-highlights/public-access/; see also the 2003 http://openaccess.mpg.de/Berlin-Declaration. For copyright issues (in conservation) the International Institute for Conservation of Historic and Artistic Works (IIC) is developing guidelines to be made available at www.iiconservation.org/resources/guidelines.

42 On the Tracking Colour work space see Østergaard 2009, 70-7, 72, figs 1-4 and 2010, 7, 8 figs 1-3 (early version); Østergaard 2012, 7-8, 9 fig. 1 (later version).

43 Iannaccone et al. 2015 is a pioneering example of this.

44 Scharff et al. 2009, 16-7; Sargent & Therkildsen 2010, 12. On light sources see also Blume 2015, 16. For a wide selection of such documentation see the plates in Brinkmann 2003 and Blume 2015.

45 As an Eschenbach Lupe x3 and a Dino-Lite AM7013MT video microscope with x20/50 to x200 zoom magnifications.

159

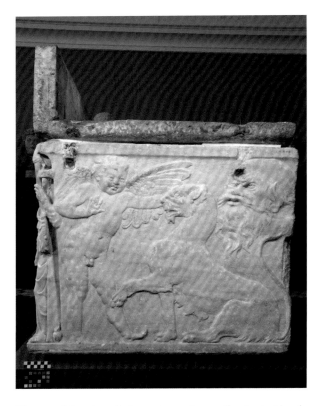

Fig. 12. Mapping of pigment remains on the short side of a Metropolitan Roman sarcophagus with Dionysus and Ariadne ('Casali Sarcophagus'). Marble. Late 2ⁿᵈ century CE, H (of chest): 68 cm. Copenhagen, Ny Carlsberg Glyptotek, inv. no. IN 843.

included in all images. These images serve as support for mapping features observed in the course of subsequent examination of the surface (Fig. 12), as well as for pinpointing the locations of non-invasive and invasive analysis.[48] As macroscopy proceeds, a need for detail photographic documentation will usually arise. The photographic documentation will therefore consist of two main sections, total views (T) organized by degrees (thus 'T 0' for frontal view) and detail views (D), and be stored accordingly.

The initial phase may reveal features which must be examined and documented under raking light using a mono-directional light source and under total blackout for exposures; if possible or desirable, the Polynomial Texture Mapping (PTM) technique may also prove useful.[49] Raking light will typically be relevant in cases with such indirect evidence of polychromy as outline incisions and differential weathering.[50]

Technical imaging

A variety of digital technical imaging techniques are used to explore features and map the spatial distribution of materials on the surface of ancient sculptures, and in some cases also to provide information on the character of materials. The systematic use of these techniques in polychromy research was pioneered by Vinzenz Brinkmann from the 1980s onwards.[51]

When using such techniques in combination, one speaks of digital multispectral imaging (MSI) to indicate that they move through the ultraviolet (UV), visible (VIS) and infrared (IR) ranges or spectra of light waves. MSI is the quickest, most affordable and technologically most straightforward means of non-invasive, non-contact analytical investigation of the polychromy of an ancient sculpture.[52]

tographic documentation often stand in an iterative relationship. Thus photographic documentation in colour[46] will be carried out at an early stage in the form of total views beginning with the front (Fig. 11a) and subsequently in 90-degree rotations of the sides and back. It is important also to photograph the sculpture from above.[47] A colour reference standard for subsequent colour balancing is

---

46   In the Tracking Colour project the camera used was a digital Canon EOS 5D Mark II with a Canon Zoom Lens EF 24-105mm and a Canon Compact-Macro Lens EF 50mm for detail photography.

47   The top surfaces can otherwise not be shown on virtual 3D models, cf. for example Graham 2012a, 74, fig. 8 'polar caps'.

48   Mapping of UV-VIS measurements: Brinkmann, Koch-Brinkmann & Piening 2010, 194, fig. 139 (Phrasikleia); mapping of sampling locations: Verri, Opper & Deviese 2010, 45, fig. 4a 'Treu Head'.

49   Earl, Martinez & Malzbender 2010.

50   Above, 6.

51   Brinkmann built on work begun in the 1960s by Volkmar von Graeve, Christof Wolters and Frank Preusser. For a bibliography of their contributions see http://www.stiftung-archaeologie.de/publicationsen.html

52   See Dyer, Verri & Cupitt 2013. A brief introduction and download of the manual is available on the British Museum website as part of the European CHARISMA project (Cultural Heritage Advanced Research Infrastructures: Synergy for a Multidisciplinary Approach to conservation and restoration). http://www.britishmuseum.org/research/research_projects/all_current_projects/charisma/technical_imaging.aspx

MSI falls into two categories, namely reflectance and luminescence imaging.[53] The former registers the radiation which the object reflects from the radiation source (reflectance imaging), the latter the radiation which the object emits in the form of luminescence (luminescence imaging). Luminescence is "the emission of light by a substance, which occurs when an electron returns to the electronic ground state from an excited state and loses its excess energy as a photon".[54] The excited electronic state is a result of the absorption of energy in the form of photons from the radiation source, triggering the transition of electrons from the ground state to the higher (excited) electronic energy state. It should be made clear here that 'luminescence' is a higher-order term encompassing two forms of luminescence, namely fluorescence and phosphorescence. In the literature on sculptural polychromy research, 'luminescence' and 'fluorescence' are used interchangeably. 'Luminescence' is the term preferred by the leading practitioner of MSI, Giovanni Verri, and will be used here.[55] In both categories of imaging, complete black-out conditions have hitherto been required; a new technique provides an alternative that may be used under ambient light conditions.[56]

Of particular value to polychromy research are the following imaging techniques:[57]

– Infrared-Reflected imaging (IRR) may reveal significant pictorial details, as has been demonstrated most recently in the investigation of polychromy on Classical Greek marble vases.[58]

– Ultraviolet-Reflected imaging (UVR) and Ultraviolet-Induced Luminescence imaging (UIL)[59]

UV-reflectography will strengthen the contrast of 'colour shadows' (Fig. 8), while UIL captures the luminescence from certain organic pigments on the surface and may also reveal otherwise invisible features of an original polychromy (Fig. 11b).[60]

– Visible-Induced Luminescence imaging (VIL), which captures the luminescence of Egyptian blue, a synthetic pigment first produced in Egypt in the 3rd millennium BCE and subsequently widely used in Classical Antiquity (Fig. 11c). The radiation source is visible light with a minimum of emission in the infrared spectrum; the pigment re-emits the energy absorbed in the form of luminescence in the infrared range, invisible to the human eye but visible in a digital image taken by a camera with the appropriate filters. Because the luminescence is found on the near-infrared range, the term NIR (Near-InfraRed) luminescence is also used instead of VIL.[61]

The images obtained through the application of the technical imaging methods just described are always to a greater or lesser extent open to interpretation, not least in the case of VIL.[62] Examination by other methods as a cross-check are, as always, to be recommended.

Microscopy

The results of macroscopy, photographic documentation and technical imaging may be followed or accompanied by more focused microscopy of relevant areas of preserved polychromy. In the Tracking Colour project, a high-end video microscope became the main microscope.[63]

---

53   Cf. Verri & Saunders 2014, 83.

54   Ganio et al. 2015, 815.

55   For a basic understanding of the terms luminescence, phosphorescence and fluorescence see Verri et al. 2008, 1-2; Verri & Saunders 2014, 83 with references.

56   Verri & Saunders 2014.

57   Infrared and ultraviolet false-colour reflected images (IRRFC; UVRFC) have to my knowledge not been relevant to sculptural polychromy research (yet?). See Dyer, Verri & Cupitt 2013, 4, 5 figs 1-3.

58   Dyer, Verri & Cupitt 2013; Brecoulaki 2014, 161; cf. Brecoulaki, Kavvadias & Verri 2014, 19-24.

59   Or frequently, ultraviolet-fluorescence imaging (UV-FL), cf. the point just made on terminology.

60   Koch-Brinkmann & Posamentir 2010, 180 figs 196-8, 182-3 (UVR and UIL of NCG IN 2564); Sargent & Therkildsen 2010, 20 fig. 10 (UIL of NCG IN 2687 Caligula).

61   Verri 2009; Ganio et al. 2015, 814-5 with references. A paper is under preparation for the Research & Technical Studies Session at the 2016 AIC Annual Meeting, entitled: "Visible-Induced Luminescence Imaging: Past, Current and Future Applications in Conservation Research".

62   On interpretation and analysis see Dyer, Verri & Cupitt 2013, 6, 8-34; Verri et al. 2008.

63   Tracking Colour main microscopes: 1) Leica M651 binocular optical surgical stereo microscope, to X26 magnification at a working distance of 15 cm, using a 150 mm lens; a 130 mm lens allowed working distance of up 30 cm with X13 magnification. Limitations: being designed for surgical functions, the lowest and uppermost parts of a full-size sculpture could not be examined. 2) The more versatile Leica DVM 5000 video microscope, now the preferred instrument. 3) A Leica DM 2500 dark field microscope for cross-section analysis.

The use of video microscopes in research on ancient sculptural polychromy was pioneered in France from 1996 onwards by Brigitte Bourgeois; such instruments became the 'work horse' of the investigations conducted by her and a French–Greek team from 1999 to 2007 on the surface features of marble sculpture from Delos. The instrument now in use by Brigitte Bourgeois is a Hirox KH-8700 with a zoom magnification to 400X and provided with sophisticated software allowing 3D and micro topographical imaging.[64] Using a Keyence VHX-500 video microscope, with a lens giving 20-175X magnification, Mark Abbe has also produced important results.[65] The case for choosing a video microscope for sculptural polychromy research has been well-stated by Bourgeois: maneuverability, rapidity of use and spectrum of magnification –[66] to which one might add the constant development of relevant digital software.

Analytical investigation

The observations made in the course of the investigations outlined above may encourage a closer look at the physical and chemical properties of the pigments discovered.[67] To this end, a suite of geophysical, physico-chemical and biochemical analyses may be applied; the sequence in which they are applied will reflect the two main categories into which they may be divided, namely non-invasive and invasive. Several of these analytical methods are applicable in both categories.[68] In the following, each category is dealt with in turn.

Non-invasive methods

These methods have in common the fact that they allow acquisition of quantitative data without contact with the historical material. It follows that these methods are applied in situ, i.e. on the sculpture itself. The term 'non-destructive' is sometimes, wrongly, used synonymously with 'non-invasive'; 'destructive' and 'non-destructive' describe two categories of invasive methodology as will become apparent below.

The standard protocol for non-invasive analysis includes the following methods:[69]

X-ray Fluorescence spectroscopy (XRF) performed in situ with a portable spectrometer (p-XRF) provides information on elements present in the pigment.[70] An advanced version of the instrument is the portable ARTAX micro-XRF (µ-XRF).[71]

Ultraviolet-Visible Spectroscopy (UV-VIS) (or UV-VIS absorption spectroscopy in diffuse reflection, to indicate the inclusion of near UV 300-400 nanometer and near IR 800-1100 nanometer bandwidths) has been in use for identifying pigments since around 1990 and has in recent years been applied in research on ancient sculptural polychromy. Its leading exponent is Heinrich Piening, working in close collaboration with Vinzenz Brinkmann

---

64   Bourgeois 2012, 31-3, 34; Bourgeois 2014b, 5-6 with note 18; Bourgeois 2014c, 77, fig. 14; micro topography, ibid. 78 fig. 17; Bourgeois & Jeammet 2014. Cf. C2RMF website report on investigation of the archaic Greek 'Kore of Lyon': http://c2rmf.fr/actualite/les-couleurs-de-la-kore (accessed February 19, 2016).

65   Abbe, Borromeo & Pike 2012.

66   Bourgeois 2012, 34.

67   The subject challenges this archaeologically trained author; when publishing the results of interdisciplinary research more attention needs to be paid by all disciplines involved to guiding the intended, but untrained reader. The instrumentation involved is always very expensive and only experienced professionals should use it. The heading of this section might have been 'Materials analysis', cf. Abbe, Borromeo & Pike 2012, 766. There are several handbooks available on analytical methods in cultural heritage conservation contexts, each with their particular strengths, but none with a focus on ancient artefacts, let alone sculpture. One may mention for example Ciliberto & Spoto 2000, with the introduction Ciliberto 2000. Abbe 2015, 174 has a very brief introduction.

68   Among recent publications demonstrating such full sequences one may mention Bottini & Setari 2007, 132-66; Scharff et al. 2009; Verri, Opper & Deviese 2010; Sargent & Therkildsen 2010a; Abbe, Borromeo & Pike 2012. Though on the subject of Gandharan sculpture, Talarico et al. 2015 is very instructive. In the following, references will be given to several more publications in connection with the individual analytical methods.

69   Bracci et al. 2014 gives a concise overview of methods.

70   Liritzis & Zacharias 2011; Abbe, Borromeo & Pike 2012, 766; Sargent & Therkildsen 2010a, 33, 47; Ganio et al. 2015, 814.

71   https://www.bruker.com/products/x-ray-diffraction-and-elemental-analysis/micro-xrf-and-txrf/artax/overview.html, cf. in situ application Leona 2009, 7, fig. 7.

and Ulrike Koch-Brinkmann.[72] The method involves the combination of UV-VIS measurements with colourmetry using chromaticity coordinates in order to estimate the colour values of the pigment traces found.[73]

Fiber Optics Reflectance Spectroscopy (FORS) is a non-invasive technique closely related to UV-VIS.[74] Its limitations are due to the lack of easily accessible libraries of comparative data.[75]

Raman Spectroscopy was applied non-invasively, using a portable set-up, in the pilot project phase leading to the Glyptotek's Tracking Colour research.[76] It was not successful, due to the interference from the marble substrate. For good results in situ use of the technique requires micro-Raman spectroscopy (µ-Raman; MRM).[77]

Invasive methods

As the term indicates, invasive methods entail physical contact with the historical materials of the original and the removal of a sample for analytical investigation. The methods of investigation used may either be non-destructive or destructive; in the latter case, the sample is destroyed in the analytical process, in the former, the material remains available for future analysis. A decision to apply invasive methods requires an awareness of contemporary conservation ethics, and more specifically, of the criteria by which such a decision may be taken. This is a wide field which cannot be surveyed in the present context. I shall restrict myself to some basic observations.

First of all, the general state of preservation of polychromy on Greek and Roman marble sculptures must be recognized for what it is: so deteriorated as to be completely out of touch with the originally intended visual effect. This stands in contrast to the rare instances of better preserved polychromy on an ancient sculpture – terracotta statuettes above all – and, especially, the almost complete and complex state of many post-antique, European polychrome sculptures. This must enter the equation when discussing whether the application of invasive methods is permissible or not – as a rule this is not a matter dealt with in publications; here, the Tracking Colour project is no exception.

Next, one must have a clear idea of the size of samples needed to permit the application of the methods dealt with in this section.[78] The sample size required for analyses has in general steadily decreased to the degree that the refinement of analytical technology has increased. Today, average samples are of a size hardly visible to the naked eye, yet a distinction is still drawn between sampling and micro-sampling, according to the minimum size required for the great variety of analyses relevant to ancient sculptural polychromy.[79] By extension, such practical aspects as methods of extracting and storing, and of safely sending samples when working with external network partners, are all part of the workings of invasive methodology. Furthermore, one must qualify modern concepts of an 'original' material by drawing attention to the 'biography' of a sculptural surface, from discovery onwards – a biography which will include 'invasive' treatment in the field and in museums.[80]

In the Tracking Colour project, guidelines for the use of invasive methods, i.e. the taking of samples, were established verbally on a professionally informed, common sense basis: there must be a sufficient volume of material remaining after sampling to allow future investigation; the reasons why a sample is needed must be closely argued; the methods of investigation must be explained and the necessary collaboration with external partners must be in place. These criteria being met, invasive methodologies were welcomed, as they are by other institutions carrying

---

72   Brinkmann, Koch-Brinkmann & Piening 2010; Piening 2010a; Piening 2014; Blume 2015, 134-6 (Heinrich Piening, Harald Theiss, Annegret Fuhrmann). The exclusive use of non-invasive methods is regarded as a given by Piening (Piening 2014, 185). UV-VIS-NIR spectrometers covering the 200-1800nm range are available and desirable, but beyond the financial reach of Piening. I thank Heinrich Piening for this information.

73   Piening 2010, 112-3; Brinkmann, Koch-Brinkmann & Piening 2010, 200-2.

74   Leona 2009, 7.

75   I thank Heinrich Piening for this opinion.

76   Berg 2009.

77   Brecoulaki, Kavvadias & Verri 2014, 155. Cf. Smith et al. 2009.

78   On this point misconceptions are frequent. Precise information in publications is the remedy.

79   On sampling generally, see for example Ciliberto 2000, 5. The average size needed for cross-sections is from 0.25 to 1 mm²; up to 2 mm² (the size of the head of a pin) may be needed for other analyses (those for organic materials especially).

80   Cf. Bourgeois 2014c.

out polychromy research.[81] This positive attitude to invasive analysis is determined by what is to be gained from it: a decisive widening of the results of non-invasive analyses, and knowledge on features of polychromy which are (as yet) beyond the reach of non-invasive methods.

The following brief overview points to some relevant invasive analytical methods, divided into three groups, the first group having to do with the identification of inorganic pigment components, the second with colourants, i.e. organic pigments, and the third, intimately related to the first two, with painterly technique, and stratigraphy in particular.[82]

1. Identifying inorganic pigments

XRF; μ-XRF; Raman Spectroscopy and μ-Raman Spectroscopy are iterative methods, repeating non-invasive analyses carried out in situ on the sculpture (see above). The designation μ indicates that method may be applied to very small (micro) samples.

X-ray Diffraction Spectroscopy (XRD)

Scanning Electron Microscopy / Energy Dispersive X-ray spectroscopy (SEM-EDX)

Fourier Transform Infrared Spectroscopy (FTIR)

Inductively Coupled Plasma Mass Spectrometry (ICP-MS) is an analytical technique used for elemental determinations. This method has special relevance for polychromy studies because it permits the study of isotopes of lead and subsequently determination of its source.[83]

Electron Micro Probe Analyzer (EMPA) for non-destructive determination of the chemical composition of small volumes of material.[84]

2. Identifying organic pigments (colourants)

Gas Chromatography – Mass Spectrometry (GC-MS) is the most important method of identifying organic components in the form of binding media and colourants in polychromy.[85] The method is destructive.

Chemical Spot tests can be done on small samples to identify a substance.[86] Such tests are also destructive.

3. Painterly technique and stone characterization

Cross-section stratigraphy through analysis of samples by polarization microscopy.[87]

Thin section marble petrography and isotopic analysis for provenancing of the stone used.[88]

Experimental reconstruction as a research tool

To my knowledge, this is an aspect of methodology which has not yet been comprehensively addressed.[89] The earliest attempts to show the polychromy of ancient stone sculptures on copies of the originals date to the middle of the 19th century;[90] still earlier are similar attempts in two-dimensional media.[91] Both techniques have been in use since then, with varying frequency. A third means of 're-introducing' colour is far more recent, namely that of digital, virtual reality techniques.[92] Of these three meth-

---

81 For example Ny Carlsberg Glyptotek; Paris, Louvre/C2RMF; London, The British Museum; Firenze, The Uffizi; Rome, Musei Vaticani and Museo Nazionale dell'Arte Orientale.

82 Pallecchi et al. 2009 for the full suite of invasive methods, there applied to wall painting, but nevertheless instructive. See also Abbe, Borromeo & Pike 2012, 766-7 and, especially, Verri, Opper & Lazzarini 2014.

83 Rosing & Østergaard 2009; Fink-Jensen 2013.

84 Therkildsen 2011, 33.

85 Andreotti et al. 2014; Santamaria et al. 2014; Verri, Opper & Lazzarini 2014, 160-1. Binding media in Fayum mummy portraits determined by NIR-FT Raman, cf. Reeler et al. 2013.

86 Feigl & Anger 1937/2012; Odegaard, Carroll & Zimmt 2005.

87 See for example Sargent 2012, 35-8.

88 Sargent 2011, 44; Therkildsen 2012, 39-41, 44-8 (NCG IN 821, IN 822, IN 826); Verri, Opper & Lazzarini 2014, 158-60.

89 On reconstructions: Brinkmann 2010, 24-7; Schmaltz 2009; Brinkmann 2010a, 20; Piening 2010; Brinkmann & Koch-Brinkmann 2010; Koch-Brinkmann, Piening & Brinkmann 2014; Verri, Opper & Lazzarini 2014; Skovmøller & Therkildsen 2014; Brinkmann 2015, 95-6; Zimmer 2016. On the pigments: Brinkmann 2010b. Virtual 3-D reconstruction: Frischer 2015; http://vcg.isti.cnr.it/roman-sarcophagi/ulpia-sarcophagus-3d/index.html (E. Siotto & R. Scopigno). On scanning: Graham 2012a; Brinkmann 2015, 97.

90 Plaster casts of slabs of the Parthenon Frieze, in the Crystal Palace as re-erected in Sydenham 1854. Cf. Nichols 2015, 74-7.

91 Quatremère de Quincy 1814, frontispiece (Phidias' chryselephantine cult statue of Zeus at Olympia).

92 See Earl et al. 2009; Graham 2012; Frischer 2015.

ods, this section deals almost exclusively with reconstructions on copies of the originals. A further limitation, as indicated by the section title, is that I shall restrict myself to a research context. What this means is that the polychromy applied to the copy is to the greatest possible extent based on (preferably published) data acquired from the original, that historical pigments are used and that the process involved is as extensively documented as possible.[93]

Practically speaking, this means going back to the early 1990s and the pioneering efforts of Vinzenz Brinkmann and Ulrike Koch-Brinkmann in their investigation of the sculptures in the west pediment of the temple of Athena Aphaia on Aegina.[94] The reconstructions were carried out on copies made of plaster and later synthetic marble. Brinkmann, Koch-Brinkmann and Heinrich Piening have since made up a core polychromy research group with the Stiftung Archäologie as its organizational basis. They have collaborated with various partners, investigating and reconstructing works with particularly well-preserved polychromy, from different collections and spanning from the Greek Archaic to the Roman Imperial period. Besides the materials mentioned earlier, crystalline acrylic glass and marble have been used.[95] In a number of cases, sequences of reconstructions have been produced over some years, reflecting the research-based, experimental archaeological character of the activity.[96] Only a few outside the Stiftung Archäologie group have produced similar work;[97] it is to be hoped that more will follow.[98]

In connection with an ongoing project to produce a research-based reconstruction of a 2nd-century CE female marble head in the British Museum[99] – the so-called 'Treu Head' – Giovanni Verri has introduced a novel method of two-dimensional reconstruction, involving projecting colours found on relevant ancient works on to an image of the head.[100] Two-dimensional reconstruction of a similarly high quality, using coloured crayons, is used by Clarissa Blume in her research on the polychromy of Hellenistic sculpture.[101]

Research-based experimental reconstructions, also described as 'approximations', are important tools in the endeavour to rediscover the lost techniques of painting on stone. It is basically a case of 'learning' by doing. The implicit recognition of our very incomplete understanding of the craftsmanship of the polychromy of Greek and Roman marble sculpture makes it clear that such reconstructions emphatically do not claim to show what a given sculpture looked like when it left the workshop in Antiquity. It would be quite absurd to assert anything of the kind. The fact is that we will *never* know, or see, what an antique polychrome sculpture looked like in its original state. What we can do is to gradually gain an understanding of many important aspects of such a work. The raison d'etre of research-based reconstruction is that it is a tool in a learning-by-doing process.[102]

Another aspect of the reconstruction is almost as important, namely that of communicating some very basic facts to a wider public: above all the fact that ancient marble sculpture *was* polychrome, not white. The research-based reconstruction – despite its limitations – is nearer to a historical reality than any faded original. The impact of this on 'ordinary' viewers cannot be overestimated; for a great majority, it is demonstrably an 'aha' experience, awakening a new interest in the ancient world.

---

93   The interesting reconstructions ('Nachbildungen') of the Kasseler Apollo and the Athena Lemnia are therefore not included: Gercke 2009.

94   The most recent overview with extensive bibliography is Haag, Brinkmann & Koch-Brinkmann 2013, 60-2.

95   For a complete inventory of the reconstructions produced within the framework of the Stiftung Archäologie, see http://www.stiftung-archaeologie. de/reconstructionsen.html. The Stiftung closed down in 2016 and its work will be carried on under the auspices of the Städelstiftung, Frankfurt am Main.

96   For example the so-called 'Peplos Kore': Haag, Brinkmann & Koch-Brinkmann 2013, 55. The portrait of Caligula in Copenhagen: Haag, Brinkmann & Koch-Brinkmann 2013, 69; Østergaard & Nielsen 2014, 270-1. Variant A of Caligula: Brinkmann & Scholl 2010, 218-25 (J. S. Østergaard).

97   The Augustus of Prima Porta: Liverani 2004a; Spada 2004. The Lateran portrait of Ariadne: Liverani 2009, 17-9; Østergaard & Nielsen 2014, 282-3 (Paolo Liverani). The Acropolis Kore 682: Schmaltz 2009. The reconstruction on a marble copy of the polychromy of an early 3rd-century CE Roman portrait of a youth, NCG IN 821: Graham 2012; Skovmøller & Therkildsen 2014; Skovmøller 2016, 150-1.

98   In this connection, the announced publication by Ulrike Koch-Brinkmann of her procedures and vast experience will be of great importance. It is encouraging that she has for some time been teaching on the subject at the University of Göttingen.

99   Verri, Opper & Lazzarini 2014; Koch-Brinkmann, Piening & Brinkmann 2014, 146-8, 151.

100   Verri, Opper, & Lazzarini 2014, 171-2. 174-5, figs 17-20.

101   As for example Blume 2015, Pls. 77, 22.29; Østergaard & Nielsen 2014, 185, fig. 25 (Blume).

102   Quatremère de Quincy also found it necessary to stress this: Quatremère de Quincy 1814, xviii.

The experimental reconstructions/approximations have therefore made up the core of the highly successful 'Bunte Götter' exhibition series and have been shown in others as well.[103] And in some museums, they have found a place as permanent exhibits, in the galleries, next to the originals – as in the Ny Carlsberg Glyptotek in Copenhagen and the Acropolis Museum in Athens.[104]

In this communicative function, as exhibition objects, the reconstructions have met with especially strong critical reactions from colleagues in classical archaeology and art history. Quite heated verbal discussions have taken place in professional fora, but seldom in print;[105] for such discussions to be constructive and bear fruit they must find a written form, and the sooner the better.

Only by reaching a common understanding of, and agreement on, the ways and means of our research will we move forward with success.

Research must be organized accordingly. This is the subject of the final section of this article.

Organization of research

The complexity of sculptural polychromy, as described in this article, requires an interdisciplinary research approach. Recognizing this is a first step which may be taken by any individual wanting to contribute to the field.[106] Mobilizing and organizing the necessary interdisciplinary resources is a different matter. This section offers some thoughts on organizational practice, or 'research scenarios'. They will seem self-evident to those who have long worked in the professions involved, but

as short-term project employment is becoming an unfortunate fact of life in all types of research it becomes necessary to ensure continuity in, and transmission of, experience by other means than those afforded in better times by long tenures.

Research scenarios

Though sculptures kept in museums are at the heart of sculptural polychromy research,[107] the initiative to organize it and the responsibility for carrying it out may lie with a variety of institutional players.[108] Museums must of course be involved by giving access to the sculptures, but also by being the prime movers, as in the case of the research at the Ny Carlsberg Glyptotek on which this contribution is based.[109] It is most encouraging to note that research activity on sculptural polychromy in museum collections is now also being directed at ancient statues from other geographical areas.[110]

Museum collections

In the present context, museums with collections of ancient sculpture may be divided into three categories, established according to criteria that are decisive for the way in which research may best be organized: the large 'world' museums, the medium-sized museums, and the smaller museums. The latter category is the most numerous one, including such important museums as the archaeological museum in Sperlonga, Italy, or the Musée Saint-Raymond in Toulouse, France. This category will

---

103 As 'Transformations: Classical Sculpture in Colour', Ny Carlsberg Glyptotek, Copenhagen 2014, cf. Østergaard & Nielsen 2014.

104 The Acropolis Museum's initiative on Archaic Colors (2012) was accompanied by an instructive booklet (Pandermalis 2012).

105 As Schmaltz 2008.

106 Working on their own, scholars can (still) make important contributions. See for example Hoft 2013 on inlaid eyes.

107 Investigation of sculpture still in situ is as important, cf. Iannaccone et al. 2015, on a sarcophagus in the catacombs of St. Mark, Marcellian and Damasus Rome.

108 As for example Università degli Studi di Firenze; Université de Sorbonne Paris IV; the Consiglio Nazionale delle Ricerche (CNR) and the Istituto Superiore per la Conservazione ed il Restauro in Italy; in France the Centre nationale de la recherche scientifique (CNRS) and the Centre de recherche et de restauration des musées de France (C2RMF; http://c2rmf.fr/actualite/les-couleurs-de-la-kore); the National Hellenic Research Foundation/Institute of Historical Research (NHRF/IHR)/Section of Greek and Roman Antiquity (SGRA) http://www.eie.gr/nhrf/institutes/igra/index-en.html.

109 Especially the project 'Tracking Colour. The polychromy of Greek and Roman sculpture in the Ny Carlsberg Glyptotek', 2009-14, with the Copenhagen Polychromy Network (CPN). The contribution made by project conservators Maria Louise Therkildsen, BA and MSc, and Rikke H. Therkildsen, BA and MSc, was vital; the generous support offered by external partners in the Copenhagen Polychromy Network is gratefully recognized. Annual preliminary reports 2009-13 are available for download at www.trackingcolour.com. See also Østergaard 2010b. The final report is expected in 2018.

110 See Pannuzi 2015. From the point of view of interdisciplinary research organization, this publication is most instructive.

not be dealt with in the brief survey below because sculptures there have only rarely been investigated for their polychromy.[111]

The large, encyclopaedic 'world' museums

These museums are situated in major cities: they include famous institutions, like the Musei Vaticani, the Louvre, the Hermitage, the Staatliche Museen zu Berlin (Antikensammlung – Altes Museum/Pergamon Museum), the British Museum, the Metropolitan Museum of Art, the Museum of Fine Arts in Boston and the J. Paul Getty Museum. The core resources required for interdisciplinary research are found in-house, namely curatorial departments and departments of scientific research and objects conservation, with spaces allowing visual examination and imaging of sculpture.[112] Other competences needed usually exist close at hand in university institutes, other categories of museums and private companies.[113] The large museums usually also have their own means of publication. Large museums therefore provide ideal conditions for establishing interdisciplinary research networks.

Institutional support and commitment from museum management is of course a prerequisite for any research in museums. The sheer size of the largest museums implies a complex decision-making process between the museum management's lower and higher echelons, and, understandably, intense competition for the often meagre resources available.

As public funding of museums is cut back, the importance of support from external sources increases. In large museums, fundraising and the concomitant co-ordination of research strategy becomes another filter through which projects must pass to become a reality. Things become even more difficult when research is in

a formative phase, like that of ancient sculptural (and architectural) polychromy. To be successful, a sculptural polychromy research project in a world museum must, therefore, be based on common interest established between upper-level museum management and its strategic priorities, the core curatorial, conservation and science departments and above all, the individuals on the staffs concerned. Win–win in aims and means will carry the day, and a lot of preparatory reconnoitering and sounding out is clearly required.

In every phase, on every level, a main strength of argument is the fact that the polychromy of ancient sculpture and architecture is of equal fascination to a wide museum audience on the one hand, and to a scholarly, scientific community on the other.

Medium-sized museums: Research networks

This category includes a number of state and regional archaeological museums, often located in major cities or university towns: well-known examples are the Staatliche Antikensammlung und Glyptothek in Munich, the Liebieghaus Skulpturensammlung in Frankfurt am Main, the Ny Carlsberg Glyptotek in Copenhagen and the Antikenmuseum Basel und Sammlung Ludwig. There are many others. They differ from their larger sister institutions in not having the same spectrum of in-house conservation capabilities. More specifically, they are rarely equipped with a conservation science unit, but usually with staff and facilities for objects conservation relevant for their collections. Only if sculpture is a dominant category will they be served by a stone conservation workshop or 'studio', as for example the Glyptotek in Copenhagen. Even then, spaces suitable for visual examination and imaging of large-scale sculpture are often not available and must

---

111 Calandra et al. 2014. The urns investigated are in the Museo Archeologico Nazionale dell'Umbria, Perugia, and in the Antiquarium comunale, Corciano.

112 This 'in-house' resource may be in the same building as the collections, as in the British Museum or the Metropolitan Museum of Art; see Leona 2009 for the set-up in the latter. In other cases, it is physically and institutionally separated from the museum. Thus, the Rathgen-Forschungslabor in Berlin/Charlottenburg (far from museums) serves the conservation science needs of all the Staatliche Museen Berlin (http://www.smb.museum/en/museums-and-institutions/rathgen-forschungslabor/home.html), while the objects conservation needs of the Antikensammlung are met by a stone workshop in the Archäologisches Zentrum not far from the Museumsinsel (http://www.smb.museum/en/museums-and-institutions/archaeologisches-zentrum/home.html), and metal and ceramic objects are conserved in the building of the Altes Museum (http://www.smb.museum/museen-und einrichtungen/antikensammlung/restaurierung.html). In Paris, the main objects conservation and scientific research resources serving the Louvre are to be found in a national centre, the Centre de recherche et de restauration des Musées de France (C2RMF; http://c2rmf.fr/).

113 Humanities in particular: ancient history, classical and medieval philology, art history, digital humanities.

be improvised. The challenge in this scenario is to establish a network of external partners. The network must be set up to provide resources in conservation science and natural science on the one hand, and humanities on the other:

Network resources in conservation science and natural science

These resources are a sine qua non, but the relevant external (potential partner) institutions and persons will often belong to a sort of professional terra incognita. Relevant partner institutions are the following:

1. Schools of Conservation. The School of Conservation in Copenhagen has been the key external partner institution in the Copenhagen Polychromy Network, established on the initiative of Ny Carlsberg Glyptotek in connection with the Tracking Colour Project.[114] Some of the reasons for this pivotal role go beyond the specific context: First and foremost, the objects conservator(s) who must necessarily be part of the museum's research team will have received their professional training at such a school. This forms a decisive link to the resources which make a school of conservation such a vital network partner in polychromy research. It can offer highly competent advice and support in matters of both objects conservation and conservation science, and also provide access to analytical instrumentation (i.e. SEM-EDX; XRF) and other equipment not available at the museum. Furthermore, both parties may profit from having students attached as interns to the museum team as part of their training, perhaps leading to a Master's thesis on the work

done.[115] For their part, the schools of conservation stand to benefit from gaining access to the international contacts of the museum partner and the data acquired may be relevant to aspects of the research being carried out at the schools themselves, in particular in technical art history and the development of preventative conservation measures in relation to ancient stone sculpture.[116]

2. Museums of natural history. Such museums may be institutionally linked to universities[117] and thus to university institutes/departments. They will always have an academic staff trained in disciplines relevant to polychromy research, most particularly geology, but also zoology and botany.[118] Besides the natural scientific competences, such network partners will also often have access to relevant analytical instrumentation.

3. Archaeometric research units. These units constitute a resource staffed and equipped to serve the humanities by conducting analyses of a variety of artefacts, both archaeological and art historical. Such units are imbedded in university institutes or affiliated to universities and/or other research organizations.[119] An archaeometric unit is attuned in a general way to the mindset of humanities researchers, to their organizational setups and the type of research questions they pose: it is therefore a very valuable network asset.

4. Digital humanities (DH). DH is a field of teaching and research at the intersection of computing and the humanities. It is found in a variety of environments, often at universities as a resource shared by several academic disciplines. Among the aspects useful to polychromy research are 3D digitization and modelling,[120] and virtual reality reconstruction of the polychromy of individual

---

114 The School of Conservation is an integrated part of The Royal Danish Academy of Fine Arts Schools of Architecture, Design and Conservation https://kadk.dk/en/school-conservation.

115 As for example Sargent 2011; Therkildsen 2012.

116 Scharff 2013.

117 As is the case of the Natural History Museum of Denmark, cf. http://snm.ku.dk/english/.

118 The possible presence of microorganisms in pigments containing marble dust; the identification of species of plants providing madder lake; the identification of plants represented on monuments (as on the Ara Pacis, cf. Caneva 2010).

119 A number of units are directly involved in polychromy research. In the Copenhagen Polychromy Network, the Cultural Heritage Archaeometric Research Team – CHART/University of Southern Denmark, Institute of Chemistry is a partner, cf. http://www.sdu.dk/en/om_sdu/institutter_centre/c_chart/research.

120 Frischer 2015, 82 and *passim*. Cf. also Graham 2012 and 2012a in collaboration with the University of Lund's HumLab and Nicol'Dell'Unto: http://www.ark.lu.se/en/research/research-groups/823); The Visual Computing Lab of Pisa (CNR, ISTI) http://vcg.isti.cnr.it/; Eliana Siotto et al. http://vcg.isti.cnr.it/roman-sarcophagi/ulpia-sarcophagus-3d/index.html and http://vcg.isti.cnr.it/Publications/ with several titles relevant for polychromy research. See also the web page of V-Must, a network of excellence composed by a large number of European infrastructures working with 3D visualization and Museums http://www.v-must.net/.

sculptures and polychrome sculpture in its architectural setting.[121]

5. Commercial partners. Polychromy research requires specialized equipment and materials. It is worthwhile establishing close collaboration with the suppliers; mutual benefit has been shown to accrue from such collaboration, i.e. as regards microscopes, scanning equipment, and, for reconstructions, 3D printing and casting.

Network resources in the humanities

Collaboration with disciplines within the humanities not usually available at the museum will mean moving in more familiar territory, involving competences found at most universities, namely classical philology, epigraphy, ancient history and art history.

Among the benefits of working with universities is the possibility of supporting MA theses in classical archaeology[122] and establishing shared, co-financed PhD fellowships,[123] all connected to the museum's research project and thus aiding all-important recruitment to the field as well as strengthening the institution's research profile. From a strategic point of view this is one of the ways in which independent or private, non-state museums may gain recognition on a par with state museums and with it access to government research funding. New insights into one's own collection may become the spectacular 'acquisitions' of the future and thus the fuel for an exhibition activity less dependent on costly loans than on international research collaboration.

Concluding remarks

Brief and uneven as it is, this attempt at a survey does not do justice to the range and sophistication of methodologies applied in research on the polychromy of Greek and Roman sculpture; nor does it give anything like a full picture of the publications presenting the results of this research. But it does reflect the very positive and accelerating pace of development in this field since the 1980s; the expression 'break-through phase' would seem justified.[124] One might even dare to hope that a point of no return has been passed, assuring polychromy its place in the equation when we try to understand Greek and Roman sculpture – were it not for the fact that obvious dangers lurk.

It seems to me that research on the polychromy of Greek and Roman sculpture is for a number of reasons still in the nature of an imperiled species. Thus, to my knowledge, the subject is not as yet generally offered as a course at universities teaching classical archaeology, affecting the vital issue of recruitment to the field. Far more serious is the lack of an institutional foothold which would ensure continuity and consequent build-up of research experience and data as well as maintenance of specialized instrumentation. As it is, research in this field is project-based, i.e. time limited; the team and networks involved will therefore again and again be broken up and dispersed. This article has made it clear that it is a field of research which requires the expenditure of considerable resources. For the results of such an investment not to have an institutional foothold would be found intolerable in other fields of knowledge.

To me, assuring an institutional foothold in the form of a permanent research unit, preferably as a joint European venture, seems the greatest challenge now facing our field. Such a unit would best reflect the relevance to 'us in the West' of the return of colour to the sculpture of Classical Antiquity.

---

121 Cf. work done at the University of Southampton's Archaeological Computing Research Group http://acrg.soton.ac.uk/, http://acrg.soton.ac.uk/projects/amazon/ and Earl *et al.* 2009; Beale & Earl 2011. See also Bernhard Frischer's work on Hadrian's Villa https://www.phf.upenn.edu/events/recovering-polychromy-statues-hadrians-villa

122 As Graham 2012, Siotto 2013, Hoft 2014, Lenzi 2014, Kopczynski 2015, Iannaccone 2015, Blume 2015.

123 As Skovmøller 2016; Verena Hoft in progress (Eberhardt Karls Universität,Tübingen).

124 That a chapter has been devoted to 'Polychromy' in the Oxford Handbook of Roman Sculpture is most encouraging, cf. Abbe 2015.

Bibliography

Abbreviations specific to this paper:
IN = Ny Carlsberg Glyptotek inventory number
NCG = Ny Carlsberg Glyptotek

Abbe, M. 2015
'Polychromy', in Friedland & Sobocinski 2015, 173-88.

Abbe, M., G. E. Borromeo & S. Pike 2012
'A Hellenistic Greek Marble statue with Ancient Polychromy Reported to be from Knidos' in *Interdisciplinary Studies on Ancient Stone. ASMOSIA 9 (Tarragona 2009). Documenta 23*, A. Gutiérrez, P. Lapuente & I. Roda (eds), Tarragona, 763-70.

Andreotti, A., I. Bonaduce, M. P. Colombini, I. Degano, A. Lluveras, F. Modugno & E. Ribechini 2014
'Characterization of natural substances in ancient polychromies', in Liverani & Santamaria 2014, 191-206.

Baroni, S., G. Pizzigoni & P. Travaglio (eds.) 2014
Mappae clavicula. Alle origini dell'alchimia in Occidente. Testo-Traduzione-Note, Saonara (Pd).

Barry, F. 2011
'A Whiter Shade of Pale: Relative and Absolute White in Roman Sculpture and Architecture', in Clerbois & Droth 2011, 31-62.

Beale, G. & G. Earl 2011
'A Methodology for the Physically Accurate Visualisation of Roman Polychrome Statuary', in *The 12th International Symposium on Virtual Reality, Archaeology and Cultural Heritage VAST* (The Eurographics Association), M. Dellepiane, F. Niccolucci, S. Pena Serna, H. Rushmeier & L. Van Gool (eds), 137-44.

Berg, R. W. 2009
'Raman spectroscopy characterization of colored pigments in archaeological materials', in Østergaard 2009, 48-67.

Blume, C. 2015
Polychromie hellenistischer Skulptur 1-2, Petersberg.

Bottini, A. & E. Setari (eds.) 2007
Il sarcofago delle Amazzoni, Milan.

Bourgeois, B. 2012
'Marbre blanc, taches de couleur. Polychromie et restauration de la sculpture grecque', in *La restauration des peintures et des sculptures. Connaissance et reconnaissance de l'oeuvre*, P.-Y. Kairis, B. Sarrazin & F. Trémolières (eds), Paris, 25-42.

Bourgeois, B. 2014
'Thérapéia. Taking Care of Colour in Hellenistic Greece', in Østergaard & Nielsen 2014, 190-207.

Bourgeois, B. (ed.) 2014a
Thérapéia. *Polychromie et restauration de la sculpture dans l'Antiquité, Technè 40*.

Bourgeois, B. 2014b
'Ètudier et conserver la polychromie antique. Vidéo-microscopie et archéologie de la surface', in Bourgeois 2014a, 3-7.

Bourgeois, B. 2014c
'(Re)peindre, dorer, cirer. La *thérapéia* en acte dans la sculpture grecque hellénistique', in Bourgeois 2014a, 69-80.

Bourgeois, B. & V. Jeammet 2014
'Peindre et repeindre sur terre cuite en Grèce hellénistique', in Bourgeois 2014a, 84-95.

Bourgeois, B. & Ph. Jockey 2010
'The Polychromy of Hellenistic Marble Sculpture in Delos', in Brinkmann, Primavesi & Hollein 2010, 224-239.

Bracci, S., R. Iannaccone, S. Lenzi & P. Liverani 2014
'Non invasive characterization of pigments on "monochromes on marble" from Herculaneum and Pompeii: new researches', in *Art' 2014. 11th International Conference on Non-Destructive Investigations and Microanalysis for the Diagnostics and Conservation of Cultural and Environmental Heritage. Madrid, Museo Arqueológico Nacional, June 11th–June 13th, 2014*, Madrid (n.p.).

Bradley, M. 2009
Colour and Meaning in Ancient Rome, Cambridge.

Brecoulaki, H. 2014
'"Precious colours" in Ancient Greek Polychromy and Painting: Material Aspects and symbolic Values', *RA 2014/1*, 1-36.

Brecoulaki, H., G. Kavvadias & G. Verri 2014
'Colour and Luxury. Three Classical painted Marble Pyxides from the Collection of the National Archaeological Museum, Athens', in Østergaard and Nielsen 2014, 152-65.

Brecoulaki, H., S. Sotiropoulou, Ch. Katsifas, A. G. Karydas & V. Kantarelou 2014
'A Microcosm of Colour and Shine. The Polychromy of Chryselephantine Couches from Ancient Macedonia', in Bourgeois 2014a, 8-22.

Brinkmann, V. 2003
Die Polychromie der archaischen und frühklassischen Skulptur, Munich.

Brinkmann, V. 2010
'Einführung in der Ausstellung. Die Erforschung der Farbigkeit antiker Skulptur', in Brinkmann & Scholl 2010, 16-27.

Brinkmann, V. 2010a
'Statues in Colour: Aesthetics, Research and Perspectives', in Brinkmann, Primavesi & Hollein 2010, 10-21.

Brinkmann, V. 2010b
'Farben und Maltechnik', in Brinkmann & Scholl 2010, 236-43.

Brinkmann, V. 2015
'Art of Many Colors. Classical Statues in their Original Appearance', in *Serial / Portable Classic*, S. Settis & A. Anguissola (eds), Milan, 95-100.

Brinkmann, V., S. Kellner, U. Koch-Brinkmann & J. S. Østergaard 2010
'Die Farbfassung des Caligula-Porträts', in Brinkmann & Wünsche 2003, 206-211 (see also the version in Brinkmann & Scholl 2010, 228-235).

Brinkmann, V. & R. Wünsche (eds.) 2003
Bunte Götter. Die Farbigkeit antiker Skulptur. Eine Ausstellung der Staatlichen Antikensammlungen und Glyptothek, München. In Zusammenarbeit mit der Ny Carlsberg Glyptotek, Kopenhagen, und den Vatikanischen Museen, Rom, Munich.

Brinkmann, V., O. Primavesi & M. Hollein (eds) 2010
Circumlitio. *The Polychromy of Antique and Mediaeval Sculpture*, Munich.

Brinkmann, V. & A. Scholl (eds.) 2010
Bunte Götter. Die Farbigkeit antiker Skulptur. Eine Ausstellung der Antikensammlung, Staatliche Museen zu Berlin in Kooperation mit der Liebieghaus Skulpturensammlung, Frankfurt am Main und der Stiftung Archäologie, München im Pergamonmuseum auf der Museumsinsel Berlin. 13.7. – 3.10.2010, Munich.

Brinkmann, V. & U. Koch-Brinkmann 2010
'On the Reconstruction of Antique Polychromy Techniques', in Brinkmann, Primavesi & Hollein 2010, 114-35.

Brinkmann, V., U. Koch-Brinkmann & H. Piening 2010
'The funerary monument to Phrasikleia', in Brinkmann, Primavesi & Hollein 2010, 188-217.

Calandra, E., L. Cenciaioli, M. Cappelletti, A. Scaleggi & P. Comodi 2014
'Policromia in Umbria. Testimonianze nelle necropolis di Casaglia e di Strozzacaponi a Perugia', in Liverani & Santamaria 2014, 71-108.

Caneva, G. 2010
Il codice botanico di Augusto: Roma, Ara Pacis. Parlare al popolo attraverso le immagini della natura/The Augustus Botanical Code: Rome, Ara Pacis. Speaking to the People Through the Images of Nature, Rome.

Ciliberto, E. 2000
'Analytical Methods in Art and Archaeology', in Ciliberto and Spoto 2000, 1-10.

Ciliberto, E. & G. Spoto (eds.) 2000
Modern Analytical Methods in Art and Archaeology, New York.

Clerbois, S. & M. Droth (eds) 2011
Revival and Invention. Sculpture through its Material Histories, Oxford, Bern, Berlin.

De Cesare, M. 1997
Le statue in imagine: studi sulle raffigurazioni di statue nella pittura vascolare greca, Rome.

Donati, F. 2014
'Linee programmatiche per il riconoscimento e lo studio della policromia sulle urne etrusche e i sarcofagi romani', in Liverani & Santamaria 2014, 129-48.

Drinkler, D. 2009
'Tight-Fitting Clothes in Antiquity – Experimental reconstructions', *Archaeological Textiles Newsletter* 49, 11-5.

Dyer, J., G. Verri & J. Cupitt 2013
Multispectral Imaging in Reflectance and Photo-induced Luminescence modes: A User Manual. Version1.0. http://www.britishmuseum.org/research/research_projects/all_current_projects/charisma/technical_imaging.aspx (Accessed March 2015).

171

Earl, G., G. Beale, J. Happa, M. Williams, G. Turley, K. Martinez & A. Chalmers 2009
'A re-painted Amazon', in *EVA London 2009: Electronic Visualisation & the Arts. Proceedings of a conference held in London 6-8 July 2009*, A. Seal with S. Keene & J. Bowen (eds), London, 20-9.

Earl, G., K. Martinez & T. Malzbender 2010
'Archaeological applications of polynomial texture mapping: analysis, conservation and representation', *Journal of Archaeological Science*, 37:8, 2040-2050.

Elsner, J. 2007
Roman Eyes. Visuality and Subjectivity in Art and Text, Princeton.

Feigl, F & V. Anger 1937/2012
Spot tests in inorganic analysis, Amsterdam.

Fine, S. 2013
'Menorahs in color: polychromy in Jewish visual culture of Roman antiquity', *Images* 6, 3-25.

Fink-Jensen, P. 2013
'An archaeometric study of lead pigments from a 1st century BCE Roman marble sculpture', in Østergaard 2013, 36-62.

Friedland, E. A. & M. Grunow Sobocinski, with E.K. Gazda (eds.) 2015
The Oxford Handbook of Roman Sculpture, New York.

Frischer, B. 2015
'Three-dimensional Scanning and Modeling', in Friedland & Sobocinski 2015, 74-89.

Ganio, M., J. Salvant, J. Williams, L. Lee, O. Cossairt & M. Walton 2015
'Investigating the use of Egyptian blue in Roman Egyptian portraits and panels from Tebtunis, Egypt', *Applied Physics A*, Volume 121, Issue 3, 813-821.

Gercke, P. 2009
'Farbige und metallbeschichtete Nachbildungen des 'Kasseler Apollon' und der 'Athena Lemnia'', in *Bunte Götter. Die Farbigkeit antiker Skulptur. Eine Ausstellung der Museumslandschaft Hessen-Kassel. 6. März–1. Juni 2009*, V. Brinkmann (ed.), Kassel, 148-55.

Graham, C. A. 2012
Applications of Digitization to Museum Collections Management, Research and Accessibility, unpublished Master's thesis in archaeology, University of Lund.

Graham, C. A. 2012a
'3D Digitization in an Applied Context: Polychromy Research', in Østergaard 2012, 64-85.

Haag, S., V. Brinkmann & U. Koch-Brinkmann (eds.) 2013
Bunte Götter. Die Farbigkeit antiker Skulptur. Eine Ausstellung des Kunsthistorischen Museums Wien in Kooperation mit der Stiftung Archäologie, München, und der Liebieghaus Skulpturensammlung, Frankfurt am Main, Vienna.

Heilmeyer, W. -D. & W. Massmann 2014
Die 'Berliner Göttin': Schicksale einer archaischen Frauenstatue in Antike und Neuzeit, Lindenberg im Allgäu.

Henke, F. 2014
Graptoi Typoi. Die griechischen und lateinischen Schriftquellen zur Farbigkeit der antiken Skulptur, unpublished PhD thesis, Ludwig-Maximilian-Universität, Munich.

Hoft, V. 2013
'Der Blick in eingelegte Augen: Griechische und römische Skulpturen in der Ny Carlsberg Glyptotek, in Østergaard 2013, 63-79.

Hoft, V. 2014
Intarsienaugen. Ein Beitrag zur Polychromie römischer Steinskulpturen, unpublished Master's thesis, Universität Hamburg.

Iannaccone, R. 2015
Tecniche di imaging innovative per la messa a punto di un protocollo integrato per la caratterizzazione dei pigmenti utilizzati nell'antichità, unpublished PhD thesis, Florence, Università degli Studi.

Iannaccone, R., S. Bracci, E. Cantisani & B. Mazzei 2015
'An integrated multi-methodological approach for characterizing the materials and pigments on a sarcophagus in St. Mark, Marcellian and Damasus catacombs', *Applied Physics A*, Vol. 121, 1235-42.

Kakoulli, I. 2009
Greek Painting Techniques and Materials from the fourth to the first century BC, London.

Kannicht, R. (ed.) 1969
Euripides, Helena. Vols 1-2. Heidelberg.

Koch-Brinkmann, U. & R. Posamentir 2010
'Ornament und Malerei einer attischen Grablekythos', in Brinkmann & Scholl 2010, 178-85.

Koch-Brinkmann, U., H. Piening & V. Brinkmann 2014
'On the Rendering of Human Skin in Ancient Marble Sculpture', in Østergaard & Nielsen 2014, 140-51.

Kopczynski, N. 2015
Couleur et matière de la statuaire romaine d'Afrique. Recherche sur la polychromie de la sculpture romaine à partier de l'étude des collections du Musée du Bardo, unpublished Master's thesis, Université de Sorbonne Paris IV.

Leka, E. 2014
'La *thérapéia* des sculptures en Gréce ancienne: le temoinage des sources textuelles', in Bourgeois 2014a, 61-8.

Lenzi, S. 2014
La policromia dei "Monochromata": la ricerca del colore su dipinti su lastre di marmo di età romana, unpublished PhD thesis, Florence, Università degli Studi.

Leona, M. 2009
'The Materiality of Art: Scientific Research and Art Conservation at the Metropolitan Museum', *The Metropolitan Museum of Art Bulletin* 67: 1, 4-11.

Liritzis, I. & N. Zacharias 2011
'Portable XRF of Archaeological Artifacts: Current Research, Potentials and Limitations', in *X-Ray Fluorescence Spectrometry (XRF) in Geoarchaeology*, Shackley, M.S. (ed.), 109-42.

Liverani, P. (ed.) 2004
I colori del bianco. Policromia nella scultura antica. Collana di studi e documentazione. Musei Vaticani, Rome.

Liverani, P. 2004a
'L'Augusto di Prima Porta', in Liverani 2004, 235-42.

Liverani, P. 2009
'Osservazioni sulla policromia e la doratura della scultura in età tardoantica', in Andreuccetti & Cervelli 2009, 9-22.

Liverani, P. & U. Santamaria (eds.) 2014
Diversamento bianco. La policromia della scultura romana, Rome.

Mandel, U. 2010
'On the qualities of the 'Colour' White in Antiquity', in Brinkmann, Primavesi & Hollein 2010, 303-23.

Marconi, C. 2011
'The Birth of an Image. The Painting of a Statue of Herakles and Theories of Representation in Classical Greek Culture', *Res: Anthropology and Aesthetics* 59/60, 145-66.

Moormann, E. M. 1988
La pittura parietale romana come fonte di conoscenza per la scultura antica, Assen.

Moormann, E. M. 2008
'Statues on the wall: The representation of statuary in Roman wall painting', in *The Sculptural Environment of the Roman Near East. Reflections on Culture, Ideology, and Power*, Y. Z. Eliav, E. A. Friedland & S. Herbert (eds), Leuven/Dudley MA, 197-224.

Moormann, E.M. 2015
'Images of statues in other media', in Friedland & Sobocinski 2015, 638-52.

Nichols, K. 2015
Greece and Rome at the Crystal Palace: Classical Sculpture and Modern Britain, 1854-1936, Oxford.

Odegaard, N.N., S. Carroll & W.S. Zimmt 2005
Material characterization tests for objects of art and archaeology, London.

Pallecchi, P., G. Giachi, M.P. Colombini, F. Modugno & E. Ribechini 2009
'The painting of the Etruscan 'Tomba della Quadriga Infernale' (4th century BCE), in Sarteano (Siena, Italy): technical features', *Journal of Archaeological Science* 36, 2635-42.

Pandermalis, D. (ed.) 2012
Archaic Colors, Athens.

Pannuzi, S. (ed.) 2015
Gandhara. Tecnologia, produzione e conservazione. Indagini preliminari su sculture in pietra e in stucco del Museo Nazionale d'Arte Orientale 'Giuseppe Tucci', Rome.

Piening, H. 2010
'From Scientific Findings to Reconstruction: The Technical background to the Scientific Reconstruction of Colours', in Brinkmann, Primavesi & Hollein 2010, 108-13.

Piening, H. 2010a
'Ein farbiges Vermächtnis – Die Farbmittel am 'Alexandersarkophag'', in Brinkmann & Scholl 2010, 202-5.

Piening, H. 2014
'UV-VIS spectroscopy in the research on ancient sculptural and architectural polychromy. Recent activities', in Liverani & Santamaria 2014, 185-90.

173

Primavesi, O. 2010
'Antike Dichter und Philosophen über die Farbigkeit der Skulptur', in Brinkmann & Scholl 2010, 28-39.

Primavesi, O. 2014
'Colourful Sculptures in Greek Tragedy', in Østergaard & Nielsen 2014, 70-9.

Quatremère de Quincy, A.-Ch. 1814
Jupiter Olympien, ou l'art de la sculpture antique considérée sous un nouveau point de vue, ouvrage qui comprend un essai sur le gout de la sculpture polychrome, l'analyse explicative de la toreutique, et l'histoire de la statuaire en or et ivoire chez les Grecs et les Romains, avec la restitution des principaux monuments de cet art et la démonstration pratique ou le renouvellement de ces procédés mécaniques, Paris. http://tools.yoolib.com/Yviewer/index.php?user=inha&filemedia_id=15371&fullscreen=1&current_image_id=3&dbk=&menu_left_visible=1&menu_left_type=signet (Accessed February 2016).

Reeler, N. E. A., O. F. Nielsen, L. Spaabæk, M. Jørgensen & H.G. Kjærgaard 2013
'Fayum mummy portraits investigated by NIR-FT- Raman microscopy', *Asian Chemistry Letters* 7:1-2, 1-12.

Reuterswärd, P. 1960
Studien zur Polychromie der Plastik. Griechenland und Rom. Untersuchungen über die Farbwirkung der Marmor- und Bronzeskulpturen, Stockholm.

Romualdi, A., P. Pallecchi, L. Pierelli & G. Tonini 2005
'Surfaces of antique marble sculptures in the Uffizi Gallery: reflection of history and image', *Surface Engineering* 21, 5-6, 378-84.

Rosing, Minik T., & J. S. Østergaard 2009
'Preliminary results from geochemical analysis of pigments on ancient Greek and Roman marble sculptures', in Østergaard 2009, 41-7.

Roueché, C., M. Holdenried & M. Scholz 2014
'Digital Epigraphy in its archaeological context: The case of Metropolis, Magnesia & Apollonia', in *Die Surveys im Hermos- und Kaystrostal und die Grabungen an den Thermen von Metropolis sowie am Stadion von Magnesia am Mäander (Ionien): Neue Methoden und Ergebnissen*, B. Dreyer (ed.), Münster, 163-79.

Santamaria, U. & F. Morresi 2004
'Le indagini scientifiche per lo studio della cromia dell'Augusto di Prima Porta', in Liverani 2004, 243-52.

Santamaria, U., F. Morresi, G. Agresti & C. Pelosi 2014
'Studi analitici della policromia antica e sperimentazione sul nano incapsulamento di coloranti con nanosilici', in Liverani & Santamaria 2014, 33-49.

Sargent, M. L. 2011
Dokumentation og undersøgelse af antik skulpturel polykromi – med focus på en romersk marmor amazone (Documentation and investigation of antique sculptural polychromy – with a focus on a Roman marble Amazon), unpublished Master's thesis, The Royal Danish Academy of Fine Arts. The School of Conservation.

Sargent, M. L. 2011a
'Recent Investigation of the Polychromy of a Metropolitan Roman garland Sarcophagus', in Østergaard 2011, 14-34.

Sargent, M.L. 2012
'Investigations into the polychromy of some 5th century BCE Etruscan architectural terracottas', in Østergaard 2012, 26-44.

Sargent, M.L., L. R. Spaabæk, M. Scharff & J. S. Østergaard 2009
'Documentation and investigation of traces of colour on the Archaic sphinx NCG IN 1203', in Østergaard 2009, 74-89.

Sargent, M. L. & R. H. Therkildsen 2010
'The Technical Investigation of Sculptural Polychromy at the Ny Carlsberg Glyptotek 2009-2010 – An Outline', in Østergaard 2010, 11-26.

Sargent, M. L. & R. H. Therkildsen 2010a
'Research on Ancient Sculptural Polychromy with Focus on a 2nd century CE Marble Amazon', in Østergaard 2010, 27-49.

Scharff, M. et al. 2009
Scharff, M., R. Hast, N. Kalsbeek & J. S. Østergaard 2009
'Investigating the polychromy of a Classical Attic Greek marble female head NCG IN 2830', in Østergaard 2009, 13-40.

Scharff, M. 2013
'Ten years of studies in ancient sculptural polychromy revisited', in Østergaard 2013, 80-6.

Schmaltz, B. 2008
'Die wundersame Vermehrung der göttlichen Buntheit', *Antike Welt* 2, 41-4.

Schmaltz, B. 2009
'Die Kore Akropolismuseum Inv. 682. Versuch einer Rekonstruktion', *JdI* 124, 75-133.

Siotto, E. 2013
Nuove tecnologie per lo studio della policromia sui sarcofagi romani: proposte per una standardizzazione metodologica, unpublished PhD thesis, Università degli Studi di Pisa.

Skovmøller, A. 2011
'The Tracking Colour Website', in Østergaard 2011, 47-55.

Skovmøller, A. 2014
'Where Marble Meets Colour: surface texturing of hair, skin and dress on Roman marble portraits as support for painted polychromy', in *Greek and Roman Textiles and Dress: An Interdisciplinary Anthology* (Ancient Textiles Series 19), M. Harlow & M.-L. Nosch (eds), Oxford, 279-97.

Skovmøller, A. 2015
Portraits and Colour-codes in ancient Rome: The Polychromy of white marble Portraits, unpublished PhD thesis, University of Copenhagen.

Skovmøller, A. & R.H. Therkildsen 2014
'A Reconstruction. Portrait of a Young Roman Man', in Østergaard & Nielsen 2014, 256-69.

Smith, D., H. Brecoulaki, G. Oikonomou, I. Kougemitrou, M. Perraki & E. Stasinopoulou 2009
'The in situ MRM first discovery of lazurite on a painted marble pyxis at the National Archaeological Museum, Athens', poster presented at the *5th International Congress on the Applica-tion of Raman Spectroscopy in Art and Archaeology, Bilbao (Spain), 14-18 Sept. 2009* (Book of Abstracts: RAA 2009).

Spada, S. 2004
'Restauro e ricostruzione della policromia dell'Augusto di Prima Porta', in Liverani 2004, 249-52.

Talarico, F., P. Biocca, G. Sidoti & M. Torre 2015
'Caratterizzazione dei materiali pittorici provenienti dal Gandhara' in Pannuzi 2015, 52-60.

Theiss, H. 2010
'A Brief Overview of the Decorative Techniques Used in Sculptural Polychromy in the Middle Ages', in Brinkmann, Primavesi & Hollein 2010, 136-53.

Therkildsen, R. H. 2011
'The Copenhagen Polychromy Network: introducing the survey protocol in documenting and investigating ancient sculptural polychromy', *Medelhavsmuseet* (Focus on the Mediterranean 6), 31-40.

Therkildsen, R.H. 2012
Antik skulpturel polykromi. En farveundersøgelse af tre romerske portrætter i poleret marmor (Antique sculptural polychromy. A colour investigation of three Roman portraits in polished marble), unpublished Master's thesis, The Royal Danish Academy of Fine Arts. The School of Conservation.

Verri, G. 2009
'The spatially resolved characterization of Egyptian blue, Han blue and Han purple by photo-induced luminescence digital imaging', *AnalBioanalChem* 394:4, 1011-21.

Verri, G., D. Comellic, S. Cather, D. Saunders & F. Piqué 2008
'Post -capture data analysis as an aid to the interpretation of ultraviolet-induced fluorescence images', in *Computer Image Analysis in the Study of Art. Proc. of SPIE-IS&T Electronic Imaging*, D. G. Stork & J. Coddington (eds), *SPIE Vol. 6810, 681002* (Bellingham 2008).

Verri, G., P. Collins, J. Ambers, T. Sweek & St J. Simpson 2009
'Assyrian colours: pigments on a neo-Assyrian relief of a parade horse', *The British Museum Technical Research Bulletin* 3, 57-62.
https://www.britishmuseum.org/research/publications/online_journals/technical_research_bulletin/bmtrb_volume_3.aspx (Accessed April 2016).

Verri, G., Th. Opper & Thibaut Deviese 2010
'The 'Treu Head': a case study in Roman sculptural polychromy', *British Museum Technical Research Bulletin* 4, 39-4.
http://www.britishmuseum.org/research/publications/online_journals/technical_research_bulletin/bmtrb_volume_4.aspx (Accessed December 2015).

Verri, G., Th. Opper & L. Lazzarini 2014.
'"In picturae modum variata circumlitio"?: the reconstruction of the polychromy of a Roman female head (Treu Head)', in Liverani & Santamaria 2014, 149-83.

Verri, G., M. Gleba, J. Swaddling, T. Long, J. Ambers & T. Munden 2014
'Etruscan women's clothing and its decoration: the polychrome gypsum statue from the 'Isis tomb' at Vulci', *British Museum Technical Research Bulletin* 8, 59-71. http://www.britishmuseum.org/research/publications/online_journals/technical_research_bulletin/bmtrb_volume_8.aspx (Accessed November 2015).

Verri, G. & D. Saunders 2014
'Xenon flash for reflectance and luminescence (multispectral) imaging in cultural heritage applications', *British Museum Technical Research Bulletin* 8, 83-92.

Zanker, P. 2000
'Bild-Räume und Betrachter im kaiserzeitlichen Rom', in A. H. Borbein, T. Hölscher & P. Zanker, *Klassische Archäologie: Eine Einführung*, Berlin, 205-26.

Zimmer, K. (ed.) 2016
Von der Reproduktion zur Rekonstruktion – Umgang mit Antike(n) II. Summerschool vom 16.–19. Juni 2014 in Tübingen, Tübingen.

Østergaard, J.S. 2003
'Der Caligula in der Ny Carlsberg Glyptotek, Kopenhagen. Ein Projekt zur Rekonstruktion der polychromen Fassung eines römischen Porträts', in Brinkmann & Wünsche 2003, 198-203 (see also the version in Brinkmann and Scholl 2010, 218-25).

Østergaard, J.S. (ed.) 2009
Tracking Colour. The Polychromy of Greek and Roman sculpture in the Ny Carlsberg Glyptotek, Copenhagen. Preliminary Report 2, Copenhagen.

Østergaard, J.S. 2009a
'The CPN Pilot Project: a brief introduction and evaluation', in Østergaard 2009, 11-2.

Østergaard, J.S. 2009b
'The CPN Main Project 2008-2011: an outline', in Østergaard 2009, 68-73.

Østergaard, J.S. (ed.) 2010
Tracking Colour. The Polychromy of Greek and Roman sculpture in the Ny Carlsberg Glyptotek, Copenhagen. Preliminary Report 2, Copenhagen.

Østergaard, J.S. 2010a
'The Polychromy of Antique Sculpture: A Challenge to Western Ideals?', in Brinkmann, Primavesi & Hollein 2010, 78-105.

Østergaard, J. S. 2010b
'The Copenhagen Polychromy Network. A Research Project on Ancient Greek and Roman Sculptural Polychromy in the Ny Carlsberg Glyptotek', in Brinkmann, Primavesi & Hollein 2010, 324-35.

Østergaard, J.S. 2011
Tracking Colour. The Polychromy of Greek and Roman sculpture in the Ny Carlsberg Glyptotek, Copenhagen. Preliminary Report 3, Copenhagen.

Østergaard, J.S. (ed.) 2012
Tracking Colour. The Polychromy of Greek and Roman sculpture in the Ny Carlsberg Glyptotek, Copenhagen. Preliminary Report 4, Copenhagen.

Østergaard, J.S. (ed.) 2013
Tracking Colour. The Polychromy of Greek and Roman sculpture in the Ny Carlsberg Glyptotek, Copenhagen. Preliminary Report 5, Copenhagen.

Østergaard, J S., M. L. Sargent & R. H. Therkildsen 2014
'The polychromy of Roman 'ideal' marble sculpture of the 2nd century CE', in Liverani and Santamaria 2014, 51-69.

Østergaard, J.S. & A.M. Nielsen (eds) 2014
Transformations. Classical Sculpture in Colour, Copenhagen.

Art Historical Studies and
Modern Greece

The Parthenon in Danish art and architecture, from Nicolai Abildgaard to Theophil Hansen[1]

PATRICK KRAGELUND

Until the final decades of the 18th century the Parthenon was virtually unknown to the world. What the temple looked like, where it was situated and how it related to its surroundings – all this, despite the widespread admiration for everything Classical, was shrouded in almost total mystery. If I may generalize, before 1800 the concept of 'antiquity' was almost wholly defined by Rome: Roman art, architecture and literature. Of course, by the mid-18th century this was beginning to be challenged, thus for instance inducing Piranesi to defend the primate of Roman as opposed to Greek architecture. As for the Parthenon, its fame and iconic status was however still eclipsed by that of the Roman Pantheon.

All this changed in the decades around 1800 – no doubt faster in the Protestant North than in the Latin South, but the trend was pan-European. A process now set in motion meant that Greece and all things Greek gradually came to replace Rome as the privileged centre of artistic and scholarly focus: not at any measurable speed, and not in the sense that Rome lost out completely, but within the Classical hierarchy a remarkable and long-lasting shift took place.[2]

With a few examples below I shall illustrate how this adulation of the Parthenon (I can find no better word) affected the Danish art and architecture of Theophil Hansen's youth, and then look at the way this early adu-

lation still influenced his late and, perhaps luckily, perhaps sadly, unfinished project for an Acropolis Museum in the final years of his life.

One of the first Danes to show clear artistic awareness of the Parthenon's Doric glory was the learned painter-philosopher Nicolai Abildgaard (1743-1809). The closest Abildgaard ever got to Greece was Paestum in the south of Italy (these were also the only Greek temples that the father of Classical archaeology, Johann Winckelmann, ever saw), but when in 1801 he embarked upon illustrating the Greek style comedy *Andria, The Girl from Andros* by the Roman playwright Terence (Terentius), he approached the task of creating an Athenian setting in a deliberately playful and capricious manner. He mixes Neoclassical buildings from Copenhagen and from a Utopian Athens to create a setting that in its emphasis on dazzling perspective has clear allusions to the ancient *scaenographia*, as famously described by the Roman architect Vitruvius. In its second painting the series has a fantasy setting of the Tower of Winds (based upon the engraving in his edition of Stuart & Revett's *The antiquities of Athens*) – and in the comedy's paradigmatic opening scene a version of the Parthenon is the dazzling *point de vue* of a street scene in a fantasy Athens (Fig. 1).[3]

The next decade saw the transition from fantasy to actual familiarity, a move resulting in a greatly increased

1   This is the text of a lecture given at a conference in January 2015 on "Theophilus Hansen and Athens', organized by the Danish Institute at Athens in connection with the Theophil Hansen exhibition at the B. & M. Theocharakis Foundation in Athens. The verbal style of the lecture has been retained and only the essential references added. I am indebted to Director Rune Frederiksen for effective planning, the creation of much fruitful dialogue and splendid hospitality.

2   Atherton 2006 is an illuminating case-study illustrating how Greece replaced Rome as the valued centre of attention; a similar process changed attitudes to Greek tragedy: Kragelund 2015, ch. 17.

3   On the *Andria* series, see Kragelund 1987, 137-85; Lederballe 2009, 139-49 (both with bibliography).

Fig. 1. *N. Abildgaard, Scene from Terence's Andria, Act I, Scene 1. Oil on canvas. 157.5 x 142 cm. Signed "N. Abildgaard 1803" (National Gallery of Denmark).*

Danish awareness of the real Parthenon.[4] In 1813, the first Classical scholars from Denmark visited and brought home knowledge; in 1818-20 followed the architect and later Royal Academy professor Jørgen Hansen Koch (1787-1860), whose drawings from Mycenae, Aegina and Athens would have given his Copenhagen Academy students a clearer idea about Greek architecture. So would the hundreds of drawings by himself and his colleagues, drawings that still form the core of the Greek collection in the Danish National Art Library (Fig. 2).[5] This was also the time when the Academy became able to give its students a more immediate impression of Greek art through the acquisition of casts from the so-called Elgin Marbles. Casts of the Phidias frieze, the metopes and the pediment figures were between 1819 and 1828 included among the canonical works exhibited in the Academy's cast collection at Charlottenborg Palace in Copenhagen. Within a decade, such time-honoured icons as the *Laocoon* and the *Apollo Belvedere* were now joined by such uppity newcomers as the *Ilissus*, the Parthenon metopes and the Phidias frieze (Fig. 3).[6] In the history of taste, this was a rapid shift of unprecedented magnitude. What added to the excitement was the sensational discovery that two fragments of Greek sculpture that had been in the Royal collections since 1688 were in fact fragments of one of the Parthenon metopes.[7] In these years the Parthenon and the Acropolis entered public consciousness as the very summit of artistic endeavour. What Theophil Hansen saw when drawing in the Academy's cast collection was, in short, an expression of the growing admiration for all

---

4   Dietz 2000 offers a panoramic survey of Dano-Greek interaction.

5   Catalogues and discussions of the Greek material in the Danish National Art Library: Bendtsen 1993; Haugsted 1996.

6   Zahle 2008, 214-37.

7   Lund & Rathje 1991, 11-56.

Fig. 2. *Christian Hansen, The temple of Erechtheum. Oil on canvas. 35.5 x 54.2 cm. 1844. Private collection (photo: Danish National Art Library).*

things Greek – the country of which, in letters from his brother Christian, he was hearing so much.[8]

In Denmark this adulation of all things Greek and widespread sympathy for the country's battle for liberty were combined with a no less fervent admiration for the nation's top cultural hero, the sculptor Bertel (or, in Italian, Alberto) Thorvaldsen (1770-1844), an artist whom Hansen throughout his life held in the highest esteem. In the cast collection of the Royal Academy of Fine Arts the tondi of the so-called 'Modern Phidias' (i.e. Thorvaldsen) would, with almost demonstrative insistence, share the space otherwise allotted to the casts of the Phidias frieze and a relief symbolically evoking the Roman Empire (Fig. 4). This is a programmatic layout strongly indicative of a specific neo-classical aesthetics that would follow Theophil Hansen throughout his life.

As observed by Villads Villadsen, in the essay re-printed in the splendid catalogue of the exhibition in Athens,[9] there is something almost symbolic in the fact that 1838, the year of Thorvaldsen's final, triumphant homecoming to Copenhagen from Rome, was also the year of Hansen's departure for Greece. Where Rome had been the arena of Thorvaldsen's rise to international fame, Athens would now become the central, permanent centre of Theophil Hansen's aesthetic project.[10]

As for Thorvaldsen, the homecoming sculptor hero was celebrated in Copenhagen and his work honoured by the decision to build him a museum. It was built with money donated by the general public, high and low, and by the city of Copenhagen – whereas the role of the monarch was deliberately, not to say provocatively, underplayed. We are close to the year of a European revolution, 1848.

8   Villadsen 2014, 222.
9   Cassimatis & Panetsos 2014.
10   Villadsen 2014, 222-31.

181

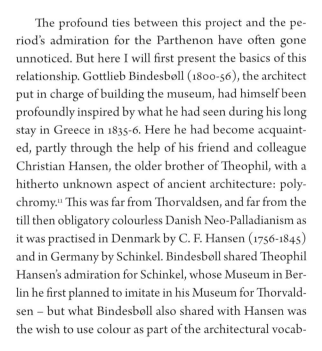

Fig. 3. *Kristen Købke, From the Cast Collection at the Royal Academy in Charlottenborg. Oil on canvas. 41.5 x 36 cm. 1830 (The Hirschsprung Collection).*

Fig. 4. *P.H. Rasmussen, The Cast Collection in the Danish Royal Academy. Oil on canvas. 47 x 44 cm. 1837. Private collection (here reproduced from Bundgaard Rasmussen et al. 2008, 234).*

The profound ties between this project and the period's admiration for the Parthenon have often gone unnoticed. But here I will first present the basics of this relationship. Gottlieb Bindesbøll (1800-56), the architect put in charge of building the museum, had himself been profoundly inspired by what he had seen during his long stay in Greece in 1835-6. Here he had become acquainted, partly through the help of his friend and colleague Christian Hansen, the older brother of Theophil, with a hitherto unknown aspect of ancient architecture: polychromy.[11] This was far from Thorvaldsen, and far from the till then obligatory colourless Danish Neo-Palladianism as it was practised in Denmark by C. F. Hansen (1756-1845) and in Germany by Schinkel. Bindesbøll shared Theophil Hansen's admiration for Schinkel, whose Museum in Berlin he first planned to imitate in his Museum for Thorvaldsen – but what Bindesbøll also shared with Hansen was the wish to use colour as part of the architectural vocabulary, thereby of course creating a spectacular framework setting for all the Thorvaldsen casts and marbles. "More Bindesbøll's Museum than mine", the old Thorvaldsen is said to have jokingly observed (Fig. 5).[12]

Rather than a Schinkel-inspired model for the museum with an internal Pantheon dome, Bindesbøll eventually opted for a massively compact format that variously underlines the sacral nature of the complex. What sustains these temple associations are the monumental scale and elevation, as well as the tomb-like gateways, each formed on an A and T modular so as to mimic Alberto (as he was called in Italy) Thorvaldsen's signature. Add to this the strong axiality that moves from the central front gateway all through the complex, en route passing over the place where Thorvaldsen was to be buried, finally to reach a kind of apsis, from where the model for the sculptor's iconic *Christ* seems to be blessing the tomb of the hero.[13]

11 Bindesbøll's pioneering use of external polychromy: Van Zanten 1977, 150-67.
12 Bruun & Fenger 1892, 104.
13 On Bindesbøll and his Museum, see Bruun & Fenger 1892, Bramsen 1959, 49-97; Millech 1960; Thule Kristensen 2013, 58-148.

Fig. 5. *G. Bindesbøll, drawing for the façade of Thor-valdsen's Museum. Pencil and watercolour on paper. 61.7 x 97.1 cm. C. 1842 (Danish National Art Library).*

Fig. 6. *The Frieze of Jørgen Sonne, with workers carrying Thorvaldsen's sculptures into his Museum. The fresco was completed in 1848. On the basis of the original drawings it was completely renewed in 1948-50 by the painter Axel Salto (here reproduced from Thule Kristensen 2013).*

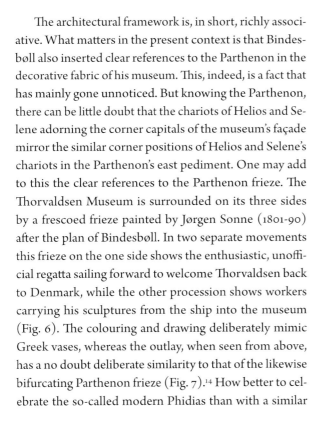

The architectural framework is, in short, richly associative. What matters in the present context is that Bindesbøll also inserted clear references to the Parthenon in the decorative fabric of his museum. This, indeed, is a fact that has mainly gone unnoticed. But knowing the Parthenon, there can be little doubt that the chariots of Helios and Selene adorning the corner capitals of the museum's façade mirror the similar corner positions of Helios and Selene's chariots in the Parthenon's east pediment. One may add to this the clear references to the Parthenon frieze. The Thorvaldsen Museum is surrounded on its three sides by a frescoed frieze painted by Jørgen Sonne (1801-90) after the plan of Bindesbøll. In two separate movements this frieze on the one side shows the enthusiastic, unofficial regatta sailing forward to welcome Thorvaldsen back to Denmark, while the other procession shows workers carrying his sculptures from the ship into the museum (Fig. 6). The colouring and drawing deliberately mimic Greek vases, whereas the outlay, when seen from above, has a no doubt deliberate similarity to that of the likewise bifurcating Parthenon frieze (Fig. 7).[14] How better to celebrate the so-called modern Phidias than with a similar

frieze celebrating how his gifts to the nation were carried into his temple?

After these examples of Danish Parthenon adulation, it is time to turn to Athens, to the project initiated in 1885, when the great finds of archaic sculpture on the Acropolis made it necessary to build a museum. Theophil Hansen was officially asked to produce the drawings. He was so proud of the project that in 1887, when he was awarded the so-called Nobel prize of architecture, the gold medal of the Royal Institute of British Architects, he donated a complete set of photographs illustrating the project to the Royal Academy in Copenhagen.[15] I published these photographs and the relevant drawings at the Vienna Symposium in 2013. Some of the drawings were shown in the exhibition in Athens.[16]

The most significant first-hand information about the project is contained in a speech by Hansen himself on the occasion of celebrating his fifty years in Athens – I edited the contemporary English translation of the speech in the above, and we now have a modern English version from Professor Marilena Cassimatis that is printed in the splendid Athens exhibition catalogue.[17]

---

14   Henderson 2005, 22 agrees that the similar layout of the friezes is significant.
15   There are brief references to the Acropolis Museum in Niemann & Feldegg 1893, 118, 127; Russack 1942, 145; Kokkou 1977, 239-41; Haugsted 1996, 343 (with thanks to Aristea Christensen in Athens for sending a copy of Kokkou).
16   Kragelund 2013, 179-92; cf. Cassimatis & Panetsos 2014, 22-8 with cat. nos. 38.1-9.
17   Cassimatis & Panetsos 2014, 26-8.

183

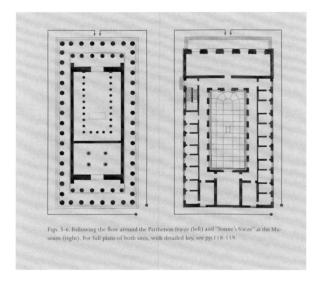

Figs. 5-6. Following the flow around the Parthenon frieze (left) and "Sonne's frieze" at the Museum (right). For full plans of both sites, with detailed key, see pp.118-119.

Fig. 7. *Plan of the Parthenon and of Thorvaldsen's Museum with position of friezes (after Henderson 2005, 22).*

Fig. 8. *Theophil Hansen, Proposed setting for Acropolis Museum. Pen and ink on paper. 32.3 x 29.7 cm. 1887 (Vienna, Academy of Arts).*

However, to understand Hansen's plans it is crucial to study the surviving drawings which show that he at some point drastically changed the position of the museum. From an early stage in the project we have a ground plan, which shows the originally intended position in relation to the Acropolis. This was in relation to what later happened much more to the east, but in its core layout it is basically identical with the later project.[18] In a later, more detailed version (Fig. 8), which further illustrates the museum's relation to the old Military Hospital (to the south of which Bernard Tschumi's New Acropolis Museum now stands), Hansen opted for a position slightly further to the west, but still with his modern stoae running parallel with the ruins of the Stoa of Eumenes that in Antiquity connected the theatres of Herodes Atticus and Dionysus.

I shall shortly return to what motivated this westward change of position and how it would affect the visitor's aesthetic experience, but first I should comment briefly on the ground plan. Hansen envisaged a large, open complex divided in two by the present-day Dionysio Areopagitou Street (Fig. 9). At each of the complex's four corners Hansen placed Corinthian tholoi connected by stoae that are closed towards the street but open towards inner courtyards. Visitors would gain access to the museum through four Ionic temple gateways. To the south of this oblong complex, where the terrain slopes rather steeply downwards, Hansen unusually places a one-storey theatre-shaped complex that opens up to an inner courtyard.

Where Hansen's stoae are visual evocations of the stoae of antiquity, the theatre shape playfully seems to resume and echo the theatres dominating the south slope of the Acropolis, adding a modern parallel to the ancient icons. So does the tetra style Ionic entry temples, the nearby temple of Nike being the ultimate model. It adds to the feeling of authenticity that the project, unusually in Hansen's oeuvre, seemingly works without elevating ramps and staircases, the stoae, tholoi and temples placed flatly on ground level. However, as the views from the

18 The early plan: Kragelund 2013, fig. 1 = Cassimatis & Panetsos 2014, fig. 38.6.

Fig. 9. *Theophil Hansen, Museum für Athen. I. Perspektivische Ansicht. 25.5 x 58.5 cm. 1887. Photograph of an ink on paper drawing in the Hansen bequest in the Danish National Art Library. In the background can be seen Hansen's Zappeion and Gärtner's Royal Palace, now the Greek Parliament.*

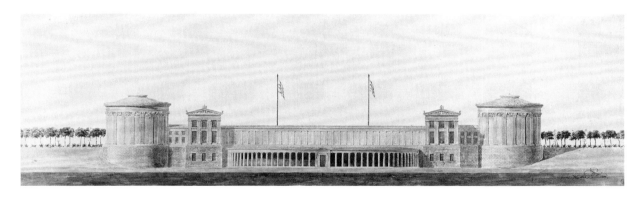

Fig. 10. *Theophil Hansen,Museum für Athen. I. Ruckwärtige Ansicht. 18 x 59 cm. 1887. Photograph of an ink on paper drawing in the Hansen bequest in the RIBA Library Drawings & Archives Collections, London.*

south rear illustrate, Hansen has used the natural slope of the area to introduce great visual variation, the substructures, which support the Museum's southbound rear façade, clearly echoing the Acropolis' raw cut walls of substruction supporting the platform of the Temple of Nike.

Seen directly from the south (Fig. 10), where Hansen intended to place a café for the visitors, the semi-circular colonnade enclosing the internal courtyard would serve as a sort of uniform pediment above which the individual segments of the complex would stand out clearly against

the green backdrop of the Acropolis. Here, from the south, with the low-slung, pavilion-style disposition of the museum's line of buildings, the layout of this complex would have been easily grasped; seen from here, moreover, an aspect that in Hansen's public oeuvre is almost unique seems to call for an explanation.

As outlined in the drawings, Hansen's project is markedly centrifugal, its central section so un-accentuated and un-emphasized that one looks in vain in his public oeuvre for a parallel. From the Athens Academy to the Vienna *Musikverein* and Vienna Parliament (Fig. 11), the disposi-

185

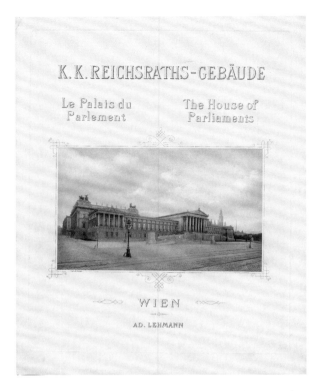

Fig. 11. *Illustration from Das K.K. Reichsraths-Gebäude in Wien von Theophil von Hansen, Vienna. 1890 (The Danish National Art Library).*

Fig. 12. *Theophil Hansen, Museum für Athen. I. Ruckwärtige Ansicht. 18 x 59 cm. 1887. Photograph of an ink on paper drawing in the Hansen bequest in the RIBA Library Drawings & Archives Collections, London with modern photo of Parthenon inserted to show Hansen's intended effect.*

tion is almost invariably the opposite, the side pavilions as it were framing, highlighting and elevating a more massive and highly ornate central section.[19] So why the departure in this, his Athenian swan song?

It is the intended change of location for the entire complex which offers the key to solving this problem. As we have seen, in his second ground plan Hansen had decided to move the whole complex slightly to the west (Fig. 8). If one carefully examines this new location, it emerges that its overriding purpose was to provide the complex with its almost demonstratively missing centre. In this location, a person standing in the Museum's axis of symmetry would have had the dramatically protruding southwest corner of the Parthenon right at his centre of vision (in Athens, one can recapture the effect by looking up at the Acropolis when standing at the corner of the Dionysio Areopagitou Street and the Parthenonos street, which is roughly where the Museum's central axis would have been). So this monumental and visually almost invasive corner was to have been the soaring *point de vue* of Hansen's whole complex, high above its very centre (Fig. 12).

In short, Hansen's project is centrifugal precisely because his modern-day buildings were meant to be seen as moving aside (humbly, as it were), providing at their centre an uncontested primary space for this venerable Doric set piece, the very icon of Classical architecture. It is clearly for this same reason that Hansen avoided using the Doric order in his exterior. Instead, he makes his project encircle and, as it were, inscribe the venerable ruin, first with flagpoles flying the national Greek flag and further out by buildings in the two other Classical orders, the Ionic and then finally the Corinthian.

Where Hansen's Ionic temples are firmly rooted in Athenian tradition, his Corinthian tholoi are, in the context, an unusually innovative element that allowed him to give his museum the kind of domed Pantheon rotunda so brilliantly introduced to museum architecture by the idol of his youth, Schinkel.[20] But where Schinkel in the *Altes Museum* imitates the Pantheon's Corinthian order, Hansen in the interior of his Athens museum pays homage to the genius loci by using the Doric. As for the Corinthian exterior of these tholoi, however, another icon of his youth may well be relevant: what are they but massively enlarged fantasy versions of the likewise Corinthian Ly-

---

19 Stalla 2014, 294-303 aptly describes Hansen's use of this modular system.

20 Hansen and Schinkel: in his diary from 1838 (Villadsen 2014, 223) the *Altes Museum* is "without doubt the most beautiful Piece of Architecture I have seen". Hansen saw himself as Schinkel's pupil: Stalla 2014, 294.

sicrates monument that Hansen had drawn in his youth, and to which he would return again and again?[21] Finally, as Professor Georgios Panetsos rightly made me aware, these tholoi resume and bring to full closure the monumental theatrical half circle of the building's south façade.

When entering the Acropolis through the gateway of Mnesikles' *Propylaea*, one sees the Parthenon at its most imposing, across a diagonal that at its centre has the temple's northwestern corner.[22] It was no doubt Hansen's intention to replicate this effect, but now from the sunlit south and from below upwards, with his low and modern buildings respectfully laid out so that they would have provided a kind of architectural frame for this compelling visual experience. This mise-en-scène function of archi-

tecture is not un-paralleled in Hansen's oeuvre. As rightly observed by Professor Alexander Papageorgiou-Venetas, Hansen's Zappeion works on similar principles, since its open courtyard 'frames' a splendidly panoramic view of the Lykabettos Mountain. The Parthenon Museum's very similar interaction of setting and architecture adds significantly to the intrinsic value of Hansen's final project.

To conclude: Hansen owed his meteoric rise to architectural stardom to his years in Athens. The links with Sinas, who financed his Athens Observatory, proved crucial when he left for Vienna – and from there the rest is history. What I hope to have shown is that he did not arrive in Greece wholly unprepared. Indeed, in the Denmark of his youth there was much that was already Greek.

BIBLIOGRAPHY

Atherton, G. 2006
The Decline and Fall of Virgil in Eighteenth-Century Germany: The Repressed Muse, Rochester, NY.

Bendtsen, M. 1993
Sketches and Measurings. Danish Architects in Greece 1818-1862, Copenhagen.

Bramsen, H. 1959
Gottlieb Bindesbøll – liv og arbejder, Copenhagen.

Bruun, C. & L. P. Fenger 1892
Thorvaldsens Musæums Historie, Copenhagen.

Bundgaard Rasmussen, B., J. Steen Jensen, J. Lund & M. Märcher (eds) 2008
Peter Oluf Brøndsted (1780-1842). A Danish Classicist in his European Context, Copenhagen

Cassimatis, M. & G. A. Panetsos (eds) 2014
'Hellenische Renaissance'. The Architecture of Theophil Hansen (1813-1891), Athens.

Dietz, S. (ed.) 2000
København-Athen tur/retur, Copenhagen.

Haugsted, I. 1996
Dream and Reality. Danish antiquaries, architects and artists in Greece, London.

Henderson, J. 2005
The Triumph of Art at Thorvaldsens Museum, Copenhagen.

Hurwit, J.M. 2005
'Space and Theme: The Setting of the Parthenon', in *The Parthenon. From Antiquity to the Present*, J. Neils (ed.), Cambridge, 9-34.

Kokkou, A. 1977
Η μερίμνα για τις αρχαιότητες στην Ελλάδα και τα πρώτα μουσεία, Athens.

Kragelund, P. 1987
"Abildgaard around 1800: his Tragedy and Comedy', *Analecta Romana Instituti Danici* 16, 137-85.

Kragelund, P. 2013
'The RIBA Gold Medal and Theophil Hansen's Plans for an Acropolis Museum in Athens', in *Theophil Hansen. Ein Resümee*, B. Bastl et al. (eds), Vienna, 179-92.

Kragelund, P. 2015
Roman Historical Drama. The Octavia in Antiquity and Beyond, Oxford.

Lederballe, T. (ed.) 2009
Nicolai Abildgaard. Revolution Embodied, Copenhagen.

21 Hansen produced a detailed reconstruction of the Lysicrates monument in 1846: Cassimatis & Panetsos 2014, fig. 8.1; with Stalla 2014, 295.
22 In Antiquity it was only when arriving at the Chalkotheke terrace closer to the Parthenon that one would have got the first full – but there, diagonal – view of the complex: Hurwit 2005, 12 (with bibliography).

Lund, J. & A. Rathje 1991
'Danes Overseas – A Short History of Danish Classical Archaeological Field-work', *Acta Hyperborea* 3, 11-56.

Millech, K. 1960
Thorvaldsens Museum. Bygningens æstetiske funktion og idé samt udviklingen i forarbejderne (Meddelelser fra Thorvaldsens Museum 1969), Copenhagen.

Niemann, G. & F. v. Feldegg 1893
Theophilos Hansen und seine Werke, Vienna.

Russack, H. H. 1942
Deutsche bauen in Athen, Berlin.

Stalla, R. 2014
"My work has always been modelled on classical antiquity': Reflections on the Structural and Decorative System', in Cassimatis & Panetsos 2014, 294-303.

Thule Kristensen, P. 2013
Gottlieb Bindesbøll – Danmarks første moderne arkitekt, Copenhagen.

Van Zanten, D. 1977
The Architectural Polychromy of the 1830's, New York, London, 150-67.

Villadsen, V. 2014
'From Copenhagen to Athens. Pages from Theophilus Hansen's Travel Diary 1838', in Cassimatis & Panetsos 2014, 222-31 (translation by Neil Stanford & Patrick Kragelund).

Zahle, J. 2008
'P.O. Brøndsted – The Resolute Agent in the Acquisition of Plaster Casts for the Royal Academy of Fine Arts, Copenhagen', in Bundgaard Rasmussen et al., 214-37.

Reports on Danish Fieldwork in Greece

The Lower Acropolis of Kalydon in Aitolia

Preliminary report on the excavations carried out in 2013-15*

OLYMPIA VIKATOU & SØREN HANDBERG

Since 2001 Danish and Greek archaeologists have collaborated in carrying out archaeological investigations at the ancient Greek city of Kalydon, close to the modern village of Evinochori in Aitolia. Work has included large-scale excavation projects as well as the study and publication of the finds. As part of the ongoing collaboration, a programme of new excavations on the Lower Acropolis was initiated in the summer of 2013. It is a joint project of the Danish Institute at Athens and the Ephorate of Antiquities of Aetolia-Acarnania and Lefkada, directed by the ephor Dr Olympia Vikatou and Dr Søren Handberg.

The Lower Acropolis area refers to a sloping plateau that surrounds an upper flat plateau known as the Central Acropolis, which at 167 m above sea level constitutes the highest point in the city (Fig. 1). The Lower Acropolis plateau is encircled by a substantial wall that connects with the city's outer defensive wall. Geophysical investigations carried out in the area in 2001-5 suggested that the plateau was laid out in an orthogonal grid, and several architectural features were identified, but no excavations were undertaken at the time.[1]

Several research questions prompted the initiation of the new excavation on the plateau. First of all, since the reconstruction of the city's topographical layout has previously primarily been based on the interpretations of the geomagnetic surveys, we wanted to test the validity of the obtained results. Secondly, we were interested in finding traces of the city that predate the Hellenistic period, which we believed could possibly be found on the acropolis. Finally, we wanted to find solid evidence for the construction date of the fortification wall that encircles the Lower Acropolis plateau. It had previously been suggested that this fortification wall might be earlier than the outer fortification circuit, and if an early construction date could be substantiated through excavations, we would also expect to find remnants of the early period of the city's history in the area behind the fortification.

During three excavation seasons (2013-5), 17 excavation trenches were opened in two different locations on the Lower Acropolis (Figs 2-3). In Area I, located approximately in the middle of the plateau, just south of the southeastern tower of the fortification of the Central Acropolis, 15 trenches were opened up, and another two trenches were opened in Area II by the wall that surrounds the Lower Acropolis plateau. The excavations in Area I have so far revealed substantial remains of a Hellenistic building that contains some undisturbed and relatively well-preserved contexts. The excavations at the Lower Acropolis wall has produced a good quantity of early material in the form of late Geometric and Archaic pottery.

*   The project wishes to thank the Greek Ministry of Culture and Sport for granting permission to carry out the fieldwork at Kalydon. The project is furthermore grateful to the following people, who have contributed to the work: S. Barfoed (responsible for the registration of finds); Chr. Kaniou (field supervisor 2013); G. Stamatis (field supervisor 2014-5); G. Lolos and S. Hoffmann (topographic surveys); G. Manthos (keeper of the archaeological area); and N. Michaelides, D. Barzis and E. Vlassi (Architecture Engineers), as well as the staff of the Ephorate. The project also wishes to acknowledge R. Frederiksen's support in initiating the new excavations, as well as the work of the 101 archaeology students and the 20 local technicians and workmen who have participated throughout the years. The fieldwork was made possible by financial support from the Carlsberg Foundation. The original documentation of the fieldwork is kept in the archives of The Danish Institute at Athens.

1   For the results of the geophysical work, see Smekalova 2011.

Fig. 1. *Aerial view of the acropolis of Kalydon from the southwest with the Lower Town in the foreground (C. Giatrakos).*

Fig. 2. *Topographic site plan of ancient Kalydon showing major monuments and the excavation trenches on the Lower Acropolis.*

The Hellenistic House on the Lower Acropolis

During the three excavation campaigns, 15 trenches covering an area of 375 m² were opened in Area I in the middle of the plateau. In this area of the plateau the terrain slopes gently downwards towards the south at an approximately 15° angle. The excavations in the area have revealed a building complex dating to the Hellenistic period (Fig. 3). When excavations began in 2013, a substantial layer of stone debris covered almost the entire area. The stone debris layer, which at the time was referred to as a "stone blanket", consisted of a very compact layer of medium-sized stones which in some places was up to 0.70 m deep. Early in the first year's excavation, it became clear that the formation of the stone debris layer had been caused by the collapse of walls belonging to a Hellenistic building with at least two construction phases.

The complete extent and the exact layout of the structure remains uncertain at this point, but it is clear that the building was bordered by streets on the western and eastern sides, and another street probably ran along the northern side of the building, which was possibly its back. Even though the layout remains somewhat uncertain, we can clearly identify two rooms, and possibly a third

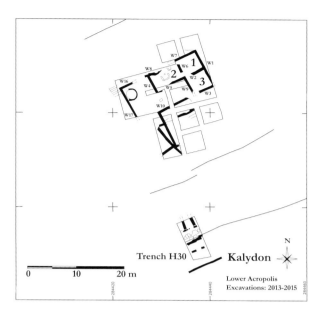

Fig. 3. *Topographic plan of the excavations in Areas I–II on the Lower Acropolis.*

room, as well as an area that seems to have served as a courtyard. The building should probably be interpreted as a Hellenistic private house. Its walls are constructed of a combination of larger roughly dressed blocks of local sandstone and smaller undressed stones. The walls are better preserved in the northern part of the building, where up to six courses of stones are preserved in some places. So far, no traces of mudbrick have been observed in connection with the walls – which were presumably completely constructed of stone, extending all the way to the roof.

In the northeastern part of the excavated area, three rooms can be identified (Rooms 1-3). The rooms are situated in the corner of the building and form an L-shape, with Rooms 1 and 3 on the eastern side and Room 2 protruding towards the southwest. A courtyard seems to have been connected with the building in the area to the south and southwest of Room 2. Wall Sections 3 and 10 form a continuous wall, although a small section of it is missing in the eastern part, and presumably constitute the southern border of the building. In the southwestern part the wall turns towards the south at a 90° angle (Wall Section 15), which might represent an extension of the

courtyard towards the south. Since this area has not been excavated yet, the full extent of the courtyard remains unclear. Excavations in this area are planned for 2016.

The northern wall of the building has been traced across four trenches (Wall Sections 7, 8 and 16) and measure 17.7 m in length. The bedrock, which lies at a higher point in the northern part of the excavated area, has in some places been used as a foundation for the wall. Most of the stones in the middle section of the wall have slid from their original position and were found within Room 2 and in the courtyard area.

Room 1

The first part of the building to be revealed when excavations started in 2013 was Room 1, situated in the northeastern corner of the building (Fig. 4). In 2015 the western half of the room was excavated down to the level above the bedrock. A clearly defined layer containing hundreds of fragments of terracotta roof tiles of Laconian type was found in this room. The layer covered the entire extent of the room and it clearly represents the debris from a collapsed roof.

No clearly identifiable floor level has so far been found, but the approximate level can be established on the basis of the stratigraphy. Almost all of the fragments of roof tiles were situated in Layer 3, whereas Layer 4 below was almost completely devoid of tile fragments and the composition of the soil was softer and of a slightly darker colour. The floor level of the room should therefore be located around the transition between Layers 3 and 4. Although apparently not completely horizontal across the whole area, this division is situated at around 137.56 m AMSL.[2] All the soil from the tile layer and Layer 4 below was sieved during excavation and substantial soil samples were collected. Several charred olive pits were found around the level of the floor during excavation (Fig. 5).

In the northern part of the room the bedrock protrudes above the floor level in two places. The bedrock protrusions are not horizontal, but slope dramatically downwards towards the east. The bedrock was here used as a foundation for the northern wall of the building, but soil has been used to fill the gaps in the foundations where the bedrock slopes.

2   Level numbers 76 and 78 (July 15, 2015).

Fig. 4. *View over Rooms 1 and 3 from the south (Søren Handberg).*

Fig. 5. *Examples of the charred olive pits found in the floor layer in Room 1.*

The bedrock hence creates sloping "platforms" that must have protruded into the room in antiquity (Fig. 4). The highest point of this bedrock outcrop in the northwestern corner of the room is at 138.56 m AMSL, which lies 1 m above the supposed level of the floor. Consequently, the bedrock must have remained exposed above the floor level in the northern part of the room in antiquity.[3]

Several intact vessels had been preserved underneath the collapsed roof. In the southeastern corner of the room a deposit with larger vessels was excavated (Figs 6-7). It included a plain ware jug, an oil lamp and a plain ware krater.[4] Fallen tiles and stones probably broke the vessels that seem to have originally been stored in the corner of the room. Comparison with contextually dated kraters from the Athenian Agora suggests that the krater should be dated to the late 3rd or first half of the 2nd century BC.[5] In close proximity to the same corner fragments of a terracotta grill were also found. A deep Hellenistic lekane was found facing upside down right on top of the bedrock "platform" at the back wall.[6] This vessel was covered by fragments of roof tiles and it seems likely that it was stored on a wooden shelf along the northern wall, from where it fell when the roof collapsed in antiquity. A broken but complete Italian Terra Sigillata plate with "Hängelippe" and the fabricant stamp [VETTI / OPTATI], from the workshop of A. Vettius Optatus, was found at the southern end of Wall Section 6 that separates Rooms 1 and 2 (Figs 8-9).[7] The plate was found at a somewhat lower level than the presumed level of the floor in Room 1. It remains unclear whether this plate was part of the original assemblage in Room 1 at the time of the collapse of the roof. The plate can be dated to the late 1st century BC or early 1st century AD, and it should perhaps rather be associated with the context of Room 2 to the west – so belonging to a later phase of reorganization of the building.[8]

The excavations in Room 1 also produced a large amount of small fragments of white and painted stucco (Fig. 10). Hundreds of fragments were retrieved, but few were larger than c. 5x5 cm and no stucco was found preserved intact on the walls. Besides white, the predominant colours on the stucco fragments were red, ochre and blue. Some of the fragments have slightly raised moldings and thin incised lines, and the whole decorative scheme is reminiscent of the style identified in Room III in the Peristyle House in the Lower Town. There the decoration consisted of an approximately 0.7 m lower white band incised

---

3   In Rooms 1 and 3 in the so-called Dema House in Attica, the natural bedrock approached the level of the floor of the rooms, but in this case it was apparently cut so as not to protrude above the floor. See Jones et al. 1962, 77-8.

4   Find nos: 20548.1 (jug); 20798.1 (lamp); 20545.1 (krater).

5   Agora 33, 105-7. Typologically the krater from Room 1 is especially close to cat. nos 208 and 214.

6   Find no. 15-1183.

7   Find no. 15-1499.

8   For the type, see *Conspectus*, Form 12.3; for the stamp, see *CVA*, 2267-81.

Fig. 6. *Deposit in the southeastern corner of Room 1; the deposit was found during excavations in 2013 among the numerous terracotta tile fragments (Søren Handberg).*

Fig. 8. *The Terra Sigillata plate with fabricant stamp found at the southeastern end of Wall Section 6.*

Fig. 9. *Drawing of the reconstructed plate.*

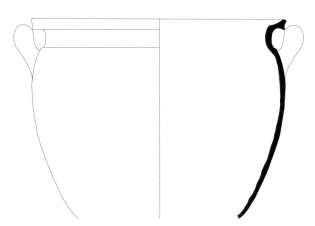

Fig. 7. *Drawing of the krater found in the deposit in Room 1 (Diameter: 22 cm).*

Fig. 10. *Examples of the fragments of stucco from the floor level in Room 1.*

Fig. 11. *Fragment of a Corinthian kotyle of the Middle Corinthian period found below the floor level in Room 1.*

with thin horizontal lines and an upper red zone.[9] Apart from the fact that more colours seem to have been used in the wall decoration in the building on the Lower Acropolis than in the Peristyle House, the decoration appears so similar in style and execution that the same craftsmen may have been employed in the decoration of both houses.

The date of the collapse of the roof must remain tentative since the majority of the finds need detailed study, but on the basis of the chronology of the objects found in situ in the room, a date somewhere in the second half of the 2nd century BC can be proposed. The overall scheme of the wall decoration can perhaps be compared to the First Pompeian Style, which would support the proposed date. The tile layer (Layer 3) also included a bronze coin.[10] It was found at the level 137.51 m above sea level,[11] which roughly corresponds to the supposed level of the floor.

Fig. 12. *The cooking installation (structure 1) and the hearth (structure 2) in Room 2; remains of the thick ash-layer is visible in the soil column in the foreground (Søren Handberg).*

---

9   Dietz 2011a, 114-20. We are grateful to Søren Dietz for sharing information about the stucco decoration from the Peristyle House with us.

10   Find no. 15-1373. The coin has not yet been properly cleaned, so it remains difficult to form an opinion about the date.

11   Level number 59 (July 17, 2015).

In Layer 4 (the layer beneath the tile debris), a single sherd of a Middle Corinthian kotyle was found (Fig. 11).[12] On stylistic grounds the kotyle belongs in the Middle Corinthian or early Late Corinthian period, and should thus be dated to the first half of the 6th century BC.[13] This date supports the assumption that this layer is below the original floor level of the room and should also give us a terminus post quem for the first construction phase of the building. Furthermore, the sherd also provides tentative evidence for earlier occupation in the area, although the fragment might also be part of the debris that had eroded down from the area further north.

Room 2

Room 2, to the southwest of Room 1, has been entirely excavated down to the yellowish sediment that lies on top of the bedrock. Six courses of stones are preserved in the western wall of Room 2, which reaches a height of c. 0.85 m. A door opening onto the courtyard was found in Wall Section 5, near the southwestern corner of the room. The door opening, which measures approximately 0.8 m. in width, was at some point in antiquity blocked by smaller stones. A rectangular pillar capital was found as a spolia used to block the opening. A baulk still covers part of the opening and the wall, which will be removed in 2016.

Two significant structures were identified in Room 2 (Fig. 12). The first structure (Structure 1) is a substantial base constructed in dry stone masonry consisting of four courses of undressed stones. The base is built up against the bedrock, which here functioned both as the lower part of the back wall of the building and as the foundation for the built-up upper part of the wall. A large Corinthian pan-tile was found on top of the base, probably placed there to facilitate a flat surface. The stone base is set on top of a low platform which extends beyond the base.[14] The platform is constructed with a frame of rectangular slabs, two of which are mortar slabs which probably originate from another building and were reused in the construction of the platform. The top of the platform

Fig. 13. *Fragments of cooking ware found in situ next to the cooking installation (Søren Handberg).*

was paved with flat stone slabs of irregular size which have only been preserved underneath a tile layer in the northwestern corner of the platform. In the corner of the mortar slab and the bedrock west of the stone structure, several sherds of Hellenistic cooking-ware vessels were found lying right on top of the pavement of the platform (Fig. 13). This area was covered with many fragments of roof tiles, which must have preserved the vessels in their original place.

Structure 2 was found to the southwest of the stone base at a slightly lower level and can be identified as a hearth. It measures 1.32 x 0.95 m and is framed on three sides by larger rectangular blocks placed vertically with

---

12   Find no. 15-1469.

13   For a parallel, see e.g. Corinth 15.3 cat. nos 590 and 608, pls 28-9.

14   A "platform" somewhat similar to the one from Room 2 was found in a late Hellenistic or early Roman house further up on the Central Acropolis; see Dietz 2001b, 231-6, and specifically fig. 168.

an opening in the southeastern corner. The northwestern side of the hearth facing the back wall of the room was presumably constructed of several smaller stones, some of which seem to have been preserved close to their original position. Inside the hearth, the bedrock was reached between 0.15 and 0.2 m below the top of the framing stones. The surface of the bedrock inside the hearth is irregular and has not been dressed. Some of the higher areas of the bedrock show signs of exposure to high temperatures and display a greyish colour: the bedrock surface was certainly used as a firing surface.

The area in front of the plateau and east of the hearth was covered with a layer of fine greyish ash that extended all the way to the wall which separates Room 1 and 2. The ash layer could most clearly be identified in an area extending around 1 m from the border of the plateau of Structure 1. The ash layer had the shape of a low mound with the highest point in front of the plateau, from where the layer sloped gradually towards the south and southeast. Closer to Wall Section 5 and the possible opening into Room 1, the ash layer was patchier and it was difficult to identify its precise contours. Soil samples were taken from both the ash layer and the soil inside the hearth for future analyses.

Only a preliminary framework of the chronological sequence of the various features in Room 2 can be presented. It seems, however, that both structures in Room 2 were in use at the same time, even though they are situated rather uncomfortably close to each other, and the hearth is at a somewhat lower level. The best indication of the synchronicity of the two structures stems from the fact that the ash layer did not overlay the hearth.

Several different formation processes may explain the presence of the ash layer. The layer is not likely to represent the debris of a collapsed roof. No pieces of charcoal were found in it, nor did it include any nails from the timber construction of the roof. In addition, no similar ash layers were found in other areas of the excavated building. The most obvious explanation therefore seems to be that the ash layer represents the residue from the hearth that was continuously deposited in the area next to

it. However, the ash might also stem from burnt offerings. Structure 1's construction is similar to altars built up of several courses of rough field stones known from depictions on Attic red-figure vases.[15] However, since traces of burning were not visible on the Corinthian pan-tile that rested on top of the stone base, it is difficult to identify it as an altar for burnt offerings. It might of course had functioned as an altar for other perishable offerings, such as fruits and vegetables or smaller terracotta figurines, but preliminary studies of the finds, as well as some of the soil samples, have yielded no evidence for this practice. Furthermore, no thymiatria have been identified among the objects from the room.[16]

The more plausible interpretation is that the base is some kind of cooking installation associated with the hearth. A similar structure, which has tentatively been interpreted as an altar by the excavators, was identified in the early Hellenistic Building D in the Poseidon Sanctuary at Kalaureia on Poros.[17] An extensive ash layer was found around the structure in Building D, and similar large ash layers are known from rooms that have been interpreted as kitchens, for instance the 0.3 m-deep ash layer in Room 2 in Building M:21-22 in the Demeter and Kore Sanctuary at Corinth, which resembles the deposit in Room 2 in Kalydon.[18]

Room 3

The room to the southeast of Room 1, which has provisionally been called "Room 3", is not well understood, and further excavations are needed in order to form a clear interpretation of the contextual situation. What is clear, however, is that a large deposit of dumped material was situated in the northeastern corner of the area (Fig. 4). The deposit included hundreds of larger fragments of Hellenistic pottery, metal objects, animal bones and ash. The highest point of the deposit abutted the eastern wall (Wall Section 1), from where it sloped downwards towards the southwest. This fact, combined with the relatively low breakage rate of the pottery found in this deposit, suggests a distinct depositional pattern where material was

15   Ekroth 2001, fig. 7.
16   We are grateful to Gunnel Ekroth for discussing this structure with us in September 2014.
17   Wells et al. 2003, 49-77 (for the altar see especially p. 60).
18   *Corinth* 18.3, 187.

Fig. 14. *The layer of terracotta tiles, which was found below the dump in Room 3 in 2015 (Søren Handberg).*

continuously and purposely dumped in the area. Underneath this dumped deposit a layer of fallen terracotta roof tiles was found (Fig. 14). This tile layer, which runs almost continuously across the room, stops abruptly at around 1.5 m from the northern wall (Wall Section 2). The southwestern wall of Room 3 (Wall Section 9) is not well-defined and only consists of a few preserved stones. A few stones are protruding from the northern section of the trench between Wall Section 9 and the tile layer. These might represent a small staircase connecting Rooms 1 and 3. The difference in height between the floor levels of the two rooms is around 0.5 m.

The Courtyard

The area to the southeast and west of Room 2, which stretches across five excavation trenches (Trenches H20, H21, H24, H37 and H38), appears to have been a courtyard associated with the building (Fig. 15). Wall Section 10, which forms the southern border of the building, turns towards the southeast at a 90° angle in the southern part

of Trench H21. It seems likely that this southern, and so far unexcavated area, should be included in the area of the courtyard. If this turns out to be the case, the layout of the building would be L-shaped.

A large isolated Corinthian pan-tile was found in Trench H21 in the courtyard area. The position of the tile is aligned with the southwestern wall of Room 2 (Wall Section 4) at a distance of 1.75 m from the wall. This distance is almost the same as the extent of the tile layer found in Room 3, and it is possible that the Corinthian tile was used as a base for a wooden pillar that would have carried a roofed portico, which would have run along the southeastern façade of Room 1 and 2. A pillar capital that was found among the material that blocked the doorway into Room 2 might have been used for this purpose. The level of the Corinthian tile, which must represent the original surface of the courtyard, and the sloping nature of the bedrock indicate that in antiquity the surface of the courtyard sloped slightly towards the south.

In the northwestern corner of the courtyard a larger circular structure was identified in 2015. The structure

199

Fig. 15. *The supposed courtyard area in the western part of the building; the Corinthian pan tile, which might have supported a wooden pillar, is visible on the right-hand side (Søren Handberg).*

measures 2.6 m in diameter and up to six courses of smaller stone slabs are preserved on the northern side. The top of the structure is covered by a number of large terracotta slabs, which form a roughly circular area. The structure incorporates the bedrock in its foundation in the western part, where the level of the bedrock is higher. Firm evidence for the date of the circular structure is so far lacking, but considering the upper level of the structure it was probably visible during the use period of the building. The structure may, however, have been constructed prior to the erection of the building. The function of the structure remains unknown, although it does not seem to have functioned as an altar, since no traces of burning was observed – neither on the terracotta slabs, nor in the area surrounding the structure. Further excavations around the structure might shed more light on its function.

A Preliminary Interpretation of the Building

On the basis of the preliminary study of the finds several observations support an interpretation that allows for at least two distinct phases of use. First of all, the original doorway between the courtyard and Room 2 was at some point in time covered up. When the blocking of the doorway took place, a new exit from Room 2 into Room 1 might have been created by removing the southeastern part of Wall Section 6. Secondly, the deposit in "Room 3" was intentionally dumped on top of the roof tiles after the roof had already collapsed.

We may then tentatively suggest that in the first phase the building consisted of two rooms (Rooms 1 and 2). These would both have had doorways opening into a roofed portico that ran along the southeastern side of the two rooms. The pillars of the portico, which were presumably of wood, were placed on large Corinthian pan tiles, of which only the westernmost in the courtyard has been preserved. In this first phase, the courtyard might already have been L-shaped and thus extended beyond the two rooms. A possible construction date for this building could be the first half of the 2nd century BC, but the finds need to be studied in more detail to corroborate this date. The first phase of the building suffered a sudden destruc-

Fig. 16. *Fill layers identified in area behind (north of) Wall Section 16 (Søren Handberg).*

tion which meant the roof collapsed, thus preserving the objects in situ in Room 1. The walls of the building, or at least a substantial part of them, must have remained standing after this first destruction.

In the second phase of the building, it seems that Room 2 was reoccupied and the doorway into the courtyard was covered up. The dump in "Room 3" could represent the clearing of debris from Room 2. Room 1 was left basically untouched, but the area may have been used as an exit way into the courtyard. The removal of the southeastern part of the wall between Rooms 1 and 2 might have occurred at this time, and might also explain the presence of the Roman plate found there. The second phase should perhaps be dated to the late 1st century BC or early 1st century AD. This sequence of events could also explain the scanty nature of the western wall of "Room 3". The reconstruction is an attempt to understand the archaeological contexts, but it must be regarded a very preliminary reconstruction that is open to future reinterpretations. A more thorough study of the stratigraphic circumstances and the associate finds will shed additional light on the contextual situation.

The Road System

The geomagnetic investigations that were previously carried out on the Lower Acropolis had already indicated that a quasi-orthogonal street grid transects most of the plateau. This hypothesis is corroborated by the results of the excavations in 2013-5.

The strongest evidence was found outside the courtyard area west of Wall Section 17. Here five steps of a staircase which lies partly outside Trench H37 were identified (Fig. 15). The staircase is part of a street that runs in a northwestern to southeastern direction towards the fortification wall to the south (see below). A similar street has been identified on the other (eastern) side of the building, although no clear traces of a staircase have been found.

Behind the northern wall of the building, a series of fill layers were identified. A tripartite stratigraphy was clearly observable in the area that borders the staircase to the west (Fig. 16). The lower layer, which rests on the bedrock, consists of a compact layer of smaller stones, possibly chips from blocks that have been worked. On top of this layer lies a soil layer of a lighter colour with fewer stones. The upper layer consists of erosion soil. It

201

Fig. 17. *The two trenches (H30 and H336) at the Lower Acropolis wall seen from the north; the T-junction of the street is visible in the foreground (Søren Handberg).*

seems possible that the entire area behind the northern wall of the building was levelled in antiquity in order to make a flat surface, thereby creating a passageway behind the northern wall of the building, or possibly a larger open space, which would also have facilitated movement between the two streets that ran on either side of the building. Evidence of similar fill layers was found in Trenches H32 and H33 at the eastern end during excavations in 2014. The finds from the fill layers should provide evidence for the date of the construction of the street system and thereby perhaps also indirectly for the date of the construction of the building. Only a preliminary study of the finds from the fill layers have been undertaken in 2015 and they await further study.

In 2015 another trench (Trench H36) was opened in Area II to the south, as a northern extension of Trench H30 at the fortification wall (see below). Here the end of the street with the staircase was found (Fig. 17). The street runs into a T-junction that connects to another street which presumably ran along the interior side of the fortification wall that encircles the Lower Acropolis plateau. The street is lined on both sides by walls. The eastern wall is slightly broader than the western wall, a fact that could suggest that the eastern wall belongs to a house construction, whereas the western wall might be a lower wall that only served to delimit the street. The two border-walls of the street do not run exactly parallel to each other, and the street is wider at its southern part where it connects with the other street. In the street that runs southwest–northeast along the fortification wall the excavations reached the level of a pavement, which consists of numerous stone slabs of various sizes. Towards the south the street is delimited by another wall, which appears originally to have had an opening that was subsequently blocked by smaller stones.

Fig. 18. *The outer face of the Lower Acropolis wall seen from the south (Søren Handberg).*

Fig. 19. *Trench H30 at the Lower Acropolis wall; the rubble fill between the outer and inner faces of the wall is clearly visible in the eastern section of the trench (Søren Handberg).*

The Lower Acropolis Fortification Wall

A substantial wall constructed of rough, irregular-sized sandstone ashlar blocks in isodomic style surrounds the Lower Acropolis plateau and connects with the outer fortification circuit. In 2014 a single 5 x 5 m trench (Trench H30) was excavated on the northern interior side of the wall, in a place where at least five courses were preserved to a height of 2.2 m (Fig. 18).[19] Before the excavations were carried out, the date of the construction of the wall was unknown, but in connection with the fieldwork carried out in Kalydon in the years 2001-5, the then director had suggested that the wall might date to the late Archaic or early Classical period.[20] The main aim of opening a trench at the wall was therefore to investigate the date of the construction of the wall.

The excavation of Trench H30 revealed that the acropolis wall is an approximately 3.6 m-thick double-faced wall

with an inner fill consisting of stone rubble and earth. Traces of the inner wall, in the form of a single row of smaller blocks running parallel to the outer wall, were found in Trench H30. The inner wall has been much disturbed, and at most two courses may be recognized. However, it is clear that this row represents the inner face of the acropolis fortification wall. This is seen in the profile of the eastern section of the trench, where the fill of the wall is clearly demarcated (Fig. 19). The fill is tightly packed with stones of various sizes and a dark soil. To the north in the profile, a completely different layer is clearly visible. This layer is of a pale brownish colour and completely devoid of stones. This layer (H30, Layer 3) is confined to the area north of the inner wall and did not continue into the rubble fill. The complete section of the acropolis wall is therefore clearly visible in the eastern baulk. Layer 3, which abuts the northern side of the inner

---

19   No excavations were carried out on the exterior side of the wall and the total number of preserved courses therefore remains unknown.

20   Dietz 2011c, 78.

Fig. 20. *Fragment of the rim of a cup-skyphos found in the fill of the Lower Acropolis wall.*

wall, continues underneath the wall, and it seems that the wall was originally set into this layer, which contained predominantly pottery of the Archaic period.

The easternmost area of the fill, called Trench H30A and measuring approximately 2 x 2 m, was excavated down to a depth of c. 0.6 m. The uppermost part of the fill was excavated separately in order to avoid contamination that might have affected the upper part of the fill material. A substantial amount of pottery was recovered from the rubble fill excavated in Trench 30A. A preliminary study of the pottery suggests that all fragments should be dated within the period from the late 8th century to the early 5th century BC. The latest pottery fragment that can be securely dated is a rim fragment of an Attic black glossed cup-skyphos with concave rim dating to the early 5th century BC (Fig. 20).[21] The evidence, in the form of the pottery fragments obtained from the fill of the wall, therefore strongly suggests a terminus post quem around 490-480 BC for the construction of the wall.

This date provides us with an unprecedented early fortification wall from Aitolia. In fact, this appears to be the earliest fortification so far attested in the whole region.[22] The substantial amount of pottery sherds dating to the late Geometric and Archaic period that was found both in the fill of the fortification wall and in the dumped fill behind the inner face of the wall most likely represents traces of earlier occupation on the Lower Acropolis in this period. So far, excavations further up on the plateau have only produced sporadic finds of Archaic material, and the accumulation of early finds in the contexts surrounding the fortification suggests a levelling of the area of the plateau in connection with the construction of the wall. It seems very likely that the area behind the fortification wall was originally similar to the situation observable at nearby Chalkis, where houses of the late Geometric and Archaic period have been unearthed on the border of the Hagia Triada acropolis.[23] The existence of an even earlier system of fortification somewhere on the acropolis of Kalydon should not be excluded – especially since Homer seems to refer to a defensive wall in his account of the story of the Kalydonian boar hunt (Homer *Il.* 9.549-51).

A Topographic Survey of the Ancient City

In 2015 a new project which aims at recording all visible ancient monuments within the archaeological area of Kalydon was initiated.[24] The overall purpose of this survey is to create a complete topographical map of the ancient city by updating the existing site plan. Such a comprehensive and systematic mapping of all ancient structures within the area has not previously been carried out. When completed, the final topographical map could be compared with the existing geomagnetic surveys as well as excavated structures in the area. The combination of the three types of evidence – the geophysical, the visible remains and the excavated features – will present us with a good overview of the topography of the entire ancient city.

The recording of the remains was carried out with the aid of a high-precision GPS system (Leica CS25 tablet with an accuracy of up to 0.01 m). The GPS coordinates of the structures were stored in a database and subsequently plotted, through GIS software, onto a topographic map of the area. In 2015 approximately 200 structures (mostly wall sections, of which most are presumed to be ancient) were

---

21   Find no. 23051-5. For a parallel, see *Agora* 12, cat. no. 578, fig. 6.

22   Funke, P. 1987. See also Frederiksen 2011, 106-7, 153-4 for the possibility that another early fortification wall encircled the Central Acropolis.

23   Houby-Nielsen & Moschos 2004.

24   The topographic survey was led by Anne Ditte Koustrup Høj.

recorded in the area of the acropolis of Kalydon. Further survey work is planned for the next couple of years.

Conclusion

The past three years of excavations on the Lower Acropolis of Kalydon have revealed the existence of a house complex of the Hellenistic period. The building seems to have sustained considerable damage not long after it was erected. The destruction, which caused the collapse of the roof, has preserved the content of Room 1 in situ. This situation is similar to the destruction, and in situ preservation of finds, observed in the so-called Peristyle House in the Lower Town, which suggest the damage to the two buildings may have been caused by the same event.

Room 2 can be identified as a cooking area, and appears to be one of the best instances of the occurrence of both a hearth and a cooking installation known from the ancient Greek world.[25] The room was probably reused, contrary to Room 1, in a second phase. According to several ancient sources, the inhabitants of the Aitolian cities were supposedly relocated to the new city of Nikopolis, which Octavian founded following his victory at the battle of Actium in 31 BC.[26] The presence of the well-preserved Roman plate dating to the late 1st century BC or early 1st century AD is therefore interesting, since it suggests some reoccupation of the site perhaps a generation after the foundation of Nikopolis.

The excavation of the wall encircling the Lower Acropolis plateau has shown that the acropolis area was most likely already fortified by early Classical times. This is the first time that a fortification wall in the Aitolia has been dated on the basis of finds from archaeological excavations. The substantial amount of Archaic pottery that was found in the levelling fill in the area of the fortification wall, as well as in the fill of the wall, in combination with previous finds of Archaic pottery on the Central Acropolis, suggests that much of the acropolis area was perhaps already inhabited by the late Geometric, or early Archaic period. These result add significant new evidence to the discussion of the process of urbanization in the Aitolian tribal society.[27]

OLYMPIA VIKATOU

Ephorate of Antiquities of Aetolia-Acarnania and Lefkada,
Ag. Athanasiou 4,
302 00 Mesologgi,
Greece,
ovikatou@culture.gr

SØREN HANDBERG

University of Oslo,
Department of Archaeology, Conservation and History,
Blindernveien 11
0371 Oslo
Norway
soren.handberg@iakh.uio.no / shhandberg@hotmail.com

Abbreviations:

Agora 12: B. A. Sparkes & L. Talcott 1970, *The Athenian Agora 12, Black and plain pottery of the 6th, 5th, and 4th centuries B. C.*, Princeton, NJ.

Agora 33: S. I. Rotroff 2006, *The Athenian Agora 33, Hellenistic Pottery: The Plain Wares,* Princeton, NJ.

Conspectus: E. Ettlinger et al. 2002, *Conspectus formarum terrae sigillatae Italico modo confectae* (*Materialien zur Romisch-Germanischen Keramik* 10), Bonn.

Corinth 15.3: A. N. Stillwell, J. L. Benson & H. N. Fowler. 1984, *Corinth* 15, 3 *The Potters' Quarter. The Pottery*, Princeton, NJ.

Corinth 18.3: N. Bookidis & R. S. Stroud. 1997, *Corinth* 18, 3 *The Sanctuary of Demeter and Kore: topography and architecture*, Princeton, NJ.

CVA: Oxé, A. 1968, *Corpus Vasorum Arretinorum: a catalogue of the signatures, shapes and chronology of Italian sigillata*, Bonn.

---

25   See Foxhall 2007 for a discussion of the ancient Greek 'kitchen'.
26   For the foundation of Nikopolis and the depopulation of the Aitolian cities, see e.g. Dietz 2009; Isager 2009.
27   See Funke 1997 for this discussion.

Works Cited:

Dietz, S. 2009
'Kalydon and Pausanias', *PoDia* 6, 217-21.

Dietz, S. 2011a
'2.1. Description of the Peristyle Building', in *Kalydon in Aitolia I. Reports and Studies. Danish/Greek Field Work 2001-2005* (Monographs of the Danish Institute at Athens 12.I), S. Dietz & M. Stavropoulou-Gatsi (eds), Aarhus, 111-25.

Dietz, S. 2011b
'4.0 General Stratigraphy', in *Kalydon in Aitolia I. Reports and Studies. Danish/Greek Field Work 2001-2005* (Monographs of the Danish Institute at Athens 12.I), S. Dietz & M. Stavropoulou-Gatsi (eds), Aarhus, 213-36.

Dietz, S. 2011c
'1.5 The city – Inside and outside the walls', in *Kalydon in Aitolia I. Reports and Studies. Danish/Greek Field Work 2001-2005* (Monographs of the Danish Institute at Athens 12.I), S. Dietz & M. Stavropoulou-Gatsi (eds), Aarhus, 77-81.

Ekroth, G. 2001
'Altars on Attic Vases: the identification of bomos and eschara', in *Ceramics in Context. Proceedings of the Internordic Colloquium on Ancient Pottery held at Stockholm, 13-15 June 1997* (Stockholm Studies in Classical Archaeology 12), C. Scheffer (ed.), Stockholm, 115-26.

Foxhall, L. 2007
'House Clearance: Unpacking the 'kitchen' in Classical Greece', in *Building Communities: House, Settlement and Society in the Aegean and Beyond. Proceedings of a conference held at Cardiff University, 17-21 April 2001* (British School at Athens Studies 15), R. Westgate, N. Fisher & J. Whitley (eds), Athens, 233-42.

Frederiksen, R. 2011
Greek City Walls of the Archaic Period, 900-480 BC (Oxford Monographs on Classical Archaeology), Oxford, New York.

Funke, P. 1987
'Zur Datierung befestigter Stadtanlagen in Aitolien. Historisch-philologische Anmerkungen zu einem Wechselverhältnis zwischen Siedlungsstruktur und politischer Organisation', *Boreas* 10, 87-96.

Funke, P. 1997
'Poligenese und Urbanisierung in Aitolien im 5. und 4. Jh. V. Chr.', in *Acts of the Copenhagen Polis Centre 4, The Polis as an Urban Centre and as a Political Community* (Det Kongelige Danske Videnskabernes Selskab, Historiske-filosofiske Meddelelser 75), M. H. Hansen (ed.), Copenhagen, 145-88.

Houby-Nielsen, S. & I. Moschos 2004
'Excavations on the Hill of Hagia Triada', *PoDIA* 4, 175-88.

Isager, J. 2009
'Destruction or depopulation of the cities in Pausanias. Nikopolis, Aetolia, and Epirus', *PoDia* 6, 201-15.

Jones, J. E., L. H. Sackett & A. J. Graham 1962
'The Dema House in Attica', *BSA* 57, 75-114.

Smekalova, T. 2011
'1.1 Magnetic surveys in Kalydon', in *Kalydon in Aitolia I. Reports and Studies. Danish/Greek Field Work 2001-2005* (Monographs of the Danish Institute at Athens 12.I), S. Dietz & M. Stavropoulou-Gatsi (eds), Aarhus, 47-58.

Wells, B., A. Penttinen & M.-F. Billlot 2003
'Investigations in the Sanctuary of Poseidon on Kalaureia, 1997-2001', *Opuscula Atheniensis* 28, 29-87.

A short-cut to Delphi

Indications of a vehicle track from a stone quarry to the Sanctuary of Apollo at Delphi

ERIK HANSEN, GREGERS ALGREEN-USSING AND RUNE FREDERIKSEN

Introduction

The following account deals with a programme of field-work in the mountains near Delphi, which was carried out in the years 2010 to 2015. The objective was to find traces of a 6 km-long roadway, which in all probability must have been laid in the years after 373 BC. The purpose of the roadway was to bring new building stones from a stone quarry today bearing the name St Elijah to the Temple of Apollo at Delphi, which lay in ruins following an earthquake in 373 BC. The fieldwork in the mountainous landscape was made possible by the hospitality extended to us by the French Archaeological School at Athens, and through the permission granted us to stay in the School's building in Delphi and the interest shown in our work by the director Dominique Mulliez and his successor Alexandre Farnoux. We would like to thank the Carlsberg Foundation for a grant which made it possible, in the spring of 2013, for us to carry out a month-long investigative survey on the mountain slopes. Permission for the work was granted by the Ephorate of Delphi and the Greek archaeological authorities, and we owe the Ephor for Delphi, Dr Athanasia Psalti, and her colleagues a debt of gratitude for their helpfulness and support in this work. The further field exploration and ensuing processing of the data were made possible by stipends from the Danish Institute at Athens, for which we are also grateful. We would like to thank Kristina Winther-Jacobsen, the Insti-tute's director, for the commitment she has subsequently invested in this publication, and for Neil Stanford's careful translation.

Regarding the field investigation and the interpretation of the observations which we made in the area, we would like to mention the great inspiration provided by a number of professionals. These include É. Bourget, D. Skorda and E. Trouki. They have conduced to our interpretations of the observations during the fieldwork. In addition, our own experiences from walks in the mountains in the years 1963-8 together with the warden of the French School's building at Delphi, the late Christos Kaltsis, have had a crucial influence on the practical organization of the fieldwork. Finally we would like to thank Tønnes Bekker-Nielsen and Per Grau Møller at the Cartographic Documentation Centre, Institute of History at Syddansk Universitet, for always being prepared to help with map readings and determining coordinates. Rune Frederiksen served as archaeological advisor to the investigation.

The article is followed by a map with indications of GPS positions referred to in numbered order in figure captions, an appendix with a list of the GPS readings, a list of sources for figures and a bibliography.

The authors
Copenhagen, December 1, 2016

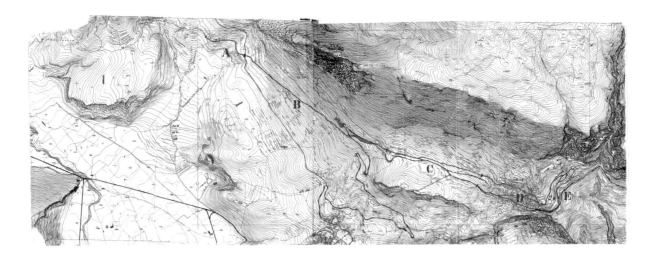

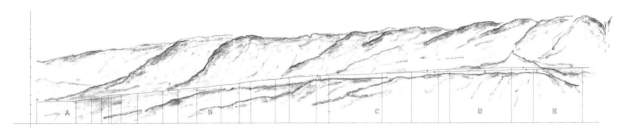

Fig. 1. *The stone quarry to the left (at A) and the sanctuary to the right (at E) are shown on this map from the 1960s. Visible between the two markings is a remarkably straight footpath. Our sketch below the map shows this path in elevation, divided into five sections from the stone quarry to the sanctuary (A–E). Also shown on the sketch of the mountainside is the percentage of increase for every 200 m towards Delphi. The sketched elevation below the map was drawn by GAU.*

How the fieldwork was structured[1]

The detailed examination of a vehicle track in the mountain slopes between a stone quarry from antiquity and the Sanctuary of Apollo at Delphi took its point of departure in the analysis of topographic maps on a scale of 1:5000, and the observations published by D. Skorda in 1991.[2] A corridor around the path drawn between the stone quarry and the modern road, which is an extension of the one to Delphi, was chosen as the area for the fieldwork.[3]

In the fieldwork the distance from the stone quarry to the sanctuary was divided up into five sections along the marked path for 6 km, as shown on the map. The sections represent the changing character of the landscape in the area. The survey on the mountain thus followed a topo-

---

1   An outline of the projected investigation was presented in a lecture at the annual meeting of the Danish Institute on April 11, 2011 at the Acropolis Museum by Gregers Algreen-Ussing, entitled "A Short Cut to Delphi".

2   Skorda 1991. We should like to thank Ms Skorda for permission to refer to her work and for the inspiring conversations we had concerning the Stone Quarry Road.

3   In the period 1963-8 this path was still passable for the Danish architecture students who surveyed/measured the sanctuary for the French School of Archaeology at Athens with a view to the publication of an atlas of the sanctuary (*Atlas*). On walks along this path we saw areas of hewing, the significance of which, at the time, was unknown to us. It was the warden of the French School, Christos Kaltsis, who was familiar with the path who gave it the name Kaltsis' Path. Today the path is impassable and has practically disappeared.

graphically accessible corridor between Amphissa and Delphi, starting from the stone quarry, which is situated 300 m lower in the landscape than the temple.

The description of the fieldwork follows the sequence step by step up to the sanctuary:

Section A includes the beginning of a vehicle track, which is to be found by the stone quarry named St. Elijah. A subsequent steep upward gradient takes the road out from the mountain towards the southeast.

Section B includes a long stretch on the southeast slope of Mount Parnassus, which leads to a small, modern church at Hosios Loukas, lying on a promontory halfway between the quarry and the temple.

Section C covers an extensive, flat, cultivated area. In relation to B it forms a mountain level at a higher altitude, which terminates at the modern town of Delphi.

Section D is marked by steep slopes in the landscape in and around the town of Delphi, wedged between the high cliffs of the Parnassus and the depths of the Pleistos Valley.

Section E is marked by a north–south oriented ridge with the so-called Bastions of Philomelos. East of this lies the sanctuary, where we suppose the vehicle track from the St Elijah quarry terminates.

The description of each section of the landscape from A to E begins with an account of the local character of each area. Within each section the local areas have been assigned a sequential number up towards the sanctuary. The most important part is described and shown through rough measurements of elevation placed over the plan on a scale of 1:150, or through photographs which may support the hypothesis of the vehicle track situation on the spot. Indications of construction work are designated as trace while specific indications of transport activity are indicated according to their actual function in the transportation work. Upward or downward gradients are given in percentages, against the background of the general consensus that c. 10% is the maximum upward gradient which a wagon with a heavy load can be hauled by a span of oxen. Directions of the compass are shown, for example, as 112° SE. They include simple compass readings on the spot and readings on a map, where GPS indications of altitude are also checked against indications of altitude on accessible maps. Unless stated otherwise, all maps and drawings are oriented with north upwards. Measurements and drawings were all undertaken on the

spot with simple tools at the scale of 1:50. Approximate measurements, the positions of which are determined with GPS, are shown in an insert.

1. Sections and arrangements of stones' contours are drawn with bold strokes.
2. Traces of ancient shaping by hewing with a sledge-hammer, chisel or wedge markings etc. are drawn in with thin strokes. The surface of the earth where it has been reinforced with pebbles is indicated by dots.
3. Delimitations of rocks and individual partial cleanings are drawn with stippled strokes. The making of scale drawings and photographs was undertaken by G. Algreen-Ussing (GAU), unless stated otherwise.
4. Hansen & Algreen-Ussing 1975 is referred to as "Atlas" throughout. Amandry & Hansen 2010, is referred to throughout as "A&H 2010".

An Inscription: Kat[estrepse]

It was an unusual event that took place in and around ancient Delphi in 373 BC, and this event is the point of departure for the following account. The great Temple of Apollo, constructed in part with the aid of the ex-iled Athenian aristocratic family of the Alkmaionidai (Hdt. 5.62), had since 505 BC been known as the most important building in the centre of the ancient world, but it was no longer looking its best. The mountainside on which the sanctuary rested, made up of fallen stone, gravel, clay and earth from the Phaedriades cliffs, had slid down. It seems conceivable that this happened in the damp autumn. Weeks of pouring rain interrupted by one violent cloudburst after another undercut the slope of the mountain, on which the numerous treasuries, monuments and terrace walls were resting on their foundations. This had catastrophic consequences for the temple, which was the third largest of its kind in the Greek world.

The enormous columns, the architrave and the cella wall enclosing the sacred space had, in the night's violent storm, developed cracks and became distorted; the first visitors in the early morning witnessed the formation of deep cracks in the poros stone of which the old temple had been constructed. The assumption of a landslide is based on a fragment of a preserved inscription which tells us that "the Temple of Apollo had been destroyed

211

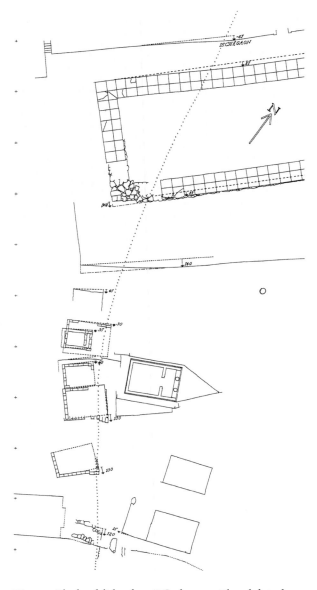

Fig. 2. *The landslide of 373 BC, drawn with red dots down the western section of the excavations in the sanctuary.*

kat[*estrepse*]" in the year 373 BC, where an earthquake is known to have happened.[4] Only the first three letters of the word given as the cause of the destruction are preserved, and we believe it should be restored as *katestrepse*, that is to say "landslide". Excavations in our own era have given us a detailed insight into what seems to have happened. Within the temenos wall of the sanctuary, ruins

have been found of a number of Archaic treasure chambers, all of which were clearly deformed by a landslide. This follows a line running down through the sanctuary from north to south. It is possible to observe the direction of the landslide from monument to monument, and even the temple terrace and the building's underlying foundations exhibit a clear effect in the line where the displacement occurred.

The assembled picture shows a movement in the terrain which cuts through the entire sanctuary. Buildings that lay across this displacement, like the temple, were destroyed or severely deformed. The monuments and buildings that lay outside the displacement, such as the column base of the Sphinx and the Athenian and Siphnian Treasuries, avoided destruction completely. This is clear from their intact foundations, which are still visible today.

Perhaps this displacement in the mountain slope happened in a matter of a few minutes and moved no more than half a metre. But it was of an immense power, and it may have happened with an ominous slowness meaning nobody could hear it in the temple. To recognize the metaphysical cracking of this divine edifice, which had been visited by innumerable pilgrims from near and far, seeking advice about their future, must have felt like the power of fate. Despite the many visible fractures and distortions, the colossal body of the temple's building doubtless still stood on its twisted foundations with its time-honoured patina and the numerous embellishments and symbols which, through time, had been added to its walls and chambers. It must have been a shocking recognition when it gradually occurred to the skilled building contractors that a repair of the old temple was out of the question.

The dreadful decision to tear the old temple down to make room for a new one was unavoidable. The entire old temple had to be demolished in order to reach the distorted foundations.

The resurrection of the temple was therefore undertaken with the serious consideration that a new, stronger foundation for the building above had to be created; there was probably also the proviso that it must still be possible to hold temple worship during the rebuilding so that pilgrims, many of whom had made a lengthy journey, would not return home bearing the news that the sanctuary was

---

4 Only *kat-* is preserved, but it is likely that the text originally read *katestrepse*, aorist of *katastrefo*; see A&H 2010, 145 and *CID* 2, 55, 4. For the earthquake see Diod. Sic. 15.48.

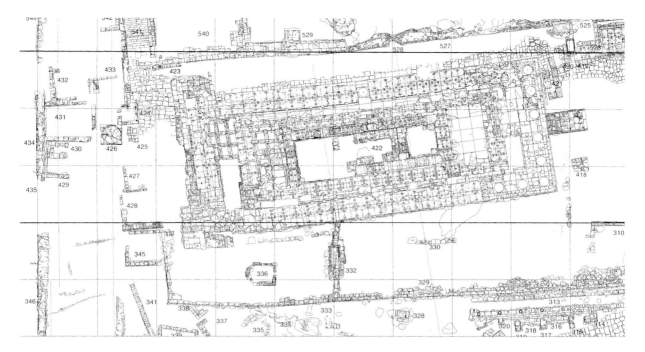

Fig. 3. *The foundations of the new temple as they appear today; between the 3 concentric frames of the foundations a binding stone framework has been inserted.*

closed. The erection of a "waiting room" up against the Ischegaon wall (Atlas 527) suggests there was such an arrangement, providing shelter for waiting pilgrims during the rebuilding.[5]

The sequence of the building of a new temple is apparent from the inscriptions which, fragment by fragment, offer an insight into the agreements, contracts and building materials which were the basis of the reconstruction of this massively important monument. It is moreover apparent from the exceptional construction of the temple foundations, which are visible today. These two sources give posterity knowledge of how, in the aftermath of the landslide, it was realized that the foundations for a monument of this size, in this location, had to be constructed according to principles which were different from those which had been used hitherto. This led to alterations in building technology in the new foundations, compared to the ones which had supported the temple that had been destroyed.

First, it was necessary to find a new, stronger kind of stone for the foundations for the columns and cella walls than the poros stone which had previously been used. Secondly, more robust joints had to be made between these new foundation stones with the aid of cramps and mandrels so that, as an assembled structure for the peristyle, cella wall and the inner colonnade, it could withstand the unstable earth pressure. Based on the actual experience this had to be taken very seriously, and it remained a concern for all construction on the sanctuary's sloping terrain. These building technological circumstances were explored in detail and described by Erik Hansen in 2010 (Fig. 3).[6]

The following account should be seen as a supplement to this examination of the temple's rebuilding. It includes the construction work in the landscape around the Sanctuary, as this was a precondition for the re-erection of the temple.

---

5 This information derives from an inscription from 355 BC, where the contractor Krémon of Argos was awarded 30 drachmas to erect a lean-to up against the Ischegaon; Poulsen 1924, 43, n. 5. But this may have happened as late as 335/34 BC: the Third Holy War in the years 356-46 would have made such activities unlikely; Bousquet 1989, 120-1.

6 A&H 2010.

A New Stone Quarry

Section A. Area A1. GPS 1.

In the period predating the catastrophe of 373 BC, the simplest constructions in the Sanctuary of Apollo were built with local limestone extracted from the nearby mountainsides. This type of stone, called "Parnassus stone", contains various kinds of limestone, which feature in many foundations, terrace walls and the surface of roads on the site. Prominent examples of the use of Parnassus stone before 373 include the terraces around the Siphnian Treasury (Atlas 123) and the large polygonal wall (Atlas 329) which forms the temple terrace. Parts of the wall enclosing the sanctuary are also made

of "Parnassus stone". If we ignore the fact that many of these stones are loose blocks of rock from the mountain slopes which have been adapted to serve their purpose in these constructions, we know of two stone quarries from which "Parnassus stone" has been extracted. One of them lies directly above the stadium, the other, called Logari, a few kilometres east of the Sanctuary of Apollo and above the Marmaria Sanctuary. Both are at a distance and in locations which made the journey to the building site where the stone was used both short and easy to manage.

In addition to these particular quarries there are also marks of wedges in practically all the rock faces surrounding the sanctuary. The many traces of extraction in the rocks demonstrate that stone was removed from the mountain's visible structure, where the quality was sufficiently high to meet the standards stipulated for construction. The two quarries in question were probably brought into existence by the quarrying of an accessible cliff, which gradually showed itself to contain stone of a usable quality at considerable depth. No solid, homogenous limestone has been found in these quarries which would meet the requirements for the new foundations of the Temple of Apollo; besides, the two quarries could not provide the necessary quantities.

Fig. 4. *View from the St Elijah stone quarry on the southern slopes of Mount Parnassus. Delphi is situated far to the left of the picture, 300 metres higher up. In the background is the port of Kirrha, situated on the Bay of Corinth; to the left in the picture, the Pleistos Valley.*

214

The actual buildings, that is to say, first and foremost the temple and the treasuries from the time before the catastrophe, were most frequently built of porous poros stone, which was brought from the quarries in the Peloponnese and subsequently transported up to the sanctuary from the port of Kirrha. In none of these monumental structures or buildings do we find the homogenous blue-grey type of stone observable in the new temple foundations.

Against this background we have to assume that in response to the desire to construct stronger foundations for the resurrection of the temple, a new stone quarry was opened soon after 373 BC which could meet the new demands. We may assume that the search for this suitable stone was one of the very first activities into which those concerned put their efforts, as supply of the stone for the new foundations was a completely necessary precondition for the subsequent re-erection of the temple's enormous superstructure. We can only guess how the search for a stone of better quality in the mountains around Delphi was actually organized.

The hard blue-grey limestone that was selected for the building of the new temple is to be found 6 km west of the sanctuary and 300 m below the level of the temple itself.[7] The relatively long distance between this stone quarry and the new temple raises some interesting questions. How did the eventual selection fall on the special deposits in the distant mountains? Next, how did they accomplish the complicated task of bringing the stones, each weighing several tonnes, up the mountainsides to the temple building site.

Fig. 5. *View from the upper level of the St Elijah stone quarry, looking west, with the plateau and the Taratsa Ravine in the background to the left.*

---

7   The stone quarry is described in modern times in 1865, and named St Elijah by the Frenchman P. Foucart, with reference to the monastery which is situated above the quarry. Later, in 1914, the quarry is more extensively described by É. Bourguet and in 1981 by P. Amandry. Rough measurements were taken by Erik Hansen (cf. Fig. 6).

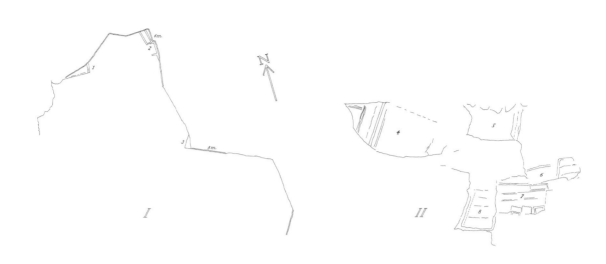

Fig. 6. *Sketch of two quarrying areas in the St Elijah quarry by Erik Hansen.*

Even in the form best suited to its use, the contractor had to evaluate whether the outcrop was of a sufficient magnitude, and how far it was situated from the building site. This evaluation must have included the character of the transport route and whether it was possible to construct a means of transport which could take the resources to the site. These matters were all essential to the opening of a quarry, not the least in the mountainous area surrounding Delphi.

In this context one crucial consideration has to be: how large must the haulage capacity be to bring the desired quantities of stone to the building site when the loads have to be pulled by oxen or mules? The increase and decrease in the upward gradients of the vehicle track impose limits on the size of the stones which could be hauled through the mountain. Thus the maximum size of the extracted stones imposes limits on the tectonic possibilities in the building work's construction and architecture.

Area A1

Section A deals with a stretch of road which may have been the point of departure for the transportation of the

Fig. 7. *A road beneath the quarry, heading east towards Delphi.*

building stones we see in the ruins of the temple. It is situated in the mountains running down towards the south below the Prophet Elijah Monastery, where the new stone quarry was opened. This expanse of the mountain brings together a number of streams to form a larger watercourse with a corridor towards the south, which runs out on the lowland between the conurbations of Itea and Kirrha. This unpaved road, below the stone quarry which runs along

Fig. 8. *Area A1. Areas of rock worn until shiny and stone pavements, looking east on the road below the St Elijah quarry. GPS 1. On both sides of the lane are numerous loose stones with marks of wedges and chisels.*

the side of it across the area, today gives access to a number of recently planted olive groves, which encircle stone spoil from the quarry. It is probably the road Bourguet described in 1914,[8] when he could see ancient roadway fragments in the make-up of the track. These fragments were not discovered in our fieldwork in this area, but it is probably the same track as the one shown in Figs 8 and 9.

The present track leads from the stone quarry at Level 242[9] up to the later modern road east, where it terminates at Level 280. The length of the track in Section A is roughly 600 m.

Even though the stone in the surface of the track just beneath the quarry is completely worn smooth in many places, one cannot attach any significance to this observa-

tion as far as the precise location of the transportation of stone is concerned. The situation of the area has, without doubt, been dissected by the course of the road used as the connection between Amphissa and Delphi right up into modern times, leaving traces of heavy traffic. The later olive plantations may have altered the road's geographical position since Bourguet saw it. But regardless of where the ancient road was situated in the mountains, the steep gradient on the last part towards Delphi would have been hard to avoid, as is apparent from the following photograph, which shows the view looking southeast from the top of the quarry. At the end of the road's gradient it turns to the left in the picture, to the east and into the mountainside on which Delphi is sited (Fig. 9).

---

8 Bourguet 1914, 335, 339, fig. 121. É. Bourguet was the first person in modern times to have seen and described a brief stretch of a road below the St Elias quarry with ancient structures.

9 Levels above sea level are provided in this way throughout the text.

Delphi's upland and mountainsides were undoubtedly well-trodden even then, not just by herdsmen and peasants with their small, terraced fields, but also by people knowledgeable about building, who, as a result of the extensive building activity generation after generation, had used the sanctuary and its immediate surroundings as a stone quarry.[10] We can therefore presuppose that the search for a new quality of stone started from the many known paths and the course of the road which led to the unusual siting of the sanctuary on the steep mountainside (Fig. 10).

There is thus a connection from the east to the sanctuary, which passed the aforementioned quarry at Logari. Another is the connecting road from the west, which runs from Amphissa through an expanse of mountain between the Prophet Elijah Monastery and the promontory Taratsa

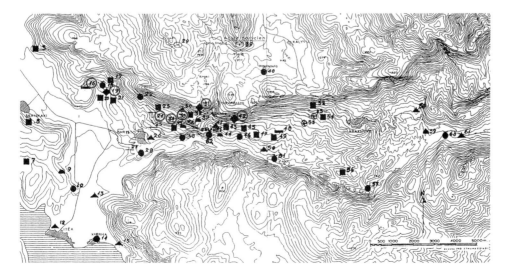

Fig. 10. *Ancient constructions in the region of Delphi. Quarries: no. 19; St. Elias: no. 31; Stadion: no. 42; Mellissi. Stretches of road: no. 16; Taratsa: no. 24; Gerospilies: no. 33; Xenia: no. 34; Elinia.*

10   Skorda 1991.

Fig. 11. *Map from 1852, which, in addition to a track between Amphissa (Salona) and Delphi, shows the stretch between the quarry and Delphi, indicated by red arrows. It also shows remains of towers and other ruins from antiquity indicated by "Tour H."; "R.H."; "Block. H".*

to the sanctuary. The last-named connecting road is to be found in a corridor in the mountains, which, seen from Amphissa, gradually rises up to Delphi on the southern mountain slopes above the plateau of the Pleistos Valley. Like so many courses of roads in the landscape, this arterial road follows the topographic conditions which display easy accessibility, and therefore has existed as a connecting road ever since the settlements of Amphissa and Delphi were founded. We have knowledge of the course of this road in the mountain from references by modern-day explorers, and it partly reappears in one of the first scientific mappings of the region, dating from 1852.[11]

It was possibly the traffic in this course of the road which led to knowledge of the locality of the St Elijah stone, in that the deposit lies in the same mountain corridor as the road. The architect of the temple and the people who knew the mountain probably began looking for new building material along the existing access road to Delphi. From these tracks their focus was directed at the outcrops of stone lying above the tracks, meaning the loading and unloading between the quarry and the transport route could be effected in a simple way, initially by using rollers

in short bursts and then by wheeled wagons through the mountainsides. This latter form of transport is a point to which we will return (Fig. 11).

A project the size of the Temple of Apollo required the quarrying of 3500 m³ of raw building stone. The visible hollows in the mountainside where the St Elijah stone was removed do not look at all impressive, however. The vertical traces in the quarry rise 30 m from an even level which has a total area of 2000 m². They divide up into 3 separate areas of quarrying along the existing road within a length of 200 m, each of which, with its traces of cutting and the use of wedges, appears as if they had only been left by the stone-cutters a week ago (Fig 12).

A view down the mountain from the quarrying areas gives an idea of the enormous piles of rock, gravel and earth that would have to have been removed to be able to get near a homogeneous, usable stone material. These heaps also contain the traces of the stonecutters' laborious liberation and initial shaping of the undressed building stones, each of which could weigh up to 9 tonnes. The eastern quarrying location seems to have been abandoned on account of the large fissures at this

11   Carte de la Gréce 1:200 000, 1852.

Fig. 12. *Aerial photograph of the St Elijah quarry, facing north; The three areas of quarrying are highlighted in red.*

point in the mountain. But one can clearly follow the carved outline of the individual building stones in two other areas of quarrying, after they came loose from the cliff. As is apparent from the aerial photograph, the three areas of quarrying lie directly above the existing road, while the grey nuances of the stone spoil form a heap of stones of slightly over half a square kilometre in area down the mountain slope.

If one estimates a waste of two thirds in connection with the quarrying of usable stone, one can calculate that in total, slightly over 10,000 m³ of stone material has been extracted from the mountainside. Quarrying of the new building stone for the Temple of Apollo was doubtlessly carefully coordinated with the actual construction process itself up at the sanctuary. But the work in the mountain, as well as the building process, was interrupted, judging

by inscriptions, for ten years from 356 to 346 BC, when the Third Sacred War was being fought.

Opening of the quarry is one of the first major tasks in the overall process. But the extensive construction work to provide a usable roadway also demanded meticulous planning. After an extensive survey, many working days were required to build the roadway through the mountains. This roadway had to be complete along its entire length before the first stone blocks could arrive at the building site to be incorporated in the foundations which were supposed to carry the temple's superstructure.

The stone quarry delivered more than 2,100 building slabs, which together had a total volume of 3,500 m³. This means that the transportation from the St Elijah quarry to the sanctuary moved slightly more than 9,500 tonnes of building stones.[12] Working from an average load of 5

12   A&H 2010, 457, in that we have in mind a specific gravity of 2.7 for this homogeneous limestone.

tonnes per trip, each moving one or more building stones, the whole task would have taken 1,900 transport trips during the years of the construction of the foundations. As we shall subsequently discuss, one must assume that these specific transport trips were all carefully coordinated with the stages of building in the sanctuary. The inscriptions concerning contracts and contractors seem to confirm the supposition that there was some kind of meticulously devised timetable for the coordination of activities between the quarry and the building, e.g. stone blocks for euthynteria, for orthostats or for floor tiles and their foundations, so that a bulky piling-up or time-wasting lack of materials could be avoided.

In this context we can try to calculate how long, on average, it would take to transport a full load of stone from the St Elijah quarry up to the building site. We could start from the 156 stones for the outermost frame of the euthynteria: these were the first building stones brought up to the site. The average weight of each of these stones is 5.5 tonnes, in that we have added 20% to the weight of the "ready" stones which we can see today lined up in a row in their original position in the foundations. The 20% corresponds to a protective layer around the stone during transportation of 3 cm which was later removed. If we work from a wagon which weighs around 1.5 tonnes, the total weight of a typical transport of these building stones would be around 7 tonnes. As draught power we should envisage 6 to 8 oxen, which together could pull this weight on a rough track surfaced with roadstones.[13] With an average upward gradient of 6% in the corridor, one should reckon on a maximum draught speed of 1 km per hour. For the euthynteria stones the most we could hope for would be 7 to 10 traction hours to bring a block from the stone quarry to the workplace at the sanctuary. So we are envisaging one day per transport, when there should also be time for breaks in which oxen and drovers can rest and satisfy their hunger and thirst.

Next we have to estimate how many trips from the quarry could be accomplished in one day. This involves considerations of how many undressed building stones can be produced per day, and how many of the arriving stones for the building site can be shaped on the site, together with how many euthynteria stones it is

possible to set in their final place per day. Whereas one can increase the number of trips without these getting in the way of each other, the situation is different in the work processes connected to the quarrying of the building stones, the dressing of them on the building site and their eventual putting in place in the temple. It is this last process in the new temple foundations which determined the rhythm of work in the St Elijah quarry. This is something of which we will acquire knowledge when we approach the building site at the temple. First, however, we will examine more closely the tracks of the stone transport on the steep mountainside, which can confirm that an actual path was made for hauling from the quarry to the sanctuary.

A Short Cut to Delphi

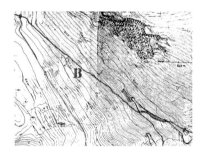

Section B. Area B 1-8
GPS 2, 3, 4

Should one become lost among the numerous tracks, which, like a fine pattern, have been trodden into the mountainside by sheep and goats, one will eventually notice a branching system of parallel paths which intersect with transverse ones. In this system there are no main streets and secondary roads, but recognizable thoroughfares which offer plenty of choices to anyone trying to find their way up the mountainside. These thoroughfares are characterized by their humble presence which does not reveal itself untill one actually walks on them. In this anonymous landscape one suddenly catches sight of a monumental row of stones which stretches out over the mountain's slope, across the rising geological formations which are oriented down towards the ravine and the val-

---

13   Landels 1978, 173-7; Korres 1993, 104.

Fig. 13. *Stone rows which in some places are made higher with an extra course; the flat façade in this terrace wall is given an even front with coarse adaptation, executed with a sledgehammer and large pointed chisel.*

ley. The large stones are lined up, side by side, in the form determined by nature. The stones are, roughly speaking, of equal size, in many cases weighing several tonnes. It is these dramatic stone rows which suggest a grandiose work of construction that engaged and combined with the principal features of the landscape. Merely the weight of a single stone, each of which was probably manhandled down from a chance place in the mountainside to a prearranged location in a stone row, demanded not only a well-organized collaboration between skilled building workers, but also tools which were capable of managing the moving of such heavy boulders on the steep slope.

The linear positioning of the stones seems to demand as a precondition a directed organization of work, the intention of which could hardly be the construction of terrace walls for the small plots of land which the slopes make possible. Neither are the older donkey paths, which can still be found in the region, flanked by stones of this size and weight (Fig. 13).

On closer inspection it turns out that the colossal stones in these terrace walls often bear traces of a coarse hewing on one side and, in some cases, wedge marks attesting to their cleavages. In the places in this stone row where the pressure from falling rocks has tipped the large

Fig. 14. *Example of the stacking of large boulders, which may have formed the foundation for the lane.*

stones over down into the valley, we can now and then see a hewn bearing surface which has been left behind in the rock. Below the terrace wall a horizontal surface is often to be observed, which may have been a roadway. The side facing the valley has almost always slipped down, however, in some places leaving the remains of very large unhewn boulders piled up in rows which supported a lane (Fig. 14).

The varying directions for the stone rows discovered show that they lie on slightly ascending levels in the mountainside, with a southeasterly orientation in the range between 112° to 125° SE. The direction can be determined more precisely in places where this direction crosses the mountain's geological structure, which at intervals shows itself in small raised ridges descending towards the Pleistos Valley. The orientation of this natural feature is around 225° SW, meaning the erected stone rows must repeatedly cross the sections of rock of the mountainside. Where this crossing occurs, the ridge has been cut away to make room for the even stretch of the road. This feature can often be observed even in modern road-building when there is a need to cut through the rises in a landscape. The vertical side in this cutting-out shows, as stated, a more precise orientation of the stone arrangements. In those places where a horizontal surface has been cut into the rock, the cutting points towards the construction of a sequence which confirms that this may have been the location of road construction, the purpose of which was to establish a track. Here the question arises as to what kind of transport such an extensive road construction was intended for. We can rule out farmers having constructed these enormous retaining walls for plots of land or access to these. The same can be said of the course of the roads we call footpaths or bridle paths for pilgrims visiting the sanctuary, which to a greater extent followed the shape of the mountainside

223

Fig. 15. *The mountainside in Section B, looking west towards the stone quarry.*

in winding routes and bends, the purpose of which was the reduction of travelling time. With this proviso, the large stone rows may point towards three possible kinds of traffic. The first is transport of the large quantities of poros stone and building materials for the construction of the temple of the Alkamaeonidai in the 6th century from the port of Kirrha, which must have left traces on the mountain and of which the observable stone rows may be a part. Another possibility is that the roadworks may have been carried out in connection with the ceremonial processions around the temple in the years 380-79.[14] A third possibility is the extensive transport work in the years after 373, when the destroyed temple from the 7th century was re-erected in the sanctuary with new foundation stones. Finally, it is an obvious interpretation that we are dealing with a roadway which has successively served all three purposes. The problematic obstacle of the mountainside created a need for a passable corridor for the efficient expediting of heavy transportation. Reuse of an earlier sequence in the landscape was of course enormously practical. Such an earlier corridor had to be maintained and extended according to the various

demands of the different aims. Herein lies a story of development, which is often characteristic of the siting of roads and tracks in general, and which in the present case suggests a surprisingly extensive programme of building work, 6 km in length across steep mountain slopes, which the present fieldwork has attempted to document (Fig. 15).

In the steep transition from the area of the mountain in which the stone quarry lies, to the relatively level south-facing mountainside which stretches towards the sanctuary in the east, the overall orientation of Kaltsi's Path alternates between 112° and 125° SE. This short cut to the sanctuary begins at Level 280 and ends at Level 484 with a total length of 2100 m. This means an average gradient of about 7%. The path in this section is pretty straight, turning after the first 1.5 km from a direction of 125° SE to a principal direction of 112° SE with local deviations. The first short stretch in the landscape has been drastically altered in modern times by new roads and by the so-called Mornos Canal. The last stretch of 500 m in this section lies close to the main road to the modern city of Delphi and cuts across it several times.

14   Forbes 1934, 104; cf. Pritchett 1980, 147.

Fig. 16. *Faint traces of a track running over a section of rock at a bearing of 114° SE in Level 362, with hewn areas. From the beginning of the vehicle track below the quarrying area itself and to the first indication B1 is roughly 1,550 m, where it has risen 120 m, giving an overall rise of 8%.*

Fig. 17. *Detail of Fig. 16, with transverse cutting.*

Area B1
Cutting into the Mountainside

The first indications of a programme of building work are to be found around Level 362. They are in the mountainside towards the Pleistos Valley, roughly 80 m above the Mornos Canal and 850 m from the place where Kaltsi's Path cuts the modern roads at Level 280-300. It is just possible to make out one or two terraces running east–west on the slope, which rises gradually.

On one of these rising levels one finds hewn areas in the rock. In one place there is also a transverse cutting which can be seen in Figs 16 and 17. GPS 2 (Fig. 16).

The transverse area of hewing may have been used as a bearing surface for a stone which was supposed to protect a roadway against sliding stones, gravel and earth from the mountainside above, which have indeed now slid. The cutting may, however, also be a gully to catch water for the thirsty oxen and their drivers after the steep journey up from the lower reaches of the mountain. A more thorough cleaning could provide the basis for a better understanding of this hewing in the middle of the mountainside's harsh landscape (Fig. 17).

225

Fig. 18. Area B2a looking towards the mountainside. This cliff with hewn areas continues its course upwards behind the tree on the right, where Area B2b is situated.

Area B2
Cuttings in the cliff with water-hole and line with arrangements of stones. GPS 3.

In the dense maquis of the mountainside a massive cliff emerges with clear signs of two hewn areas, which have arrangements of stones on their upper side. They lie about 150 m closer to the sanctuary than B1, at around Level 383. This means a average gradient of about 14% (Fig. 18).

Area B2a
Horizontal surface with water hole.

In the drawing of B2a (Fig. 19) one sees the vertical downward cutting of the rock of c. 1.4 m², and in a corre-

sponding flat surface below at 5.1 m². Both surfaces have been dressed with a sledgehammer and a coarse pointed chisel. In the horizontal surface a natural irregular hole has been widened out. It measures 42 x 32 cm, with a depth of 28 cm. Across this surface are faint parallel lines along the mountain in the direction 123° SE. They are probably markings produced by successive cutting away of the rock, or in a subsequent levelling. On the slanting upper part of the rock are spread cuts from a point chisel which were probably intended to channel water down to the small water basin. People who frequent the mountain claim it is often full of water.[15] Below the horizontal level in the rock lie a number of large stones, which may have come from a foundation for the aforementioned levelled

15   For example, Lambros Altiparmakis, formerly employed by the museum, who drew our attention to the place and the water hole.

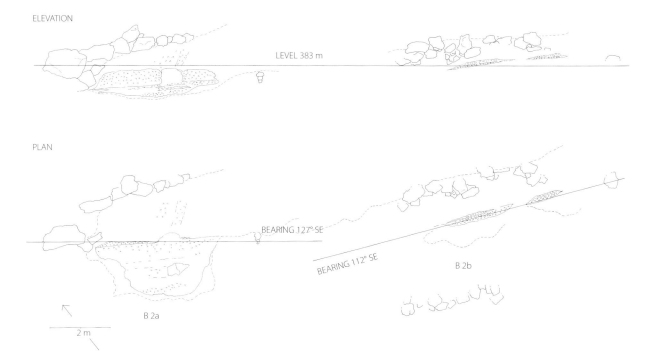

ELEVATION

LEVEL 383 m

PLAN

BEARING 127° SE

BEARING 112° SE

B 2b

B 2a

2 m

Fig. 19. *Areas B2a and B2b, elevation and plan of the hewing of a larger area of rock with a protecting arrangement of stones laid on top. Scale 1:150. The horizontal red line in the elevation shows Level 383. In the plan the red line shows the compass direction 127° SE in 2a and 112° SE in 2b. The sketch shows the bisected area. The course displays a presumed turning of the road.*

Figs 20. *Area B2a seen from above. The faint stripes in the surface may derive from successive cutting of the cliff. The hewing was carried out with a sledgehammer and coarse pointed chisel.*

area that has slid down. This relatively large surface may, if occasion arose, have served as either a halt or a "lay-by".[16] At the very top a protective arrangement of stones has been laid on top of nine large stones. They are all so heavy that it would take a team of workers with the aid of some kind of equipment to bring them down from the mountainside into their places (Figs. 18 and 19).

Area B2b
Hacked-out line in the rock.

Eight metres east of Area B2a a 4 m-long linear cut has been made in the rock with a sledgehammer and coarse chisel. It has a gradient of 15% and begins 40 cm higher than the surface in 2a. The overall length of the two areas is 16 m and exhibits an upward gradient of 8%. The cutting

---

16   Bourguet 1914, 338.

Fig. 21. *Area B2b looking west, with Area B2a behind the trees; large stones of irregular shape are laid above the straight cutting.*

Fig. 22. *Area B2b seen from the valley side; the beginning of the linear cutting which rises to the right is visible in the background, while traces of the foundation for the lane is visible in the foreground.*

in 2b is in the direction 112° SE, so 11-15° towards the north in relation to the orientation in Area 2a. The intention of this may have been to find secure purchase for the upper side of a roadway in the steep slope (Fig. 21).

Areas 2a and 2b represent the only place where we can determine that there was a significant turn in what we regard as a vehicle track for the heavy building stones from the St Elijah quarry. The relatively large flat area in Area 2a may be a "lay-by" or "passing place", but could also be interpreted as a horizontal underlying layer which makes a turning possible in the transportation of the heavy building stones. We will return to this below (Fig. 18-19).

É. Bourguet's Road

Area B3

The straight stretch up over the mountainside from Area B2b to the modern main road's first 180° swing from Delphi towards the lowland is about 400 m. If one follows the orientation in the clusters of heavy stone which show themselves, now and then, in the vicinity of Kaltsis' Path on this stretch, the elevation rises from Level 383 to Level 431. This means an upward gradient of roughly 12%. In this ascent towards Delphi the mountainside rises more

Fig. 23. *Big clusters of colossal boulders below the place where the modern road from Delphi to Itea takes a 180° turn for the first time; they may be foundations for the roadway and seem to be in situ, at an orientation of 125° SE.*

steeply. The area seems to be dissected by many faint intercutting paths which can be sensed in the levels of the mountain. They may be connected with the many surviving arrangements of stones which are to be found further down towards the valley and which may have links with the many different connecting tracks that must have been used from the port at Kirrha up to the sanctuary and in the subsequent cultivation of the mountainside. These tracks for animals, however rare, have stones of the size we find in the aforementioned stone clusters around Kaltsis' Path (Fig. 23).

Area B3
Double track with "sidewalk". GPS 4.

To our surprise we discovered an area with a double track. This means two parallel hollowed-out cavities in the rock at a distance of 145 cm apart. These are without doubt ruts for a wheeled wagon, since the surface of the rock in between rules out the use of a stone sledge on rollers. Visible in the rock between the two wheel-ruts is a strip of superficial cutting with a point chisel which has the same orientation as the roadway. We interpret this as a preliminary orientation mark for the course of the roadway in the mountain, which would have been marked out by persons who knew the mountains well in advance of the subsequent construction work (cf. Fig. 50). The area is dominated by massive projections which slope precipitously. They often leave narrow passages for the roadway in the steep mountainside. At this point the building workers have therefore hacked out an even stretch in the slope of 60 cm along the roadway, as a kind of sidewalk, to create an overall passage for wagon, oxen and drivers of about 3 m (Fig. 24).[17]

If we assume that the breadth of road necessary for a team of two oxen is about 160 cm,[18] the pavement at this point can compensate for the sloping rock surface close to the southern wheel-rut toward the valley. If this was the case it would not be possible for either oxen or drivers to find a foothold there. At the same time the sidewalk provides the option of hauling at an angle to the mountainside. The crooked pull would prevent the wagon from sliding off down into the valley.

The hauling at an angle can also be explained with the narrow parallel hewn areas in the line where the lower wheel-rut towards the south has its direction. These parallel hewings, which get displaced to a lower and lower level, indicate that the sloping rock created problems for the construction of a wheel-rut that could keep the wagon at a reasonable angle. The hewn areas in the rock create a rake of about 10° for the wagon, which must be the limit for carrying out the stone transportation. For this the wheel's axle's clearance comes over the rock surface, between the wheel-ruts. The surface is of such an irregular character, despite having been worked, that here we must be dealing with transport on a wagon which had a wheel

17 A corresponding "sidewalk" can be found on the upper side of the Koile Road up to the Acropolis in Athens (personal observation G. Algreen-Ussing, Sept. 2015).

18 We are assuming a breadth of 5 English feet for a span of two oxen. Burford 1960, 13.

Fig. 24. *Two parallel wheel-ruts cut into the rock in Area B3, seen from above looking south; the track is cut into the cliff-side with a "sidewalk".*

Fig. 25. *Elevation and plan of Area B3 with two sections; scale 1:150.*

LEVEL 428 m

SECTION A

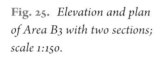

2 m

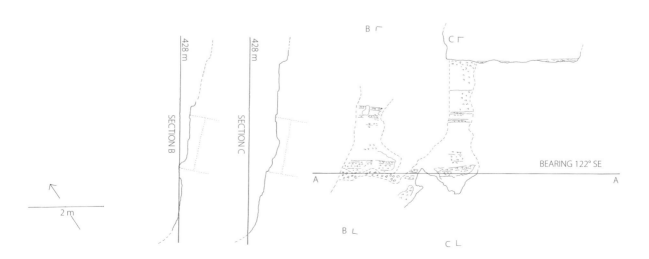

428 m

428 m

SECTION B

SECTION C

B ⌐ C ⌐

A — BEARING 122° SE — A

B ∟ C ∟

Fig. 26. *Left wheel-rut seen towards Delphi; above is the edge of the sidewalk.*

Fig. 27. *The right wheel-rut seen across the roadway; it appears to have been recut several times.*

diameter of 80 cm minimum. If there is evidence of wagon transport here, we conclude that they must have used the entire length of the vehicle track. This is our justification for only talking about a wagon with wheels and rejecting the idea of a stone sledge pulled on wooden rollers. The term "wheel-rut" is something to which we will return (Fig. 25).

The wheel-ruts lie at around Level 428 with a direction around 126º SE, in that they turn slightly inwards toward the mountain. They appear to have a steep gradient on this short section, which can be measured to around 17%. Even the cutting of the double track was done with a point chisel and the rock surface between the wheel-ruts has been worked. The distance between them is, from centre to centre, 145 cm, with a depth of from 5 to 12 cm with flat bottom and a breadth up to 25 cm,[19] which is clearest in the upper wheel-rut, looking north.

About 20 m towards Delphi several transverse "steps" have been laid across the direction of the wagon track in B3, which suggests the passage later was used as a donkey path. These steps lie on the fallen stone and piles of earth. Their "stepwise" positioning may in part have been intended to provide some respite to the donkeys, instead of keeping them moving constantly on a continually sloping, ascending or descending surface; this stepping was also a way of diminishing the erosion effect of a running watercourse, which can be very damaging to a sloping roadway bedded on earth (Figs. 26 and 27).

D. Skorda's short cut

Areas B4 to B8. GPS 5-10.

Area B4

The transition from Area B3 to Area B4 happens through a steep slope in the mountainside. It is precisely at this point on the slope that the modern road has been con-

---

19   For a comprehensive survey of gauges see Pritchett 1980, 195 in which he concludes that the standard width of ancient Greek wheel tracks is 140 cm, with a few deviations. But the rock-cut ruts over the Isthmus (Diolkos) show an axle breadth of 150-60 cm, according to Raepset 1993 possibly because of special wagons. We are grateful to Tønnes Bekker-Nielsen for this important reference.

231

Fig. 28. *Area 4a looking east, where the tracks in Areas B4 – B8 are on a line. GPS 5.*

structed across the roadway we are examining. It is difficult, therefore, to see how the vehicle track can be followed from Area B3 over to Area B4 above the modern road, where we find lengthy stone rows, hewed points in the rock and numerous wheel-ruts, lying in an extension of each other.[20] Their general orientation in the roadway changes to 112° SE. The distance from the tracks in Area

B3 to those in Area B4 is about 100 m, with a rise of 11 m. This works out as 12% in a straight line (Fig. 28).

The overall length of the Areas B4-B8 is 550 m. The rise for the first 300 m, which cut their way up into the slope of the mountainside, is barely 10%. The final 250 m, which make up the area from B7 to B8, consist of an even plateau which is terminated by a new slope across the orientation of the vehicle track, the uphill gradient of which is roughly 20%. This slope is partly concealed by modern building debris, which makes it difficult to determine its profile. Standing at the top of the slope is the new, small Church of Hosios Loukas, which forms the transition to Section C.

Arrangements of stones and massive hewings in areas of the rock link Areas B4a and B4b. They protect the roadway against sliding stones, pebbles and earth and bear witness to an impressive building work which would have demanded a lot of man-hours (cf. Fig. 29). In many places bearing surfaces have been cut for the stones, each weighing several tonnes, in the solid rock of the mountain. In other places the rows of stones have been found in the eroded falls of rock. In some cases the wedge-marks show that the stones were split. Often the façade facing the road has been worked with a sledge hammer and point chisel, so that here the violent natural shapes of the stone rows form a curiously uniform sequence facing the roadway, which follows this formation. In some places the great stones lie interlocked with each other in several courses, having thus formed a

LEVEL 440 m

BEARING 113° SE

Fig. 29. *Elevation and plan of Areas B4a and B4b, both of which bear traces of a track channel for the wheels.*

20 Cf. Skorda 1991, no. 24, Gerospilies (route).

Fig. 30. *The orientation of the stone configurations around 113° SE continues through Areas B 5, 6, 7 and 8 – in all a stretch of roughly 550 m.*

Fig. 31. *Area B4a; hacked out wheel-ruts in a direction of 113° SE at Level 440, GPS 5.*

more durable bulwark against the mountain's movements and rockslides since, according to our reckoning, they were set into the mountain shortly after the catastrophe of 373 BC. This was followed by the building of the roadway itself, of the foundations of which we have pitifully few remains, since these slid down the mountainside.

Area B4a

The fact that we can talk about a deliberately laid vehicle track for transportation in this area is because we can already see the initial evidence of such transport within the first 25 m in Area 4a. There is a single wheel–rut cut down into the upper part which may once have been the course of a wagon across the rock surface at this point (Figs. 30 and 31).

Even though no excavations were undertaken during the fieldwork, and only a few instances of superficial cleaning were carried out, the base for the roadway between the two rock surfaces, which it passes, looks as though it is merely stamped earth, reinforced with pebbles. One can see on the rough measurements of Area B4a that the cleaned field with small pebbles right up to where the roadway is led into the hacked-out tracks in the rock surface. The field is shown with dots. At the same time it is possible to see that the rut in the rock is cut in the form of a fan, which may be a way of steering a wagon wheel into a delimited field in the surface of the rock.[21]

The running surface is flat-bottomed, with a width of about 25 cm and soft edges up to the surrounding rock surface. Visible in many places along the edge are cuts made by a point chisel. The nearest surrounding rock is shaped with a point chisel, forming a flat, ascending surface. The naturally occurring depressions in this surface seem to be filled with pebbles. In the eastern termination of this indication of traffic is a v-formed channel in the surrounding under-layer of pebbles, which may be a sign that the wagon had a considerable rake at this point. It may also have been formed by another type of wagon wheel, from the use of the roadway once the transportation of stone ceased. The drawing (Fig. 32) shows another two areas which are covered by pebbles: an area above

---

21   On Malta one can see fan-shaped "entrances" in the so-called "cart-ruts" when they run from a surface of earth into the soft limestone, which later hardens on the surface through calcification. On Malta these tracks are produced by wear and tear, in contrast to the Greek ones which were intentionally cut. This is one of the causes of the many parallel tracks on Malta. Algreen-Ussing 1992.

233

Fig. 32. *Elevation and plan of Area B4a; scale 1:150.*

the roadway's protective row of stones and an area where the layer of pebbles covers the roadway. In either case this may be a donkey track made at a later date.[22] Presumably the lowest was laid first and then the uppermost later, due to the successive filling up with stone, grit and earth from the mountain above. Both stretches of pebble layers are doubtless the vestiges of Kaltsis' donkey track.

Area 4b

16.5 m to the east there is a brief stretch of a channel for wheels, which is a continuation of that found in 4a. It has the same orientation, but it was only possible to clean a very small patch.[23]

As is apparent from the rough measurement in Fig. 29, the row of large stones above the track is laid on this cliff. Here too there are wedge marks from the splitting of larger stones, and some with the coarse marks of sledgehammer and pointed chisel. The rock itself has been worked with bearing surfaces for arrangements of stones as a base for the subsequent construction of the terrace walls.

Area B5

The first visible stone rows in Area B5a lie spread out on a gently sloping terrain with a few rock projections in the fallen grit and detritus from the modern road above. It

---

22   Pikoulas 1999, 250-5.

23   During our fieldwork we only had permission to clean small patches. The track lay on the mountainside in such a way that if we could have cleaned a larger area, we might possibly have found a complete section in the roadway and its ruts.

Fig. 33. *About 40 cm of uncovered wheel rut, which continues the rut in 4a, visible in Fig. 29.*

was possible to pull a stretched rope over all the arrangements of stones from a point in 4b, which showed that the scattered larger stones in Area 5a followed the same direction, around 112° SE, with a gradient of 12%. On the front of the largest stone there are hewed areas made with a sledgehammer and a point chisel. Some have wedge marks which suggest a splitting of the stones. Both above and below the stone configurations there are traces of a road surface with small loose stones, which suggests a later donkey path.

The consummate precision in the stone configuration, which combines an orientation determined according to direction with an incline determined according to functional considerations, presents an astonishing insight into the organization and practical execution of the building work. The scattered stones in B5a–b form a stretch of about 47 m overall, of which only a single trace has come to light in the roadway (Fig. 34).

Area 5b

This wheel rut bears the marks of wear and tear and erosion, with a few chisel cuts in the sides. It rises in a gentle slope at around Level 448. The total length is 270 cm, with a depression in between the two cuttings of 70 cm. The direction is 111° SE. The minimum width of the wheel-rut is 20 cm, with soft edges of 6 cm from the flat bottom. In the transverse fissure between the two areas of rock there is a filling of pebbles. The hewing shows faintly fan-shaped entrances for approaches to Delphi (Fig. 36).[24]

---

24 Cf. Note 22.

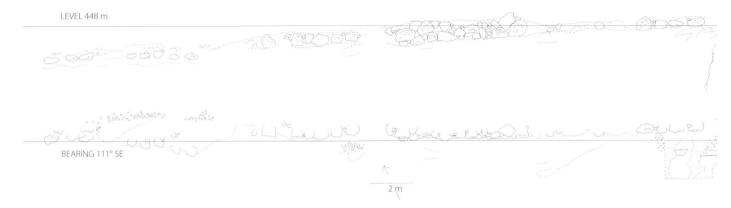

LEVEL 448 m

BEARING 111° SE

2 m

Fig. 34. *Elevation and plan of Areas 5a and 5b.*

With some cleaning around the rock surface, the earth shows itself to be reinforced with stones and pebbles. But it is hard to be sure whether this was produced by detritus from the cutting of the facades of the terrace wall above, or with the intention of reinforcing the roadway. Above the terrace wall there were remains of a road surface of small stones. Alongside the terrace of 5b, facing the valley side there is a heap of large stones on a lower level about 6 m below the track we see in Fig. 37. By and large they follow the

orientation of the lane and may have been the remains of a foundation for the building up of the roadway into a larger version of the same, but it may also contain stones which have slid down from the upper arrangements (Fig. 37).

Area B6

11.2 m in the direction of Delphi from Area 5b there is more evidence of the possible track. It is a rut 120 cm long

Fig. 35. *A wheel-rut in two sections at a bearing of 111° SE at Level 448, GPS 6; the vehicle entry points towards Delphi are shaped like fans.*

LEVEL 448 m

BEARING 111° SE

SECTION

A

A

A

2 m

Fig. 36. *Elevation and plan of a worn rut in Area B5b; scale 1:150.*

cut down into the rock, forming an extension of 5b, but turning a little towards the east: its direction is 104° SE at Level 448. An oblong stone of 25 cm, which fits into a cavity, has been inserted into the cutting. The stone appears to have been shaped and worn on the upper side.[25] The ruler indicates the direction of the track, which is 104° SE.

This location is special because the rock close to the rut falls steeply down towards the valley. A foundation for the roadway on this side would demand extensive construction work. It is therefore possible that the roadway's upper rut lies underneath the fallen stone from the mountainside, just as was the case with B3 (Fig. 38).

At any rate the construction of the roadway might have been fairly extensive in this steep location. But it cannot be physically pointed out since the mountainside, shortly after the track found in B6 is covered with a large cone of building spoil from the construction of the modern road above. It conceals the next 40 to 50 m of the mountainside under which the roadway must have run (Fig. 40).[26]

25 In Malta too, stones are found inserted into the chalk to guide traffic, especially in places where a number of tracks intersect.

26 The cone is drawn in on the Greek military map from the 1960s.

Fig. 37. *Remains of a support wall below the track in Area B5b.*

237

Fig. 38. *Photo of rut B6 when looking east toward Delphi, GPS 7. The running surface is 120 cm long with a flat bottom 30 cm wide. The direction of the rut follows the ruler.*

Fig. 39. *Detail of the rut B6, with the inserted stone.*

Fig. 40. *Area B 7 looking west, where the stone-settings along the track come out of the "rubbish cone." Orientation is 112° SE at around Level 450.*

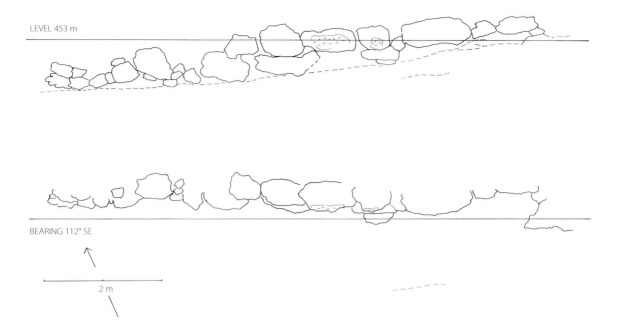

LEVEL 453 m

BEARING 112° SE

2 m

Fig. 41. *Elevation and plan of a stone row in Area B7. The lowest stones are situated directly on the rock and are loosely fitted. A number of stones have been worked with a coarse sledgehammer. GPS 8.*

Area B7

The landscape of the mountainside towards Delphi, southeast of the cones of detritus, changes to a flat surface with a very slight rake which also stretches up above the modern road. It is covered with earth which bears the marks of cultivation (Fig. 40).[27]

On the edge of this surface facing the valley lies a stone row of 16.5 m, orientated 112° SE. The distance in a straight line to the track in Area B6 is about 56 m. The stone row is a continuation of the aforementioned configurations of stones which are built up in connection with the quarry road. The row of stones gives the impression of being a foundation for a minor terracing, which could support the roadway. This assumption is based firstly on the fact that the area above approaches a horizontal surface, which does not necessitate having an extensive foundation. Secondly it is a general characteristic of the few visible foundations towards the valley that they are more irregularly built up than the upper façade towards

the roadway, which has been the object of much more meticulous workmanship.

The site of the flat plateau at Gerospilies is delimited to the south by a pronounced edge facing the valley. It appears about 50 m south of Area B7. The configuration of the boulders along this edge forms a large curve, which for the first 100 m has a direction of 125° SE but then turns towards the following Area B8, orientation 106° SE (GPS 9). This sequence may possibly be parallel to the vehicle track at this point, or it may come up from the lowland and the port of Kirrha. This relatively flat, cultivated plateau in the mountainside may, in this connection, have formed an accessible entrance corridor for a number of sequences from the west and the south which run in the direction of the sanctuary from the landscapes below. They thus get around the steep rock wall by 1.5 km, which is visible on the map (Fig. 1). It separates the landscape in which Chrisso lies from the land above, in which the modern city of Delphi is situated (Fig. 42-43).

27   Above the modern road, tucked into the mountainside, there are deep wheel tracks in the roadside at Level 468, which point up towards the tower, Skorda 1991 designates them by the number 23; Gerospilies. GPS 10.

239

Fig. 42. *A covered outflow at the edge which goes round the flat, cultivated level at the site Gerospilies; in the background, the Pleistos Valley. GPS 9.*

Fig. 43. *The outlet, which is possibly a land-drain off the cultivated area, seen from outside the edge*

Area B8

Towards Delphi the flat area east of B7 terminates in a small ridge which rises up to above Level 500. In modern times, the small church of Hosios Loukas was built on this promontory. The promontory has the form of a 20 m-high slope with a rake of roughly 20%, which the direction of the roadway will overcome. The ascent is based on an

Fig. 44. *The 3 hollowings-out C, B, A, seen from above the promontory looking west; there are probably more of these "post-holes" buried under the detritus*

estimate, because the slope on the upper part is overlaid with discarded building materials, mainly building stones. On the lower part of the ascent the rock emerges at certain places. It was here that three four-sided cavities, roughly 20 cm deep, were found, cut with a point chisel in the solid rock; an additional one, broken on one side and situated 10 m to the south of the others, is possibly a fourth (Fig. 44).

The three square holes lie not quite on a line but follow an approximate orientation of 92° SE. The middle one, B, lies with its surface at Level 485. There are probably more instances of such holes. It is conceivable that they were used as bollards, which could secure the towing ropes with some kind of tackle on the steep slope, as is known elsewhere.[28] One reason for hauling the heavy loads up into the roadway's previous orientation – rather than dragging the loads of stone around the slope, following the course of the modern road – may be rooted in the difficulty with the relatively large turnings, which, if occasion should arise, would involve both wagon and the hitched-up oxen. To haul the wagon up the steep slope with the aid of tackle must, however, because of the rake of the wagon have necessitated the securing of the loads of stone in the timberwork of the wagon (Figs 45-48).[29]

---

28   Korres 1995, 103, figs 28-9.

29   If this route over the promontory was also used for transport from the port of Kirrha, from which the 4 m-long, 8 tonnes architraves in poros for the temple's superstructure had to be hauled, there seem to be good reasons for these bollard holes.

Fig. 48. *Detail of Fig. 47.*

Fig. 45. *Lowest posthole A at Level 483; it was probably rectangular and measures c.17cm on the measurable side and at the bottom less than 18 cm.*

Fig. 46. *The middle hole B at Level 485. It is very nearly intact, with sharp edges, and measures 18 x 18 x 20 x 16 cm with a depth of 20 to 24 cm. GPS 11.*

Fig. 47. *The uppermost hole C, at Level 486, situated 3.1 m above hole B; it is similarly well-preserved.*

Fig. 49. *Friedrich Nerley, Buffaloes Hauling a Block of Marble, 1831-1844.Thorvaldsens Museum, Copenhagen.*

Road and Wagon – Digression 1

Figure 49 features pairs of oxen pulling a wagon with a block of marble, on which the name Thorvaldsen is written. The scene is from a quarry in Italy and the painting shows the wagon with rigid axles, carrying a block weighing some 6 tonnes, hauled by 6 oxen. To the left is a man who is pushing the right front wheel with a long, robust pole so that the wagon is put correctly into the turning which can be seen in the rough track and which corresponds to the torque exerted by the oxen. This shift in the orientation of the wagon seems to correspond to that which occurred from Area 2a to 2b in Section B (Fig. 49).

Studying this painting enables us to form an idea of the considerations which had to be explored by those who knew the mountains well, as well as by wagon makers, when it was decided to open a stone quarry 6 km west of the sanctuary. One of the most difficult tasks was negotiating the expected rises and falls in the road used for transporting the stones. It was the task of locals familiar with the mountains to pick out the most coherent route on this particular mountain. The challenge, however, was just as much a question of the wainwrights' ability to construct a vehicle which, with its load of several tons, would be able to stand the combined hauling power of the many oxen. In this context the character of the roadway and the capacity of the wagon imposed limitations on how heavy and large the stones could be which were to be hauled up to the temple building site.

Our knowledge of Greek temple building shows that the stone sizes in the building's individual elements were all established in a mutual relationship, and this also applied to the foundation stones which went into the rebuilding of the temple at Delphi. The question was how large and heavy the stones which the architect could expect to have made available to him would be while projecting the new foundations. How would the construction work of the trackway be carried out on the mountainside so that he could answer this question, which was so crucial for the temple's architecture?

The first sketch shows the recommended course of a route on the mountain that the building work should follow. That is, markings on the mountain for a roadway which, from area to area, could be linked with rises which

243

Fig. 50. *Phase 1.*

Fig. 51. *Phase 2.*

were surmountable for the harnessed oxen. In individual places – e.g. in Area B3 – areas of surface shaped by hewing the rock are visible, which have indicated the direction of the tracks, but are not part of them. They can be interpreted as guiding markings put there by those familiar with the mountains for the construction workers around the course of the roadway in that spot. By means of this guidance, the building work could be commenced in several spots at the same time. The first thing was that the workers cleared a broad track and then cut away the frequently occurring minor cliffs, in the direction shown by the markings in the rock surface. Where the rake of the mountain was so large that the building workers estimated that the outer side of the roadway could not be built up sufficiently to provide purchase for oxen and drivers, they hacked out a "pavement" in the upper side of the slope, as is apparent in B3 (Fig. 50).[30]

The situation in the second sketch shown in Figure 51 is the building up of the foundation of the roadway and the construction of the protective terrace wall above the road. But before the cutting in the sketch could proceed, large rough stones for the foundation of the roadway were pushed down into place. Now and again they are laid in cut-out bearing surfaces, where it was necessary to secure their position on the steep mountainside. The same procedure was followed in the terrace wall above, which is visible in, for example, Area B4, where the side facing the roadway has been turned into an even façade (Fig. 51).

As the third stage in the construction of the roadway, ruts were cut for the wheels. The ruts have a width of between 15 and 25 cm and are flat at the bottom. Their width meant that a wagon wheel with a width of 10 cm would have been able to roll in the rut with less turning,

30 Cf. B3.

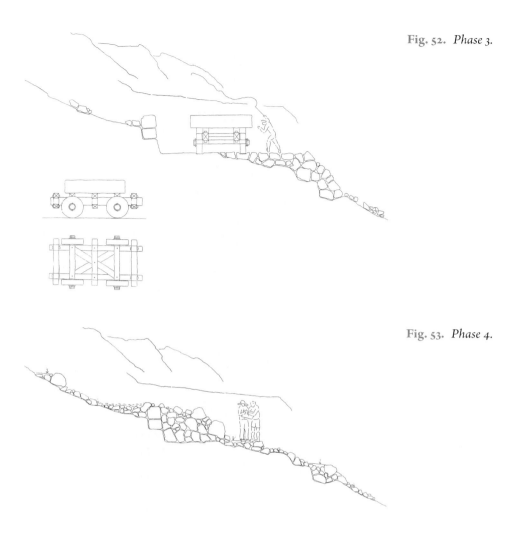

Fig. 52. *Phase 3.*

Fig. 53. *Phase 4.*

without subjecting the rectangular chassis of the wagon to excessive stress. For the same reason the hub was quite definitely not constructed too tightly around the axles, so the wheels could be turned slightly to the side on the axles. This is probably what is depicted happening to the left of the wagon in the painting shown in Figure 49. For this reason, the gauge of the wagon is difficult to determine; from centre to centre of the wheel-ruts may be measured to an average of 145 cm in the case of B3. This means free running for a wagon with traditional gauge. Taking as our point of departure the painting shown (Fig. 49), we have drawn in the sketch a wagon with rigid axles and a wheel diameter of minimum 80 cm, i.e. it fits between the wheel-ruts in Area B3.

We envisage the construction of the wagon as beams mortised and held together with dowels and robes. It would have had an overall weight of some 1.5 tonnes and was perhaps built of recycled wood from the dismantled temple roof, which was both seasoned and of good quality. The stone shown on the wagon is one of the many euthynteria stones, each weighing 5.5 tonnes (Figs. 52 and 53).

The last sketch shows the condition of the quarry road today. The piling up of stones which have slid down apparently happens right on the surface of the roadway after the terrace wall has been filled up on the upper side and has therefore forfeited its protective function – preventing stone slide. On this fill a donkey track has often been laid with a covering of small stones, until this too becomes swallowed up in the embrace of the mountain.

245

The Roads to Delphi

Section C, GPS 12-16

Area C1-5

Figure 54 shows the view of the town of Delphi from the west. The plots of land in this western part of Section C are divided up by numerous rows of stones, which are composed of what are called "handstones", meaning they can be carried and set into the ground by one or two people. Cultivation in the area must have happened more or less simultaneously with the growth of modern Delphi, which absorbed the plots of ground cultivated by the older village of Kastri. North of the modern road large stones are seen now and then which may derive from the transport track.

If one follows the orientation established hitherto up over the slope at the Church of Hosios Loukas, the landscape spreads out into open, easily accessible slopes, which today are cultivated in small plots of ground. About 1 km southeast of the church one can see, across this area of cultivated land, the modern conurbation of Delphi. The making of the vehicle track, but not least the transport of the heavy building stones in the extensive level expanse after the drive up from Section B, must have been a welcome relief after the day-long drive from the stone quarry to the temple. The numerous small stone rows show how the slight slopes of the plateau are divided into horizontal field boundaries across the ascent of the mountain. Traces of the transport of stone to the sanctuary are, for this reason, fewer and less noticeable than in Section B.

Area C1

The point where the church garden meets the mountain is marked by a short stretch of large stones, each weighing several tonnes. The positioning of these stones in a row requires the combined effort of many people. As the orientation of the row is roughly 104 degrees SE, and at the same time constitutes the continuation of the "bollard

Fig. 54. *View of the town of Delphi from the west.*

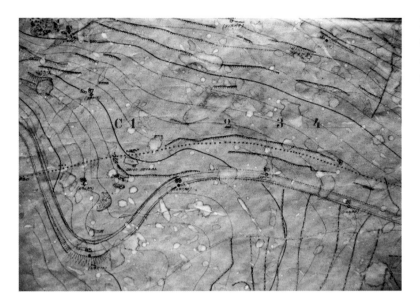

Fig. 55. *A map from 1965 of Area B8 and the western part of Section C; indications of the course of the stone quarry road are labelled C1, C2, C3 and C4*

Fig. 56. *Section C2. Bearing surface in rock.*

holes" in Area B8,[31] we regard it as part of the course of the vehicle track (Fig. 55).

The map in Figure 55 shows the area around the new Church of Hosios Loukas, where the row of large stone blocks lies in the northern part of the churchyard in Area C1. East of the church there are several stretches of stones forming corridors, where there are indications of the course of the stone quarry road, which we have labelled C2, C3 and C4.

Areas C2-4

33 m southeast of the church garden there are cut-out cavities in the sections of rock which appear between

---

31   A closer examination of the church area was difficult as it was fenced in and locked. At Level 510, north of the church, are the tower foundations Skorda 1991 has indicated as no. 23 on her plan as Gerospilies.

Fig. 57. *Section C3. Long wedge marks.*

Fig. 58. *Section C4. Extensive rockcuttings.*

the plots of ground, in a line 123 m long. Here there are large oblong marks of the wedges used to split the rock. On top of the rock are bearing surfaces for stone rows with an orientation of 104° SE, where the level increases slightly from 500 to 506. These refer back to the square "bollard holes" found on the slope in Area B8.

Area C2

In Figure 56 we see the promontory with cut-out bearing surfaces and large stones carefully positioned on top of these. The direction is approximately 104° SE and the level around 502. In fact the split of the rock and the shaped

bearing surfaces suggest an arrangement of stones, which can be interpreted as part of the construction of the vehicle track (Fig. 56).

Lying on a brief stretch of roughly 14 m in this course are rows of erect stones which are visibly in situ. A labour-intensive building task of this character would hardly have been brought about in connection with the cultivation of the earth and the establishment of cultivation plots. We are in no doubt that here one confronts the remains of building work which served to extend the track in Section B. Above the erected stones we find again a surface of small stones which at the same time indicates that Kaltsis' Path may have followed this route (Fig. 57).

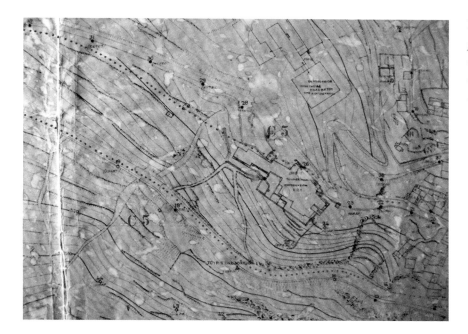

Fig. 59. *The most easterly part of the same map shown in Fig. 55, depicting an upper and lower approach to Delphi, labelled C5.*

Area C3

In Figure 57 we notice large lengthwise wedge marks in the rock and bearing surfaces. Above the cliff there are the remains of a surface covering with small stones. About 30 m to the SE from C2 is an area of rock with wedge marks and splitting of the rock which form an extension of C2. The track is situated in level 502 (Fig. 58).

Area C4

Part of the rock has been cut away in a line which continues the previous track (Fig. 58). The roadway apparently lay below the cliff (GPS 14). Roughly 14 m south there are parallel formations of stones which form a corridor in which the roadway probably had its course (cf. the map in Fig. 55).

Roughly 20 m further southeast and as a continuation of C3 is a large section of rock sticking up out of the ground, in which unusually deep wedge marks were left. The wedges probably split a part of the rock to make a passage for the roadway which clearly lay on the south side of the three aforementioned built-up tracks. In this stretch stones were later laid across the course of the roadway. The resulting flat levels are surfaced with small stones, as is the case in other places on Kaltsis' Path. Lying about 20 m south of the hewn areas and parallel with these is the modern road to Delphi.

Areas C5a and C5b

The nearer one gets to the sanctuary from the west, the more the River Pleistos' deep, funnel-shaped valley cuts into the steep mountain slopes of the Phaedriads. The landscape's alternating levels from Section C to Section D split the modern approach roads to Delphi into a number of co-ordinated tracks at Level 524, roughly 600 m southeast of the Church of Hosios Loukas. We are assuming that the same thing happened when the contractors established the course of the heavy stone transports to the sanctuary in Delphi, even though the actual track of their course gets lost in the modern urbanization. A dividing up of these transports from the St Elijah quarry is justifiable on the intractable mountainsides among which the sanctuary is located. Where it was possible, the approach roads for the transports were laid as early as possible on levels which corresponded to the work places where the heavy building material was to be used. The ground of our supposition is that there was already a differentiation of roads in Section C with regard to the final destination where the building materials were to be used. About 550 m after the road up to the Church of Hosios Loukas, the outcrop of even larger stones north of the modern road is interpreted as a division of the transport roads into one which ascends, and a lower one which tends to follow the steep edge to the Pleistos Valley (Fig. 59).

249

Area C5a
The upper approach road. GPS 15.

The upper stretch of the road, of about 550 m in the eastern part of Section C, rises from Level 525 to Level 568 with an upward gradient of some 8%. Earlier at this height, rows of heavy stones had been observed between the hotels Amalia and Delphi Palace,[32] which could indicate the position of the vehicle track at this level. These configurations of stones were observed by such people in Delphi as D. Skorda and L. Altiparmakis. They were later removed in connection with the building of the hotels and the rerouting of the modern road. We are assuming that these rows of stones indicated a probable position of the transportation of stones up to the temple area, which lies on Level 571, i.e. 3 m higher up the mountain.

Area C5b
The lower approach road. GPS 16.

Indications of a lower roadway are to be found in three formations of stones on Level 538 and Level 544 and in the garden area below the Delphi Palace Hotel (Fig. 60). The lowest stone rows are, generally speaking, parallel to the same orientation and form terraces which are 5 to 10 m wide and 20 m long. The formation is built up with large rough stones, as we see in Section B, with an orien-

Fig. 60. *C 5b seen from the roadside in the lower modern road; GPS 16.*

tation of 117° SE.[33] It is probable that the construction of these flat levels answered a need linked to the transport work, either from the stone quarry or from the port of Kirrha. The rise from the fork between C5a and C5b in the main road to the lower approach is 3% and was probably connected to a road to the Sanctuaries of Apollo and Marmaria (Fig. 60).

The Town of Delphi

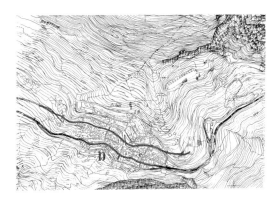

Section D
Area DI, II and III

The course of the vehicle track in and through the modern town of Delphi is difficult to find. Every year streets, stairs and urban development change the steep terrain into which the town is built. But when H. Convert drew the town's new plan for the area west of the sanctuary when the excavations commenced, he first undertook a meticulous field examination of the terrain in which the town was to be sited. This resulted in a mapping of the landscape in 1892, before the town was actually built. This mapping is the closest we can get to the landscape through which the various courses of the vehicle track were laid – it is improbable that this course went either over or under Convert's topographical map. Convert's map shows the field boundaries and the terracing which were built up by the population of the village of Kastri in the nearby upland, west of the large cliff which separates this upland from the village and the sanctuary it concealed under it. As a basis for his preliminary sketch for a town plan, Convert

---

32   Formerly the Hotel Xenia with garden plan. Architect: D. Picionis, ca. 1960.

33   Cf. Skorda 1991, no. 34, Elinia.

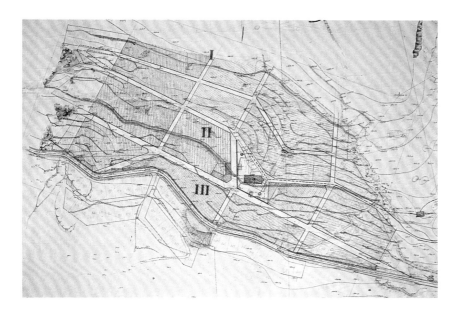

Fig. 61. *Part of Convert's map of 1892.*

used meticulous level indications of the elevations and a concluding summary in the level lines of the map. At the same time he drew in a number of details, which partly show the heaps of large blocks of stone in the western part of the area, which suggest defensive works, the course of smaller stone formations which demarcate numerous small plots of ground and finally the watercourses which form a confluence. In addition Convert put his signature into his landscape plan, which shows a number of burial grounds and cut-out areas in the mountain ridge, forming a barrier between Sections D and E, in the latter of which the sanctuary is located (Fig. 61).

Three phenomena emerge from the map which arouse our interest in how the quarry road may have fitted into this area. Two water ditches appear to connect the western part of Section D with the eastern one. They are horizontal in outline with small inclinations towards the outflow, and run across the area following the structure of the fields. In addition, below, there is the modern road which connects our Section C with our Section E through Section D.

The uppermost water ditch is about 480 m long and has its western point of departure at Level 592. For approximately every 100 m from here the level on this ditch is 601, 602, 604, and 604, respectively, in the eastern ter-

Fig. 62. *The road to Kirrha and the Gulf of Corinth seen from a donkey track in the vicinity of Kastri at the end of March 1836. Water-coloured drawing by M. Rørbye.*

251

mination towards the cliff in Section E. The overall rise in this 600 m-long sequence is less than 3%. Water Ditch II runs across the fields below Ditch I. It is roughly 600 m long and has its western emergence at Level 565. For every 100 m from here the levels on this ditch are 563, 561, 560, 569, 571 and 573, respectively, in the eastern termination in the ridge in Section E. The overall ascent gradient in this sequence is less than 2%. The modern road on the edge of the valley is about 500 m long, and has its western point of departure at Level 533. For every 100 m from here, approximately, the levels on the road's upper part are 533, 542, 543, 533 respectively, and run thereafter along the edge around the fall in the cliff towards the Pleistos Valley at Level 535. The greatest rise in this sequence is less than 4%. In addition Convert shows three drains under the road towards the edge of the Pleistos Valley and a broad donkey track, which winds up from the valley to this road. On the map this path leads up to the opening in the cliff, which forms the termination of Ditch II. This route into the village of Kastri and to Marmaria is clearly linked to a number of paths from the port of Kirrha, which wound up through the steep mountainsides as pointed out by D. Skorda (Fig. 65).

The three sequences are interesting as they connect elements in areas of the landscape in Section C and E in a way that could coincide with the abandoned roadways laid for the transport of stone in Section D. The surprising horizontal location of the water ditches across the undulating terrain may be a reuse of the road constructed earlier, which led into the area of the sanctuary. Such a hypothesis is supported by the positions where they terminate in both west and east. The position of the arrangements of stones which have been observed between the aforementioned hotels around Level 565 in Section C coincides with the emergence of Ditch II. Were one to follow this ditch to its termination in the mountain ridge in the east, this termination occurs at the same point as one of the few accessible openings into the area of the sanctuary. It is also in this opening that one sees many graveyards and hewn areas from the past, suggesting a passage of considerable symbolic significance. Against this background it is our hypothesis that the main road for stone transport from St Elijah lay along this line.

The position of the mentioned western terrace around Level 540 in Section C would be suitable for a vehicle track, which twists round below the barrier formed by the cliff towards the area of the sanctuary. This sequence furnishes possibilities without major ascents, not just to the lower area of the sanctuary but also to Marmaria. The present modern road runs on the same level at an average level of 535. The termination of the uppermost ditch in Convert's landscape is connected to an opening in the barrier, formed by the cliff at Level 603, which leads in to the uppermost part of the sanctuary, where the theatre is situated. The final destination for the three passages we will look at more closely in the following section.

The Arrival of the Vehicle Track in the Sanctuary Area

Section E
Area E1 and E2

Just before the undressed building stones from the St Elijah Quarry reached the building site, where they received their final dressing and were given their final positioning, they had to travel over one of the most difficult stretches in their 6 km-long journey. This is the ridge with the Bastions of Philomenos,[34] which, west of the temple, array themselves like a protective rampart around the concave slope of the sanctuary. The area of rock forms a continuous barrier of over 700 m across the course of the vehicle track. It stretches north from the foot of Mount Parnassus' mountain massifs at Level 730 and

34 Bommelaer 1991, 217.

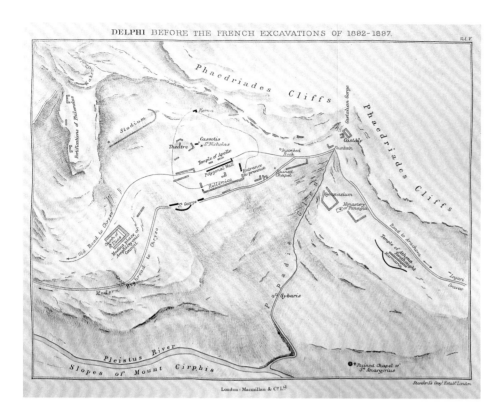

Fig. 63. *Chandler's sketch. The "old road" runs above the churchyard of St. Elijah and leads to the area around Portal C (Atlas 435), while the "modern one" runs below the churchyard and the enclosing wall around the sanctuary.*

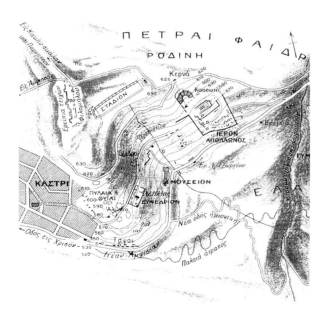

Fig. 64. *Keramópoullos 1917; part of map showing the mountain ridge, with access roads, retaining and terrace walls, as well as the Bastions of Philomelos, rock-cut tombs, small stone quarries and the location of the Synedrion.*

down to a dramatic edge at Level 520, which forms an almost vertical drop of 300 m to the deep river bed of the Pleistos Valley at Level 140. When this ridge is passed it would have been the first time in the day-long journey that the workmen, drivers and their team of oxen caught sight of the colourful monuments in the sanctuary, in the midst of which the great temple stood like a ghost of its former self.

There are few openings in the lengthy cliff which could be penetrated by the heavy transports from St Elijah. The openings have, however, been widened and re-laid in modern times so that, to the same extent as the landscape below the town of Delphi, they have left no trace of the passage of the vehicle track. In addition to Convert's mapping from a time before the excavations, which also covers the landscape around the village of Kastri, there are two informative sketch maps which can contribute to an understanding of where these approach roads were leading. One is a sketch dating from R. Chandler's visit to Delphi, which was published in 1776. It shows two roads which, at that time, led into the sanctuary. Chandler differentiates between an "*Old Road to Chryso*" and a "*Modern Highroad to Chryso*". They both have a connection to

253

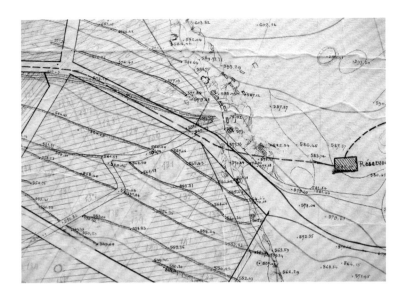

Fig. 65. *Detail of Convert's working sheet with levels.*

the temple area,[35] where the aforementioned openings were used as gateways to the sanctuary. The old road on Chandler's sketch reappears in Covert's map as a donkey track, linking itself to the termination of Ditch II and the transition to Section E. Thereafter, Chandler's way leads into the sanctuary in the area around Portal C (Atlas 435) (Fig. 63).

The other informative sketch map of approach roads was drawn by Keramópoullos in 1917, shortly after the termination of the excavations. Here we see the thoroughfare we have posited as a main road for stone transport linked to Ditch II at Level 570. Hereafter its course has been theorized to follow the retaining and terrace walls which lead on to the area around Portal C (Atlas 435) above the St Elijah churchyard. It follows Chandler's "Old Road". On his map, Chandler calls the ruins in the churchyard the "Meeting place of the Amphictyonic Council", while Keramópoullos dubs it the "Synedrion". Also drawn on this map is a passage right up via the Stadium close to the aforementioned stone quarry (Fig. 64).

There seem, therefore, to be four passages past the mountain ridge separating Section D from Section E. First is a north passage which lies just under the marked rise in the mountain at the very top, around Level 716 above the

Stadium. It connects the upper level in Section D with the concave delimitation of the sanctuary and gives access to a steep mountain path up to the fruitful landscape of Parnassus, which today is known as the Path of Pausanias. The local stone quarry above the Stadium mentioned earlier lies close to this transition. Transports of building stones from this quarry doubtless used this defile when construction work was taking place west of the sanctuary area, such as at the aforementioned bastions. But this passage did not affect stone transports for the rebuilding of the temple. Further down the mountain ridge is another passage at Level 620, which was intended for transports to the upper area of the sanctuary in a direction pointing to the theatre. This has a connection to Ditch I and was not of any significance for the temple rebuilding.

Lying below is the third passage over the mountain ridge. It is connected to Ditch II. The opening in this passage is the largest and most accessible, and it is the one described by Chandler and Keramópoullos. The passage up over the mountain ridge through this opening is, in our opinion, the most probable for the course of the vehicle track into the sanctuary. We presume, again judging by the topography, that the roadway for the stone transportation follows a turning at a level between 570-80 over towards

35 Chandler 1776, sketch map and its Superscription: *Delphi before the French Excavations of 1892-1897*, may contain later additions.

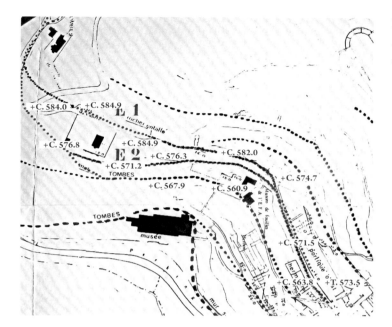

Fig. 66. *Section of Le Plan Général de Delphes, Trouki 1993. Our additions and levels are indicated in red. West is up on this map.*

the present churchyard, which is the area Keramópoullos chose as the location for the Synedrion. At this level there are occurrences of cutting and wedge marks in the areas of rock and groupings of stones both above and below the churchyard, showing an instance of a building technique which corresponds to that used for the foundations and terrace walls linked to the vehicle track in this area. The distance from the passage over the western side of the ridge via Chandler's "Old Road" to Portal C (Atlas 435) is roughly 700 m. The passage itself has a rise of 13%. Thereafter both rises and falls for the stone transports are less than 6% on the course we believe it followed.[36] We have not found actual cut tracks for the transport to the temple, nor have we had the opportunity to conduct cleanings on the places where one might expect to find such traces (Fig. 65).

Working from this basis it is probable that, following this passage over the mountain ridge, the vehicle track splits up into several divisions, two of which we will point out with E1 and E2 on Fig. 66. They are described and mapped in E. Trouki's insightful examination of the approach roads to the sanctuary.[37] The supplementary vehicle track E2 to the main road for the transportation of stone from the St Elijah quarry runs below the present churchyard, along the wall 17-O and meets the main road roughly 85 m after the foundation wall 16-O between two groups of stones at Level 573. Finally there was probably the course of a road along the edge to the Pleistos Valley, heading for the areas below the sanctuary and Marmaria (Fig. 66).

36   This hypothesis concerning the route of the transport of the stone by wagon is based on Convert's levels. In this we distance ourselves from the suppositions put forward by H. Pomtow (1889, 80-2). Here Pomtow puts forward two reasons why this stretch of road cannot be a wagon route; his observation of the 6 steps cut in the rock wall along the way and the track's ascent in and over the western cliff. Both of these are hard to point out today. As mentioned in Chapters 3 and 5, there are steps in the track for the stone transport which date from a later, different use of the sequence/route. It is difficult to tell whether this is the case in this vehicle track which we believe was laid around 366 BC. Regarding the ascent in the defile, this is hardly a crucial barrier to transport by wagon. We should like to thank Anne Jacquemin for this interesting reference.

37   Trouki 1993 (unpublished). The year before we knew of this study, most of the walls with relation to the vehicle tracks' concluding stretch were drafted and photographed during the fieldwork, with a view to a taking of measurements. It was made redundant by the thesis, which we thank J.-F. Bommelaer for having shown us. The following numbering of walls refers to E. Trouki, whom we would like to thank for permission to use her informative plans in our investigation. Cf. Fig. 66.

Where the Vehicle Track Comes to an End

The probable principal direction of the stone quarry road is the area around Portal C (Atlas 435) at the western pediment of the temple, where the entrance must have been at a level between 571 and 573 in a course between wall 7-O and wall 4-O in E. Trouki's enumeration, i.e. at the same level as the temple's future foundations.

We are in no doubt that there was a main road here for the transports and building workers, which was put in motion in connection with the rebuilding of the temple. The terrace wall, 4-O, which is more than 65 m long, forms the final, necessary termination of transport roads E1 and E2 into the Sanctuary and was begun, we believe, as the first stage in the overall plan for the rebuilding.[38] Above this road the wall forms a terrace the height of which was somewhere around Level 574. In Chandler's sketch it looks as if the old road ran over precisely this spot. It is here one would imagine the first "cutting area" to be for the shaping of the heavy building stones from the St Elijah stone quarry, before they were hauled in to the new foundation for the temple. This may at the same time support the idea of the construction of a storage area for the undressed building stones on the slope in front of wall 5-O and the cutting places located closer to the temple on the terrace on top of the wall 4-O. Above this terrace the mountain slope rises up to the place where the future portico was constructed. The termination of the vehicle track at E1 and E2 leads into this storage area and the cutting area along Wall 16-O, 6-O on to Wall 5-O, at Level 574, which is suggested by E. Trouki in Fig. 66 and the sketch in Fig. 68. The walls, as stated, bear all the marks of the same coarse hewing in the arrangement of stones, except for Wall 5-O which is built in a fine polygonal technique. Both this and the façades of the Hermeion in Wall 9-O as well as the rear Wall 7-O are built in a 5th-century manner, i.e. long before Wall 4-O was erected and the roadway we are studying was laid (Fig. 67).

As there was above the main road in Levels 573-1, there may also have been delimited plateaus below the road.

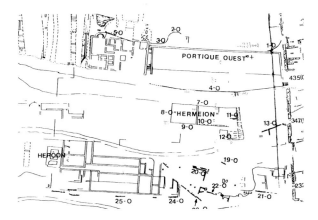

Fig. 67. *Detail drawing of the terrace area around the Hermeion. Trouki 1993, Fische no. 65.*

One example is the plateau at the Hermeion,[39] which formed a terrace at roughly Level 568, and below this again at Level 565 along the foundations of Wall 9-O and 10-O. The location of these terraces was chosen for the storage and shaping of easy-to-handle building materials, such as wood, iron and lead.

We believe that it was on these terraces, in proximity to the building process as such, that the so-called hangars and ateliers were erected. They might be above or below the main road as described in the inscriptions,[40] and thereby have formed workplaces for the preparation of the building elements which could immediately be brought into their designated places when required by the construction process.

A supplementary arrival at the sanctuary runs first along the edge to the sheer drop down to the Pleistos Valley. This divides into several branches on Trouki's layout plan. One goes up over the mountain ridge at Level 560 below the churchyard at Wall 17-O. Here follows an extensive promontory with a number of minor quarries with wedge marks and burials, which reaches into the sanctuary's concave area through an opening in the eastern edge of the rock wall. Small fillings of fissures in the rock are

---

38 The arrangement of stones is not homogeneous in its entire length, but constructed using a building technique which can be rediscovered in many of the foundations and terrace walls which seem to be associated with the vehicle track in this section. There is also a certain similarity to the building technique which is employed in the terraces in front of the Lesche of the Knidians (Atlas 604), and some of the tower foundations which D. Skorda has observed.

39 Trouki 1992, 106, fig. 7. Sketch and dating with reference to J. Bousquet 1988, 107.

40 A&H 2010, 454-6, no. 46 B II, 47 A II, 56 I A and 59.

observable here, using a building technique comparable to the other foundations along the vehicle track in this area. We are assuming that on this level there was a passage down the level of the Hermeion, where the transport of lighter building materials was possible. This passage is shown as a dotted line in our addition to Trouki's plan (Fig. 66). This roadway runs out on the foundations of Hermeion's lower walls 9-O, 10-O and 12-O Levels 568-4, from which, according to Trouki's observations, there may be access for steps or ramps to the terraces above via 8-O and 11-O and possibly into the Sanctuary itself along Wall 13-O on Level 564 at Portal B' (Atlas 347).

The lowest stretch follows the edge to the valley at Level 540, round below the large mountain ridge. This southern connection to the area from the west, distinguishes itself, as already mentioned, as early as Section C. Using this approach road from the west means that during the last 3 km through Sections C, D and E, the ascent gradient can be kept below 1% before reaching the southern delimitation of the sanctuary, or the limestone temple in Marmaria on the other side of the Kastalia Ravine, where it is visually apparent that stone from St Elijah has also been used.[41]

Canopies and sheds – Digression 2

The following sketches illustrate a possible site and elevation of the location of the building site in the suburb of Thyiai west of the sanctuary. Our suggestions as to their practical fitting out with storage area, cutting area, canopies and storage sheds were formed based on the information provided by the inscriptions and the arrangements of stones which are described by E. Trouki, together with an inscription from Levadia about the building process itself (Fig. 68).[42]

The sketch Fig. 68 shows the location of workplaces, canopies and sheds outside the western ring wall (Atlas 346-434-435). Workshop 46 B-I-II below the main road for the storage and working of stone and wood is about 100 m². It is in all likelihood one of the first canopies which was set up in the years 343-1 BC. It was assembled along Wall 7-O for the cutting of poros stones into sima blocks, and later for the making of the wooden construction for the temple roof. It is closed by the side wall and a front wall of a single layer of brick with an average height of 2.7 m. The structure supports one side of a pitched roof, and can be divided up into 2 lengths of roughly 13 and 21 m with a depth of 3.2 m. The quantity of raw mudbrick needed has been estimated at around 4390 stones. Below the Hermeion the canopy 59 was erected against Walls 9-0 and 10-O with a length of 25 m, according to the inscription from 336 BC.[43] It is an open-post construction which is closed by two gables in mudbrick as an open drying shed for 60 pine beams from Macedonia. About 700 mudbricks were used for walls in the gables. After the foundation stones and orthostats from St Elijah were brought in for the temple foundations from the cutting places above the main road in the years 344-33, two canopies, each 24 m long, were erected here against Wall 4-O. They stand with the north-facing openings in a post construction, and were the sculptor's workshop (47 A II and 56 1 A). They are of a height and length which permitted the setting-up and carving of 2 x 12 pediment figures.[44] The back walls on 4-O are made as double-skin walls and the four side walls in the gables are of mudbrick, totalling 14,745 individual bricks. All together this comes to 19,836 raw mudbricks for the aforementioned buildings.[45] This corresponds very accurately to the delivery of 20,000 bricks, according to Contract 56 IA (Fig. 69).[46]

---

41 Bommelaer, 1991, 69. In this investigation of a vehicle track from the St. Elijah quarry to the Temple of Apollo we have not examined the approach roads which may have used the floor of the Pleistos Valley and then an ascent to the sanctuaries through the olive groves below Marmaria. If we look away from the stone transports to the Temple of Apollo we notice for the whole sanctuary that transports must also have travelled to the following monuments based on the investigations described by, in particular, Bommelaer 1991 and Amandry 1981, The Theban Treasure Chamber (Atlas 124), The Kings of Argos (Atlas 113), The Rhodian Chariot (Atlas 406), The Column of the Dancer (Atlas 509) and The Thessalian Base (Atlas 511), as well as a number of smaller bases.

42 Cf. Note 53.

43 A&H 2010, 456

44 A&H 2010, 455.

45 We have used the dimensions to be found on the raw mudbricks at Delphi today: 31.3 x 31.3 x 7.8 cm.

46 A&H 2010, 455.

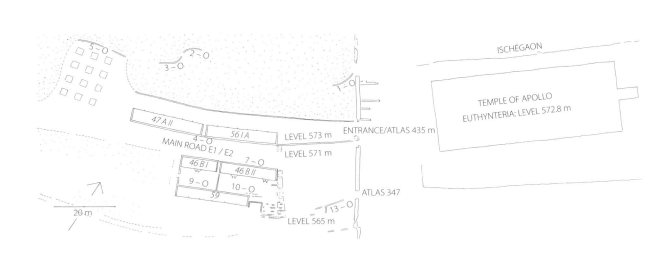

Fig. 68. *Plan showing the possible location of workplaces, canopies and sheds the western ring wall and the relation to the outline of the Temple of Apollo.*

Visible at the top is the terrace which lies over Wall 4-O. Here the stones from the quarry were given their final dressing, as described in Stages of Work I and II. Later the two north-facing ateliers were erected for work on the pediment figures. Below Wall 4-O is the main road into the sanctuary which brings to an end the road from the St Elijah quarry.

On the terrace under the main road formed by the Hermeion, sheds were set up for the storing of wood for the temple's coffered ceiling. At the bottom of the section is the drying shed for the wooden beams from Macedonia, the back of which is Wall 9-O and 10-O in Trouki's numbering.

The Rebuilding of the Temple

Shortly after the earthquake in 373 BC and its fatal consequences for the old temple, a coordinated plan of activity appears to have been devised for the many tasks entailed by such a rebirth. In all likelihood the plan was expounded in a detailed description, though all we know of this is a fragmentary inscription with references to a *syngrophos* (Doric for *syngraphos*),[47] which we today would designate as a masterplan. The plan covered the 20 years it took to recreate the great temple.

From the many stones and other traces left behind and the practical preconditions for the work, we can conclude that both outside on the mountain and inside the sanctuary a long series of projects were brought about which were closely co-ordinated according to this plan. But every participating individual could only realize his part of the project if he collaborated carefully in this common endeavour, from the stone quarry to the building site. There must have been an astonishingly well-thought-out plan for the joint project before it was set in motion.

---

47   See A&H 2010, 462, 464. Cf. LSJ s.v.

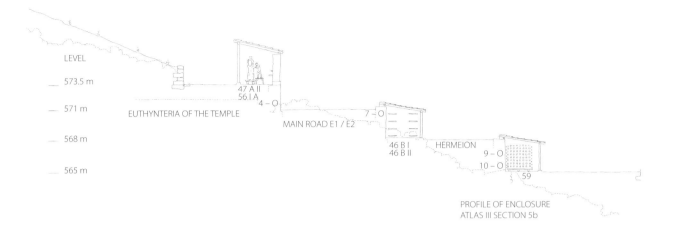

Fig. 69. *Elevation. East-facing section of canopies and sheds positioned on the terraces above and below the main road, which runs at Level 471. Behind the buildings the profile of the western ring wall is drawn in from the Atlas, section 5b.*

Turning to the temple square itself, we observe extensive demolition and the cleaning up of the damaged building elements in the temple. It was especially the construction of the foundations which attracted attention, since it was here that the key was to be found to the prevention of future movements in the building.

For this reason the demolition of the old temple was one of the first tasks commenced in 366 BC,[48] and it left the former foundations under the old temple as an open, cleared surface. This so-called hypeuthynteria, under the previous euthynteria in poros, had to be trued up and adapted to answer the new demand for a stronger enlarged euthynteria, which was now to be laid in the robust stones from the St Elijah quarry and fastened together with metal clamps (Fig. 71).

The first undressed stones for the outermost frame in the euthynteria, each weighing roughly six tonnes,[49] may have already been cut free of the quarry shortly after 366 BC and stood ready to be hauled over the mountain on the newly-laid vehicle track to the sanctuary. On their arrival at the storage yard below Wall 5-O, each individ-

ual stone, still retaining its coarse protective layer on all sides, with the requisite dimensions, was examined for cracks and its surface checked by the architect. The stones which had been approved were then, one by one, hauled up to the terrace above Wall 4-O and turned over to the stone-cutters, who initiated the first of a cycle of seven phases of work through which each building stone passed in the temple's rebuilding.[50]

1. First, what was to become the underside of the euthynteria blocks were cut to level with broad anathyroses along the edge, while the area within these is cut slightly deeper with coarser chisels.

2. The same procedure is carried out with three sides of the stone which are cut into right angles on the bottom surface. Both this and the sides' anathyroses are checked and marked with red lead and polished. After the first uniform working of each individual, approved stone from the quarry, they were considered standardized building elements waiting to be hauled in to become part of the new temple foundations.

---

48 A&H 2010, 467.

49 Calculated from an average size of these stones in situ with a density of 2.7 and allowing for a 20% protective layer.

50 This first and the following descriptions of seven work-flows follow the procedures which are to be found in the inscription in Bundgaard 1946, which deals with the temple ruin in Levadia. The building stones in Delphi and in Levadia seem in many tectonic respects to resemble each other.

259

Fig. 70. *A. Tournaire's 1902 reconstruction of the sanctuary shows where the dominating Temple of Apollo presented itself to good advantage after the rebuilding, which was completed in the year 327 BC.*

3. But before they could be fitted into the euthynteria, the fourth, unworked side of the already laid euthynteria stones in the frame had to be collectively trued up following the temple's modules. This truing up is also checked and marked with red lead and polished.

4. In addition there must have been an adaptation of the old hypeuthynteria layer which was cut to function as a bearing surface for the new rows in the euthynteria underneath, and also the bearing surfaces for the joists which bind them together.

5. One stone was laid at a time on top, where the bearing surfaces between hypeuthynteria and the new stone were finally adapted to fit each other, as well as the two side surfaces to those already laid. The joins between them were checked and marked with red lead and polished with stone powder before the final approval was given by the architect.

6. Finally, all the oil and grinding agent was washed off the joins with citric acid. Then the stone from the St Elijah quarry was at long last fitted into its permanent position and ready to be secured with cramps in situ.

7. Finally the overall surface was trued up by aligning with the laid stone and their end surfaces according to the same guidelines as before and marked red lead, grinding and truing up the curvature with the use of levelling blocks carved in dry wood from a wild olive tree.

If we assume that 12 teams of men working together two and two and in the four work teams from III to VI, we can assume that it would take a total of 18 days for each work team to lay a stone in the outermost frame of the euthynteria. Taking a point of departure in the creation of this frame for the foundation, which consists of 156 euthynteria stones, the quarry on St Elijah mountain would have to deliver at least one of these very heavy stones every third day to enable each of the six teams to work continually on the rebuilding, which took place in the years 366-56 BC. If this hypothesis is accurate, it would have taken 16 working months[51] to lay the foundation frame and probably the same for the euthynteria frame inside, which had to support the cella wall and its orthostats. The shift between the stage of the work in the first

---

51 This is a supposition which depends, to a great extent, on the winter weather. December and January can be so rainy that it the oxen could have been denied foothold. In these months there is also the danger of heavy snow, which would hinder transportation in the higher mountains.

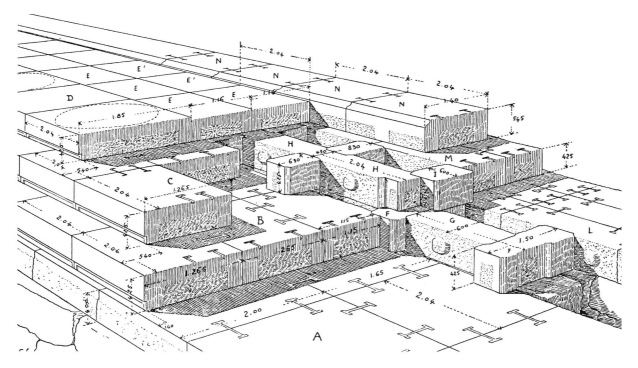

Fig. 71. *The Temple of Apollo's foundations on the long side of euthynteria; they were built in their entirety with stone blocks from the St Elijah quarry.*

two and the third work phases depends, however, on the quarry being capable of delivering more stones to I and II than the rhythm of the work demands in III to VI, and thus contributing to the creation of a stockpile of standard stones which could even out the effects of any instances of delay in the quarrying or in the subsequent transport. The planned changes in the pace of the building need deliveries of St Elijah stone for the foundation, poros stone for the superstructure and shaped wood for roof and ceiling construction may also be significant for the work rhythm in the stone quarry. For instance, in the building phase in which the peristyle is erected in poros stone, it would be conceivable to have a period when storage yards and cutting areas and workshops all concentrated on this task. This would give the St Elijah quarry workers more time. Judging by the inscriptions all the columns and part of the entablature in poros stone were complete when war broke out in 356 BC. When the war of 356-46 BC was over, the inscriptions show that the first floor tiles and

orthostats from St Elijah began to arrive at the building site, which signifies that work was completed on the foundation frame that lay within the peristyle. This occurred in the years after 343 BC and includes some of the heaviest loads of stone. An orthostat with its protective layer can weigh up to 8.5 tonnes. Emerging in the same period were a number of stones from the quarry which formed joists for the floor tiles and a fairly small frieze of 66 decorated stone blocks, which were set up in the cella wall in 335 BC. The joists and floor tiles, orthostats and frieze display what is at first sight complicated carving, the first on account of the way they must be made to fit constructively into the building and the last because of their decorative shape. In all, 2131 St Elijah building stones were used in the total construction, having an overall volume of 2959 m³.[52] They constitute about half of the total volume of stone in the finished building work. This circumstance also shows the crucial significance of the discovery of the new stone in the distant expanse of mountain had for the rebuilding.

---

52 A&H 2010, 457, fig. 18.22.

Appendix

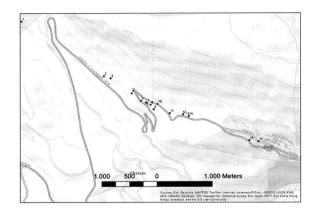

Latitude	Longitude	Altitude (m)	GPS no.
38,496405	22,451705	239.4	1
38,489171	22,465106	366.3	2
38,488900	22,466191	389.1	3
38,486889	22,469646	428.4	4
38,485895	22,471161	440.03	5
38,485686	22,471941	447.6	6
38,485652	22,472068	448.2	7
38,485393	22,472722	450.4	8
38,484790	22,473210	456.0	9
38,485492	22,473845	478.9	10
38,484274	22,475822	490.6	11
38,484118	22,477992	499.5	12
38,483894	22,478908	502.4	13
38,483879	22,478893	507.9	14
38,480546	22,490244	561.1	15
38,480678	22,488750	543.9	16

Sources for Figures

GAU = G. Algreen-Ussing
A&H 2010 = Amandry & Hansen 2010
Atlas = Hansen & Algreen-Ussing 1975

Fig. 1: Greek map sheets; 5391.1/5392 .7/6301.4/6302/2/2/6301.3//6302.4 ; 1:5000; 1966. The sketched elevation below the map was drawn by G. Algreen-Ussing.
Fig. 2: A&H 2010, part of Fig. 1.8, p. 153.
Fig. 3: Survey 1965, G. Algreen-Ussing. Atlas, Plan 12.
Figs 4-5: GAU.
Fig. 6: A&H 2010, fig. 6.
Fig. 7: Bourguet 1914, 337.
Figs 8-9: GAU.
Fig. 10: Skorda 1991, Dépliant I.
Fig. 11: Carte de la Grèce 1:200,000, Paris 1852.
Fig. 12: Amandry 1981, with red additions.

Figs 13-44: GAU.
Figs 45-8: Survey conducted together with Museum staff and Yannis Skorda. Fig. 49 Photograph by Lennart Larsen. Sincere thanks are due to Tobias Fischer-Hansen for providing this informative reference.
Figs 50-54: GAU
Fig. 55: Collotype of map on a scale of 1: 2000 / 1965; Delphes, Plan du Site 1965, Ministere. EFA no. IA 8587. The original has never been found.
Figs 56-8: GAU
Fig. 59: see fig. 55
Fig. 60: GAU.
Fig. 61: Unpublished map, H. Convert G 2/ "Village avant des fouilles et

Villages modernes" Echelle 1/1000. 1892 EFA No. 254. Modified by GAU. Reproduced with permission from the French School at Athens.
Fig. 62: Statens Museum for Kunst, Copenhagen; Sketch from Kastri by M. Rørbye, 1836. INN. NR.1974-32.
Fig. 63: Chandler 1776.
Fig. 64: Kérmopoullos 1917.
Fig. 65: Nouveau Village, EFA: G2. Ech. 1:1000.
Fig. 66: Le Plan Général de Delphes, Trouki 1993, unpublished.
Fig. 67: Trouki 1993, Fiche no. 65.
Figs 68-9: A&H 2010,. 454-62.
Fig. 70: Tournaire 1902, pl. 9.
Fig. 71: Courby 1927, fig. 21.

Bibliography

Abbreviations

Atlas
E. Hansen & G. Algreen-Ussing, *Fouilles de Delphes 2.26, Topographie et Architecture, Sanctuaire d'Apollon, Atlas,* Paris 1975.

A&H 2010
P. Amandry & E. Hansen, *Fouilles des Delphes 2, Le temple d'Apollon du IVe siècle,* Paris 2010.

Cited works

Algreen-Ussing, G. 1992
'På sporet af en gåde', *Sfinx* 15.3, 99-105.

Amandry, P. 1981
Notes Critiques, Chroniques et Rapports *BCH* 105.2, CV-1981, II, 714-21, Paris.

Bommelaer, J.-F. 1991
Guide de Delphes, le site (E.F.A. Sites et monuments 7), Paris.

Bourguet, É. 1914
Les ruines de Delphes, Paris.

Bousquet, J. 1989
Corpus des inscriptions de Delphes, Vol. 2 (index by D. Mulliez), Paris.

Bundgaard, J. A. 1946
'The Building Contract from Lebadeia', *Classica et Mediaevalia: Revue Danoise de philologie et d'histoire* 8, 1-43.

Burford, A. 1960
'Heavy Transport in Classical Antiquity', *The Economic History review,* New Series,13.1, 1-18.

Chandler, R. 1776
Travels in Greece or an Account of a Tour, Vol. 5, Oxford.

Courby, F. 1927.
Fouilles des Delphes 2, Topographie et architecture, La terrasse du Temple, Vol. 3, Paris.

Forbes, R. J. 1934
Notes on the History of Ancient Roads and their Construction, Amsterdam.

Foucart, P. 1865
Mémoire sur les ruines et l'histoire de Delphes, Paris.

Keramópoullos, A. 1917
Topographia ton Delphon, Athens.

Korres, M. 1995
From Pentelicon to the Parthenon, Athens.

Landels, J. G. 1978
Engineering in the Ancient World, London.

Pikoulas, Y. A. 1999
'The Road Network of Arkadia', in *Defining Ancient Arkadia. Symposium, April, 1-4 1998. Acts of the Copenhagen Polis Centre,* Vol. 6, T. H. Nielsen & J. Roy (eds), Copenhagen, 248-319.

Pomtow, H. 1889
Beiträge zur Topographie von Delphi, Berlin.

Poulsen, F. 1924
Den Delfiske Gud og hans Helligdom, Copenhagen.

Pritchett, W. K. 1980
Studies in Ancient Greek Topography 3, *Roads,* Berkeley.

Raepset, G. 1993
'Le diolkos de l'Isthmus à Corinth', *BCH* 117, 233-56.

Skorda, D. 1991
'Recherches dans la vallée du Pleistos', in *Delphes, Centenaire de la "Grand Fouille" Realisée par École Francaise d'Athènes (1892-1903),* J.-F. Bommelaer (ed.), Strasbourg 1992, 39-66.

Trouki, E. 1992
'La Terrasse dit de "l'Hermeion". Travaux du centre de recherche du Proche-Ouest et le Gréce antique 12. Centenaire de la "Grande fouille" realisée par l'Ecole Francaise d'Athènes (1892-1903)', in *Delphes. Centenaire de la 'Grande Fouille' réalisée par l'École française d'Athènes (1892-1903). Actes du colloque Paul Perdrizet, Strasbourg, 6-9 novembre 1991,* J.-F. Bommelaer (ed.), Leiden, 95-108.

Trouki, E. 1993
Soutenements et Periboles de Delphies. Construits en pierres travaillees, Strasbourg. Unpublished.

263

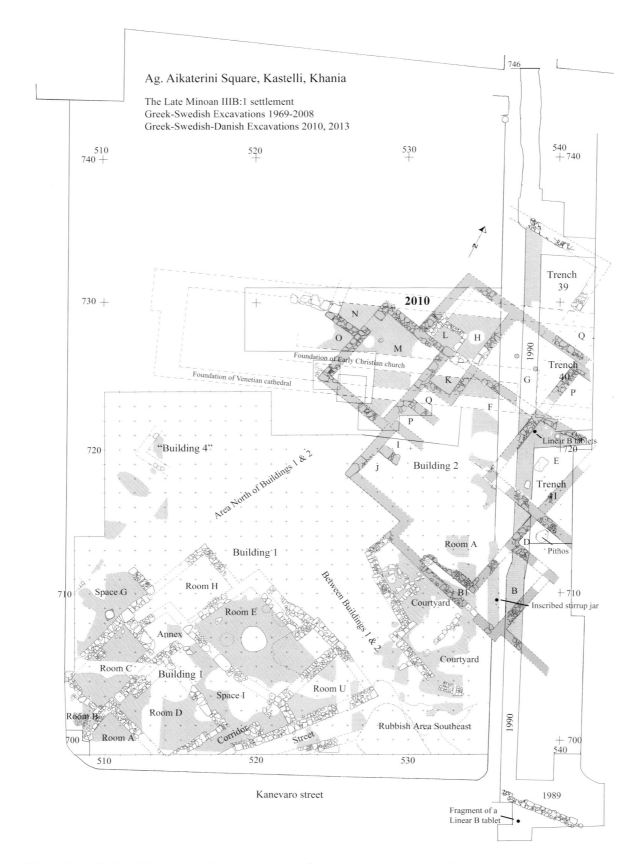

Fig. 1. *General plan of the site after the 2013 excavation (crosses indicate 10 m squares).*

The Greek-Swedish-Danish Excavations 2013

A short preliminary report

ERIK HALLAGER
& MARIA ANDREADAKI-VLAZAKI

From August 1 until October 2, 2013, excavations were conducted in three large trenches in Parodos Kanevaro and one small trench within the Ag. Aikaterini Square, while minor works and restorations were also carried out in the old excavations (Fig. 1).[1] The aim of the excavation was to explore as far as the modern habitation permitted the LM IIIA:2/IIIB:1 Building 2, where Linear B tablets and an inscribed stirrup jar had previously been found.[2]

Results of the excavation

Below the cement of the modern road a layer of gravel of varying thicknesses was reached, which had been laid down in order to level the Square after the bombardment during World War II. Of the post-Antique architectural remains, we excavated a Venetian wall foundation known from previous excavations as W1-028 in the southern part of the trench;[3] two wall foundations of the Early Christian basilica – reused in the Venetian period – were also exposed. Between these wall foundations, 5 tombs of the Venetian period were registered, only one of which had human bones preserved. In this tomb several humans (both male and female, young and adult) had been buried with coins and jewellery (Fig. 2); at first glance

Fig. 2. *Tomb in the Venetian cathedral with victims from an epidemic.*

1   The excavation took place under the general direction of Dr. Maria Andreadaki-Vlazaki, with Dr. Ann-Louise Schallin and Dr. Erik Hallager as co-directors. The on-site work was directed by Dr. Erik Hallager, assisted from the Greek side by Anastasia Ntini, and from the Scandinavian team by Dr. Tomas Alusik, Robin Rönnlund, Naja Werther and architect Ann Pedersen. Eftikia Protopadaki represented the ephorate and the Kastelli Project. The artefact studies were directed by Birgitta Hallager assisted by Stella Petrakis and Alexia Grammatikaki. Water sieving and investigation of the material was directed by Dr. Anaya Sarpaki. We are extremely grateful to the following institutions for their financial support, without which the excavation would not have been possible: The Institute for Aegean Prehistory, Kungl. Vitterhets Historie och Antikvitets Akademien, Herbert och Karin Jacobssons Stiftelse, Augustinus Fonden and the Kastelli Project.
2   Hallager, Vlazaki & Hallager 1992; Andreadaki-Vlazaki & Hallager 2007, 17-20.
3   From the Northeast Building, cf. *GSE* I, 133-4.

Conjectural reconstruction of the Early Christian basilica

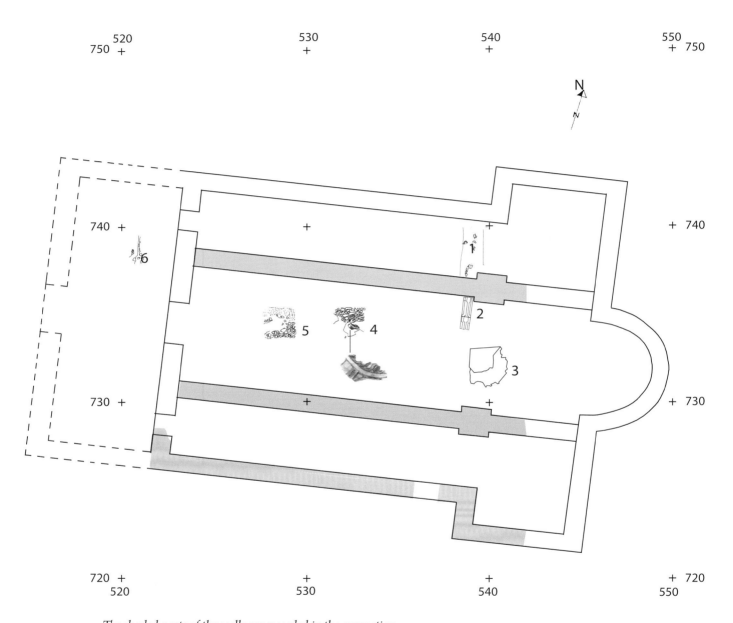

The shaded parts of the walls are recorded in the excavation.

1. *Floor fragments with fragments of mosaics at c. 13.43 m. 2. Parapet with top levels at 13.76 and 13.70 m.*
3. *Floor and floor bedding from the 2013 excavation; top level of floor at 13.48 m.*
4. *Floor with mosaic and floor bedding; mosaic floor at 13.37 m.*
5. *Trench B3 with floor bedding of mosaic floor at c. 13.36 m.*
6. *Fragment of mosaic which may perhaps be in situ at 13.60 m*

Fig. 3. *Conjectural reconstruction of the Early Christian basilica (crosses indicate 10 m squares).*

Fig. 4. *Geometric floor exposed in Trench 39, destroyed by later pits with the preserved part of one of the circular "ovens" (right); facing northwest.*

they looked like victims of an epidemic. The Venetian cathedral was built over the partly ruined Early Christian basilica and thanks to the 2013 excavations it was possible to make a conjectural cross-shaped reconstruction of the basilica with two wings protruding 2 m from the main structure (Fig. 3) – a shape often seen in Early Christian basilicas. In ground plan and size our basilica recalls the Great Basilica on the Vrina Plain in Albania.[4]

The Archaic, Classical, Hellenistic and Roman periods were represented by stray finds, mainly roof tiles. The Geometric period, i.e. the Late Geometric period, was richly represented in the northern half of the excavated area. Dominant in these deposits were the remains of three 'ovens' – large shallow pits with a diameter of c.

Fig. 5. *Worked horn from the Geometric deposits.*

2 to 2.4 m, coated with clay plaster and filled with large amounts of ash (Fig. 4). No artifacts were found in them and the interpretation of their function will have to await the analyses of the ash. Several floor levels were connected

---

4 Molla 2013. 204, fig. II2.3.

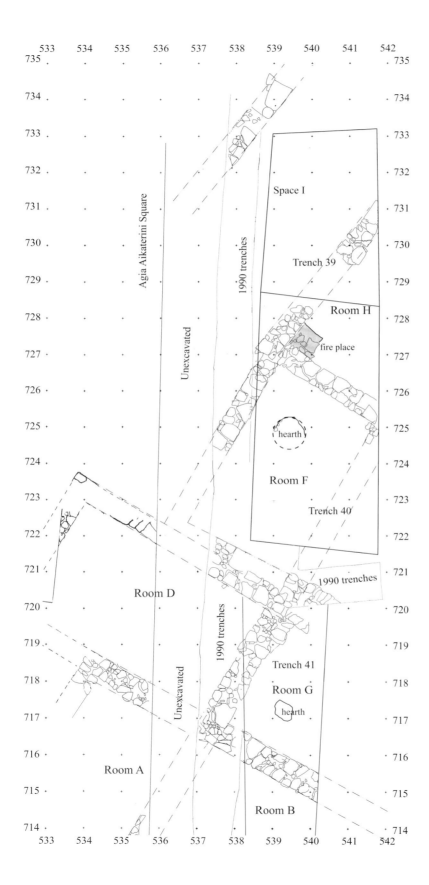

Fig. 6. *Plan of the LM IIIC settlement; the crosses indicate 1 m squares. Scale 1:100.*

Fig. 7. *Fragment of a small model of a boat (left) and unusually large bobbin (right).*

Fig. 8. *Sherd from an LM IIIC krater.*

to these ovens, and they all contained large amounts of animal bones which still need to be studied. One, however, has been identified as a worked horn (Fig. 5).

LM IIIC

The LM IIIC period was richly represented in all the excavated areas (Fig. 6). In the very northern part, which was an open area from the beginning of the LM III to the end of the Geometric period, a single floor level was observed. South and east of the open area parts of four rooms were unearthed. The two northern rooms (F and H) were constructed upon the LM IIIB:2 debris while the two southern rooms (G and B) had cut away the LM IIIB:2 debris resulting in floors resting directly upon the LM IIIB:1 destruction level. In the western corner of Room H a square structure was observed which might have functioned as a fireplace. In Room F fragments of three successive floors were excavated, the earliest of which had a circular hearth in the northern part of the room. On the latest floor of this room were found several pithos fragments, as well as a bobbin and the fragment of what appears to be a small terracotta model of a boat

(Fig. 7). Also in Room G, a small irregular hearth/fireplace was observed on the floor together with a thick layer of charcoal. Some kind of industrial activity may have taken place here, although only a single whetstone was found on the floor. The little that could be excavated in Room B revealed no interesting finds.

To a large extent the LM IIIC habitants used the existing walls of the LM IIIB:2 period, while it appears that a double wall was constructed in the southern part of Room F. In two other instances new constructions of the LM IIIC period could be discerned, both in Room G. The floors of this period were more or less empty as also noted in earlier excavations,[5] while the pits and unstratified deposits of the period yielded some fine pottery (Fig. 8).

LM IIIB:2

The LM IIIB:2 period was mainly recognized in the northern part of the excavated area since, in the southern part, it had been dug away in the LM IIIC period (cf. above). In the open area to the north (Space I, Fig. 6), two floor levels of the period were found. The inventoried pottery

5   *GSE* II, 193.

Fig. 9. Small juglet from LM IIIB:2 floor in Room H.

connected to these floors consisted mainly of fragments from drinking vessels and closed decorated liquid containers, while a few fragments from trays and a single cooking dish were also recorded. The LM IIIC fireplace in Space H was a construction of the LM IIIB:2 period, but raised above the floor level on which a small juglet was found (Fig. 9). Room F – the outline of which could be relatively safely reconstructed – measured 5 x 3.2 m. In this room, which preserved only one floor level, part of a large central hearth was also preserved and narrow double grooves at a right angle were observed in the surface of the hearth (Fig. 10).[6] The hearth was taken out and kept for further studies. No complete or restorable vessels were found on the floor, while a few tools in stone and bone, a hook in bronze and a spindle whorl were recorded. Room P of the LM IIIA:2/B:1 period (Fig. 1) was reused in the LM IIIB:2 period. The small portion of this room that could be excavated produced a largely undisturbed floor deposit with ten vessels (Fig. 11) and large fragments of a pithos. Among the small finds discovered was a mortar lying on its side and an unusual small stone pendant (Fig. 12).

The architecture of the LM IIIB:2 period consisted almost entirely of new constructions with very well-built walls (Fig. 13, WS 1316).

Fig. 10. The northern part of Room F in the LM IIIB:2 period. In the lower left corner is seen the preserved part of the large square hearth with clear traces of fire. To the right of the hearth is seen the top of a LM IIIA:2/IIIB:1 wall. Facing north.

6   Compare Building 1, Room E, cf. *GSE* IV, 89-99.

Fig. 11. *Shallow bowl from floor deposit in Room P.*

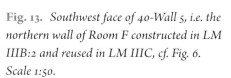

Fig. 12. *Unusual small stone pendant from floor deposit in Room P.*

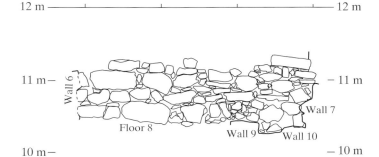

Fig. 13. *Southwest face of 40-Wall 5, i.e. the northern wall of Room F constructed in LM IIIB:2 and reused in LM IIIC, cf. Fig. 6. Scale 1:50.*

WS 13-16. Trench 40-Wall 5, SW face

Fig. 14. *Fragment of a figurine and two steatite beads (or spindle whorls) from the LM IIIB:1 floor deposits in the open area north.*

Fig. 15. *Fragment of a terracotta model of a chariot from the LM IIIB:1 deposits in the open area north.*

271

Fig. 16. *Trench 40, facing north. The original, lower floor of Room G with bedrock protruding is seen in the lower left half, and on the right side the reused Room P. The wall crossing above these rooms is the north wall of LM IIIB:2/IIIC Room F, cf. Fig. 13.*

LM IIIA:2/IIIB:1

The LM IIIA:2/B:1 period was well attested by the excavation of Building 2. Remains of the period were observed in the open area to the north, as well as in Space Q and Rooms G, E and D (Fig. 1). The open northern area revealed five floor levels of the period (one LM IIIA:2 and four LM IIIB:1). The inventoried pottery connected to these floors consisted mainly of decorated (and a few plain) drinking vessels and fine decorated liquid containers. Among the remaining shapes rhyta were predominant. Furthermore, the fragment of a large stirrup jar with possible traces of a Linear B inscription was found.

Among the small finds three fragments of figurines and two steatite beads were collected (Fig. 14) and a fragment of a chariot was discovered in a small shallow pit between the floors (Fig. 15).[7] Space Q, like the open area, is situated outside Building 2 and in this space two LM IIIB:1 floors were found at a c. 0.30 m lower level than those in the open area.

In Trench 40 we excavated parts of two rooms in Building 2: Room G and Room P. Room G measured c. 5 x 4.2 m. In 2013 one column base was disclosed in a position indicating that the room had two column bases on the central length axis of the room, as seen for exam-

7 A similar figurine was found in 1989, cf. Hallager & Tzedakis 1988, 24 and Hallager, Vlazaki & Hallager 1990, 28, pl. 1b.

Fig. 17. *Small decorated stirrup jar from the floor deposit in Room G.*

Fig. 18. *Pithos found in Room D during excavation; facing southwest.*

ple at Sissi and Quartier Nu at Malia.[8] In the northern part of the room, bedrock was protruding c. 0.15 m above the latest floor (Fig. 16). Clear traces of fire were noted in the room. On the floor some stone tools and a spool were found, together with two small decorated stirrup jars probably fallen from shelves (Fig. 17). A test trench was made in the floor and the original floor of the LM

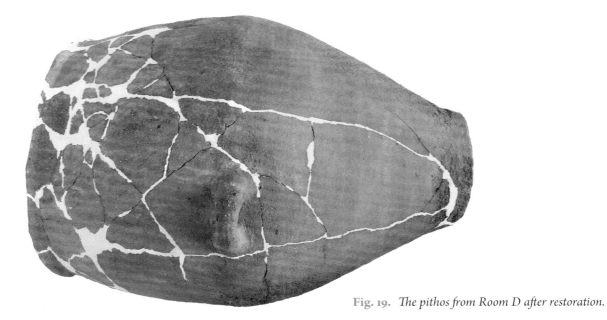

Fig. 19. *The pithos from Room D after restoration.*

---

8   Other rooms with two column bases are found for example in Sissi halls 3.1 and 4.11, cf. *Sissi* III, fig. 4.4 and at Malia Room X$_{22-23}$, cf. Driessen & Farnoux 1994, fig. 2.

Fig. 20. *Half of a double vase found inside the pithos.*

help thinking that the activities may be partly concerned with preparations of offerings to the deities. In contrast with the 1990 excavations in the same room,[10] the pottery discovered in 2013 was very fragmented.

The most exciting find in 2013, however, came from the small part of Room D that was excavated. Here, very close to the north corner of the narrow room (Fig. 1), a complete decorated pithos was discovered (Fig. 18). This pithos was unusual not only in its decoration, with white painting on a dark background, but above all in its position and its content (Fig. 19). A pit had been dug into the floor in order to fit the pithos which was lying on its side, and must have been used as a small storeroom. Inside the pithos 18 grinders and percussion stones, two mortars, two slab stones, a fragment of obsidian, a wedge-shaped piece of worked ivory, the lower part of two large closed vessels, a broken, very burnt lid, half a double vase with a small animal on the handle (Fig. 20) and an uninscribed, unburnt clay tablet were found. To our knowledge such a find is unique for Bronze Age Crete.

The architecture of Building 2 is rather impressive and two important features were revealed during the 2013 excavations. First was the discovery of the northern wall, exposed in Trench 40. Together with the small fragment exposed in 2010,[11] this enabled us to reconstruct 10 m of the north façade of the building, which after a small break continued eastwards (Fig. 1). The reconstructed north corner of the building was investigated in 2014.[12] During the 2010 excavation a large part of Space M was excavated and a conjectural reconstruction of the west corner of the space was indicated on the plan.[13] In 2013 we wanted to verify this reconstruction and consequently a small trench (2 x 2.2 m) was opened between the Early Christian and the Venetian wall foundations. After the topsoil was removed, we did indeed find the well-constructed west corner of Space M (Fig. 21). Until now 16 rooms/ spaces have been identified in Building 2, which covers an area of no less than 350 m².

IIIA:2 period was found c. 0.2 m below the later floor. The neighbouring Room P seems to have been reused in the LM IIIB:2 period (cf. above). Further south, in Trench 41, excavation continued in Room E where Linear B tablets were found in 1990. This room also proved to be relatively large, measuring c. 5 x 3.5 m. In addition to the two small fireplaces noted in 1990,[9] a larger centrally placed hearth was discovered in 2013. On the floor close to the hearth, a large mortar together with a few grinders were recorded. In a soil/ash sample taken from the hearth and close by, many seeds were recorded: a large amount came from figs, some from lentils, barley, wheat, broken legumes, olives and weeds. Obviously some kind of industrial activity took place in this room. Considering the Linear B tablets found in the same room – one of which clearly mentions offerings to Zeus and Dionysos – one cannot

---

9   Hallager, Vlazaki & Hallager 1992, 63 and fig. 2.

10   Hallager, Vlazaki & Hallager 1992, 67-70, fig. 4 and pl. 2.

11   38-Wall 4, cf. Hallager, Tzedakis & Andreadaki-Vlazaki 2014b, 215 and fig. 15.

12   Cf. this volume, p. 283.

    13   Hallager, Tzedakis & Andreadaki-Vlazaki 2014b, 214, fig. 8.

Fig. 21. *The west corner of Room M of LM IIIA:2/B:1 building 2, discovered between the wall foundations of the Early Christian basilica (left) and the Venetian cathedral (right); facing east.*

Earlier periods

Outside Building 2 in the area of Space Q, within Trench 40 (Fig. 1), 0.8 m of earlier deposits were excavated. The north wall of Building 2 was observed to be partly dug into a large pit of the LM IIIA:1 period, almost without small finds. Only a broken loom weight and a large piece of pumice were recorded. Below and partly around the pit, a deposit was noted above a beaten earth floor that was also of the LM IIIA:1 period. Below this floor, two layers with mainly LM II pottery were observed, at the bottom of which a new floor of LM I or LM II date was found. This floor contained no finds in situ, and in the deposits above only a single loom weight was recorded. The area under investigation was rather small and no walls could be connected to the two floors found here. The floors that were exposed north of Building 2 (in Trench 39) were discovered at a 0.25-0.30 m higher level. In Trench 39, how-ever, a wall fragment of the LM IIIA:1 period was discov-ered. The wall in question (Wall 3 in Trench 39) was both constructed and dismantled during the LM IIIA:1 period since it was surrounded by soil of that period on its three exposed sides. The wall fragment is interesting because at one end was placed a large square sandstone block which must have been the base for a wooden doorpost (Fig. 22). This is the only example from Khania where such door bases have been observed in buildings constructed after the Neopalatial period. The LM IIIA:1 deposits in this area (c. 0.40 m thick) revealed very few small finds: a few piec-es of obsidian, a few stone tools and a small slag. The top of the deposits contained many smaller stones, probably functioning as the bedding for the latest LM IIIA:1 floor. In this layer numerous fragments of conical cups plus six complete ones were recorded (Fig. 23). We did not exca-vate Neopalatial or earlier layers.

275

Fig. 22. *Part of a wall with a door base (without antae) in the LM IIIA:1 deposit in Trench 39; facing northeast.*

Old excavations

A few cleanings and restorations in the old excavations were carried out. Due to the excavations in 2005 in the very southwestern corner of the Ag. Aikaterini Square (Δ9),[14] a small baulk of soil above Room B of Building 1 became exposed. It was decided to excavate this baulk in order to investigate further the unique floor of the room, which earlier excavations had shown to be at least partly constructed of broken potsherds.[15] The 2013 excavation exposed a large portion of this floor (Fig. 24), and it also revealed that the northern part of the room had not been covered by pot sherds. On the other hand a large mortar was found up against Wall 5 in Trench 17. The sherds still embedded in the floor consist of several types of vessel with different paint and decoration. Among the

sherds, pithos fragments with 'string' impressions were recorded. One base is visible with dark brown circles on a white background, and a rim with red paint. Several of the sherds look as though they have been crushed in situ, since they fit perfectly together. Several types of pottery are visible, from the coarser wares to the finer decorated vessels. Apart from a rim and a base, most of the fragments are body sherds. The many colours, from brown to red, and the arrangement of the sherds give the impression that one is looking at a mosaic floor.

In 2005 a row of stones that looked like cover-stones for a drain was observed in the open Square in the triangle between House I and House III.[16] This row of stones was cleaned – and it did prove to be the cover for a drain running from the south corner of House III to the main drain

---

14 Seen plan in Andreadaki-Vlazaki & Hallager 2014, fig. 1.

15 *GSE* VI, 48-9.

16 Andreadaki-Vlazaki & Hallager 2014, 202 and fig. 14.

Fig. 23. *Floor packing for the latest LM IIIA:1 floor with several complete and many broken conical cups; facing north.*

Fig. 24. *Floor constructed of broken pot sherds in LM IIIB:1, Building 1 Room B. In the background behind the black and white scale is seen a mortar placed up against the wall. Facing north.*

in the South Street.[17] The direction of the drain points directly towards the south corner of House III, Room A, which may have been an open room.

Summary

The 2013 excavation gave new and important evidence from almost all periods. From post-Antiquity we were especially happy to find the evidence that made it possible to make a conjectural plan of the early Christian basilica, and understand how the wall foundations were reused when the Venetian cathedral was constructed. The Geometric period revealed the three large 'ovens', evidence of industrial activities that have not previously been recorded in Khania. In earlier excavations we had observed an extended reuse of LM IIIB:2 buildings in the LM IIIC period. This was also the case in the 2013 excavations, but for the first time we observed that parts of the LM IIIB:2 deposits had been removed in order for the LM IIIC buildings to be constructed. From the LM IIIB:2 period we noted especially the large, well-constructed hearth in Room F. The north wall of the LM IIIA:2/B:1 Building 2 was identified and it was revealed that Room G probably had two column bases – a feature not noted previously in Khania. Room E revealed further evidence of industrial activities, with its large, square central hearth. To our knowledge the horizontally placed pithos used as a 'storeroom' for stone tools, broken pottery and a few other items is unique for Minoan Crete. Concerning the LM IIIA:2/IIIB period, the open area north of Building 2 is interesting with its finds of many fine decorated drinking vessels and liquid containers, supplemented with a few

---

17   The exposed stones of the drain is seen, this volume p. 287, fig. 18, and the main drain in the South Street is seen in Hallager, Tzedakis & Andreadaki-Vlazaki 2014a, 183, fig. 10.

figurines and a couple of steatite beads. It is therefore tempting to suggest that this area might have been used for feasting. If so, it would further emphasize the importance of Building 2.

ERIK HALLAGER
Østerøgade 4, 8200 Aarhus N
Denmark
klaeh@hum.au.dk

MARIA ANDREADAKI-VLAZAKI
Hellenic Ministry of Culture and Sports
20-22 Mpoumpoulinas, 10682 Athens
Greece
mvlazaki@culture.gr

Abbreviations

GSE: *The Greek-Swedish Excavations at the Agia Aikaterini Square Kastelli, Khania 1970-1987* (Skrifter utgivna av Svenska Institutet i Athen, 4°, XLVII:I-VII), E. Hallager & B.P. Hallager (eds).

Vol. I. *From the Geometric to the Modern Greek Period*, Stockholm 1997.

Vol. II. *The Late Minoan IIIC Settlement*, Stockholm 2000.

Vol. IV. *The Late Minoan IIIB:1 and IIIA:2 Settlements*, Stockholm 2011.

Sissi III: *Excavations at Sissi* III, *Preliminary report on the 2011 campaign* (Aegis 6), J. Driessen et al., Louvain 2012.

Bibliography

Andreadaki-Vlazaki, M. & E. Hallager 2007
'New and unpublished Linear A and Linear B inscriptions from Khania', *PoDIA* 5, 7-22.

Andreadaki-Vlazaki, M. & E. Hallager 2014
'Excavations at the Agia Aikaterini Square, Kastelli, Khania 2005 and 2008: a preliminary report', *PoDIA* 7, 195-207.

Driessen, J. & A. Farnoux 1994
'Mycenaeans at Malia?', *Aegean Archaeology* 1, 54-64.

Hallager, E., M. Vlazaki & B. P. Hallager 1990
'The first Linear B Tablet(s) from Khania', *Kadmos* 29, 24-34.

Hallager, E., M. Vlazaki & B. P. Hallager 1992
'New Linear B Tablets from Khania', *Kadmos* 31, 61-87.

Hallager, E. & Y. Tzedakis 1988
'The Greek-Swedish Excavations at Kastelli Khania. 1. The 1989 excavations, 2. The 1990 excavations', *AAA* 21 [1993], 15-55.

Hallager, E., Y. Tzedakis & M. Andreadaki-Vlazaki 2014a
'The Greek-Swedish Excavations at Kastelli, Khania 2001: a preliminary report', *PoDIA* 7, 175-93.

Hallager, E., Y. Tzedakis & M. Andreadaki-Vlazaki 2014b
'The Greek-Swedish-Danish Excavations at Kastelli, Khania 2010: a preliminary report', *PoDIA* 7, 209-20.

Molla, N. 2013
'The Great Basilica: a reassessment', in *The Archaeology and Histories of an Ionian Town* (Butrint 4), I. L. Hansen, R. Hodges & S. Leppard (eds), Oxford, 202-14.

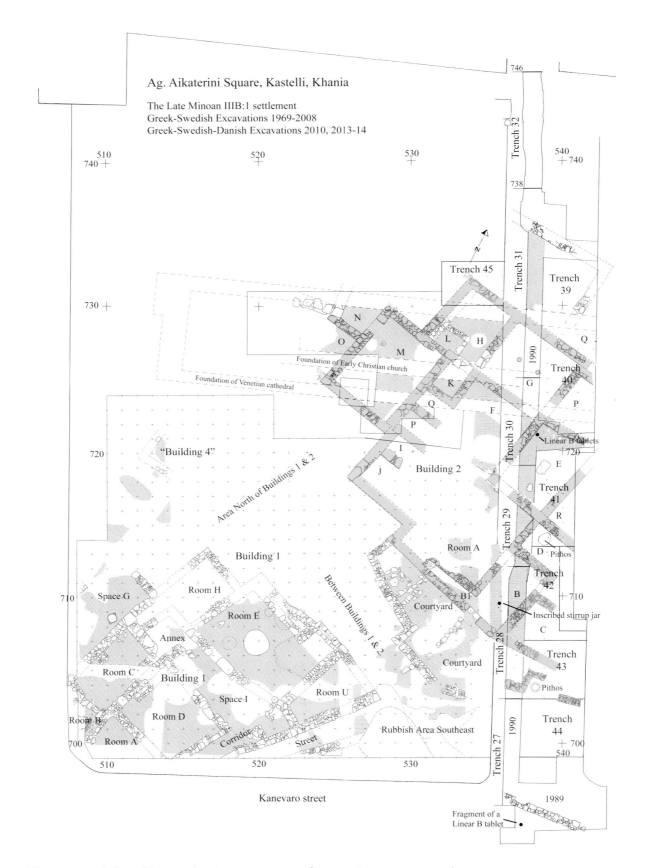

Fig. 1. *General plan of the site after the 2013 excavation (crosses indicate 10 m squares).*

The Greek-Swedish-Danish Excavations 2014

A preliminary report

ERIK HALLAGER
& MARIA ANDREADAKI-VLAZAKI

From August 4 until September 30, 2014, excavations were conducted in three large trenches in Parodos Kanevaro and one trench within the Ag. Aikaterini Square, while a minor restoration was also carried out in the old excavations (Fig. 1).[1]

Results of the excavation

As in the 2013 excavation, a layer of gravel of varying thicknesses was reached immediately below the modern road. Of the post-Antique architectural remains, in the southern part we excavated the eastern wall of the Southeastern building from the Venetian period.[2] Stratified above the wall of the Venetian period we found an Ottoman building measuring 12.4 x 6.2 m, which had its western wall in common with the Gazoseria previously excavated.[3] The finds of many small coins and broken Turkish pipes indicate the presence of a Turkish coffee house in this building. In the northern part, inside the Ag. Aikaterini Square, part of the aisle wall of the Early Christian basilica and the later Venetian cathedral was laid free, and a child's burial was recorded within the church. In this part of the excavation it was also observed that during the Turkish period, when the cathedral became a mosque, a heavy

Fig. 2. *Sherd from Geometric krater.*

foundation wall measuring roughly 2 x 2 x 2 m had been constructed, the purpose of which remains enigmatic.

From the remaining post-Minoan times, the Byzantine, Roman, Hellenistic, Classical and Archaic periods were represented by stray finds, mostly in the form of roof tiles and amphorae. The Geometric period was richly represented in large pits containing some interesting pottery (Fig. 2). Within the area of Room B (see Fig. 3), a heavy deposit of the period was located, and from this came an exciting find: the fragment of a Linear A tablet with two new ligatures not previously seen in the corpus of Linear A (Fig. 4). However, no structures of the period were recorded.

1   The excavation took place under the general direction of Dr. Maria Andreadaki-Vlazaki with Dr. Ann-Louise Schallin and Dr. Erik Hallager as co-directors. The on-site work was directed by Dr. Erik Hallager, assisted from the Greek side by Anastasia Ntini, and from the Scandinavian team by Dr. Tomas Alusik, Robin Rönnlund, Naja Werther and architect Ann Pedersen. Eftikia Protopadaki represented the ephorate and the Kastelli Project. The artefact studies were directed by Birgitta Hallager assisted by Stella Petrakis. Water sieving and investigation of the material was directed by Dr. Anaya Sarpaki. We are extremely grateful to the following institutions for their financial support, without which the excavation would not have been possible: The Institute for Aegean Prehistory, Kungl. Vitterhets Historie och Antikvitets Akademien and Herbert och Karin Jacobssons Stiftelse.
2   *GSE* I, 140-2.
3   *GSE* I, 86-94.

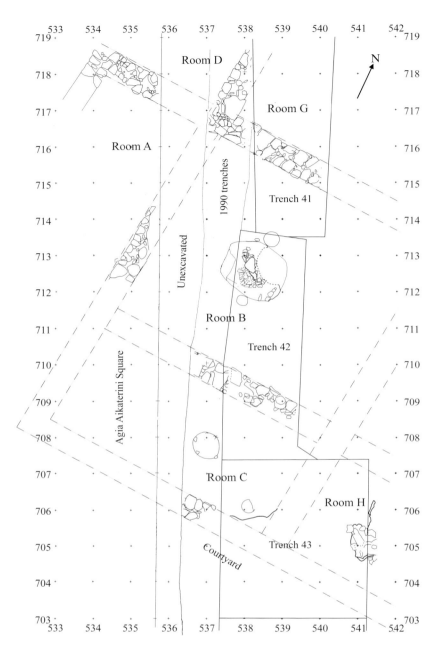

LM IIIC

The LM IIIC period provided interesting results (Fig. 3). Parts of two, or perhaps three rooms/spaces were excavated. The northernmost, Space B, had also been excavated in 1990 and 2005.[4] It was a space measuring 5.2 by at least 5.3 m. Within the space, five floor levels were observed and connected to these were two hearth/ovens, presumably placed in the centre of the space. The later one was constructed on top of the collapsed earlier one. It was built as a typical hearth of the period on a bedding of broken potsherds, covered with clayish earth and

4   The results will be presented in *GSE Supplementum*, forthcoming.

Fig. 4. *Fragment of a Linear A tablet with remains from four lines; the last signs in both line 1 and line 2 are new signs in the corpus of Linear A. Scale 1:1.*

Fig. 5. *Sherds from several broken pithoi found above the upper hearth in Room B; facing south.*

finally given a plastered surface. It measured 1.60 x 1.40 m. Over this hearth was built a vault of broken pithos sherds, probably plastered in *kouskouras* (Fig. 5), thus functioning as an oven. The original oven, placed exactly below the latter hearth/oven, belonged with the earliest LM IIIC floors and was of a very different nature. An oval groove was dug c. 0.25 m into the floor and coated with a clay lining covered with a very thin layer of plaster. The oven was built up in clay and as far as the remains indicate, it had a combustion chamber below. The floor of the oven was also constructed in clay and it appears to have had a hole with a diameter of c. 0.15 m at the centre. Over this floor, a shallow dome was constructed. North and south of the hearth/oven(s), two column bases (?) were noted. They were of different sizes, but their centres were in both cases 1.80 m from the walls, and they probably functioned as bases for a wooden support. On the floors of Space B were found several stone tools, many pieces of obsidian and a piece of lead; in a small pit between the floors an exquisite bead was recorded (Fig. 6). South of Space B was identified another room/ Space C. However, only fragments of the northern and southern walls were preserved, indicating a width of 2.80 m. All other architecture in this space had been destroyed

Fig. 6. *Pierced faience bead.*

by later activities. We do, however, believe for several reasons that it was divided into two compartments. In 1990 a small circular hearth was found in Space C,[5] while in 2014 an oven was found in the eastern part. These two

5   Hallager & Tzedakis 1988, 45 and fig. 24.

Fig. 7. *The LM IIIC oven in Space H; facing southeast.*

Fig. 10. *Rather unique terracotta object.*

Fig. 8. *Lower left corner of a linear A tablet with remains of three signs. Scale 1:1.*

fireplaces probably belonged to separate rooms and if the conjecturally reconstructed eastern wall of Space B was prolonged southwards, one would have a natural dividing line between the two spaces – now baptized C and H. Two LM IIIC floor levels were recognized in both spaces. Close to the conjectural south corner of Space C a large jar had been partly sunk into the floor, on which a few stone tools and pieces of bronze were recorded. Space H also revealed two floor levels into which an oven had been constructed. This oven was built from stones covered with *kouskouras*, and an almost spherical stone closed the hole through which the heat would have reached the cooking pots (Fig. 7). Large fragments of a cooking pot were found inside the oven.

Concerning the LM IIIC period in general, it should be noted that when Space B was constructed the underlying LM IIIB:2 deposits had been cleared away – exactly as was noted in Space G in the 2013 excavation.[6] Great effort had been made to construct this LM IIIC area, apparently for industrial activities.

LM IIIB:2

The LM IIIB:2 was poorly represented in terms of architecture and floor deposits. Although it is possible to reconstruct the outline of Rooms I (situated above Room D of

Fig. 9. *Worn pestle.*

6   Cf. this volume p. 258.

Fig. 11. *Fragment of an animal figurine en face.*

Fig. 12. *The hour-shaped unique vessel/stand.*

the LM IIIB:1 period, cf. Fig. 1) and B, no floors were found there since they had been dug out in connection with the constructions in the LM IIIC period. A few small pits and deposits were recorded within those two rooms, however, and in the lower floors of LM IIIC, Space C, some good deposits with LM IIIB:2 pottery were observed. Further south in the Courtyard Area, two floor levels (44-Floor 5 and 7) with a few deposits were recorded. According to the levels, it is clear that the LM IIIB:2 courtyard sloped towards the southeast.[7] In one small deposit below Floor 7, a small fragment of a Linear A tablet was discovered (Fig. 8). In Trench 45 inside the Ag. Aikaterini Square, three floor levels were recorded on the northern side of the LM IIIB:1 wall (38-Wall 4), indicating that this wall was reused in the IIIB:2 period. This was probably a prolongation of the open area in the north recognized in 2013.[8] The major finds of the period, however, came from pits. The largest was 44-Pit F, located in the very southwestern corner of the excavated area. It produced 89 kg of pottery and may perhaps be connected to the large 20-Pit B.[9] Pit F contained surprisingly few small finds, among which is the larger part of a horn, a fine stone tool (Fig. 9), a KS-whorl and a small fragment of a stone vase. The northern Trench 45 also revealed a few productive pits with much pottery but almost without small finds, the only interesting one being a terracotta grinder (?) (Fig. 10).

LM IIIB:1

Inside the Ag. Aikaterini Square, in Trench 45, we expected to find in the north corner of Room H a thick layer of LM IIIB:1 debris, as we did during the excavations in 2010.[10] Most of the area was disturbed, however, by a Turkish foundation wall (cf. above) – but in the eastern part a small area was left undisturbed, and it fulfilled our expectations. The Turkish structure had almost completely destroyed the northwestern wall (38-Wall 4), while the outer foundation, set against a thick MM III/LM I rubbish deposit, was recognized below the LM IIIB:2 reuse of the wall. It was thus possible to reconstruct the northern corner of Building 2 and also to observe that it was set deep into deposits of the Neopalatial period.

In the southern part, the LM IIIB:1 period was richly represented. In Room D, where a painted pithos was discovered in 2013,[11] four floor levels were recorded at a c. 0.20 m depth. The room appeared in its original construction to be L-shaped. In connection with the floors excavated here 15 grinders, one whetstone and the head of an animal figurine (Fig. 11) were recorded. In the same deposit as the figurine, a unique cylinder-shaped vessel was recorded (Fig. 12). Most of the finds in this room were clustered

---

7   LM IIIB:2 courtyard, cf. *GSE* III, 86-90.
8   Cf. this volume p. 267-268.
9   *GSE* III, 114.
10   Hallager, Tzedakis & Andreadaki-Vlazaki 2014, 213.
11   Cf. this volume, p. 272.

Fig. 13. *LM IIIB:1 lid from Room C; the handle on top was missing.*

of such a wall could be recognized. This means that we have, as yet, no indication of the eastern (or southeastern) limit of Building 2. Upon the upper floor of the room, four footed cups, one decorated lid (Fig. 13), a handleless cup and some pithos fragments were recorded. Upon the lower floor, two footed cups and the lower third of a broken pithos were recorded. The room might perhaps have functioned as a small storeroom. Except for a few pieces of obsidian, no further finds were observed on the floors.

South of Room C, in the Courtyard Area outside Building 2, a complete pithos was found. It was sunk into the LM I/LM IIIA:2 deposits with roughly half the pithos visible above the floor level (Fig. 14). The pithos was discovered while excavating a large Turkish/Venetian pit, and the content of this pit was found in the upper 0.58 m of the pithos, below which only Minoan soil was found. In this deposit a complete LM IIIB:1 jar (Fig. 15), the major part of a plain, stemless kylix, many bones including the horn of a goat, plaster fragments, a loom weight and pieces of mother of pearl were recorded. Around the pithos, a built structure was noted, the extension and nature of which remain uncertain due to later activities. The pithos is now exhibited in

close to the mouth of the pithos, inside which 18 grinders and 4 more or less complete vases had been stored.[12] Room B, where three floors were recorded, did not reveal any significant finds. Room C, however, revealed two floor deposits with some pottery in situ. The southern wall of the room was the southern outer wall of Building 2, constructed at an odd angle compared to the remaining part of the building. In connection with Room C, we had also expected to find an eastern wall, but due to the activities of the Venetian, Turkish and Modern periods, no traces

Fig. 14. *Complete pithos set in an LM III B:1 floor of the Courtyard south of Building 2.*

12 Cf. this volume, p. 272.

Fig. 15. *Near-complete jar found inside pithos.*

Fig. 16. *Restored pithos exhibited in the Museum during the 2014 season.*

the Archaeological Museum (Fig. 16). From the Courtyard Area south of Room C, three floor levels were noted at a slightly lower level than seen further west,[13] thus displaying the same pattern as noted in the LM IIIB:2 period. On these floors only a few stone tools were recorded.

LM IIIA:1/LM II

Activities of the LM II and LM IIIA:1 periods were noted in all trenches except the one inside the Agia Aikaterini Square. In Trenches 42 and 43, a clear rehabitation in the LM I House III was observed. In some cases, the LM I debris had been cleaned down to the floor surfaces of the LM I period, while in other instances parts of the LM I floors had been destroyed. A few new floors were laid during the period. Among the very few finds from these deposits can be mentioned a game marker (TC 048). In the large square south of House III, the situation was very similar to that observed in earlier excavations in that several new floors had been constructed upon the LM IB destruction debris.[14] One construction which most likely belonged to this period was the fragment of a very large oven recorded in the very southeastern part of the excavated area (Fig. 17). It was constructed on a thick bedding of *kouskouras* and it had an 'air duct' leading from the north into the back part of the oven.

LM I

The LM I period gave important new information about House III and the large square surrounded by Houses I, II and III. The south corner of House III and an entrance to this house were discovered (Fig. 18). The corner block measured 0.80 x 0.40 m and the entrance was situated in the southern part of the southeastern wall, next to the corner block. It consisted of a huge threshold (partly covered by LM IIIB:1 walls), probably measuring 1.20 x 0.80 m. The centre of the threshold was nicely worn. Inside, very close to the south corner, the arrangement for the pivot hole was found, revealing that the door would have opened inwards. The floor of the room was even, very well-constructed and plastered, with larger sand grains included. The entrance room measured 2.75 in width and was at least 7 m long. The walls had a lining of *kouskouras* which had probably also been covered with plaster. Up against the southeastern wall (42-Wall 7), a door with two typical Γ-shaped door bases led into Room B, which was probably a rather nar-

---

13   LM IIIB:1 and LM IIIA:2 floors in the courtyard. cf. *GSE* 4, 157-69 and 238-41.
14   See *GSE* V, 97-108, 183-187.

Fig. 17. *Remains of a large oven or kiln from the LM II/ IIIA:1 period.*

row room with a width of 1.75 m and an unknown length. No finds of the LM I period were made since both rooms had been cleaned of destruction debris and reused during the LM II and LM IIIA:1 period (cf. above).

Outside the entrance, 0.10 m below the level of the threshold, a pavement in good limestone was recorded (Fig. 19). The second row of slabs was found at a 0.04 m lower level, while the beginning of a third row was at a 0.18 m lower level than the first. This shows that the pavement of the courtyard sloped towards the south, which fits very well with the fact that the paved part of the square excavated 11 m further south was found at a 0.77 m lower level.[15] The deeper part of the paved square was covered with a few earthen floors during the LM I period, which were again covered with floors and deposits in the LM II and LM IIIA:1 periods (cf. above). This is also the reason why there were no finds of the LM I period in situ. In the destruction debris, a large ashlar block was recorded around 538/701.5. In previous excavations four worked ashlar blocks were found scattered in the Square outside House I, Room Q, while another was recorded in the Square around 536.5/699.5. The purpose of these scattered

ashlar blocks and a fallen pithos[16] in the Square has not yet been satisfactorily explained.

In the northern part inside the Ag. Aikaterini Square, in Trench 45, a heavy levelling deposit of the LM I/MM III period was excavated. This deposit started outside the LM IIIB:1 Building 2 at a level more than 0.50 m above the LM IIIB:1 floor inside the building. Clearly this deposit had been levelled away in connection with the construction of Building 2. Below, or rather in the levelling deposit outside the building and below the LM IIIB:1 floor, a wall-like structure came to light. It consisted of larger stones facing southeast and smaller fist-size stones in a rather loose soil on the northwestern side. The direction of this wall (?) diverges slightly from the two neighbouring LM I houses, Houses III and V (Fig. 20). Until further investigations can be carried out, the function of the wall remains uncertain. What was interesting, however, was the discovery up against it on its southeastern side of a child burial. The infant had been buried in a small earthen pit and covered by three small stone slabs (Fig. 21).[17] There were no grave goods so the grave can only be dated to MM III/LM I or earlier.

---

15   For this slabbed floor, cf. Hallager & Tzedakis 1988, 22.
16   Andreadaki-Vlazaki & Hallager 2014, 202 and fig. 14.
17   Cf. McGeorge, this volume.

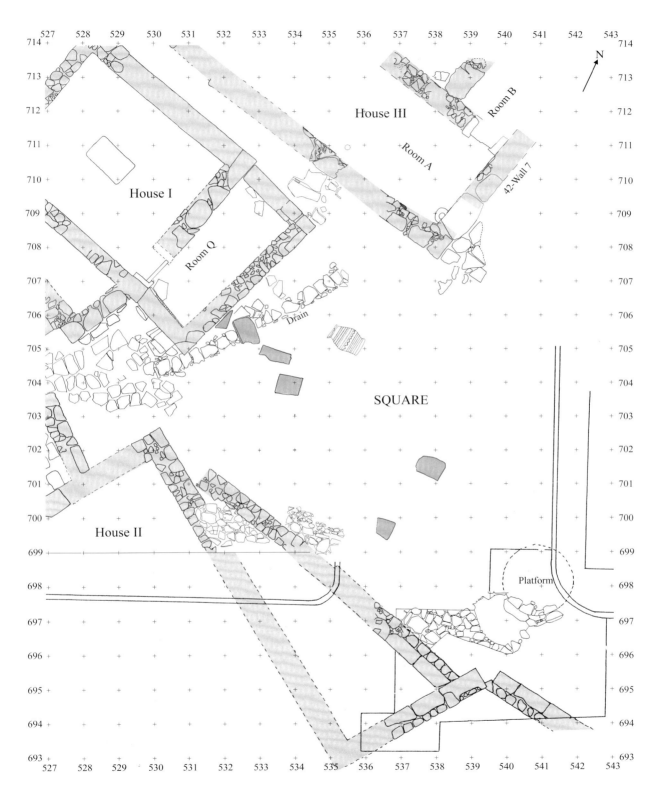

Fig. 18. *Plan of the LM I Square surrounded by Houses I, II and III; the dark shaded stones are the scattered ashlar blocks. The crosses indicate 1 m squares.*

289

Fig. 19. *South corner of House III. Behind the slab stones of the courtyard the impressive threshold is partly covered by LM II and LM III walls. Facing northwest.*

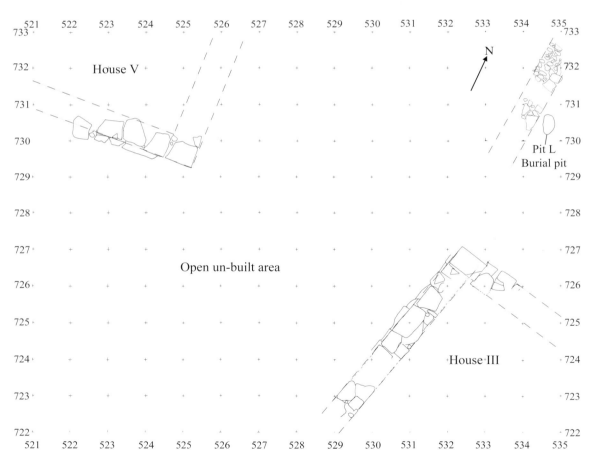

Fig. 20. *Plan of the north corner of House III and the south corner of House V, as well as the wall-like structure behind which the child burial was discovered in Pit L. Scale 1:100.*

Fig. 21. *Position of the child burial. On the left side the wall-like structure, and to the right of that three (not well-cleaned) stone slabs which covered Pit L. Seen from above; north up.*

Summary

The major aim of the 2014 excavation in the modern road Parodos Kanevaro was to investigate Building 2 of the LM IIIA:2/IIIB:1 period and the courtyard south of this building, as far as the modern habitation permitted. Concerning the architecture, our work confirmed that the north corner of the building existed as we had reconstructed it, and our theory that part of the LM I deposits had been dug away to construct the building was also confirmed. We discovered the southern outer wall of the building and saw that it had changed direction compared to the remaining part of the building. Towards the southeast no perimeter wall was found, which means that our earlier statement that the building covered an area of at least 350 m² still holds true. Inside the building we now have a clearer understanding of Rooms B (completely excavated), C and D. The courtyard provided the surprising find of a complete, sunken pithos, probably placed in a small shed. In addition to this we now have a much better understanding of the LM I House III, with the discovery of its southern corner and its entrance, and of the large LM I square surrounded by the town houses. The LM II/IIIA:1 periods revealed a pattern similar to the earlier excavations, with the only difference being that a very large oven was constructed in an open area in this period. The LM IIIB:2 period was relatively poorly represented, while the LM IIIC period with its ovens added important new evidence. The post-Minoan periods yielded new evidence of the Venetian, Turkish and Modern periods. Concerning single finds, two were outstanding: the fragment of a Linear A tablet with two new signs in the corpus of Linear A, and a cylinder-shaped vessel which to our knowledge has no parallels in the Minoan pottery repertoire.

ERIK HALLAGER
Østerøgade 4, 8200 Aarhus N
Denmark
klaeh@hum.au.dk

MARIA ANDREADAKI-VLAZAKI
Hellenic Ministry of Culture and Sports
20-22 Mpoumpoulinas, 10682 Athens
Greece
mvlazaki@culture.gr

Abbreviations

GSE: The Greek–Swedish Excavations at the Agia Aikaterini Square Kastelli, Khania 1970-1987 (Skrifter utgivna av Svenska Institutet i Athen, 4°, XLVII:), E. Hallager & B.P. Hallager (eds).

Vol. I. *From the Geometric to the Modern Greek Period*, Stockholm 1997.

Vol. III. *The Late Minoan IIIB:2 Settlement*, Stockholm 2003.

Vol. IV. *The Late Minoan IIIB:1 and IIIA:2 Settlements*, Stockholm 2011.

Vol. V. *The Late Minoan IIIA:1 and LM II Settlements*, Stockholm, forthcoming.

Supplementum. Late Minoan IIIA:2 to Modern Greek from Excavations 2001, 2005 and 2008, Stockholm, 2016.

Bibliography

Andreadaki-Vlazaki, M & E. Hallager 2014
'Excavations at the Agia Aikaterini Square, Kastelli, Khania 2005 and 2008 – a preliminary report', *PoDIA* 7, 195-207.

Hallager, E. & Y. Tzedakis 1988
'The Greek–Swedish Excavations, Khania 1989, 1990', *AAA* 21 [1993], 15-55.

Hallager, E, Y. Tzedakis & M. Andreadaki-Vlazaki 2014
'The Greek–Swedish–Danish Excavations at Kastelli, Khania 2010: a preliminary report', *PoDIA* 7, 209-20.

McGeorge, P. J. P. 2016
'The Pit L Baby Burial: Evidence of immigrants in MMIII Kydonia?', *PoDIA* 8, 293-303.

The Pit L Baby Burial – Hermeneutics
Implications for immigration into Kydonia in MMIII/LMI

P. J. P. MCGEORGE

Context

This infant burial was discovered in the Ag. Aikaterini Square excavation on Kastelli Hill in 2014.[1] The infant was buried in Pit L, a shallow oval hollow c. 9-14 cm deep and 50 cm long by 30 cm wide, sealed by 3 stone slabs, the widest of which was 35 cm. No grave offerings were found. The burial was stratified below the LM IIIA:2/B:1 Building 2, which in this part of the excavation was constructed deep in the Neopalatial layers. It is therefore securely dated to the MM III/LM I period. At the present time it is the earliest occurrence of an intramural subfloor pit burial in West Crete.[2]

Skeletal Remains

During the 2014 excavation, some cranial fragments, long bones and ribs of an infant were recovered from Pit L. More skeletal material was retrieved from the residue after water sieving 9 litres of surrounding soil, substantially increasing the amount of material recovered.[3] The residue included all of the twelve partially formed, unerupted deciduous teeth; the metacarpals, metatarsals, manual and pedal phalanges; a distal femur fragment, three fragments of a fibula and further cranial fragments including the greater wing of the left sphenoid and three ear bones, reaffirming that water sieving and residue analysis significantly improve the retrieval of fragile skeletal material.

Cranium

The cranial vault bones were eggshell thin and broken into many fragments (Fig. 1); porosity and radial lesions were noted on the endocranial surfaces of the occipital and parietals (Figs 1-3). Denser elements, such as the petrous bones (the right measuring: 29.18 mm long x 16.62 mm wide; the left: 27 mm long x 14.83 mm wide), the left greater wing of the sphenoid (22.22 mm long by 14.97 mm wide) and some tiny ear bones illustrated in figures 4-6, survived more or less intact. The measurements of the incus bone are 6.35 mm wide by 6.01 mm long.

Fig. 1. *Some of the larger occipital and parietal fragments with endocranial lesions.*

---

1   See the preliminary report in this volume p. 286 with indication of the find spot, fig. 20, and a photograph, fig. 21.

2   An earlier intramural pithos burial of a child in an EMII context is attested at Nopigeia in West Crete, see discussion and ref. in n. 27, below.

3   Many thanks to Anaya Sarpaki, who sieved the residues for organic remains.

Fig. 2. *Magnification of occipital endocranial lesions.*

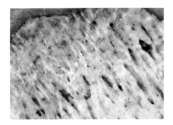

Fig. 3. *Magnification of parietal endocranial lesions.*

Fig. 4. *Right and left petrous bones.*

Fig. 5. *Greater wing of the left sphenoid.*

Fig. 6. *Ear bones – incus, malleus.*

Dentition

Twelve tooth germs (see Fig. 7) recovered from the residue were identified as the following:

$$\frac{d\ c\ b\ \mid a\ b\ c\ d}{c\ a\mid a\quad c\ d}$$

Mesiodistal crown diameters and crown heights are recorded in Table 1.

Since tooth germs begin to develop prenatally, they are good criteria for gestational age determination. Incisors, which begin initial calcification at 4 to 4.5 months in utero, have 60-80% of their crowns formed at birth, whereas canines approximately 30%, while first molars have a complete occlusal cap, maxillary molars being more completely calcified than other molars.[4] This infant's incisor and canine development corresponds to a full-term embryo, however, the occlusal caps of the molars are not complete, while the enamel of the incisors appears malformed (see Fig. 7).

Measurements in mm	Mesiodistal Crown D	Crown Ht
Upper R lateral incisor	4.08	3.87
Upper L central incisor	6.24	3.92
Upper L lateral incisor	4.69	3.52
Lower R central incisor	3.75	4.32
Lower L central incisor	3.90	4.39
Upper canine	4.62	3.28
Upper canine	[4.09]	3.13
Lower R canine	3.42	2.80
Lower L canine	3.02	2.22
Upper L molar	6.36	3.62
Upper R molar	6.37	3.51
Lower L molar	6.54	3.69

Table 1. *Tooth measurements.*

4   Scheuer & Black 2000, 156.

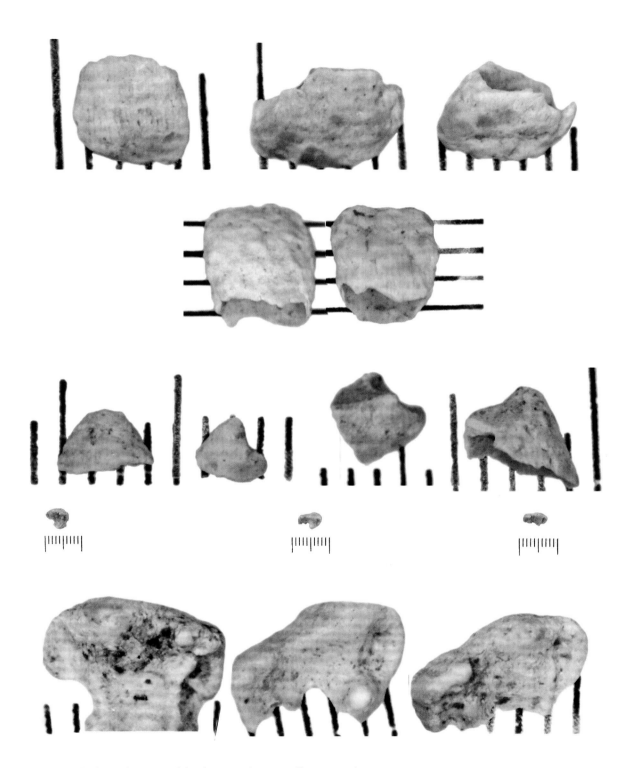

Fig. 7. *Partially formed crowns of deciduous teeth on a millimetre grid.*

Fig. 8. *Right scapula, the clavicles and the right distal humerus shaft.*

Fig. 10. *Right ulna.*   Fig. 11. *Manual phalanges.*

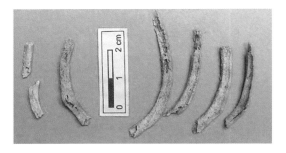

Fig. 9. *Right radius.*

Fig. 12. *Ribs.*

Post-Cranium

The baby's upper torso and limbs are represented by the clavicles, the right scapula and the right distal humerus (Fig. 8), the right radius (Fig. 9) and ulna (Fig. 10), some manual phalanges (Fig. 11) and a collection of ribs (Fig. 12). The only complete long bone was that of a right radius measuring 49.82 mm, its length corresponding to that of a 39-week embryo.

Table 2 records the measurements of the complete manual phalanges.

Proximal manual phalanges	mm	Distal manual phalanges	mm
Ray 1 (thumb)	6.91	*Ray 1 (thumb)*	5.82
Ray 2 (index)	9.85	*Ray 5 (?)*	2.57
Ray 3	10.5		

Table 2. *Measurements of complete manual phalanges.*

The lower limbs are represented by the femurs, tibias and fibulas, metatarsals and pedal phalanges, which are illustrated in Figs 13-15. Measurements of the incomplete long bones and of the metatarsals and pedal phalanges are recorded in Tables 3-4.

Conclusion

Despite the fragility of the pit burial and the noticeable absence of the pelvic bones and vertebrae (Fig. 16), enough of the skeleton is present to conclude that it was probably a low birth weight, full-term baby. Enamel hypoplasia is a correlate of low birth weight infants.[5] Lesions like those on the internal surfaces of the occipital and parietal bones, illustrated in Figs 1-3, may have a variety of causes in young children,[6] but in newborn babies the most likely causes are either bacterial infection transmitted through the placental blood supply or foetal distress due to poor maternal nutrition. In preterm infants intra-cranial haemorrhage may occur as a result of vitamin

5   Seow, Humphrys & Tudehope 1987, 221-5.
6   Lewis 2004, 82-97.

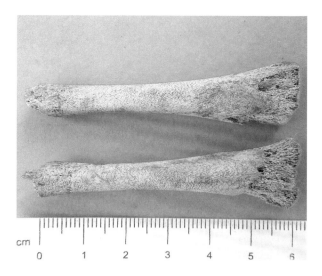

Fig. 13. *Femurs.*

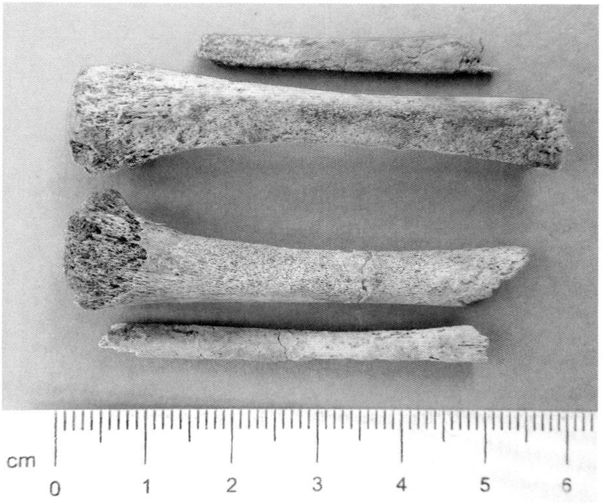

Fig. 14. *Tibias and fibulas.*

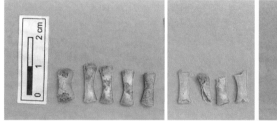

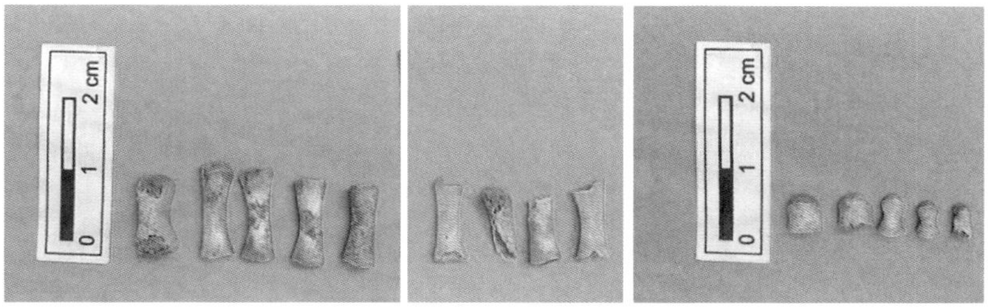

Fig. 15. *Metatarsals and pedal phalanges.*

Bone	mm
R Scapula	31.98
R Glenoid Ht.	8.35
R Clavicle	31.18
L Clavicle	16.94
R Humerus	30.98
R Ulna	32.85
R Femur	62.48
L Femur	61.59
R Tibia	52.23
L Tibia	55.01
R Fibula	45.01
L Fibula	35.82

Metatarsals	mm
1st	11.42
2nd	13.06
3rd	13.55
4th	12.37
5th	11.87

Proximal pedal phalanges	mm
Ray 1 (big toe)	5.38
Ray 2	5.77
Ray 3	4.72
Ray 4	4.50
Distal pedal phalange	2.37

Table 3. *Measurements of incomplete bones.*

Table 4. *Measurements of complete bones.*

297

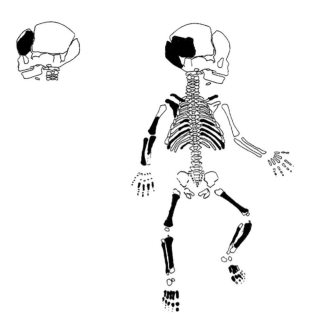

Fig. 16. Infant skeleton, dark areas preserved.

or mineral deficiency. Perinatal death might have been due to poor maternal nutrition, poor hygiene or neonatal infection. Nevertheless, it should be noted that even today in the developed world, with advanced technology, it is more often than not impossible to diagnose the precise cause of a perinatal death.

Discussion:

The Pit L baby burial is the second infant burial to be found in the Ag. Aikaterini Square excavation. A similar burial in a shallow pit was found previously under the LM IIIB:2 floor of a house,[7] less than a metre from the hearth in the centre of room E, which measured 6.5 x 4.5 m². Two iliac bones in an excellent state of preservation were the only surviving remains of the burial of a premature infant of c. 37 weeks gestation. There were no gifts. Items recorded on the beaten clay floor were two bowls, found in dif-

ferent corners, a small tripod cooking pot and a cooking dish, which suggested that the room was a domestic area used for the preparation of food.

Interments inside a house, or in an open area such as a courtyard, but within a settlement, are designated intramural, in contrast to burials in extramural cemeteries. Intramural burial of infants either inside or outside a home, often in areas where domestic activities took place, are characteristic of the earliest settled communities of the Near East. Such burials have also been found at Neolithic Knossos;[8] the Minoans, however, normally buried their dead extramurally.

On the Greek mainland, intramural burial of infants was practised throughout the Bronze Age with interments in earth-dug graves, stone-lined cists or pots, or under large sherds (see locations in Fig. 17). At some sites, such as Asine, with 57 infant or child burials (forty-five in pits, six in pithoi, five in cists and one in a brick enclosure), they occur in significantly large numbers.[9] By contrast, in the Minoan Bronze Age intramural burials of infants or children are relatively scarce, although now known at several sites throughout the island.

The highest concentration of infant burials of various types has been found at the Knossos Stratigraphical Museum Extension site, where the majority of graves are pit burials, while a few pit burials have been found at Gypsadhes[10] and the Unexplored Mansion (see Table 5).[11] Elsewhere, intramural infant burials appear sporadically, in small numbers. So far there is only one cist burial from the Unexplored Mansion at Knossos, but there are eight pot burials from six different localities, dating to the EM II (Nopigeia), LM IA (Petras and Sissi) and to LM IIIA2/IIIB periods at Palaikastro, Knossos and Phaistos (Fig. 17)[12].

Most of the burials found at the Knossos Stratigraphical Museum Extension site were dated to the post-Palatial LM

---

7   O. & E. Persson 2003, 276; McGeorge 2003, 301-3.

8   Evans 1964, 132-240; McGeorge 2013, 1-20.

9   Frodin & Persson 1938.

10   Hogarth 1899-1900, 70-84.

11   Popham 1984.

12   MacGillivray, Driessen, Macdonald & Smyth 1988, 259-82; McGeorge forthcoming.

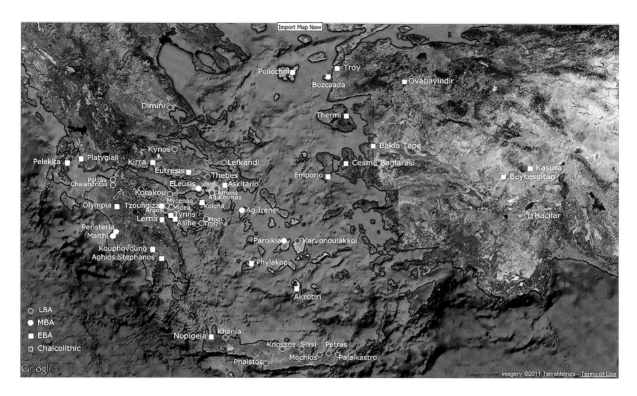

Fig. 17. *Bronze Age sites with intramural infant burial.*

IIIC/Subminoan period and their appearance was attributed to the ingress and cultural influence of Mycenaeans.[13] The Minoans had prospered from trade that flowed between Crete and the mainland, but a shift in the relationship with the Mycenaeans becoming politically dominant is undeniable once Linear B began to be used for official administrative documents.[14] The new proto-Greek-speaking overlords adopted a syllabary and an administrative system very like the one they had overrun. Late Minoan Crete became a Mycenaean dominion, submitting to a change of language and aesthetic tastes, and new divinities. However, the date of the Linear B tablets is contested. Most people accept an LM IIIA:1/A:2 date for the fire in

which the tablets were baked,[15] but a recent reappraisal of the data suggests LM IIIB:1 as the time of the destruction.[16]

In Crete, apart from the Early Minoan pithos burial at Nopigeia, the evidence suggests that intramural burials occurred progressively from the LM I period. In East Crete (Fig. 17) there are intramural, infant, pot burials that pre-date the warrior burials and the Linear B tablets: the one at Petras in an inverted pithos is dated to LM IA;[17] two at Sissi in pyxis-type vases are also dated to LM IA.[18] At Mochlos what must be assumed to have been a subfloor pit burial, since it was recovered after floatation of the deposit, was dated to LM IB.[19] Moreover, the pit

13   Warren 1980-1, 73-92; Warren 1982-3, 63-87; though some could be early, cf. McGeorge & Warren, forthcoming.

14   The ascendancy of a Mycenaean warrior caste is seen earlier at Knossos, signalled by the appearance of burials with weapons in LMII. Hood 1952; 1956.

15   Popham 1970.

16   For the thoroughly documented alternative argument, see Hallager & Hallager, 2015, 99-124.

17   McGeorge 2012, 291-304.

18   Dreissen 2011.

19   Soles & Walker 2003, 135-47, pls 32-6.

Site	Burials	Date	Types
Nopigeia Kissamos	1	EM II	Pithos
Gypsadhes	1	LM IA or IB	Pit
Unexplored Mansion	4	LM IA	1 cist/3 pits
Stratigraphical Museum	23	MM IIIB (?) /LM IA LM II-SM Hellenistic/Roman	Pits (16 +) 1 built grave 1 under lekane 1 under quern 1 on stone/block
Petras	1	LM IA	Pithos (inverted)
Sissi	2	LM IA	Pyxis-type vases
Mochlos	1	LM IB	Pit
Palaikastro	1	LM IIIA2/IIIB	Decorated amphoroid krater
Phaistos	2	LM IIIB	Double-handled globular cooking jar / tubular vase
Khania	1 1	MM III/LM I LM IIIB2	Pit Pit

Table 5. *Bronze Age sites in Crete with intramural burials.*

burials at Gypsadhes and the Unexplored Mansion have been dated to LM IA or IB. There are several possible explanations, one being that it is a mainland-derived idea introduced by Mycenaean elements in the population entering Crete earlier than is generally believed.

However, intramural burial of infants is not a uniquely Mycenaean burial rite. Syro-Palestinian peoples had practised the intramural burial of infants in jars ever since the invention of pottery[20] and had long established contacts with the Minoans[21] According to Levantine mythology

the entrance to the netherworld was Mt. Knkny, the name of which is a derivative of the Ugaritic, Akkadian, Aramaic and Canaanite words for 'storage jar' (*knkn*), referencing the use of storage jars for burial.[22] Knkny is mentioned specifically in the Ugaritic Tale of Aqhat,[23] recorded in the early 14th century BC.[24] Since trade was the portal for the intangible ebb and flow of ideas, religious beliefs and customs that paralleled the flow of goods and people, the rite may have been practised by immigrants, or the practice may have come about through cross-cultural consumption of an attractive ideology.[25]

---

20   McGeorge 2013.

21   They believed Kothar, their god of technology, resided in Crete; Cline 1995, 276.

22   Astour 1980; Pritchard 1969, 139, quoted by Ilan 1995, 136.

23   McGeorge 2013, 1-20.

24   The text, written down in alphabetic cuneiform by the scribe Ilimilku, was found at Ras Shamra in the house of the High Priest, which was destroyed by an earthquake in 1365 BC. See Schniedewind & Hunt 2007, 8-29.

25   Burying infants in domestic contexts may be related to primitive perceptions of the mechanisms of human reproduction, fertility and customs, which were believed to promote the generation/regeneration of new life. See McGeorge 2012.

At present, only one Early Minoan intramural jar bur-ial dated to EM II is known in West Crete at Nopigeia, Kissamos, almost 60 miles or 100 km across the sea from Cape Malea in the Peloponnese. A three-year-old child was interred with two obsidian blades, in a pithos (c. 0.50 cm tall) at the corner of a building in an open area paved with pebbles.[26] The pithos lay on its side in a shallow pit, the mouth of the jar pointing westwards. In this period, Nopi-geia appears to have had contacts with the Peloponnese,[27] where intramural burial was practised. Although several Bronze Age settlement sites have been excavated in West Crete since the 1960s,[28] only Nopigeia in the early Bronze Age and Kastelli Khania in the late Bronze Age have pro-duced intramural infant burials.

Intramural burials of similar early date to that at Nopigeia have been found at many island sites across the Aegean, in the North Aegean, Dodecanese and Cyclades. Specifical-ly, Early Bronze Age intramural infant burials are known from the islands of Astypalaia,[29] Samos, Lesbos, Chios, Limnos, Melos, Thera, Paros and Aegina.[30] These burials may be linked to a wave of immigration from Asia Minor where Early Bronze Age sites with intramural burials are numerous (Fig. 17),[31] and/ or from further East, where such burial customs had been practised from time imme-morial.[32] Moreover, according to historical tradition re-corded by Herodotos and Thucydides, the Aegean islands were colonized by immigrant Carians and Phoenicians[33] who, along with troublesome pirates, were later expelled by Minos.[34]

Fig. 18. *Asia Minor.*

Recent events in the Mediterranean have made us all aware that human migrations are motivated by many lay-ered dynamics. Interestingly, all the LM intramural burials on Crete have been found at centres with vibrant overseas contacts that might have attracted foreigners seeking new opportunities, or foreigners who came involuntarily. Lin-ear B tablets mention women, possibly sold into slavery, engaged in weaving, giving their cities of origin, which some Mycenologists identify with place names in West-ern Anatolia.[35] The case against using symbolism from diverse cultural origins to distinguish between Minoans,

---

26 Karantzali 1997, 66-81.

27 A study of EM ceramics from the Nopigeia area posited that the recipes/technological expertise used to manufacture the pottery originated in the Peloponnese. See Nodarou 2011.

28 Debla, Kastelli Khania, Nerokourou, Nopigieia, Samonas and Stylos.

29 Investigation of a 3rd-millennium BC settlement on the headland of Vathy, Astypalaia unearthed Early Bronze Age pot burials of newborn infants in 2012 and 2013. One of the containers was a wide-mouthed jar sealed with a stone lid. Micro-excavation of the contents revealed near the base of the vase an imprint of the cloth in which the infant had been wrapped. A second infant was found in a two-handled EC I bowl. See BCH 2013 Chronique des Fouilles en Ligne no. 4703. Information and references were kindly provided by Prof. A Vlachopoulos.

30 McGeorge 2013, 2.

31 At Bakla Tepe, Çeşme-Bağlararası, Troy, Alişar, Boğazköy, Kalınkaya, Kusura, Beycesultan, Hacılar II, Ovabayındır and more. See Stech-Wheeler 1974, 415-25; Massa & Şahoğlu, 2011.

32 McGeorge 2013.

33 Carians from southwest Anatolia, and Phoenicians from Syro-Palestine.

34 Herodotos 1.171; Thucydides I. 8.

35 Ventris & Chadwick 1973, 156, 410 identify: Miletus/Mi-ra-ti-ja; Lemnos/Ra-Mi-ni-ja; Knidus/Ki-ni-di-ja; Zephyria/Ze-pu-ra and Asia/A-swi-ja, see Unal 1991.

Mycenaeans or other ethnicities in the Late Minoan burial record has been argued vigorously, offering high status competition as an alternative explanation.[36] However, an infant subfloor pit burial without offerings does not infer high status; nor does it appear to be a typically Minoan burial practice.

In conclusion, the recently excavated pit burial, dated to MM III/LM I,[37] could be evidence of the spilling into West Crete, earlier than is generally believed, of mainlanders/Mycenaeans, or perhaps other foreigners practising this burial rite, drawn to Minoan Crete at the height of her prestige and prosperity.[38] Such an early occurrence of intramural infant burial suggests that a subtle migration process may have been active in MM III, initiating gradual transformation of the population's social and genetic matrix, earlier than was previously supposed and prior to the usurpation of political power by a proto-Greek speaking Mycenaean élite who were backed, as we now know, by military might.[39]

P. J. P. MCGEORGE
British School at Athens
35 Evoikou, 19009 Rafina
Greece
tinamcgeorge@gmail.com

---

36 Preston 2004, 321-48.

37 In absolute dates: 1700-1450 BC, according to Whitelaw 2000, 223-6.

38 The people who buried their dead in the LM IIIA:2 pit caves excavated at Palama Street may have been immigrants from the East; see Hallager & McGeorge 1992, 28.

39 Documented by the very impressive Achaean warrior tombs, including shaft graves, excavated southeast of the Kastelli settlement, near the modern law courts in Khania. See Andredaki-Vlazaki, Rethemiotakis & Dimopoulou-Rethemiotaki, 2008, 102.

Bibliography

Andreadaki-Vlazaki M., G. Rethemi-otakis & N. Dimopoulou-Rethemio-taki (eds) 2008
From the Land of the Labyrinth Minoan Crete from 3000-1100 BC Essays, Athens.

Astour, M. C. 1980
'The netherworld and its denizens at Ugarit', in *Death in Mesopotamia* (Papers read at the XXVIe Rencontre Assyriologique Internationale, Mesopotamia 8), B. Alster (ed.), Copenhagen, 227-38.

Cline, E. H. 1995
'Tinker, Tailor, Soldier, Sailor: Minoans and Mycenaeans abroad', in *Politeia. Society and State in the Aegean Bronze Age* (Aegaeum 12), R. Laffineur & W.-D. Niemeier (eds), Liège, 265-83.

Dreissen, J. 2011
Excavations at Sissi. Vol. II. *Preliminary Report on the 2009-2010 Campaigns*, Louvain.

Evans, J. D. 1964
'Excavations in the Neolithic settlement of Knossos 1957-60. Part I', *BSA* 59, 132-240.

Frodin, O. & A. W. Persson 1938
Asine. Results of the Swedish Excavations 1922-1930, Stockholm.

Hallager, B. P. & P. J. P. McGeorge 1992
Late Minoan III Burials At Khania (SIMA 93), Gothenburg.

Hallager, E. & B. P. Hallager 2015
'When the saints go marching in', in *Ein Minoer im Exil, Festschrift für Wolf-Dietrich Niemeier*, D. Panayiot-opoulos, I. Kaiser & O. Kouka (eds), Bonn, 99-124.

Hood, S. 1952
'Late Minoan Warrior-graves from Ayios Ioannis and the New Hospital Site near Knossos', *BSA* 47, 243-77.

Hood, S. 1956
'Another warrior grave at Ayios Ioannis, near Knossos', *BSA* 51, 81-9.

Hogarth, D. G. 1899-1900
'Knossos: II. Early Town and Cemeteries', *BSA* 6, 70-84.

Ilan, D. 1995
'Mortuary Practices at Tel Dan in the Middle Bronze Age: A reflection of Canaanite Society and Ideology', in *The Archaeology of Death in the Near East* (Oxbow Monograph 51), S. Campbell & A. Green (eds), Oxford, 117-39.

Karantzali, E. 1997
'Στοιχεία Πρωτομινωικής Κατοίκησης στα Νοπήγεια Κισάμου', *ΑΔ* 47-8 (1992-1993), Α' Μελέτες, 66-81.

Lewis, M. E. 2004
'Endocranial lesions in non-adult skeletons: understanding their aetiology', *International Journal of Osteoarchaeology* 14, 82-97.

MacGillivray, J. A., J. Driessen, C. Macdonald & D. Smyth 1988
'Excavations at Palaikastro, 1987', *BSA* 83, 259-82.

Massa, M. & V. Şahoğlu 2011
'Western Anatolian Burial Customs during the Early Bronze Age', in *Across, The Cyclades and western Anatolia during the 3rd millenium BC*, V. Şahoğlu & P. Sotirakopoulou (eds), Istanbul.

McGeorge, P. J. P. 2003
'Intramural Infant Burials in the Aegean', in E. Hallager & B. P. Hallager (eds), *The Greek Swedish Excavations at the Agia Aikaterini Square Kastelli, Khania 1970-1986 and 2001 3, 1 The Late Minoan IIIB:2 Settlement* (ActaAth-4°) (Appendix 2), Stockholm, 301-3.

McGeorge, P. J. P. 2012
'The intramural infant jar burial at Petras: context, symbolism, eschatology', in *Petras Siteia: 25 Years of Excavations and Studies* (MoDIA 16), M. Tsipopoulou (ed.), Athens, 291-304.

McGeorge, P. J. P. 2013
'Intramural Infant Burials in the Aegean Bronze Age, Reflections on symbolism and eschatology with particular reference to Crete', in *Le Mort Dans La Ville, Pratiques, contexts et impacts des inhumations intra-muros en Anatolie, du début de l'Âge du Bronze à l'époque romaine*, Olivier Henry (ed.), Istanbul, 1-20.

McGeorge, P. J. P. forthcoming
'Due Sepolture A *Enchytrismos* Del TMIIIB In Una Casa A Festos', in *Il complesso della Casa a ovest del Piazzale I de Festòs (scavi 1965-1966)* (Quaderni di Archeologia Cretese, Università di Catania – Monografie), A. Padova (ed.).

McGeorge, P. J. P. & P. Warren forthcoming
Intramural Burials from the Knossos Stratigraphical Museum Excavations 1978-1981.

303

Nodarou, E. 2011
Pottery production distribution and consumption in Early Minoan West Crete: an analytical perspective (BAR International Series 2210), Oxford.

Persson, O. & E. 2003
'A Note on the Foetus', in *The Greek Swedish Excavations at the Agia Aikaterini Square Kastelli, Khania 1970-1986 and 2001 3, 1 The Late Minoan IIIB:2 Settlement* (ActaAth-4°), E. Hallager & B. P. Hallager (eds), Stockholm, 276.

Popham, M. R. 1970
The Destruction of the Palace at Knossos. Pottery of the Late Minoan IIIA Period (SIMA 12), Gothenburg.

Popham, M. R. 1984
The Minoan Unexplored Mansion at Knossos (BSA Supplement 17), London.

Preston, L. 2004
'A Mortuary Perspective on Political Changes in Late Minoan II–IIIB Crete', *AJA* 108, 321-48.

Pritchard, J. B. 1969
Ancient Near Eastern Texts Relating to the Old Testament, Princeton.

Scheuer, L. & S. Black 2000
Developmental Juvenile Osteology, Oxford.

Schniedewind, W. M. & J. H. Hunt 2007
A Primer on Ugaritic Language, Culture, and Literature, Cambridge, 8-29.

Seow, K. W., C. Humphrys & D. I. Tudehope 1987
'Dental enamel defects in low birth weight children', *Paediatric Dentistry* 9:3, 221-5.

Soles, J. & C. Walker 2003
'Human Skeletal Remains', in *Mochlos IA: Period III. Neopalatial Settlement on the Coast: The Artisans' Quarter and the Farmhouse at Chalinomouri. The Sites* (Prehistory Monographs 7), J. Soles & T. M. Brogan (eds), Philadelphia, 135-47.

Stech-Wheeler, T. 1974
'Early Bronze Age Burial Customs in Western Anatolia', *AJA* 78, 415-25.

Unal, A. 1991
'Two peoples on both sides of the Aegean: Did the Achaeans and Hittites know each other?', in *Essays on Anatolian and Syrian Studies in the 1st and 2nd millennium BC*, H. I. H. Prince Takahito Mikasa (ed.), Wiesbaden, 16-44.

Ventris, M. & J. Chadwick 1973
Documents in Mycenaean Greek (2nd ed.), Cambridge.

Vlachopoulos, A. G. 2013
BCH 2013. Chronique des Fouilles en Ligne no. 4703 accessed December 13, 2015. http://chronique.efa.gr/index.php/fiches/voir/4703/

Warren, P. M. 1980-1
'Knossos Stratigraphical Museum Excavations, 1978-80. Part I', *Archaeological Reports* 27, 73-92.

Warren, P.M. 1982-3
'Knossos Stratigraphical Museum Excavations 1978-82. Part II', *Archaeological Reports* 29, 63-87.

Whitelaw, T. 2000
'Beyond the Palace: A Century of investigation in Europe's oldest city', *Bulletin of the Institute of Classical Studies* 44, 223-6.

'Finding Old Sikyon', 2015
A preliminary report

RUNE FREDERIKSEN, KONSTANTINOS KISSAS, JAMIESON DONATI, GIORGOS GIANNAKOPOU-LOS, SILKE MÜTH, VASSILIOS PAPATHANASIOU, WOLFGANG RABBEL, HARALD STÜMPEL, KATHA-RINA RUSCH & KRISTINA WINTHER-JACOBSEN

In memory of Anastasios Orlandos and Serapheim Charitonidis

The project 'Finding Old Sikyon' is a cooperation between the Ephorate of Antiquities of Corinth, the National Museum of Denmark, the Danish Institute at Athens and the Institute of Geoscience of the Christian Albrechts University of Kiel.[1] It is planned as a five-year project, the actual running permit covering the first two years. The project was conceived by former Director of the Danish Institute at Athens Rune Frederiksen with the aim of identifying the exact location and major features of the city, prior to its relocation in 303 BC to the plateau of Vasiliko by Demetrios Poliorketes. The project studies the topography of the pre-Hellenistic city and its surrounding landscape, hoping to identify the course of the city walls, the location of the harbour, major public spaces, monumental architecture and dwelling quarters with houses, streets etc. Rescue excavations of the Archaeological Service and the Archaeological Society at Athens have already brought significant evidence to light, and the project intends to conduct a systematic search for the city in order to understand its main elements, material, size, form and topography. This, however, is intended to serve the greater purpose of answering general questions of Archaic and Classical urbanism, as it is a very rare case that a major Archaic and Classical polis was given up at a clearly defined date and never built over afterwards, either by later ancient or larger medieval or modern settlements. Old Sikyon will thus – as one of the rare examples in the Greek motherland – allow us to study in detail the genesis and processes of development of an important city between natural growth and systematic planning. Moreover, the archaeological investigation of Old Sikyon will allow us to mirror the accounts of the written sources on this very active centre of art in seizable archaeological remains and thus to evaluate their reliability. Finally, it will inform us about the structure and organization of a famous centre of art and culture in comparison with other such centres like Corinth and Athens.

The five-week field season during the summer of 2015 was directed by Dr. Rune Frederiksen (now Ny Carlsberg Glyptotek, Copenhagen). With the assistance of Giorgos Giannakopoulos, Dr. Kristina Winther-Jacobsen (now Director of the Danish Institute at Athens) directed the intensive systematic survey with the participation of twenty students from the Universities of Copenhagen, Aarhus and Southern Denmark, as well as two students from the National and Kapodistrian University of Athens. Vasilis Oikonomou directed the finds registration. Geophysical survey was carried out by the research team 'Archeo-Geophysics' of the Institute of Geoscience,

---

1 The project obtained authorization for 2015 and 2016 with a Ministerial Decree (ΥΠΟΠΑΙΘ/ΓΔΑΠΚ/ΔΙΠΚΑ/ΤΕΕΑΕΙ/68688/379/29.06.2015). The synergasia is directed by Dr. Konstantinos Kissas, Director of the Ephorate of Antiquities of Corinth and Dr. Silke Müth of the National Museum, Denmark.

Fig. 1. *GIS map of the research area with the rivers and plateau.*

Christian Albrechts University of Kiel under the direction of Prof. Wolfgang Rabbel, and Eastern Atlas GmbH & Co, Berlin under the direction of Burkart Ullrich. Dr. Jamieson Donati of the Institute for Mediterranean Studies applied remote sensing methods to the project area.

The area under examination is located in the marine plain of Kiato and is defined by the Asopos river towards the south, the Helisson river towards the north, the east slopes of the plateau of Hellenistic Sikyon towards the west and the sea towards the east (Fig. 1). Several archaeological sites identified since the 1960s are located within the project area, such as Ayios Konstantinos, Ayios Nikolaos, Moulki, Syriona, Chtiri, Palaiochori, Dragatsoula and Merkouri (Fig. 1).[2]

In 2011 Yannis Lolos published his synthesizing study of Sikyonia in Hesperia Supplements, but systematic archaeological research in Sikyon has up to now focused mainly on the Hellenistic city. The American School of

Classical Studies excavated major parts of the theatre between 1896 and 1898, and during the 20th century excavations conducted by the Archaeological Society at Athens brought additional monumental structures to light, i.e. the temple, the gymnasium-palaistra, the long stoa and parts of the theatre's koilon.[3] From 2004 until 2008 a survey took place on the Hellenistic plateau under the cooperation of the Ephorate of Antiquities, the University of Thessaly, the Institute for Mediterranean Studies at Rethymnon and the University of York.[4]

The mission of the Archaeological Service in the area goes back to the 1960s, producing important knowledge for the topography of pre-Hellenistic Sikyon. During the emergency excavations for the suburban railway (2003-7) and the national highway Corinth-Patras (since 2008), residential structures, workshops, cemeteries and ancient roads have come to light.

---

2   ΦΕΚ 282/B/26.04.1969, ΥΑ 9309/18.04.1969.

3   Brownson & Young 1893, Earle 1889a; 1889b; 1893; Fiechter 1931; Fossum 1905; Krystalli-Votsi 1984; 1988; 1991a; 1991b; McMurtry 1889; Orlandos 1933; 1934; 1935; 1936; 1937; 1938; 1939; 1940; 1947; 1952; 1954; 1955; 1956; Petrakos 1989; Philadelpheus 1926.

4   Lolos et al. 2007; 2012.

Systematic Intensive Survey

The aim of the systematic intensive survey is to understand the settlement pattern in the plain of Kiato from a diachronic perspective. The survey area – approximately 8 square km – occupies the western part of the Vocha marine plain, which spreads from Corinth to Kiato and consists of three marine terraces with only minor altitude variations between them. The highest altitude of 121 m is found on the eastern slopes of the Hellenistic plateau. Generally, the landscape appears homogeneous except for the hills of Palaiochori and Tragana.

Apart from Asopos and Helisson, the two rivers constituting the southern and northern boundaries of the project's area, the landscape is highly hydrogenous due to many streams, as well as artificial channels for watering the fields. The northeast of the area is occupied by the town of Kiato and the northwest by the modern settlement of Moulki, with secondary settlements at Palaiochori and Tragana. The area is intensely cultivated, the crops consisting mainly of apricot trees, citrus trees and vineyards, as well as olive trees and vegetables.

Very few structures are recorded in situ on the surface in the area included in the permit, and recent as well as current emergency excavations at the railroad and the national highway have demonstrated that part of the survey area is covered with a layer of alluvial sedimentation up to 1.5 m thick. This sedimentation complicates the interpretation of the results of both the side-by-side and the geophysical survey. The remote sensing survey also documents the strong morphological forces at work in the survey area (see below).

The survey area was subdivided into zones according to existing toponyms: Ayios Konstantinos, Ayios Nikolaos, Kamaratiza, Moulki, Syriona, Merkouri, Chtiri, Zogeri, Dragatsoula, Palaiochori, Tragana-Dourvationa, Lakkos, Valtos and Ayios Ioannis (Fig. 1). Supported by local knowledge, natural and cultural features, such as changing elevations and roads, were used to define the boundaries of the zones. Initially, the ambition of the 2015 campaign was focused on the area immediately north of Asopos and east of the plateau of Hellenistic Sikyon, where the emergency excavations of the Archaeological Service and the Archaeological Society at Athens have

revealed the in situ remains of Classical habitation (Ayios Konstantinos, Kamaratiza and Syriona, see also below). However, due to the complications of the thick sedimentation and poor visibility in general we chose to prioritize survey units with high visibility within the entire survey area. Consequently, the survey results give a patchy image, but we have managed to sample all the zones during the first season.

Methodology

The systematic intensive methodology and research strategy was adapted for the conditions in the Plain of Kiato by Kristina Winther-Jacobsen, based on experiences from *The Troodos Archaeological and Environmental Survey Project*, *The Dzarylgac Survey Project*, and the *Where East meets West* project.[5] Four teams carried out the fieldwork and the daily processing of the finds, supervised by Vasilis Oikonomou. Each team worked as an individual unit of four people supervised by a team leader.

Initially the aim was only to survey ploughed or harrowed fields with 75-100% visibility. However, visibility proved to be the great challenge, because more fields than expected were covered with thick vegetation. Visibility was recorded in ranges of 25%. Visibilities over 75% were recorded in 47% of the units surveyed.

Field boundaries were used to delimit the survey units, and the research area is characterized by fields of greatly varying sizes. In order to achieve sufficient spatial resolution the survey units were never larger than 60 x 50 m, but the majority of fields were much smaller. When fields were larger than 60 x 50 m, they were subdivided into multiple units. In fact, the mean size of the survey units is approximately 1165 m². The 50 m limit was determined by the size of the team and the spacing of the field walkers (see below). When fields where shorter than 50 m, a smaller area was surveyed with fewer people, with 4 field walkers along a 40 m line and so on (Fig. 2).

Two approaches to the surveying were employed:

1. A fully quantitative method consisting of intensive survey with field walkers spaced at 10 m intervals.

---

5   Given et al. 2013a–b; Bilde, Attema & Winther-Jacobsen 2012; Winther-Jacobsen 2015. See also Bekker-Nielsen & Winther-Jacobsen, this volume. Extensive literature on the issues of planning a survey is referred to in these studies.

Fig. 2. *Archaeological surveying on the plain (Photo: Kristina Winther-Jacobsen).*

According to this method, the field walkers cross the survey unit, collecting all finds larger than a thumbnail (a so-called total collection) in a 1 m transect line, thereby producing a quantitative sample from a 10% coverage of the total surface.

2. In areas of significantly high density of finds we employed a qualitative survey method, collecting diagnostic sherds over the entire surface after the systematic, intensive survey.

As an experiment we developed a new method for fields with poor visibility, which involved raking the 1 m transect lines. The raking produced conditions of 100% visibility, allowing us to collect all the finds from 10% of the surface. Of course the raking displaced the finds, but with two people working together, one could dedicate their attention exclusively to looking for finds. Although the data produced by this method are quantitative, we will treat them separately in the analysis.

Architectural fragments and remains of structures, as well as some unquantified ceramic assemblages, were recorded as *Places of Special Interest* with coordinates.

The finds were recorded according to the chronotypological system, which entails creating a hierarchical classification according to fabric, manufacture, surface treatment, function and period.[6] The advantage of the chronotypological system is that it facilitates the mapping of finds' densities quantitatively according to different periods. Chronotypes range from very precisely dated, well-researched types of pottery such as *Tableware, Bell-crater, Handle, Classical period,* which would be abbreviated TWBCH-Cl. At the opposite range are generic chronotypes consisting of finds lumped together based on observations of broader physical characteristics. Such chronotypes may be assigned to multiple periods, e.g. the *Mud stone group* (Msg-), defined by a characteristic inclusion. The *Mud stone group* is an endemic group and more research is required to date it and locate its exact prove-

6   Winther-Jacobsen 2013, 29-30.

Fig. 3. *GIS map of the units surveyed and PO-SIs recorded in 2015 with the zones indicated.*

nance, but based on morphology the fabric was probably used to produce pottery over an extended period of time.

The advantage of the chronotypological system is that function is at the heart of the classification system, and since we are mapping functions all finds are important.[7] No finds are discarded; all finds are analyzed and finally become part of the interpretation.

For spatial mapping of the finds' densities, the data are exported from the Access database to a Geographical Information System (GIS) in order to create spatially coherent density maps. For the density maps, total densities are extrapolated from the 10% coverage, then multiplied by 10 and divided by square metres. The project applies two ways of correcting for visibility: 1) maps with extrapolated visibilities, and 2) maps with uncorrected visibility, where units in which visibility should affect the densities are marked by a signature.

Results

During the 2015 campaign we surveyed 578 survey units covering an area of 0.79 square km (Fig. 3). Distribution according to zones is as follows: 30 SU in Ayios Konstantinos, 29 SU in Ayios Nikolaos, 35 SU in Kamaratiza, 72 SU in Moulki, 32 SU in Syriona, 49 SU in Merkouri, 81 SU in Chtiri, 32 SU in Zogeri, 60 SU in Dragatsoula, 38 SU in Palaiochori, 31 SU in Tragana-Dourvationa, 43 SU in Lakkos, 35 SU in Valtos and 11 SU in Ayios Ioannis.

A total number of 52.326 pottery fragments and 17 lithics, as well as 85 architectural artefacts were collected, washed, counted and described; the most important specimens were drawn and photographed. A pottery inventory was created, consisting of 328 sherds after the first season. This inventory works as a reference collection of the chronotypes for future seasons.

All the data are entered into the database, but we have only made preliminary studies of the material, and a detailed study of chronology awaits the 2016 season. We may, however, present the following preliminary observations. First of all the surface revealed far richer traces of the buried past than we had dared to hope for, based on our knowledge of the geomorphology of the landscape of Sikyon. The finds date from the Late Neolithic/Early Bronze Age to the present day, but material from the Classical period is predominant.

The density map including the pottery of all the periods is characterized by a high degree of heterogeneity (Fig. 4). Even accounting for visibility, highly variable densities have been recorded in adjoining fields, which may be interpreted in two ways: either the settlement was not contiguous, or post-depositional disturbance has been highly heterogeneous. Densities over 1 per square metre were recorded in 23% of the units. The highest densities, 5 to 6.8 sherds per square metre, which is approximately equivalent to the second highest category in the urban survey on the Hellenistic plateau, where the plough zone is

---

7   Winther-Jacobsen 2010, 67-70.

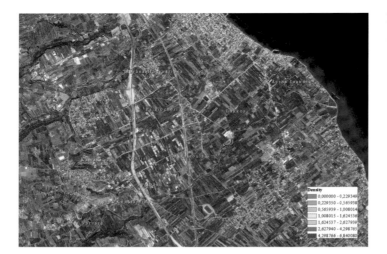

Fig. 4. *GIS raw density map with the zones indicated.*

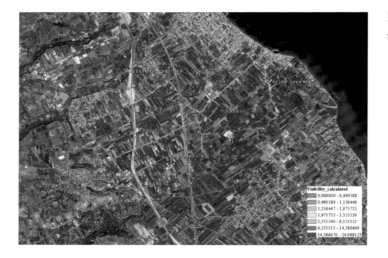

Fig. 5. *GIS density map corrected for visibility with the zones indicated.*

Fig. 6. *GIS raw density map of Ayios Konstantinos, Ayios Nikolaos and Kamaratiza.*

relatively thin, were recorded in 3 units.[8] Due to the lack of continuity between the fields surveyed, we cannot at present say anything conclusive about the diffusion of finds, whether it represents a contiguous pattern or many separate settlements. All the zones investigated yielded finds, although numbers dropped as we moved north towards Moulki and east towards Kiato, where modern activity is also more intense. The slopes immediately east of the plateau yielded the highest densities as well as the largest and best preserved fragments, indicating that the buried structures from which the finds originate are well-preserved. Although this is an intensely farmed area, a few structures were even preserved in situ on the surface. In this area the finds date from the Bronze Age to the present day, but finds of the Classical period are ever predominant.

The preliminary overview of the entire survey area appears to confirm existing theories on the location of the pre-Hellenistic city, based on emergency excavations. Elevated densities are recorded predominantly on the second and third marine terraces directly north of Asopos. Towards the north this area includes Kamaratiza and Zogeri. The distribution within the area is not homogeneous, but densities of more than 1 sherd per square metre are very rare outside this area. Correcting for visibilities does flatten the data, but cannot explain the heterogeneity on its own (Fig. 5).[9] Apart from extending the areas of relatively higher densities in the individual zones, at this poor chronological resolution the corrected visibilities do not seem to affect the overall distribution pattern (see individual zones below). This is also the area where emergency excavations have revealed architectural remains of habitation. Additionally, graves seem to line up along the edge of the second marine terrace, which actually cuts directly through the area with elevated densities.

Places Of Special Interest (POSI) from 2015 consist of remains of seven structures in situ, 53 architectural fragments and some pottery assemblages (Fig. 3). Three wells/cisterns were identified at the edge of Ayios Konstantinos close together (see below). The other four structures are wall remains located at Ayios Konstantinos, Chtiri and Kamaratiza. The architectural fragments

Fig. 7. *Well at Ayios Konstantinos (Photo: Kristina Winther-Jacobsen).*

consist mainly of ashlar blocks, but capitals and bases of both the Doric and Ionic order were also recorded.

The individual zones

Ayios Konstantinos is located on the southeastern slope of the Hellenistic plateau just below the rocky outcrop, with the earliest settlement remains of the area. From the current terrain it is obvious that the area consisted of multiple smaller terraces. As indicated above, Ayios Konstantinos is an area of high archaeological significance. Pottery densities were generally high and Classical period material made up a significant proportion of the recorded finds, and architecture has been found in as well as ex situ (Fig. 6). Three wells/cisterns were identified at the edge of Ayios Konstantinos close together (Fig. 7). In the same area several looters' pits revealed pottery, as well as fragments of polychrome pebble mosaics, though no architectural remains were observed. In this area, previous excavations revealed a pebble mosaic of the late 5th–early 4th century BC at a vineyard next to the chapel of Ayios Konstantinos, and Vassilios Papathanasiou of the Ephorate recorded the remains of a mosaic during works for establishing a pipeline close by.[10] Finds densities

8 Lolos et al. 2007, 282, fig. 5. The highest was 7-12 sherds per square metre.

9 The necessary discussion of the methodology of correcting for visibility and its potential is too complex for this report.

10 Orlandos 1939, 122-3; Papathanasiou personal comment. For other mosaics' fragments deriving from the plain without further specification of the exact find spot, see Orlandos 1936, 83; Orlandos 1937, 94; Orlandos 1947, 59-60.

Fig. 8. *Southeast view of Kamaratiza towards the Asopos from the Plateau (Photo: Kristina Winther-Jacobsen).*

are high at Ayios Konstantinos, and there appears to be a general correlation between high finds densities and increased numbers of architectural fragments in several zones. Corrected densities seem to homogenize or flatten the distribution pattern.

Ayios Nikolaos is a more homogeneous landscape, apart from the northwestern corner, where it slopes upwards towards the Hellenistic plateau. At the church of Ayios Nikolaos several spolia have been collected over the last few years by the Archaeological Service, but their precise original contexts are unknown. In general, densities at Ayios Nikolaos are more homogeneous and the proportion of post-Classical material is higher compared to Ayios Konstantinos. The corrected visibilities extend the area of relatively high densities. There are no recorded excavations at Ayios Nikolaos.

Kamaratiza is located on the eastern slope of the Hellenistic plateau and like Ayios Konstantinos consists of multiple smaller terraces (Fig. 8). The area is charac-

terized by high densities in general and there is a strong correlation between the high densities and architectural fragments, many of which derive from the Hellenistic city wall. The corrected visibilities extend the area of relatively high densities. The pre-Hellenistic element appears not to be as significant among the finds in this area. In 2007 and 2009 the Ephorate conducted an excavation of a Roman road leading to the Hellenistic plateau under the direction of Athanasios Tsiogas. Burials of the same period and a cistern were found at the sides of the road.[11]

Moulki consists of two geological zones, a homogeneous plateau below the Hellenistic plateau and a lower flood plain along the southern bank of Helisson River. The visibility on the flood plain was generally too low to survey, while access to the higher plateau was restricted by the modern settlement of Moulki. Due to these restrictions the interpretation of the observed data is less secure, but if observed tendencies are to be believed, finds appeared to be dating mainly to post-Classical or even post-Antique

11   Tsiogas 2013; Papathanasiou & Maragoudaki 2013, 129.

Fig. 9. *Southeast view of the lowest marine terrace from Palaiochori (Photo: Giorgos Giannakopoulos).*

times. During emergency excavations, the Archaeological Service recorded a water pipe, a small quarry and fragmentary structures, as well as a Late Archaic to Hellenistic roadside necropolis at the location of the tollbooth.[12] Several burials of the 4th and 3rd centuries BC, pits opened in the smooth bedrock, have been excavated on the slope of plateau west of Moulki, in the area called Gkraves.[13] Additionally, on the southwestern border of Moulki in the Karampetsos vineyard an old emergency excavation brought to light another pebble mosaic, dated to c. 400 BC.[14]

Syriona cuts across the second and third marine terraces but generally the landscape is homogeneous, apart from the strip of fields adjacent to the north bank of Asopos. The old and the recent National Highway emergency excavations have brought to light a complex of domestic remains, often with mosaics, workshops and technical works as well as graves, which span from the Early Geometric to the Classical period.[15] The surface finds, however, appear less promising. This is probably due to the 1.50 m-thick layer of sedimentation covering the structures recorded by the emergency excavations.

Merkouri is located on the second marine terrace. The highest densities are mainly associated with areas previously excavated by the Archaeological Service, e.g. in the Kollias, Protopappas and Kostouros plots, which brought to light a pebble mosaic of the 5th century BC and other fragmentary structures potentially interpreted as private houses and workshops.[16] One survey unit in the southern part proved particularly interesting. The topsoil has been recently removed mechanically, and the highest density in the zone was recorded in this field, clearly indicating that the thickness of sedimentation is a significant factor which needs to be explored. The preliminary study of the assemblages suggests that tablewares and cooking wares make up a significant proportion.

Chtiri cuts across the second to third marine terrace and is dominated by middle-range densities. In general, assemblages from Chtiri are more heterogeneous. Zogeri is located on the third marine terrace, but generally finds are very similar to those at Chtiri. In Chtiri and Zogeri

---

12   Papathanasiou, personal communication.

13   Orlandos 1933, 75-6; Orlandos 1937, 91; Kasimi 2004, 138; Papathanasiou & Maragoudaki 2013, 128.

14   Orlandos 1947, 59; Lolos 2011, 273-4.

15   Charitonidis 1968, 124; Papathanasiou & Maragoudaki 2013, 116, 127.

16   Krystalli 1968, 165-6; Krystalli Votsi 1976; Papathanasiou 2012, 152-4.

Fig. 10. *Geomagnetic survey in summer 2015 (Photo: Rune Frederiksen).*

an extended necropolis dating from the Late Archaic to the Roman period has been excavated by the Archaeological Service.[17] Nonetheless, in both zones emergency excavations have revealed structures or even complexes of multiple structures of the Classical or Early Hellenistic period, preliminarily interpreted as private houses and workshops.[18]

Dragatsoula and Palaiochori are located on the second and third marine terraces. Both zones, as well as the settlement patterns, are dependent on the change in level. Generally assemblages are heterogeneous and densities in the middle to low range. The general drop-off in densities as we move from west to east is first clearly observable in this area. At Dragatsoula, Vassilios Papathanasiou excavated a quarry of oolithic limestone, while Late Helladic and Classical necropoleis have been excavated at Palaiochori.[19]

Tragana-Dourvationa is located on the second marine terrace and access is restricted by the modern homonymous settlement. Generally, assemblages are heterogeneous and densities are in the low range.

Fig. 11. *Parallel resistivity and seismic measurements in summer 2015 (Photo: Wolfgang Rabbel).*

---

17 Krystalli 1968, 164-5; Krystalli Votsi 1984, 65; Krystalli Votsi 2013; Balla 2013; Papathanasiou – Maragoudaki 2013, 128.

18 Archive of the Ephorate of Corinth. Emergency excavations at Zarkotos, Papakyriakos and Kampardi plots.

19 For the quarry, see Papathanasiou 2012, 155; Papathanasiou – Maragoudaki 2013, 125. For the necropoleis, see Orlandos 1937, 92-4; Papathanasiou 2012, 154-6; Papathanasiou 2013; Papathanasiou & Maragoudaki 2013, 127; Anagnostopoulou & Kasimi 2014, 474-6.

Fig. 12. *Radar measurements in summer 2015 (Photo: Rune Frederiksen).*

Lakkos, Valtos and Ayios Ioannis are located on the lowest marine terrace, which is dominated by the modern settlement of Kiato (Fig. 9). In this area the drop-off in densities is remarkable, with many survey units without any recorded finds. The exception is one survey unit at Valtos that has a very high density of finds. Trial trenches that produced no finds were dug in a field less than 50 m to the west, suggesting that the high density of the survey unit is an isolated phenomenon, possibly a farmstead. The proportion of cooking wares appears to be significant and in terms of chronology the Roman element is noteworthy. The area east of Lakkos, in the town of Kiato, is hypothetically a strong candidate for the ancient harbour area. The hypothesis is mostly based on the large Basilica of the 5th century AD and the adjacent Magoula hill, where three graves of uncertain date have been excavated by the Archaeological Service.[20]

Geophysical Prospection

Aim and methods

The main objective of the geophysical survey was to discover remains (e.g. building structures, streets, open spaces, etc.) of the pre-Hellenistic city of Sikyon. The primary method of the survey was extensive geomagnetic mapping (Fig. 10). In areas where the magnetic survey showed significant anomalies, electrical resistivity, georadar and seismic measurements were applied to gain more insight into the nature of these anomalies (Figs 11-12).

Geomagnetic surveying is one of the classical geophysical methods used in archaeological prospection because it enables mapping of large areas very quickly, depending on local conditions. For magnetic surveys the contrast in magnetization between the cultural elements (e.g. remains of walls, streets or tombs) and the surrounding material is important. In case of a low contrast, objects might not be detectable at greater depth. Another factor regarding the penetration depth is the size of the object: the larger the object, the greater the penetration.

Geoelectric surveying is one of a number of geophysical investigation methods which are able to deliver more detailed information than the magnetic data. The geoelectric method measures the specific electric resistivity of the subsurface, which is affected mainly by porosity, water saturation and clay content of the soil.

Georadar (GPR) is – conditions providing – like the magnetic method very suitable for answering archaeolo-

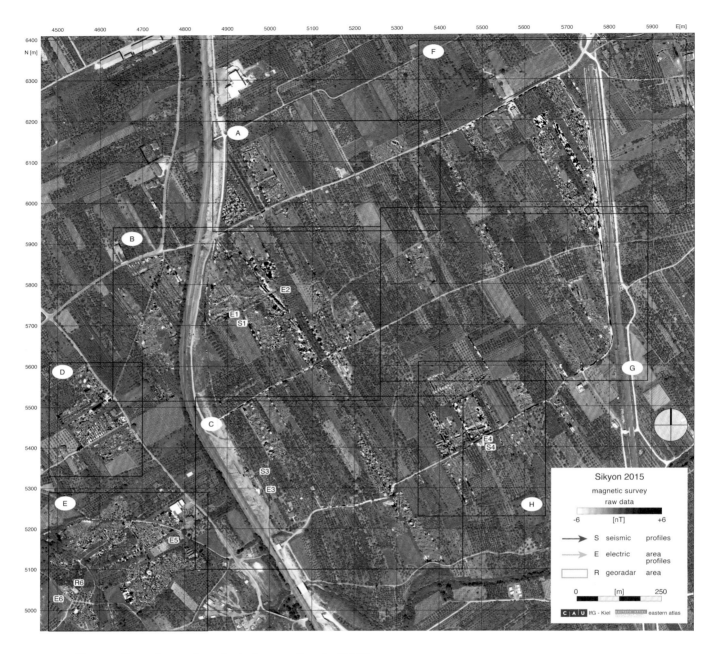

Fig. 13. *General map of geophysical prospections in Old Sikyon, 2015.*

gical questions due to its excellent vertical resolution. A short high-frequency electromagnetic pulse is sent into the subsurface and all its reflections are recorded over a certain time (comparable to reflection seismics).

In the seismic survey, mechanical (seismic) waves are used to explore the underground. For near-surface applications, waves are produced with a sledgehammer or a vibration device ('shot'). Geophones positioned along a profile record the amplitude and return time of the seismic waves. In general, differentiation is made between reflection and refraction seismics, which differ in the configurations of shot points and geophones.

For topographical positioning, a local coordinate system was set up, which was later used by both teams for the stationing of their respective differential GPS base stations.

Results (Fig. 13)

In Syriona, a flat area next to the rescue excavations was used to test the different geophysical methods (Fig. 14). The advantage of using this location for the tests was that the depth of the cultural layer and the size of the expected buildings were known. In the magnetic map, the tests showed nothing but dark patches that coincided with the geoelectric anomalies. The geoelectric results showed a zone of higher resistivity values in a depth corresponding with the cultural layer (1.5-2 m). Due to the depth of 2 m, the resolution was not as clear as if the houses were lying within the first metre under the surface. It is important to mention, however, that the orientations of the anomalies did match the direction of the known house walls.

The whole survey area was subdivided into smaller areas (Areas A–H), and only find spots of potential importance will be reported on. In Area A, which is located at Zogeri and Chtiri, the most prominent anomaly is a cross-like structure (A1, Zogeri; see Fig. 15), and the most obvious interpretation of this would be a crossroad. An alternative interpretation is, however, possible: the anomaly may be caused by a mud-brick wall. A geoelectric profile on the spot should be able to resolve this ambiguity, and rule out one of these two most likely options. South and southwest of this area, more anomalies point to a street grid in approximately the same orientation.

In the eastern part of Area B (Chtiri), a broad double magnetic maximum (B2) more than 150 m in length with high amplitudes runs slightly off this orientation from the northwest to the southeast, and merges into one in its further progress, while the area around appears rather quiet in the magnetic map (Fig. 16). Here, an electric profile was measured, which shows a 3 m-wide and 1.5 m-high block of high resistivity in a depth of c. 1.5 m. Perhaps it can be connected to a wall, but further methods need to be applied here to arrive at a correct interpretation. South of this, the magnetic map is characterized by a disrupted pattern of a rather rectangular orientation, which could point to a former building development in this area.

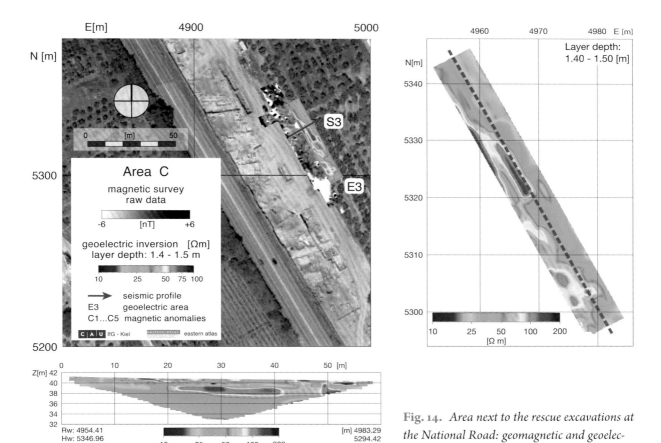

Fig. 14. *Area next to the rescue excavations at the National Road: geomagnetic and geoelectric results.*

317

Fig. 15. *Possible crossroads (A1) in geomagnetic results in Zogeri.*

Indications for the densest occupation are found in Area E, located in the zone of Ayios Konstantinos immediately to the east of the southernmost spur of the plateau. Here, the magnetic map shows many small-scale magnetic anomalies. In comparison to other areas, these small-scale anomalies do not appear to be caused by metal on the surface, but might be indicators of an ancient surface. Several continuous linear structures may be interpreted as streets that form a roughly rectangular pattern. Additional geoelectric investigation applied in the same area (E5) was able to detect two parallel high-resistivity lineaments which can be interpreted as walls (Fig. 17). Moreover, a narrow zone with a thickness of about 1 m and resistivities of 100 to 200 Ωm in a depth of 0.5 to 1 m could indicate the depth of the cultural layer in this area. In combination with the adjacent walls, it might also be the floor of a large building.

In the very south of Area F (F3, Dragatsoula), where it overlaps with Area G, there is a trapezoidal anomaly that is interesting due to the arrangement of maximum and minimum with the maximum always on the inside and the minimum always on the outside (see Fig. 13). This structure on the edge of the second marine terrace, close to the new train track, might be connected to an ancient quarry, traces of which have been found nearby.

In the western part of Area H (Merkouri), a magnetic maximum between two minima runs for around 140 m roughly in an east–west direction (H2, see Fig. 18). At a little bend to the north, the northern minimum separates from the other two anomalies. A geoelectric profile (E4) is marked by a block of very high resistivity (over 250 Ωm) at the place of the magnetic maximum (Fig. 19). A seismic profile (S4) likewise shows an anomaly, which has the shape of a ditch. The interpretation of these structures, however, still requires more detailed investigation. It is not clear if these combined anomalies can be connected with a defensive system.

The general picture points to a city centre close to the southeastern spur of the plateau, with extensions or suburbs and further peripheral structures in the extended area of the second marine terrace. There are some candidates for larger walls, which might mirror parts of the town's defenses in its different phases.

Remote Sensing Archaeology in Sikyon

For the summer of 2015, attention focused on a zone slightly less than 1 square km immediately below the eastern plateau of the Hellenistic city (Fig. 4). Results were based on a high-resolution multispectral (4-band) WorldView-2 image from 11 April 2014, as well as four historical aerial photographs (1945, 1960, 1972, 1987) and an ASTER GDEM 2 for digital elevations.

The analysis shows that the landscape within and around the target has been altered by anthropogenic and environmental factors since the middle of the 20th century. One obvious and remarkable element is the change of crops in the 1960s. In 1945, fields are mostly void of trees and orchards, while by the 1960s, orchards predominate, and by the 1970s the area was densely filled with trees, as we know it today. The courses of small rivers and seasonal streams were more evident in 1945 than they are now. Branches of the Asopos River appear to have impacted the southern and southeastern area of the target zone more than is the case today.

Remote sensing identified a large number of surface anomalies in the target zone that likely relate to palaeo-channels. This was to be expected, since the area is still quite hydrologically active. As such, there is an increased

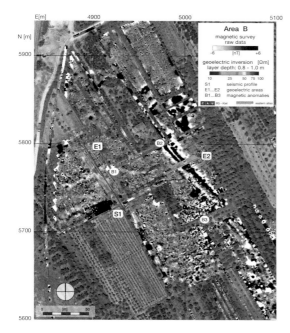

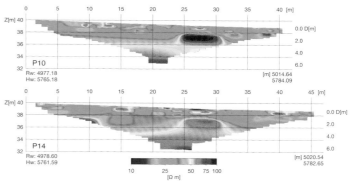

Fig. 16. *Long double magnetic maximum (B2) and geoelectric profile (E2) in Chtiri.*

likelihood of soil erosion and/or alluvial sedimentation, which can often affect the preservation of subsurface features of archaeological interest and the ability of remote sensing and geophysical methods to identify them.

Very few anomalies in the target appear to be from features other than palaeochannels (Fig. 20), which may be explained by the density of trees and orchards that limit the identification of surface anomalies using satellite

and aerial remote sensing methodologies. To overcome this issue, the project aims to apply LiDAR (Light Detection and Ranging) in the future, since it can identify surface details regardless of vegetation and tree growth. One rectilinear anomaly (c. 70 x 25 m) in Chtiri was identified in the 1945 aerial photograph, but for most of its parts, this unfortunately now lies under the new National Road (Fig. 21). A roughly circular anomaly of c. 20 m in

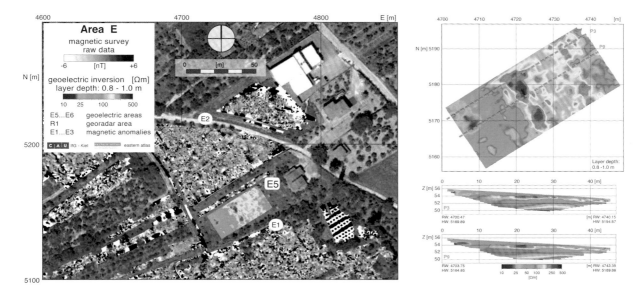

Fig. 17. *Geoelectric depth slice and depth profiles (E 5) of possible parallel walls in Agios Konstantinos.*

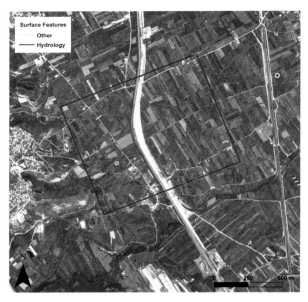

Fig. 18. *Long magnetic maximum between two minima (H2) in Merkouri.*

Fig. 20. *Surface anomalies (mostly palaeochannels) identified from the WordView-2 satellite image and its feature enhancement indices.*

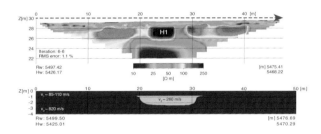

Fig. 19. *Geoelectric depth profile E4 and underground model of seismic velocities (S4) at the magnetic maximum (H2) in Merkouri.*

diameter was noted in Ayios Nikolaos and needs to be further explored by geophysical prospection.

The coastal plain of Vocha has long been recognized as a region where Roman centuriation still persists in the morphology of modern field boundaries. Two systems have so far been identified: one related to the Roman colony of Corinth founded by Caesar, and another related to a second wave of colonization during the Flavian period.[21] It is notable in this context that field boundaries were vir-

tually unchanged between the 1945 aerial photograph and the 2014 WorldView-2 satellite image. Internal divisions of some fields have been altered, but by and large the same boundaries have been retained since 1945. An analysis of the alignments of modern field boundaries in a 2 km² area around the target shows that a great majority of them cluster in narrow ranges with southwest–northeast orientations. The broader characteristics of field boundary alignments in the Sikyonian coastal plain and the possible relationship to Roman centuriation and/or an earlier Greek system of land division need to be explored more extensively in the future.

Conclusions

Combining the preliminary surface observations and the knowledge from previous emergency excavations, there can be little doubt that the western part of Old Sikyon occupied the east slopes of the Vasiliko plateau. The Asopos River makes up the southern boundary, and the northern and eastern boundaries we hope to be able to locate more precisely in 2016.

21 Romano 2005.

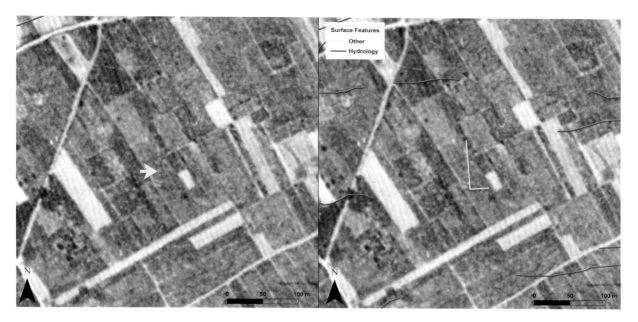

Fig. 21. *Rectilinear surface anomaly identified from the 1945 aerial photograph, now for most parts lying under the National Road.*

This is also supported by the geophysical investigations. After the prospection in 2015, much work still remains to be done in order to complement the obtained data. Especially in the areas where we have gained information about the subsurface with the geomagnetic method, electric and seismic profiles have to be produced. The geoelectric and the magnetic data have to be combined, so that ideally a model can be created that fits all datasets. Moreover, extended geophysical investigation in fields not yet measured in 2015 will supply further information. This will include, for example, the investigation of the presumed harbour area of the town.

Remote sensing in the target area entails different qualities of results. The fact that few subsurface features of possible archaeological value were identified with the above datasets does not necessarily mean that features will not be found with other methods, or even other datasets from different extraction dates. On the other hand, an interesting outcome of remote sensing was the reconstruction of the palaeoenvironment within and around the target. At some point in the past, since Antiquity, the region was heavily impacted by rivers and streams. Soil erosion and soil accumulation, and their likely influence on the preservation of any potential archaeological features, are important considerations for future site exploration and interpretation.

RUNE FREDERIKSEN
Ny Carlsberg Glyptotek
Dantes Plads 7, 1556 Copenhagen V
Denmark
rufr@glyptoteket.dk

KONSTANTINOS KISSAS
Ephorate of Antiquities of Corinth
Archaia Korinthos, 20007
Greece
kkissas@hotmail.com

GIORGOS GIANNAKOPOULOS
Ephorate of Antiquities of Corinth &
Danish Institute at Athens
Archaia Korinthos, 20007
Greece
giorgos.giannakopoulos@diathens.gr

VASSILIOS PAPATHANASIOU
Ephorate of Antiquities of Corinth
Archaia Korinthos, 20007
Greece
jamesvpapathanasiou@yahoo.gr

JAMIESON DONATI
Institute for Mediterranean Studies
Melissinou and Nikephorou Foka 130,
74100 Rethymno, Crete
Greece
jcdonati@ims.forth.gr

SILKE MÜTH
National Museum of Denmark
Frederiksholms Kanal 12, 1220 Copenhagen K
Denmark
silke.muth-frederiksen@natmus.dk

WOLFGANG RABBEL
Christian Albrecht University of Kiel,
Institute for Geosciences
Otto-Hahn-Platz 1, 24118 Kiel
Germany
wrabbel@geophysik.uni-kiel.de

HARALD STÜMPEL
Christian Albrecht University of Kiel,
Institute for Geosciences
Otto-Hahn-Platz 1, 24118 Kiel
Germany
stuempel@geophysik.uni-kiel.de

KATHARINA RUSCH
Christian Albrecht University of Kiel,
Institute for Geosciences
Otto-Hahn-Platz 1, 24118 Kiel
Germany
krusch@geophysik.uni-kiel.de

KRISTINA WINTHER-JACOBSEN
The Danish Institute at Athens
Herefondos 14, 10558 Athens
Greece
kwj@diathens.gr/kwjacobsen@hum.ku.dk

Bibliography

Anagnostopoulou, A. M. & P. Kasimi 2014
'Νομός Κορινθίας', *ArchDelt* 61 Β΄1 (2006), 474-6.

Balla, F. 2013
'Αρχαία Σικυώνα: Η Αποκάλυψη Τμήματος Νεκροταφείου Ελληνιστικής Εποχής', in *Athenaia 4, The Corinthia and the Northeast Peloponnese, Topography and History from Prehistoric Times until the End of Antiquity*, K. Kissas & W.-D. Niemeier (eds), Munich, 491-508.

Bilde, P. Guldager, P. Attema & K. Winther-Jacobsen (eds) 2012
The Dzarylgac Survey Project (Black Sea Studies 14), Aarhus.

Brownson, C. & C. H. Young 1893
'Further Excavation at the Theatre of Sicyon in 1891', *The American Journal of Archaeology and the History of the Fine Arts* 8:3, 397-409.

Charitonidis, S. 1968
'Κορινθία', *ArchDelt* 21 Β΄1 (1966), 124.

Earle, M. L. 1889a
'Excavations by the American School at the Theatre of Sikyon II. Supplementary Report of the Excavations', *The American Journal of Archaeology and of the History of the Fine Arts* 5:3, 286-92.

Earle, M. L. 1889b
'Excavations by the American School at the Theatre of Sikyon III. A Sikyonian Statue', *The American Journal of Archaeology and of the History of the Fine Arts* 5:3, 292-303.

Earle, M. L. 1893
'Further Excavation at the Theatre of Sicyon in 1891', *The American Journal of Archaeology and the History of the Fine Arts* 8:3, 388-96.

Fiechter, W. 1931
Das Theater in Sikyon, Stuttgart.

Fossum, A. 1905
'The Theatre at Sikyon', *AJA* 9, 263-76.

Given, M., A. B. Knapp, J. S. Noller, L. Sollars & V. Kassianidou (eds) 2013a
Landscape and interaction: the Troodos Archaeological and Environmental Survey Project, Cyprus 1, Methodology, analysis and interpretation (Levant Supplementary Series. London: Council for British Research in the Levant), Oxford.

Given, M., A. B. Knapp, L. Sollars, J. S. Noller & V. Kassianidou (eds) 2013b
Landscape and interaction: the Troodos Archaeological and Environmental Survey Project, Cyprus 2, The TAESP landscape (Levant Supplementary Series. London: Council for British Research in the Levant), Oxford.

Kasimi, P. 2004
'Νομός Κορινθίας', *ArchDelt* 53 Β΄1 (1998), 138.

Krystalli, K. 1968
'Κορινθία', *ArchDelt* 22 Β΄1 (1967), 164-6, pls 124α–β.

Krystalli-Votsi, K. 1976
'Nouvelle Mosaïque de Sicyone', *BCH* 100:2, 575-88.

Krystalli-Votsi, K. 1984
'Νομός Κορινθίας', *ArchDelt* 31 Β΄1 (1976), 65, pls 58α–δ.

Krystalli-Votsi, K. 1988
'Ανασκαφή Σικυώνος', *Prakt* 1984, 241-2.

Krystalli-Votsi, K. 1991a
'Ανασκαφή Σικυώνος', *Prakt* 1987, 66-8.

Krystalli-Votsi, K. 1991b
'Ανασκαφή Σικυώνος', *Prakt* 1988, 30-1.

Krystalli-Votsi, K. 2013
'Πυρά Ταφικού Μνημείου από τη Σικυώνα', in *Athenaia 4, The Corinthia and the Northeast Peloponnese, Topography and History from Prehistoric Times until the End of Antiquity*, K. Kissas & W.-D. Niemeier (eds), Munich, 509-18.

Lolos, Y. 2011
Land of Sikyon: archaeology and history of a Greek city-state (Hesperia supplement 39), Princeton.

Lolos, Y. A., B. Gourley & D. R. Stewart 2007
'The Sikyon Survey Project: A Blueprint for Urban Survey?', *JMA* 20, 267-96.

Lolos, Y. A., B. Gourley, A. Sarris, C. Hayward, C. Trainor, E. Kiriantzi & N. Papadopoulos 2012
'Surveying the Sikyonian plateau: integrated approach to the study of an ancient cityscape', *Proceedings of the 5th Congress of the Greek Archaeometric Society*, Athens, 305-26.

McMurtry, W. J. 1889
'Excavations by the American School at the Theatre of Sikyon I. General Re-

port of the Excavations', *The American Journal of Archaeology and of the History of the Fine Arts* 5:3, 267-86.

Orlandos, A. 1933
'Ἀνασκαφή Σικυῶνος', *Prakt* 1932, 63-76.

Orlandos, A. 1934
'Ἀνασκαφή Σικυῶνος', *Prakt* 1933, 81-90.

Orlandos, A. 1935
'Ἀνασκαφή Σικυῶνος', *Prakt* 1934, 116-22.

Orlandos, A. 1936
'Ἀνασκαφή Σικυῶνος', *Prakt* 1935, 73-83.

Orlandos, A. 1937
'Ἀνασκαφή Σικυῶνος', *Prakt* 1936, 86-94.

Orlandos, A. 1938
'Ἀνασκαφή Σικυῶνος του 1937', *Prakt* 1937, 94-6.

Orlandos, A. 1939
'Ἀνασκαφαί Σικυῶνος', *Prakt* 1938, 120-3.

Orlandos, A. 1940
'Ἀνασκαφαί Σικυῶνος', *Prakt* 1939, 100-2.

Orlandos, A. 1947
'Ἀνασκαφαί Σικυῶνος 1941', *Prakt* 1941, 56-60.

Orlandos, A. 1952
'Ἀνασκαφή Σικυῶνος', *Prakt* 1951, 187-91.

Orlandos, A. 1955
'Ἀνασκαφή Σικυῶνος', *Prakt* 1952, 387-95.

Orlandos, A. 1956
'Ἀνασκαφή Σικυῶνος', *Prakt* 1953, 184-90.

Orlandos, A. 1957
'Ἀνασκαφή Σικυῶνος', *Prakt* 1954, 219-31.

Papathanasiou, V. 2012
'Νομός Κορινθίας', *ArchDelt* 56-59 Β´ 4 (2001-4), 152-6.

Papathanasiou, V. 2013
'Μυκηναϊκό και Κλασικό Νεκροταφείο στην Αρχαία Σικυῶνα', in *Athenaia* 4, *The Corinthia and the Northeast Peloponnese, Topography and History from Prehistoric Times until the End of Antiquity*, K. Kissas & W.-D. Niemeier (eds), Munich, 479-89.

Papathanasiou, V. & E. Maragoudaki 2013
'Sikyon', in *Ancient Corinthia*, K. Kissas (ed.), Athens, 113-29.

Philadelpheus, A. 1926
'Note sur le Bouleuterion (?) de Sicyone', *BCH* 50, 174-82.

Romano, D. G. 2003
'City Planning, Centuriation and Land Division in Roman Corinth: Colonia Laus Iulia Corinthiensis and Colonia Iulia Flavia Augusta Corinthiensis', in *Corinth* 20, *The Centenary, 1896-1996*, C. K. Williams & N. Bookidis (eds), Princeton, 279-301.

Tsiogas, A. 2013
'Ἀνασκαφική Ἔρευνα σε Οικόπεδο στη Θέση Καμαράτιζα Αρχαίας Σικυῶνας', in *Athenaia* 4, *The Corinthia and the Northeast Peloponnese, Topography and History from Prehistoric Times until the End of Antiquity*, K. Kissas & W.-D. Niemeier (eds), Munich, 519-24.

Winther-Jacobsen, K. 2010
From Pots to People: A ceramic approach to the archaeological interpretation of ploughsoil assemblages in Late Roman Cyprus (BABESCH Supplement 17), Leuven.

Winther-Jacobsen, K. 2015
'Contextualising Neoklaudiopolis: a glimpse at settlement dynamics in the city's hinterland', in *Landscape and settlement dynamics in Northern Anatolia in the Roman and Byzantine period* (Geographica Historica 32), K. Winther-Jacobsen & L. Summerer (eds), Stuttgart, 83-100.